THE CAMPAIGN OF WATERLOO

THE CAMPAIGN OF

WATERLOO

A MILITARY HISTORY

BY

JOHN CODMAN ROPES

Member of the Massachusetts Historical Society, the Military Historical Society of Massachusetts,
and the Harvard Historical Society; Fellow of the American Academy of Arts and Sciences
and the Royal Historical Society; Honorary Member of the United States Cavalry
Association, etc. Author of "The Army under Pope," in the Scribner
Series of "Campaigns of the Civil War"; "The First
Napoleon, a Sketch, Political and Military," etc.

The Naval & Military Press Ltd

Published by

The Naval & Military Press Ltd
Unit 5 Riverside, Brambleside,
Bellbrook Industrial Estate,
Uckfield, East Sussex,
TN22 1QQ England

Tel: +44 (0) 1825 749494
Fax: +44 (0) 1825 765701

www.naval-military-press.com
www.nmarchive.com

In reprinting in facsimile from the original, any imperfections are inevitably reproduced and the quality may fall short of modern type and cartographic standards.

PREFACE

THE need of another narrative of the campaign of Waterloo may not be at first sight apparent. There has been a great deal written on this subject, and much of it has been written by eminent hands. The last and the most unfortunate campaign of the great soldier of modern times has naturally attracted the repeated attention of military historians. Jomini, Clausewitz, Charras, Siborne, Kennedy, Chesney, Vaudoncourt, La Tour d'Auvergne, Thiers, Hooper, and many others have sought to explain the almost inexplicable result,— the complete defeat in a very brief campaign of the acknowledged master of modern warfare. One would suppose that the theme had been exhausted, and that nothing more remained to be said.

But several circumstances have contributed to render the labors of these writers unusually difficult. In the first place, the overthrow of Napoleon, which was the immediate result of the campaign, operated to prevent a satisfactory account of it being given to the public from the French point of view at the time when the facts were fresh in men's minds. The Emperor, exiled at St. Helena, could indeed give his story; but, unable, as he was, to verify or correct his narrative by citations from the orders that were given at the time, and by conferring with the officers who had served under him, he has left us an account, which, though by no means without historical value, is yet so defective and erroneous in parts that it has aroused in the minds of men who are not alive to the great difficulties which always attend the composition of a military narrative, and who are not concerned to make fair allowance for the unavoidable and peculiar difficulties of one writing in the circumstances which surrounded Napoleon at St. Helena, grave doubts as to the trustworthiness of his recollection and even as to his veracity. The chief officers of the army have also rendered little assistance to the historian. Ney was shot a few months after the battle. Soult, Grouchy, d'Erlon and others were forced into exile. No detailed reports were ever made by them. The royal government did not concern itself about this episode in the experience of their predecessors. What the French commander and his subordinates had to say about the campaign came out by degrees, and much of it only after long years of waiting. Many of the narratives were written and published before all the facts had become known,—hence were necessarily more or less imperfect.

With a few exceptions, too, the histories of this campaign have been gravely affected by the partisanship of their authors. It is well-nigh impossible for Thiers and La Tour d'Auvergne to admit any fault, for Charras and Quinet to admit any merit, in Napoleon's management of affairs. It is equally difficult for the majority of English writers to avoid taking sides against the Emperor in any of the numerous disputes to which the campaign of Waterloo has given rise. These influences have operated in many cases to deflect the narrative of the military operations into a criticism of those who have written from the opposite standpoint.

Nevertheless, all this discussion has not been by any means without use. We have had many obscure corners cleared up, many seemingly inexplicable problems solved, and we are now in possession, taking all our information together, of nearly all, if not quite all, the facts. It only remains to collect and co-ordinate them in a spirit of impartiality. This is the task attempted in the present volume. It may be added that the narrative and discussions will be confined to purely military topics.

In the treatment of the subject, Napoleon will naturally be the central figure. The campaign was his campaign, planned and executed by him, frustrated by his opponents. It will be our endeavor to get at, as nearly as we can, his intentions, his expectations, his views from day to day of the facts of the case, so that we may, if possible, carry a personal interest into the varying fortunes of those eventful days. This will be found entirely consistent, it is believed, with an equally careful attempt to view events from the standpoints which the English and Prussian commanders must have occupied from time to time during the campaign.

The general method of Colonel Chesney in his "Waterloo Lectures" is adopted; that is, the chapters will first contain a statement or narrative, and, afterwards, notes. In these we shall have occasion to examine most of the controversies concerning this campaign. Those persons who do not care for these discussions can read the chapters *seriatim*.

Those controversies which would occupy too much space if given in the text proper will be found in appendices.

A partial list of works relating to the campaign is prefixed.

A map of the theatre of war in Belgium and another of the field of Waterloo are inserted in the book.

For those students who desire to follow the campaign more carefully, an Atlas has been prepared, which is sold separately. It contains a general map of the whole theatre of war, eleven maps of Belgium, showing the varying positions of the three armies during the campaign, and two maps of the field of Waterloo, in which the topographical features are shown by contour lines taken from the government survey, and on which the positions of the troops are set down at the commencement and close of the battle. The references in the text to maps are to the maps in this Atlas.

Copies of all the important orders and despatches will be found in Appendix C.

The author desires to express his thanks for valuable manuscripts, books and references kindly furnished him by Major General R. Oldfield, R. A., and Colonel F. A. Whinyates, R. A.; also for many useful suggestions, and for assistance in many ways, to Major W. R. Livermore, Corps of Engineers, U. S. Army, and Captain A. H. Russell, Ordnance Department, U. S. Army.

He desires also to acknowledge the aid rendered him by M. Eugène Wenseleers, Barrister of the Court of Appeal, Brussels, in ascertaining the location of the Chateau Marette, at Walhain, where (and not at Sart-à-Walhain, as has been generally believed) Marshal Grouchy was when he heard the sound of the cannon of Waterloo.

99 Mount Vernon Street:
Boston: June 1, 1892.

J. C. R.

NOTE TO THE THIRD EDITION.

Since the publication of this book the writer has been put in possession of facts which have led him to reverse his opinion of the truth of the story that the Duke of Wellington rode to Wavre on the evening of the 17th of June, 1815.

J. C. R.

99 Mount Vernon Street:
Boston: May 17, 1893.

CONTENTS.

	PAGE
PREFACE	i
CHAPTER I: THE PLAN OF CAMPAIGN . . .	1
The general military situation	2
Reasons for taking the offensive	2, 3
Napoleon decides to move against Wellington and Blücher	3
Positions of the Anglo-Dutch and Prussian Armies	3, 4
Napoleon's plan	4
As stated in Gourgaud's Narrative	4
And in the "Memoirs"	5
The other plans which were open to him . .	6
His expectation that Blücher would accept battle single-handed	7, 8
NOTE TO CHAPTER I	9
Napoleon's plan distinguished from certain other plans attributed to him	9
Alison's view that he threw himself between the two allied armies	10
Condemned by Wellington and Clausewitz . .	10
But adopted by Hooper and Quinet . . .	11
Rogniat's theory, that Napoleon ought to have aimed at seizing both Quatre Bras and Sombreffe on the first day	12
Jomini's belief, that he did have this intention .	12
Adopted by La Tour d'Auvergne	13
And by Charras	13
Their view opposed to that of Napoleon, Wellington and Clausewitz	13
Napoleon desired and expected a battle with the Prussians	14, 15

CONTENTS.

CHAPTER II: THE FRENCH ARMY 16

The army as affected by Napoleon's return from Elba 16
Confidence of the soldiers in Napoleon . . . 17
Lack of confidence in the high officers . . . 17
Napoleon's choice of Soult to take Berthier's place . . 17
Soult's unfitness for the position of chief-of-staff . . 18
The five corps-commanders 18
Estimate of the defects of the French general officers by Napoleon and by Charras 19
Probability of the truth of their views . . . 19
What Napoleon expected from his lieutenants . . 20
Marshal Ney sent for at the last moment . . 20
Sudden appointment of Marshal Grouchy to the command of the right wing 21
Napoleon's error in not taking Marshal Davout with him 22
Estimate of Napoleon's own bodily and mental vigor at this period 23–24
Portrait of Napoleon by General Foy . . . 23
Estimate of the French Army 24
It was not the best army which Napoleon had ever led 24
But it was a better army than either that of Wellington or of Blücher 25
Its strength and composition 25–28

NOTE TO CHAPTER II 29

Napoleon's health—Gardner—Ségur . . . 29
The Gudin story 30
Napoleon more or less a sufferer; but on the whole possessed of good health and strength . . 30, 31

CHAPTER III: THE ALLIED ARMIES . . . 32

Strength and composition of the Prussian army . 32, 33
Location of the different corps 33
Temper and spirit of the army 34
Marshal Blücher 34
The Duke of Wellington's army 34
Its strength and composition 35–38
Location of the various divisions 38
Merits and defects of the several parts of the army . 39

CONTENTS.

The generals: the Prince of Orange	40
Lord Hill,—Sir T. Picton	40
The Duke of Wellington	40
The internal economy of the three armies	41, 42
That of the French army	41
That of the English army	42
That of the Prussian army.	42

NOTE TO CHAPTER III 43

Defects peculiar to the inexperienced English regiments 43

CHAPTER IV: THE FIFTEENTH OF JUNE: NAPOLEON. 44

Napoleon assembles his army near Charleroi .	44, 45
He addresses it at Avesnes on the 14th	45
His letters to his brother Joseph and to Davout confirm the view above given of his plan of campaign	45
The general order of movement issued on the evening of the 14th of June	45, 46
Accident in the transmission of his orders to General Vandamme on the 15th	46
Desertion of General Bourmont	47
The operations in the centre under Napoleon's immediate supervision	47
Positions of the centre and right on the night of the 15th and 16th	48
Operations of the left wing. Arrival of Ney .	48, 49
He pushes the divisions of Bachelu and Piré to Frasnes	49
And leaves those of Jerome and Foy at Gosselies .	49
Backwardness of the 1st Corps	50–52
At 3 A. M. of the 16th one division had not arrived at the Sambre .	51
D'Erlon to blame for this tardiness .	52
Napoleon's own summary of the situation on the evening of the 15th .	53
He had purposely abstained from occupying Sombreffe	53
He expected Blücher to fight the next day for the preservation of his communications with Wellington	53

CONTENTS.

He gets a few hours' sleep during the evening of the 15th 54

NOTES TO CHAPTER IV 55
 1. Marshal Ney's lack of a proper staff 56
 2. Discussion of the results of the operations on the 15th . . . . 56 et seq.
 Jomini and Charras consider them incomplete and unsatisfactory 56
 A. The question, as regards the non-occupation of Sombreffe on the evening of the 15th . . 57–61
 Rogniat's criticism 57
 Napoleon's answer 57
 Charras and Jomini 58, 59
 Re-statement of Napoleon's plan and expectations . 59
 The plan suggested by Rogniat, Jomini and Charras no improvement on that of Napoleon . . 60
 B. The question as regards the non-occupation of Quatre Bras on the evening of the 15th . 61–63
 (1.) Reasons why the effect on Blücher of the occupation of Quatre Bras might be different from that of the occupation of Sombreffe . 61
 (2.) The occupation of Quatre Bras on the evening of the 15th not necessary to Napoleon's scheme . 62
 3. Reasons why Napoleon blamed Ney for not having occupied Quatre Bras on the 15th . . 63
 4. Did Napoleon give Ney a verbal order to seize Quatre Bras on the 15th? 64
 The statements of Gourgaud and the Memoirs . . 64
 The statement in the Bulletin of the Army, sent off in the evening of the 15th 65
 The published statement of Marshal Grouchy in 1818 that he heard the Emperor blame Ney for having disobeyed his orders to seize Quatre Bras on the 15th . . . . . . 65, n. 28
 The subsequent hearsay evidence of little value . 66–67
 The Bulletin much the best evidence that we have 67–69
 That no mention is made in the written orders of the 16th of the verbal order of the day before, is not material 69

CHAPTER V: THE FIFTEENTH OF JUNE: BLUCHER AND WELLINGTON 70

Blücher on the 14th ordered his army to concentrate at Sombreffe 70
And without consulting Wellington 70
The nature of the understanding between them . 70 *et seq.*
Müffling's statement generally misunderstood . . 71
There was every intention to act in concert, but no definite agreement as to details 72
Bülow's disobedience of orders 73
Gneisenau's remissness in not giving him full information of the situation 73
Wellington's desire to protect Ghent and Brussels . 74
He retained his headquarters at Brussels . . 74
He thought it probable that the French would advance by way of Mons 74
Hence he would not hastily move in force in the direction of Quatre Bras 75
The Prince of Orange hears of the French advance . 76
And brings word of it to the Duke at Brussels at 3 P. M. of the 15th 77
Wellington's first orders were issued between 5 and 7 P. M. 77
They were simply for the concentration of the various divisions of his army 78
But they implied that Nivelles and not Quatre Bras was likely to be the point of concentration for the whole army 78
Information that Blücher is concentrating at Sombreffe arrives in the evening at Brussels . . 78
And Wellington issues, about 10 P. M., his "After Orders" which direct a general movement towards the east 79
Difficulty of reconciling the evidence as to the subsequent orders of the Duke 79
The Duke's official report states that he ordered the whole army to Quatre Bras in the early morning of the 16th 80
Müffling's statement 80
The Duke's conversation with the Duke of Richmond . . . . 81, n. 37

CONTENTS.

The instructions issued to Colonel de Lancey have been lost 81
The orders to Hill in the early morning of the 16th . 82
They indicate that no decision for a concentration at Quatre Bras had then been reached . . . 83
This inference may be also drawn from the halt of Picton's division at Waterloo 83
It has even been maintained that as late as 10 A. M. of the 16th the Duke had not decided to hold Quatre Bras . . . . 84, n. 50
But the Letter of the Duke to Marshal Blücher and the "Disposition" of Sir W. De Lancey contradict this supposition 85
Character and meaning of the "Disposition" . . 86
The "Disposition" evidently the foundation of the Letter to Blücher 87–88
Taken together, they show that the Duke ordered a concentration of his army at Quatre Bras in the early morning of the 16th 88
But not until after he had given the orders above mentioned to Hill and Picton 88
His decision was probably arrived at while he was at the Duchess of Richmond's ball . . . 89

NOTES TO CHAPTER V 90
  1. The Duke's "Memorandum on the Battle of Waterloo" 90
  Its surprising statements 90
  2. No definite plan of action agreed on by Wellington and Blücher in the event of a French invasion 91
  3. Wellington does not deserve credit for promptness in deciding to concentrate at Quatre Bras 92
  4. Wellington's original intention of concentrating at Nivelles considered 93
  It is approved by Colonel Maurice 93
  A. But when Wellington knew that the French main army was in front of Blücher at Sombreffe he could run no great risk in concentrating at Quatre Bras 94

CONTENTS.

B. His fault was in delaying to issue the order to do so 94
If his orders had been strictly carried out, Ney would have occupied Quatre Bras without opposition, and been able to assist Napoleon at Ligny 95
C. Napoleon attached great importance to Quatre Bras, and gave Ney a large force in order to make sure of its acquisition 95, 96
5. The extent of the cantonments of the allied armies criticized 96
Opinion of Sir James Shaw-Kennedy 96
Opinions of Charras and Napoleon . . . 97, 98
6. Napoleon's criticism on Blücher for fixing Sombreffe as the point of concentration for his army, well supported 98
But his censure of Wellington for concentrating at Quatre Bras undeserved 99
Because this decision of Wellington's was based on Napoleon's having already concentrated in front of Sombreffe 99, 100

CHAPTER VI: THE DUTCH-BELGIANS . . 101
Prince Bernhard of Saxe-Weimar occupies Quatre Bras in the afternoon of the 15th . . . 101
And is attacked by Reille's advance between 5 and 6 P.M. 101
The other brigade of Perponcher's division, Bylandt's, ordered there also 102
The Prince of Orange arrives at Quatre Bras at 6 A.M. of the 16th 102

NOTE TO CHAPTER VI 103
Maurice's criticism on the occupation of Quatre Bras by the Dutch-Belgian generals . . 103
But the fact that they knew of the concentration of the French and Prussian armies near Sombreffe fully justifies their course 103, 104

CHAPTER VII: THE MORNING OF THE SIXTEENTH OF JUNE: WELLINGTON . . 105
The Duke leaves Brussels about 7.30 A.M. of the 16th 105

And rides at once to Quatre Bras 106
His letter to Blücher 106
Comparison of the statements in the Letter with those in the "Disposition" of Sir W. De Lancey 107–108
He evidently accepted the "Disposition" as conclusive 108
He rides over to Brye to confer with Blücher . . 108
And returns to Quatre Bras between 2 and 3 P. M. . 109
No doubt expecting to find a large part of his army there 109
Delbrück's theory, that the Duke deliberately misrepresented the situation of his army, entirely unsupported 109, 110

NOTES TO CHAPTER VII 111
  1. Actual positions of Wellington's divisions at 7 A.M. of the 16th 111–113
  2. Whether, if the Duke had known the truth, he would have stayed at Quatre Bras,—*quære* . 114
  3. Wellington badly served by his subordinates in the matter of the transmission of intelligence from the front 114–115

CHAPTER VIII: THE MORNING OF THE SIXTEENTH OF JUNE: NEY . . . 116
Ney returns from Charleroi to Gosselies at 2 A.M. . 116
And at first orders Reille to set out at once for Frasnes 116
But afterwards changes his mind, and allows Reille, with the divisions of Jerome and Foy, to remain in Gosselies 117
He ought to have sent them to Frasnes at once . . 117
And to have filled their places at Gosselies with the divisions of the 1st Corps 118
He does nothing to bring up the 1st Corps till late in the forenoon 119
Soult's first order to him on the 16th . . . 120
Received about 6 A.M., and answered before 7 A.M. . 120
Ney then returns to Frasnes, leaving Reille at Gosselies, with instructions to march to the front at once on receipt of orders from army headquarters 120

About 9 A.M. Reille receives word from Girard that the Prussians are massing at Fleurus	121
And at 10 A.M. he reads the Emperor's letter to Ney, brought by Flahaut	121
But defers his march to Frasnes till he gets further orders from Ney	122
He gets further orders, and leaves Gosselies at 11.45 A.M.	122
Soult's second order directs Ney to march on Quatre Bras	122
The Emperor's letter to Ney	123
The 1st and 2d Corps and Kellermann's cavalry are all put at Ney's disposal	123
The third order to Ney from Soult that morning	123, 124
Its peremptory character	124
Ney refuses fully to obey his orders	124
His unwillingness to take the risks which they involve	124
He proposes to keep half his force in reserve	125

NOTES TO CHAPTER VIII 126

1. Summary of Ney's conduct on the morning of the 16th 126
2. He evidently did not intend to obey his orders strictly 127
3. The light his conduct on the 16th throws on his failure to seize Quatre Bras the day before . 127
4. No criticism can be made on Napoleon and Soult . 128
5. Why Napoleon did not send Ney an earlier order to seize Quatre Bras, answered in Chapter IX . 128

CHAPTER IX: THE MORNING OF THE SIXTEENTH OF JUNE: NAPOLEON . . 129

Ney and Napoleon at Charleroi during the night of the 15th and 16th	129
Napoleon, impressed by the backwardness of d'Erlon, decides to wait until the left wing is ready	130
The formal order to Ney to seize Quatre Bras not given until Ney's report of the state of his command had arrived — between 8 and 9 A.M.	131
The advance of the centre and right also delayed to conform to the movements of the left	131, 132

Napoleon's expectations as to the forwardness of
Ney's command 132, 133
Napoleon prepares and sends letters to Ney and
Grouchy, in view of the possible withdrawal
of Marshal Blücher 134, 135
He seems to have thought this probable . . . 136
But he made every preparation for encountering the
enemy in force both at Sombreffe and at Quatre
Bras 137
The 6th Corps regarded as a reserve for the whole
army 138

NOTES TO CHAPTER IX 139
1. The censure generally passed on Napoleon for
his delays on the morning of the 16th not
deserved 139
Opinions of Wellington and Clausewitz . . . 139, n. 5
2. Ney not responsible for the backwardness of
the 1st Corps during the night . . . 140
3. Ney's inactivity on returning to Gosselies . 140
4. No evidence thus far of indolence or irresolution on the part of Napoleon . . . 140
5. Error of supposing that he ever thought of
pressing on to Brussels between the two allied
armies — Chesney and Clinton . . . 141
His letters to Ney and Grouchy conclusive as
to this 141, 142
His object was to destroy the allied armies in succession — Jomini 142

CHAPTER X: THE BATTLE OF LIGNY:
BLUCHER'S DECISION TO ACCEPT
BATTLE NOT DEPENDENT ON WELLINGTON'S ASSURANCE OF SUPPORT . 143
Blücher concentrated his army without receiving
any assurance of support from Wellington . 143
He got Wellington's letter about noon of the 16th . 144
Wellington arrived at Brye at 1 P.M. . . . 144
Their conversation 144
Wellington gave no unconditional promise . . 145
Blücher's decision to fight was arrived at before he
heard from or saw Wellington . . . 146
And on entirely independent grounds . . . 147

CONTENTS.

NOTE TO CHAPTER X 148
   Blücher's reasons for deciding to accept battle at
      Ligny as given by Damitz 148
   He was unwilling to retreat 148
   Suggestions of Ollech and Delbrück not of any
      value here 149
   Blücher expected to concentrate his whole army of
      120,000 men 149
   And was unwilling to change his decision when he
      found he could not count upon Bülow's arrival . 150

CHAPTER XI: THE BATTLE OF LIGNY . . . 151
   Position of the Prussian army at Ligny . . . 151
   Napoleon examines the position 152
   The most obvious plan of battle was to turn the
      Prussian right 152
   But Napoleon decides to attack the centre . . 153
   Positions taken by the French 153, 154
   The 2 P. M. order sent to Ney to coöperate with
      the main army 154
   The battle begins at 2.30 by attacking Ligny and
      St. Amand 154
   The 3.15 P. M. order to Ney 155
   Napoleon determines about half-past five o'clock to
      put in the Guard 156
   The unexpected appearance of d'Erlon's Corps
      causes a delay of nearly two hours . . . 157
   The attack by the Guard breaks the Prussian centre . 158
   The Prussians fall back to Brye and Sombreffe . 159
   Losses of the Prussians and French . . . 159
   The non-employment of the 6th Corps . . 159, 160
   Extent of the victory 160, 161
   It was not equal to Napoleon's hopes, but it had
      disposed of the Prussians for a time . . 161, 162

NOTES TO CHAPTER XI 163
   1. Napoleon's delay in beginning the battle . . 163
   His reasons considered 164
   2. His plan of battle criticised by Rogniat and
      others 164
   Napoleon's reply to Rogniat 165

His reasons for taking the course he did . . . 165
The criticism of Davout and Clausewitz considered . 166
3. Clausewitz's doubts as to the decisive result of Ney's movement 167
The question fully stated and Napoleon's expectations justified 167
4. What Napoleon had a right to expect from Ney . 168
5. Whether Napoleon's plan was the best, considering that he could not absolutely rely on Ney's coöperation . , ... 169
6. Why Napoleon did not order d'Erlon to remain and take part in the battle 170
He must have assumed that d'Erlon had come upon the field for this purpose 170
And there was not time to send him orders . . 170
7. Napoleon's skill well displayed at Ligny . . 171
Clausewitz's review of the battle 171-173
He points out that Napoleon was more economical in the use of his troops than Blücher . . 171
Severe and unwarranted criticism of Marshal Davout on Napoleon's tactics 173
Napoleon not responsible for the error which brought d'Erlon on the field 174
8. Whether Napoleon was wise in arresting the progress of the battle on the appearance of the strange corps (d'Erlon's),—*Quære* . . 174-175
9. Napoleon to be censured for not having made use of the 6th Corps 175

CHAPTER XII: THE BATTLE OF QUATRE BRAS 176
Résumé of Marshal Ney's doings in the forenoon of the 16th 176
He should have ordered Jerome and Foy to Gosselies in the early morning 177
He scattered his command instead of uniting it, as he was ordered to do 177
He begins the action at 2 P. M., with the divisions of Bachelu, Foy and Piré 178
Jerome's division arrives at 3 P. M. . . . 178
Wellington returns to Quatre Bras at 2.30 P. M. . 178
Picton's division arrives at 3.30 P. M. . . . 178

CONTENTS.

Alten's division arrives at 5 P. M.	179
At this hour Ney has only the 2d Corps on the field	179
Reasons for the non-arrival of the 1st Corps	179
Its delay in starting	180
Its leading division — Durutte's — turned off by an aide of the Emperor's from Frasnes towards St. Amand	180
The corps is seen approaching St. Amand about 5 P. M.	180
It must, therefore, have left the Charleroi road at Frasnes about 4.30 P. M.	181
This was two hours and a half after Jerome's division had passed through Frasnes	181
Responsibility of Ney and d'Erlon for this extraordinary state of things	181
Marshal Ney not to blame for recalling D'Erlon to Quatre Bras	181
It was probably the staff-officer who carried the 2 P. M. order who turned the 1st Corps off from the turnpike	182
For the non-arrival of Kellermann's cavalry Ney alone was responsible	182
He ordered it to remain in the rear at Frasnes and Liberchies	182, 183
In this he deliberately disobeyed orders	183
He finally, at 6 P. M., puts in one brigade of Kellermann's Corps	183
Which is at first successful, but is afterwards driven back with loss	184
The French retire to Frasnes	184
The casualties on both sides	184
If d'Erlon's Corps had not been turned off, it is probable that Wellington would have been badly beaten	184, 185
If Ney had concentrated his whole command between 12 M. and 2 P. M., Quatre Bras would probably have been evacuated	185, 186
In this case Ney could have spared 10,000 or 20,000 men to assist Napoleon	186
Criticism on Marshal Ney's management	186
Wellington's skilful handling of his troops	187, 188

CONTENTS.

NOTES TO CHAPTER XII 189
   1. Charras' erroneous statements as to Ney's orders in regard to the employment of Kellerman's cavalry 189
   2. Napoleon's mistakes in his account of the matter in his Memoirs 190
   But his principal censure on Ney for not having got his command together and used it as a whole, is fully borne out 191
   3. Curious error of Siborne's 191
   4. Jomini's defence of Reille's delay to march to Frasnes 192
   It overlooks the necessity of occupying Frasnes in any event, and therefore cannot be accepted . 193
   5. Baudus' account of his carrying an order from Soult to d'Erlon 193
   Reasons for thinking that this order must have been directed to Ney 194
   Baudus probably carried the duplicate of the 3.15 P. M. order to Ney 195
   The evidence on certain minor points conflicting . 196

CHAPTER XIII: THE SEVENTEENTH OF JUNE: NAPOLEON 197
   Résumé of the campaign up to date . . . 197
   Napoleon had no reason for delay 197
   He had a disposable army composed almost entirely of fresh troops 197
   Reasons for thinking that the Prussians might soon recover from the defeat of Ligny . . . 198
   Opportunity open to Napoleon of overwhelming that part of Wellington's army which was at Quatre Bras 199
   Napoleon's inactivity on this morning . . . 200
   Probably the result of fatigue 200
   Ney sends no report to the Emperor . . . 200
   Soult's first order to him to move on Quatre Bras . 201
   Napoleon presumes that Wellington has long since fallen back 201
   Napoleon's lack of energy and activity this morning . 202
   Before noon, however, the 6th Corps and the Guard are ordered to Marbais 203

Second order to Ney at noon	203
Girard's division of the 2d Corps left at Ligny	203
Napoleon's reasons for supposing that Blücher had retired on Namur	203, 204
Of which the principal was that he had on the day before employed so large a part of his army in holding the Namur road	204
Pajol captures some prisoners and a battery on the road to Namur	205
Napoleon's neglect to send out cavalry to explore the country to the north	205
Napoleon determines to send Grouchy with the 3d and 4th Corps to pursue the Prussians	206
His verbal orders to Grouchy, and Grouchy's remonstrances	207
Grouchy's points not well taken	207
Grouchy's denial that he ever received on that day a written order	208
Berton reports a whole Prussian corps at Gembloux	209
The Emperor, then, in the absence of Soult, dictates to Bertrand an order to Grouchy	209
Full text of this order	209, 210
This order changes entirely the task assigned to Grouchy	210
He is to ascertain whether the Prussians intend to separate from the English or to unite with them to cover Brussels or Liége in trying the fate of another battle	211
And is left full discretion as to his course in either event	211
Strength and composition of his command	212
He reaches Gembloux that evening	212
And writes to the Emperor a report in which he says he shall try to separate the Prussians from Wellington	212, 213
Strength of Wellington's force at Quatre Bras	214
At Quatre Bras the Emperor in person leads the pursuit of the English	214
His remark to d'Erlon	215
Interesting picture of the march by the author of "Napoléon à Waterloo"	215

Skirmish at Genappe	216
The English take up positions south of the hamlet of Mont St. Jean	216
NOTES TO CHAPTER XIII	217
1. Napoleon not to be blamed for not having pursued the Prussians in the early morning of the 17th. Clausewitz's opinion	217
2. Napoleon probably would not have detached Grouchy had he known that the Prussians had retired on Wavre	218
3. Effect on the contemporary historians of Grouchy's concealment of the Bertrand order—*e. g.*, on Clausewitz	218
4. Curious survival of this effect on historians who wrote after the order had come to light	219
On Chesney	219
On Maurice	219
On Hamley	221
On Hooper	222
5. Whether the Bertrand order was sufficiently explicit. Charras' opinion	222
6. The reasons for directing Grouchy on Gembloux considered	223
7. Valuable suggestions of Maurice as to the reasons which induced Napoleon to suppose that the Prussians had retreated to Namur	223
8. It was an error for Napoleon to trust to the probabilities, when so much was at stake	224, 225
CHAPTER XIV: THE SEVENTEENTH OF JUNE: BLUCHER AND WELLINGTON	226
Zieten and Pirch I. fall back towards Wavre	226
Renunciation of the line of Namur	226
But a general concentration at Wavre not necessarily implied	226
Although it was rendered possible by Gneisenau's action	227
Gneisenau unwilling to renounce all hope of union with the English	228
Although he recognized the difficulties attending it	228
And doubted whether he could rely on Wellington	229
Blücher carried off the field to Mellery	229

CONTENTS.

Hardinge's story of the discussion between Blücher and Gneisenau 230
The Prussian generals decide to march to join Wellington 230
Movements of Thielemann and Bülow . . . 231
Admirable conduct of the Prussian corps-commanders 231
The Prussians fall back on Wavre 232
Leaving a detachment at Mont St. Guibert . . 232
The artillery trains arrive at Wavre at 5 P. M. . 232
Wellington at Quatre Bras on the morning of the 17th 233
His message to Blücher sent through Lieut. Massow . 233
Blücher replies about midnight, promising support . 234
Wellington's uncertainty during the day and evening of the 17th 234
The risk which he ran 235, 236
NOTES TO CHAPTER XIV 237
1. Maurice's correction of Siborne . . . 237
2. The story of the Duke's ride to Wavre on the evening of the 17th 238–242
Lockhart's brief statement 239
Lord Ellesmere's denial of Lockhart's statement . 239
The story as told by the Rev. Julian Charles Young 239–241
Mr. Coltman's recollection of his father's statement about it 241
Reasons for rejecting the story 242
3. Napoleon's criticism on the course of Wellington and Blücher after the battle of Ligny . . 243
Clausewitz denies that Wellington ran any risk . 243
His view not tenable 244
The question of the advisability of running the risk stated 244
CHAPTER XV: THE EIGHTEENTH OF JUNE: GROUCHY AND BLUCHER . . . 245
Grouchy's letter from Gembloux of 10 P. M. not really satisfactory 245
But Napoleon and Soult do not give him further instructions or any information . . . 246
Napoleon thinks Grouchy may arrive by the bridge of Moustier and sends Marbot to look out for him . 247

CONTENTS.

Grouchy was acting under the Bertrand order	248
Which laid upon him the task of ascertaining the intentions of the Prussians	249
And then left him entire liberty of action	249
Errors of Gardner and Maurice as to this latter point	249, 250
Grouchy at 10 P. M. of the 17th issues his orders for the next day to move on Sart-à-Walhain at 6 and 8 A. M.	250
But at daybreak he has learned that the Prussians had retired on Brussels	251
Yet he does not change his orders	252
He should have marched for the bridge of Moustier at daybreak	253
Opinion of Jomini	253
Opinion of Clausewitz	253
Opinion of Charras	253
Grouchy neglects to reconnoitre to his left	254
He arrives at Walhain and stops at the house of M. Hollert, a notary	255
He writes a despatch to the Emperor	255
Analysis of this despatch	255, 256
The sound of the cannon of Waterloo is heard	256
Grouchy's plain duty	256
Gérard's advice	256
Grouchy refuses to follow it	257
And resumes his march on Wavre	257
Condition of the roads and bridges	258
Grouchy might have crossed the Dyle after having arrived at La Baraque	259
Three general misconceptions	259
1. As to the place where the sound of the cannon was heard	259
2. As to the necessity of marching by way of Mont St. Guibert	259
3. As to the resistance to be expected at the bridges	260
Grouchy might have been across by 4 P. M.	260
Positions of the IVth and IId Prussian Corps at that moment	261
And of the Ist Corps	261
Probability that Grouchy would have arrested the march of Bülow and Pirch I.	261

Zieten's march, however, would not have been interfered with	261
Bülow reaches St. Lambert at noon	262
Pirch I. and Zieten do not leave Wavre till nearly noon	262
Tardiness of these movements	263
Accounted for by Gneisenau's distrust of Wellington	263
His postscript to the letter to Müffling	263
His doubts as to Wellington's accepting battle dispelled by the sound of the cannon of Waterloo	264
The combat at Wavre	264, 265
The bridge of Limale carried by the French between 6 and 7 P.M.	265
Soult's 10 A.M. order to Grouchy	265
Analysis of this order	266
Its main object	266
It furnishes no justification for Grouchy's course	267
Inconsistency between this despatch and the instructions given to Marbot	268–270
The despatch probably not revised by Napoleon	270
The 1 P.M. order to Grouchy	270, 271
Both despatches show that Napoleon was relying on Grouchy	272
The postscript to the second shows that the Emperor had become alarmed	272
NOTES TO CHAPTER XV	273
1. The wisdom of detaching Grouchy with 33,000 men considered	273
This course was decided on when it was believed that the Prussians had retreated on Namur	273
For Grouchy was not needed for the battle with the Anglo-Dutch army	274
But the Bertrand order shows that Napoleon feared that Blücher might have undertaken to join Wellington	274
In which case he would have had a long start by the time when Grouchy could move	275
Yet Napoleon adhered to the original decision to send Grouchy off, although he gave him a distinct warning	276
Risks incurred by this course	276

It would have been far safer to have taken Grouchy and his two corps with the main army	. . .	277
2. Kennedy's reason against the detachment of Grouchy	. . . . . .	277
But it was not to beat Wellington that Grouchy was needed, but to keep off Blücher	. . .	278
3. Importance of treating independently of the conduct of Napoleon and Grouchy	. . .	279
4. Hamley's opinion as to Grouchy's proper course given and commented on	. . . .	280
5. The probable results, if Grouchy had marched for Moustier at daybreak	. . . .	281
It would seem that he might easily have concealed the object of his march	. . . .	281
Charras, however, is of a different opinion	. .	282
Examination of his views	. . . . .	282
Probability that Grouchy could have effected a crossing at Moustier and Ottignies by 11 A.M.		283
And that Bülow would have stopped to concentrate his corps and fight	. . . . . .	283
And that Pirch I. and Thielemann would have reinforced Bülow	. . . . . .	284
Zieten, however, if he chose to do so, might have continued his march	. . . . .	284
6. Charras' view as to the difficulty of Grouchy's effecting a crossing after he had arrived at La Baraque	. . . .	284
His statements as to the Prussian force in the vicinity of the lower bridges unsupported	.	285
7. It is generally stated that Grouchy was at Sart-à-Walhain when he heard the sound of the cannon of Waterloo	. . . .	286
Statements of the different narratives	. . .	286, 287
He was, however, at Walhain, at the Chateau Marette, then the residence of M. Hollert, the Notary of Nil St. Vincent	. . . .	287, 288

CHAPTER XVI: THE BATTLE OF WATERLOO 289

Napoleon examines the allied position at 1 A.M. . . 289

Early in the morning he again goes to the front to see if the English are there 290

CONTENTS.

His expectation of victory 290
The *rôle* which he expected Grouchy to play . . 290
He does not seem to have drawn the very natural inference that Wellington was expecting Blücher; or, if he did, he certainly did not act upon it 291
The rain ceased about 8 A. M. 291
The original intention was to begin the battle at 9 o'clock 292
But Drouot suggested delay and Napoleon acquiesced . 292
Napoleon forms the army in three lines . . . 292
His delay in beginning the action criticised . . . 293
And his neglect to send word to Grouchy . . . 294
Every hour's delay a gain to Wellington . . . 294
Whose army was unequal to the shock without the assistance of the Prussians 294
Kennedy's explanation of Wellington's course . . 295
Risks that Wellington took 295
Wellington had had the field surveyed . . . 296
Description of the English position 297
Composition and strength of Wellington's army . . 298
Positions of the various troops 299
Hougomont and La Haye Sainte 300
Strength and composition of the French army . . 301
Positions of the corps 301
Napoleon's plan of battle 302
Establishment of a great battery east of the Charleroi turnpike 302
It has been universally commended 303
The attack on Hougomont, ordered as a preliminary to the main attack, which was to be on the centre, very rashly and carelessly conducted 303, 304
The assault by d'Erlon's Corps 304-307
Formation of the troops 305
No assignable reason for such a peculiar and unwieldy formation 305
The attack is made and repulsed 307
Napoleon sees the Prussians on the heights of St. Lambert 307
Capture of La Haye Sainte 307
The great cavalry attacks on the English centre . . 308

CONTENTS.

They were made against troops in good condition to stand them	308
Napoleon is called away at 4 P. M. to take charge of the resistance to the Prussians	308
Necessity of maintaining the Charleroi road and Planchenoit against their assaults	309
Napoleon's personal supervision needed	309
The great cavalry charges	309
They accomplish little and the cavalry is ruined	310
French batteries placed to the south of La Haye Sainte enfilade the English line west of the turnpike	310
But this was only done to a limited extent	310
The attack by the heavy cavalry of the Guard	311
Napoleon succeeds in repulsing Bülow	311
The battle against the English not actively carried on after the cessation of the cavalry attacks	312
But the English line at this period becomes from various causes very weak. Kennedy's description of it	312
What Napoleon might have accomplished against the English had he not been fighting the Prussians at this time	313
The fight with the Prussians terminated, Napoleon returns to the front	314
Wellington has made every effort to restore his line; its condition to the west of the pike	314
Ney is ordered to make preparations for an attack to be made by the Imperial Guard	315
Disposition at this time of the various battalions of the Guard	15, 316
Strength and composition of the attacking force	316
The Emperor leads up and hands to Ney two regiments of grenadiers and two of chasseurs	317
They are formed in columns of battalions and march in *échelon*, the right in advance	317
Premature attack of a body of French horse on the left of the Guard	317
No support furnished by Reille	318
Admirable conduct of d'Erlon	318

CONTENTS.

The leading battalions of the Guard strike Maitland's brigade of guards	319
Captain Powell's account	319
The leading battalions of the Guard are beaten .	320
General Maitland's account	321
Skilful and gallant conduct of Sir C. Halkett .	322
The left and rear battalions of the Guard continue to advance	323
But are attacked in flank by the 52d regiment .	324
And are completely overthrown	324
The failure of the attack largely due to the absence of supports	324
Arrival of the van of Zieten's Corps on the field .	324
The French right wing retires in confusion . .	325
Charge of the cavalry-brigades of Vivian and Vandeleur	325
Exertions of Napoleon to restore order . . .	325
He is finally forced to retire	326
The French retreat blocked at Genappe . .	326
The result of the battle due to the intervention of the Prussians	327
Probable course of Zieten if Grouchy had detained Bülow and Pirch I.	328
Grouchy, however, not solely responsible for the defeat	328
NOTES TO CHAPTER XVI	329
1. The French tactics generally censured . .	329
Napoleon and Ney both to blame	329
Injurious effect on the French chances of success of Napoleon's absence at Planchenoit . . .	330
The attack on Hougomont criticised . . .	330
The defence of Planchenoit praised . . .	331
2. The English tactics exceedingly good . .	331
3. The attack of the Imperial Guard . . .	331
A. No foundation for the hypothesis of two columns	332
B. The claims of the 52d regiment considered .	333
The notion that it was only the skirmishers of the Imperial Guard who were driven off by Maitland's brigade refuted by the testimony of eye witnesses	334
The great credit due to Colborne	335

CONTENTS

4. Napoleon's reasons for ordering the attack considered 336
Zieten's intervention not anticipated 336
The English reported as growing weaker . . . 337
Ney ordered and expected to support the attack by Bachelu's division and by cavalry on the left . 337
Ney disappoints the Emperor's expectations in both respects 337
The charge of the Guard might have been properly supported 338
Contrast between Ney and Wellington . . . 338
Note on Ney's state of mind . . . . 338, n. 22
5. Wellington's course in leaving 18,000 men at Hal and Tubize, not to be defended . . . 339
6. As to the effect upon the Prussians of the appearance of Grouchy's force marching from the Dyle 339
7. The rout of the French army due to the irruption of Zieten's Corps 340
The comparative weakness of the Anglo-Dutch army at the close of the action 341
8. Relative responsibility of Napoleon and Grouchy for the intervention of the Prussians . . . 341
Both are responsible for it 342

CHAPTER XVII: CONCLUDING OBSERVATIONS 343
The principal points treated of in this book . . 343–350

APPENDIX A.

On some characteristics of Napoleon's Memoirs . 351
Injustice done Napoleon by Charras and others . 351
Peculiarity of Napoleon's memory 352
He recalls his expectations, but not the tenor of the orders which he gave 352
Illustration from the orders sent to Ney on the afternoon of the 16th 352
The same thing probably true as to the order sent to Grouchy 353
The orders given in the "Memoirs" were probably never sent 354
And the Bertrand order, which was sent, was forgotten 354

CONTENTS. xxxi

APPENDIX B.

On Marshal Grouchy and the Bertrand order	355
Denials by Marshal Grouchy in his pamphlets published in Philadelphia that he received on the 17th any written order.	355
He relied on the fact that no copy of the Bertrand order was among the major-general's papers	356
Publication of the order in 1842	357
It is now recognized in the Grouchy Memoirs	357
Original text of the Bertrand Order	358
Grouchy's report to the Emperor dated Gembloux, 10 P. M., June 17, given in full	359
It is in reality a reply to the Bertrand order	360
Mutilation by Marshal Grouchy of the text of this report	360
Object of the change	360
No doubt as to the correct reading	361

APPENDIX C.

I.	Napoleon's Address to his army, June 14, 1815	362
II.	Order of movement, June 14, 1815	363
III.	Order to the Count Reille, 8.30 A. M., June 15, 1815	366
IV.	Order to the Count d'Erlon, 10 A. M., June 15, 1815	367
V.	Order to the Count d'Erlon, 3 P. M., June 15, 1815	367
VI.	Subsequent Order to the Count d'Erlon, June 15, 1815	367
VII.	Order to Gen. Noguès, 3 A. M., June 16, 1815	368
VIII.	Bulletin of the army, June 15, 1815, evening	369
IX.	Wellington's first Memorandum of Orders, June 15, 1815	370
X.	Wellington's letter to the Duc de Feltre, 10 P. M., June 15, 1815	371
XI.	Wellington's "After Orders," 10 P. M., June 15, 1815	371
XII.	Extract from Wellington's Report of the Operations, June 19, 1815	372

XIII.	Wellington's Conversation with the Duke of Richmond, June 16, 1851	373
XIV.	Wellington's Orders to Lord Hill, June 16, 1815	374
XV.	Extract from Wellington's "Memorandum on the Battle of Waterloo"	374
XVI.	Wellington's Letter to Blücher, 10.30 A. M., June 16, 1815	376
XVII.	Soult's first order to Ney, June 16, 1815	377
XVIII.	The Emperor's Letter to Ney, June 16, 1815	377
XIX.	Count Reille's Letter to Ney, June 16, 1815	379
XX.	Ney's Orders to Reille and d'Erlon, June 16, 1815	379
XXI.	Soult's formal Order to Ney to carry Quatre Bras, June 16, 1815	380
XXII.	Soult's second Order to Ney to carry Quatre Bras, June 16, 1815	381
XXIII.	Flahaut's Letter to the Duke of Elchingen	382
XXIV.	Napoleon's Letter to Grouchy, June 16, 1815	382
XXV.	The 2 P. M.—June 16th—Order to Ney	383
XXVI.	The 3.15 P. M.—June 16th—Order to Ney	384
XXVII.	Soult's Letter to Ney, June 17, 1815	384
XXVIII.	Soult's Order to Ney, 12 M., June 17, 1815	385
XXIX.	Capt. Bowles' story of Wellington at Quatre Bras, June 17, 1815	386
XXX.	Grouchy's report to Napoleon from Sart-à-Walhain, 11 A. M., June 18, 1815	386
XXXI.	General Order of preparation for the Battle of Waterloo, June 18, 1815	387
XXXII.	Order for the attack to begin at 1 P. M., June 18, 1815	388
XXXIII.	The 10 A. M.—June 18th—Order to Grouchy	388
XXXIV.	The 1 P. M.—June 18th—Order to Grouchy	389

MAPS.

(At end of this volume.)

THE THEATRE OF WAR.

THE FIELD OF WATERLOO AT 11 A. M., JUNE 18, 1815.

A PARTIAL LIST OF WORKS RELATING TO THE CAMPAIGN.[1]

ALISON:
History of Europe from the commencement of the French Revolution to the Restoration of the Bourbons in 1815. By Archibald Alison, LL. D. New Edition with Portraits. Vols. XIII and XIV. Wm. Blackwood & Sons, Edinburgh & London, MDCCCL.

BATTY:
An Historical Sketch of the Campaign of 1815, illustrated by Plans of the Operations and of the Battles of Quatre-Bras, Ligny and Waterloo. By Captain Batty, of the First or Grenadier Guards. 2d Edition, Considerably Enlarged. London, 1820.

BAUDUS:
Études sur Napoléon. Par le lieutenant-colonel de Baudus, ancien aide-de-camp des Maréchaux Bessières et Soult. 2 Vols. Paris: Debécourt: 1841.

BERTON:
Précis, historique, militaire et critique, des batailles de Fleurus et de Waterloo. Avec une Carte. Par le Maréchal-de-Camp Berton. Paris: Delaunay. 1818.

BIBLIOGRAPHY OF THE CAMPAIGN:
Prepared, with critical estimates, in October, 1875, by Justin Winsor, now Librarian of Harvard College, in Bulletin No. 35 of the Public Library of the City of Boston, of which Mr. Winsor was then Librarian. It includes a notice of Maps and Plans.
Colonel Chesney gives a list of works cited by himself just after the Table of Contents in his Waterloo Lectures.
Colonel Maurice in his book entitled "War,"— London and New York: Macmillan & Co., 1891,— gives in the Appendix, pp. 128 *et seq.*, a list of books relating to the campaign of Waterloo,— with comments and estimates.

BROWNE:
Wellington: or Public and Private Life of Arthur, first Duke of Wellington. By G. Lathom Browne. London, W. H. Allen & Co. 1888.

BULLOCK'S DIARY:
Journal of R. H. Bullock, 11th Light Dragoons. English Historical Magazine. July, 1888.

---

[1] Where these works are cited in this book they are cited by the word which is printed in capitals; as ALISON, BATTY, BAUDUS.

CAMPAGNE DE LA BELGIQUE:

Contenant
1. L'Ode sur la Bataille de Waterloo ou de Mont St. Jean:
2. Relation Belge sur la Bataille de Waterloo, et de la part qu'y a prise la troisième division militaire du Royaume des Pays Bas:
3. Relation Française, par un témoin oculaire:
4. Campagne de Walcheren et d'Anvers; 1809:
5. Relation Anglaise, traduite sur le texte, publiée à Londres en Septembre dernier.

Bruxelles, 1816. (With a portrait of the Prince of Orange, and maps.)

CHARRAS:

Histoire de la Campagne de 1815: Waterloo: Par le Lt-Colonel Charras. 5me Édition, revue et augmentée. Avec un Atlas nouveau. Leipzig: F. A. Brockhaus. (No date.)

CHESNEY:

Waterloo Lectures: A Study of the Campaign of 1815. By Colonel Charles C. Chesney, R. E., late Professor of Military Art and History in the Staff College. Third Edition. London: Longmans, Green & Co. 1874.

CHURCHILL'S LETTER:

Letter to his father written by Major Chatham Horace Churchill, of the 1st Foot Guards, Aide to General Lord Hill. (Waterloo Roll Call, pp. 2, 14, 92, and Appendix.) The letter was first printed in the Life of Sir William Napier, pp. 175 *et seq*. It was reprinted, with some omissions and some additions, in an English magazine called Atalanta, in November, 1887, where it erroneously said to have been "hitherto unpublished." The writer's name is not given. Mr. Dalton, the compiler of the Waterloo Roll Call, states in the Appendix (p. 235) that a copy of the letter is in his possession. It would be well worth while to republish it textually with notes.

CLAUSEWITZ:

Der Feldzug von 1815 in Frankreich. Hinterlassenes Werk des Generals Carl von Clausewitz.

Zweite Auflage. Berlin: Ferd. Dümmler's Verlagsbuchhandlung: 1862.

CLINTON:

The War in the Peninsula, and Wellington's Campaigns in France and Belgium. With original maps and plans. By H. R. Clinton. London: Frederick Warne & Co. 1878.

CORRESPONDANCE de Napoléon 1er, publiée par ordre de l'Empereur Napoléon III.

Tome XXVIII.

Tome XXXI. Œuvres de Napoléon 1er à St. Hélène. Paris: Imprimerie Impériale. 1869.

COTTON:
A Voice from Waterloo: a history of the battle, &c. By Sergeant-major Edward Cotton, late 7th Hussars.
Fifth Edition, revised and enlarged. Printed for the author. London. R. Green. 1854.

CRAAN, W. B.:
Plan du Champ de Bataille de Waterloo. Bruxelles: 1816.

DAMITZ: Histoire de la Campagne de 1815: Par le major de Damitz, officier prussien, d'après les documents du Général Grolman, Quartier-Maître-Général de l'armée prussienne en 1815.
Traduite de l'Allemand par Léon Griffon. Avec Plans. 2 Volumes. Paris. Correard. 1840.

D'AUVERGNE:
See La Tour d'Auvergne.

DAVOUT:
Histoire de la Vie Militaire, Politique, et Administrative du Maréchal Davout, Duc de Auerstaedt, Prince d'Eckmühl. D'après les documents officiels. Par L. J. Gabriel de Chenier. Paris: Gosse, Marchal & Cie: 1866.

DOCUMENTS INÉDITS:
Documents inédits sur la campagne de 1815, publiés par le Duc d'Elchingen. Paris. 1840.

DRAME DE WATERLOO:
Le Drame de Waterloo: Grande Restitution Historique. Avec un plan. 3me edition. Paris: Au Bureau de la Revue Spiritualiste. 1868.

DROUET:
Le Maréchal Drouet, Comte d'Erlon. Notice sur la vie militaire, écrite par lui-même et dediée à ses amis. Publiée par sa famille. Avec portrait. Paris: Gustave Barba: Libraire Éditeur. 34 Rue Mazarine. 1844.

ELLESMERE:
Essays on History, Biography, Geography, Engineering, &c. Contributed to the Quarterly Review: By the late Earl of Ellesmere. London: John Murray. 1858.

FRAGMENTS HISTORIQUES:
See Grouchy.

FRASER: Letters written during the Peninsula and Waterloo Campaigns.
By Sir A. S. Fraser. London: 1859.

FRASER:
Words on Wellington — the Duke — Waterloo — the Ball. By Sir Wm. Fraser, Baronet. London. John C. Nimmo: 1889.

GARDNER:

Quatre Bras, Ligny and Waterloo. A narrative of the campaign in Belgium in 1815. By Dorsey Gardner. London: Kegan Paul, Trench & Co. 1882.

GAWLER:

The Crisis and Close of the Action at Waterloo. By an Eyewitness. Dublin. Richard Milliken & Son: 104 Grafton Street. 1833.

GÉRARD:

1. Quelques Documents sur la Bataille de Waterloo, propres à éclairer la question portée devant le public par M. le Marquis de Grouchy. Par le Général Gérard. Paris: Denain: Novembre, 1829. (With a Map.)

2. Dernières Observations sur les Opérations de l'aile droite de l'Armée Française à la Bataille de Waterloo, en réponse à M. le Marquis de Grouchy. Par le Général Gérard. Paris: Denain: 1830. (With a Map.)

3. Lettre à MM. Germain Sarrut et B. Saint Edme, Rédacteurs de la Biographie des Hommes du Jour. Paris: 12 Mars, 1840.

GIRAUD:

The Campaigns of Paris in 1814 and 1815, etc. Translated from the French of P. F. F. J. Giraud by Edmund Boyce. 2d Edition, enlarged. London. 1816.

GNEISENAU:

Das Leben des Feldmarschalls Grafen Reithardt von Gneisenau. Vierter Band. 1814, 1815. Von Hans Delbrück. Fortfetzung des Gleichnamigen Werkes von G. H. Pertz. Berlin. 1880.

GOMM:

Letters and Journals of Field-Marshal Sir William Maynard Gomm, G. C. B. From 1799 to Waterloo, 1815. Edited by Francis Culling Carr-Gomm. London: John Murray. 1881.

GORE:

An Historical Account of the Battle of Waterloo; intended to elucidate the topographical plan executed by W. B. Craän, J. U. D. Translated from the French, with explanatory notes, by Captain Arthur Gore, 30th Regiment of Foot. With Plates. London. Printed for Samuel Leigh. 1817.

GOURGAUD (original):[1]

Campagne de dix-huit cent quinze: ou Relation des Opérations Miliaires qui ont eu lieu en France et en Belgique, pendant les Cent Jours. Écrite à Sainte Hélène. Par le Général Gourgaud. Paris: 1818.

GOURGAUD (translation):

The Campaign of 1815. Written at St. Helena by General Gourgaud. London: 1818.

---

[1] Our citations are from this (original) edition.

GRENADIER GUARDS:

The Origin and History of the First or Grenadier Guards. By Lieut. Gen. Sir F. W. Hamilton, K. C. B. In three volumes. London: John Murray. 1874.

GROUCHY:

1. Observations sur la Relation de la Campagne de 1815, publiée par le Général Gourgaud, et Réfutation de quelques unes des Assertions d'autres écrits relatifs à la bataille de Waterloo. Par le Maréchal de Grouchy. Philadelphie. 1818.

2. The same, with omissions and changes. Philadelphia, 1819.

3. The same title except that the author's name is given as "le Comte de Grouchy." Reprinted, with many omissions and changes, from the Philadelphia edition of 1819. Paris: Chez Chaumerot Jeune, Libraire, Palais Royal. 1819.[1]

4. Doutes sur l'Authenticité des Mémoires historiques attribués à Napoléon et première réfutation de quelques unes des assertions qu'ils renferment. Par le Comte de Grouchy: Philadelphie: Avril, 1820.

5. Fragments Historiques relatifs à la Campagne de 1815 et à la Bataille de Waterloo. Par le Général Grouchy.
Lettre à Messieurs Méry et Barthélemy.
Paris: Firmin Didot Frères, 20 Novembre, 1829.

6. Fragments Historiques, &c.
De l'influence que peuvent avoir sur l'opinion les documents publiés par M. le Comte Gérard.
Paris: Firmin Didot Frères, 20 Decembre, 1829.

7. Le Maréchal de Grouchy du 16 au 19 Juin 1815. Par le Général de Division Sénateur Marquis de Grouchy. Paris. E. Dentu. 1864.

8. Mémoires du Maréchal de Grouchy. Par le Marquis de Grouchy, officier de l'état-major. vol. 4. Paris: E. Dentu. 1874.

GURWOOD:

The Despatches of Field Marshal the Duke of Wellington. Compiled from official and authentic documents, by Lieut.-Colonel Gurwood. Vol. XII. London: John Murray: 1838.

HAMLEY:

The Operations of War explained and illustrated. By Edward Bruce Hamley, Colonel in the Army, etc. Second Edition. William Blackwood & Sons. Edinburgh and London. 1869.

HILL:

The Life of Lord Hill, G. C. B. By the Rev. Edwin Sidney, A. M. Second edition. London: John Murray: 1845.

HISTOIRE DE L'EX-GARDE:

Depuis sa formation jusqu'à son licenciement. Paris: Delaunay: 1821.

---

[1] Unless otherwise stated, our quotations are from this edition.

HOOPER:

Waterloo: the Downfall of the First Napoleon: A History of the Campaign of 1815. By George Hooper: author of "The Italian Campaigns of General Bonaparte." With Map and Plans. London: Smith, Elder & Co. 1862.

IMPERIAL GUARD:

See Histoire de l'Ex-Garde.
See St. Hilaire.

JOMINI (original):

Précis Politique et Militaire de la Campagne de 1815, pour servir de supplement et de rectification à la Vie Politique et Militaire de Napoléon racontée par lui-même. Par le Général J. Paris: 1839.

JOMINI (translation):[1]

The Political and Military History of the Campaign of Waterloo. Translated from the French of General Baron de Jomini, by Capt. S. V. Benét, Ordnance Dept. U. S. Army. Second Edition. New York: D. Van Nostrand: 1862.

JONES:

The Battle of Waterloo, with those of Ligny and Quatre Bras, described by eye-witnesses, and by the series of official accounts published by authority. To which are added Memoirs of F. M. the Duke of Wellington, F. M. Prince Blücher, the Emperor Napoleon, etc., etc. Illustrated by Maps, Plans, and Views of the Field, and Thirty-four Etchings from Drawings. By George Jones, Esq., R. A. Eleventh Edition, enlarged and corrected. London: L. Booth: Duke Street. 1852.

KENNEDY:

Notes on the Battle of Waterloo. By the late General Sir James Shaw-Kennedy, K. C. B., acting at the time of the battle on the Quarter-Master-General's Staff of the Third Division of the Army. London: John Murray: 1865.

LA TOUR D'AUVERGNE:

Waterloo: Étude de la Campagne de 1815. Par le Lieutenant-Colonel Prince Édouard de La Tour d'Auvergne. Avec Cartes et Plans. Paris: Henri Plon: 1870.

LEEKE:

The History of Lord Seaton's Regiment (the 52d Light Infantry) at the Battle of Waterloo. By the Reverend William Leeke, M. A. 2 vols. London: Hatchard & Co. 1866.

LOBEN SELS:

See Van Loben Sels.

---

[1] Our citations are from this translation.

LOCKHART:

The History of Napoleon Buonaparte. By J. G. Lockhart. Third edition. 2 vols. London: John Murray. 1835.

The History of Napoleon Buonaparte. Reprinted from the Family Library. London: William Tegg. 1867.

MARÉCHAL DE GROUCHY EN 1815:

See Grouchy.

MAURICE: ARTICLES ON WATERLOO:

By Col. J. F. Maurice, R. A. From the United Service Magazine. Vol. 123. In the years 1890 and 1891.

MÉMOIRES (original):

Mémoires pour servir à l'Histoire de France en 1815, avec le plan de la bataille de Mont St. Jean. Paris: 1820.

MEMOIRS (translation):

Historical Memoirs of Napoleon. Book IX. 1815. Translated from the original Manuscript by B. E. O'Meara. London: Printed for Sir Richard Phillips & Co. 1820.

MERCER:

Journal of the Waterloo Campaign. Kept throughout the Campaign of 1815. By the late General Cavalié Mercer, commanding the 9th Brigade Royal Artillery. In 2 vols. Wm. Blackwood & Sons, Edinburgh & London. 1870.

MORRIS, O'CONNOR:

See O'Connor Morris.

MUDFORD:

An Historical Account of the Campaign in the Netherlands in 1815 under his Grace the Duke of Wellington and Marshal Prince Blücher. By William Mudford. Illustrated. London. 1817.

MÜFFLING: PASSAGES:

Passages from my Life; together with Memoirs of the Campaign of 1813 and 1814. By Baron von Müffling. Edited with notes by Col. Philip Yorke, F. R. S. Second Edition, revised. London: Richard Bentley, New Burlington Street. 1853.

Part II., beginning with page 197, contains an account of the Waterloo Campaign.

MÜFFLING: SKETCH:

A Sketch of the Battle of Waterloo, to which are added the Official Despatches of Field Marshal the Duke of Wellington, Field Marshal Prince Blücher, and Reflections on the Battles of Ligny and Waterloo. By General Müffling. With Craän's Map of the Field. Sixth Edition. Waterloo. H. Gérard, Publisher. 1870.

MUQUARDT:
Précis de la Campagne de 1815 dans les Pays-Bas. Bruxelles. Libraire Militaire C. Muquardt: Merzbach and Falk, Éditeurs. 1887.

NAPIER:
Life of General Sir William Napier, K. C. B., Author of the "History of the Peninsular War." Edited by H. O. Bruce, M. P. 2 vols. London: John Murray. 1864.

NAPOLEON:
See Correspondance.
" Mémoires.
" Memoirs.

NAPOLÉON À WATERLOO:
Souvenirs Militaires. Napoléon à Waterloo, ou Précis rectifié de la Campagne de 1815. Avec des Documents nouveaux et des Piéces inédites. Par un ancien officier de la Garde Impériale, qui est resté près de Napoléon pendant toute la campagne. Paris: J. Dumaine, 1866.

NIEMAN'S DIARY:
The Journal of Henri Nieman of the 6th Prussian Black Hussars. From the English Historical Magazine for July, 1888.

O'CONNOR MORRIS:
Great Commanders of Modern Times, and the Campaign of 1815. By William O'Connor Morris. London: W. H. Allen & Co.: 1891.

OLDFIELD:
Letters on the Battle of Waterloo. MSS. By John Oldfield, Captain and Brigade-Major, Royal Engineers.

OLLECH:
Geschichte des Feldzuges von 1815 nach archivalischen Quellen. Von Ollech, General der Infanterie. Berlin: 1876.

O'MEARA:
See Memoirs.

PAJOL:
Pajol, Général en Chef. Par le général de division Comte Pajol — son fils ainé. 3 vols. Paris. Firmin Didot Frères. 1874.

PASCALLET:
Notice Biographique sur M. le Maréchal Marquis de Grouchy, Pair de France, avec des Éclaircissements et des Détails historiques sur la Campagne de 1815 dans le midi de France, et sur la Bataille de Waterloo. Par M. E. Pascallet, Fondateur and Rédacteur en chef de la Revue Générale, Biographique, Politique and Littéraire. 2e Edition. Paris. 1842.

QUINET:
Histoire de la Campagne de 1815. Par Edgar Quinet. Paris: Michel Lévy Frères. 1862.

RELATION BELGE:
See Campagne de la Belgique.

ROGNIAT:
Réponse aux notes critiques de Napoléon sur l'ouvrage intitulé "Considérations sur l'Art de la Guerre." Paris. 1823.

SIBORNE:
History of the War in France and Belgium in 1815. Containing minute Details of the Battles of Quatre Bras, Ligny, Wavre and Waterloo. By Capt. W. Siborne; Secretary and Adjutant of the Royal Military Asylum Constructor of the "Waterloo Model." 2d Edition. 2 vols. London T. & W. Boone: 1844. With an Atlas of Maps and Plans.

STANHOPE:
Notes of Conversations with the Duke of Wellington. 1831-1851. By Philip Henry, 5th Earl Stanhope. New York, Longmans, Greene & Co. 1886.

ST. HILAIRE:
Histoire, anecdotique, politique et militaire, de la Garde Impériale. Par Emile Marco de Saint-Hilaire. Paris: Eugène Penaud. 1847.

SUPPLEMENTARY DESPATCHES:
The Supplementary Despatches, Correspondence and Memoranda of Field Marshal Arthur, Duke of Wellington, K. G. Edited by his son, the Duke of Wellington, K. G. Volume X. London: John Murray. 1863.

THIERS:
History of the Consulate and the Empire of France under Napoleon. By M. A. Thiers. Vol. XX. London: Willis and Sotheran. 1861.

TREUENFELD:
Die Tage von Ligny und Belle-Alliance. Von v. Treuenfeld, Premier-Lieutenant im 2 Hessischen Infanterie-Regiment No. 82. Mit 11 Karten. Hanover, 1880. Helwing'sche Verlags-Buchhandlung: Schlägerstrasse 20.

VANDAMME:
Le Général Vandamme et sa Correspondance. Par A. Du Casse. 2 Vols. Paris: Didier et Cie. 1870.

VAN LOBEN SELS:
Précis de la Campagne de 1815 dans les Pays-Bas. Par le major d'artillerie E. Van Löben Sels, aide-de-camp de S. A. R. le Prince Frédéric des Pays-Bas. Avec Plans. Traduit du Hollandais. La Haye: Chez les Heritiers Doorman: 1849.

VAUDONCOURT:
Histoire des Campagnes de 1814 et 1815 en France. Par le Général Guillaume de Vaudoncourt. Tome Quatrième. Paris. 1826.

xlii PARTIAL LIST OF BOOKS RELATING TO THE CAMPAIGN.

VAULABELLE:

Campagne et Bataille de Waterloo. Par Achille de Vaulabelle. Bruxelles. 1853.

WATERLOO LETTERS:

Waterloo Letters. A selection from original and hitherto unpublished letters bearing on the operations of the 16th, 17th and 18th June, 1815, by officers who served in the campaign. Edited, with explanatory notes, by Major General H. T. Siborne, late Colonel R. E. Illustrated with numerous Maps and Plans. London: Cassell & Co. Limited. 1891.

WATERLOO ROLL CALL:

The Waterloo Roll Call. By Charles Dalton, F. R. G. S. London. Wm. Clowes & Sons, Limited. 13 Charing Cross, S. W. 1890.

WELLINGTON:

See Gurwood, and, also, Supplementary Despatches.

CHAPTER I.

THE PLAN OF CAMPAIGN.

NAPOLEON entered Paris on his return from Elba on the twentieth of March, 1815. His first endeavor, after quieting the not very formidable movements of the royalists in the south and west of France, was to open communications with the great powers. He proclaimed his policy to be strictly one of peace, and we have every reason to believe that his intentions were sincerely pacific. But his agents were turned back on the frontier. The nations of Europe refused to treat with him on any terms, and entered into an offensive and defensive alliance against him with the avowed purpose of driving him from the throne of France. The armies of the neighboring powers began immediately to concentrate on the border, and even Russia set her troops in motion for the general attack upon France and her Emperor.

To meet this formidable coalition Napoleon bent all his energies. The army had, since his first abdication, been reorganized, and many high commands had naturally been given to the chiefs of the royalist party. Much had to be done before the new arrangements, necessitated by the re-establishment of the Imperial government, could be effected.

These changes in the military organization of the country required time. Besides, Napoleon was not desirous to precipitate matters. He was naturally solicitous not to appear to commence an avoidable war. He was, moreover, much occupied with domestic politics, but of his dealings with the chambers and of his new constitution we do not propose to speak.

Besides increasing and reconstituting the army, work was begun on the fortifications of the principal cities.

By the first of June, no change having taken place in the relations of France with her neighbors, it became incumbent on the Emperor to decide what he would do.

The situation was, in brief, as follows: Two large armies, one composed of English, Dutch, Belgian and Hanoverian troops, with contingents from Brunswick and Nassau, the whole under command of the Duke of Wellington, the other composed of Prussians, Saxons, and other Germans under Marshal Blücher, lay scattered in their cantonments in Belgium to the north and east of the rivers Sambre and Meuse. On the eastern frontier, the Austrians were collecting a formidable force, and were expecting to be reinforced in July by a powerful Russian army. If Napoleon should maintain a strictly defensive attitude, France would again be the theatre of hostilities, as in the previous year. True, time would be gained by the delay, and time was most important for filling the ranks of the army, completing the fortifications, manufacturing ammunition, and generally putting the country into a state of defence. But when the invasion came, it would be made in overwhelming force. It was possible, certainly, to hope for the repetition of the exploits of 1814, for victories like Champ Aubert, Montmirail and Rheims; on the other hand, bloody and indecisive battles like those of Brienne, Laon, and Arcis-sur-Aube were to be expected with equal probability. The thing for Napoleon to do, if possible, was to reduce this tremendous disparity of numbers, and this could only be effected by beating his enemies in detail. If he could dispose of the armies of Wellington and Blücher now, he would have so much the better chance against the Austrians and the Russians. And Napoleon undoubtedly hoped that if fortune should favor him in 1815 as in 1805 and 1806, for instance,—if he should be able to repeat in Belgium the astonishing successes of Austerlitz and Jena,—he would not find it impossible to make peace with his father-in-law, the Emperor of Austria, and that Russia, whose interests in the war were remote and really theoretical, would willingly retire from the contest. When we add to this that Napoleon's *forte* was the offensive, that his genius was specially adapted for enterprising and daring strategy, we are not surprised that he should have decided to move at once, with all his available force, upon the armies of Wellington and Blücher.[1]

These armies were, as has been stated, lying in their cantonments on and behind the Belgian frontier. (See Map 1.) Their front covered, roughly speaking, an extent of a hundred miles, from Namur and Huy on the east to Mons and Tournay on the west. They were distributed in numerous towns and villages, some of these being as far back as forty miles from the frontier. With the location of the various detachments Napoleon was undoubtedly, to a great extent, acquainted. He calculated that Wellington's forces, which were scattered over a wide extent of country, could not be concentrated in less than two days; and that it would require more than one day for Blücher to assemble the four corps of which his army was composed.

The high-road, which runs from Charleroi north through Quatre Bras, Genappe and Waterloo to Brussels, ran between these armies,—that of the Duke of Wellington lying to the westward of the road and that of Marshal Blücher lying to the eastward of it. The Prussians lay considerably closer to the frontier than the English and Dutch. Wellington's headquarters were at Brussels;

---

[1] See Clausewitz, chaps. 8, 14.

Blücher's at Namur. The turnpike, which runs from Namur through Quatre Bras to Nivelles, was the main avenue of communication between these two armies.

The Prussian lines of supply extended by way of Liége and Maestricht to the Rhine; the English by way of Ostend and Antwerp to the sea. The bases of the two armies were thus situated in opposite directions. It was, of course, probable that if either of these armies should be obliged to retreat, it would retreat towards its own base. But to retreat towards its own base would be to march away from its ally. On this peculiarity in the situation Napoleon's plan of campaign was, to a great degree, founded. The situation was far more favorable for him than if the 220,000 men in Belgium had all belonged to one army, for now, not only were there two armies, under two commanders, in whose operations he might safely count upon the existence of more or less misunderstanding and failure fully to meet each other's expectations, but the two armies were bound, in case of disaster to either or both, to follow lines of retreat which were wholly divergent.

We are now prepared to consider Napoleon's plan. He proposed to assemble his own forces with all possible secrecy in the neighborhood of Charleroi,— near the point of junction of the two opposing armies. He expected that, on the first news of his approach, the two armies would respectively concentrate, and then endeavor to unite. He expected that the Prussians, being less scattered than the English, and being likely to know of the approach of the French before the English could possibly hear of it, would be the first to concentrate, and he expected therefore to encounter them alone and unsupported by their allies.

The statement of Napoleon's plan of campaign in Gourgaud's narrative is as follows:— [2]

---

[2] Gourgaud, pp. 42, 43.

"The Prussian army, having intimation of the enemy's intentions eight or ten hours before the English, would accordingly be first concentrated. Hopes were even entertained of attacking the Prussians before their four corps were united, or of obliging them to fall back in the direction of Liége and the Rhine, which was their line of operations; and by thus separating them from the English, to create an opportunity for new combinations.

"In these calculations, the characters of the enemy's commanders were much to be considered. The hussar habits of Marshal Blücher, his activity and decided character, formed a strong contrast with the cautious disposition, the deliberate and methodical manner of the Duke of Wellington. Thus, it was easy to foresee, that the Prussian army would be the first to be concentrated, and also that it would evince more decision and promptitude in hastening to the aid of its ally [than the English army would if the Prussians should be the first to be attacked]. If Blücher had only two battalions ready to act, he would be sure to employ them in support of the English army; but there was reason to believe that Wellington, unless his whole army was united, would not attack the French to succor Blücher. All these considerations rendered it desirable that the attack should be commenced against the Prussian army; it necessarily would, so we thought, be the first to be concentrated, and this turned out to be the fact."

To the same effect the Emperor says in his "Memoirs":—[3]

"The [Prussian] army was to assemble in rear of Fleurus. * * * In the night between the 14th and 15th, confidential messengers returned to the French headquarters at Beaumont, and announced that everything was tranquil at Namur, Brussels and Charleroi; this was a happy presage. To have thus succeeded in concealing from the enemy the movements which the French army had made for the last two days, was to have already obtained a great advantage. The Prussian army found itself obliged either to establish a point of concentration further back than Fleurus, or to receive battle in that position without being able to be assisted by the Anglo-Dutch army. * * * All the measures of Napoleon had therefore for their object to attack the Prussians first."

---

[3]Corresp., vol. 31, pp. 195, 197, 198.

In a word, Napoleon believed that the allied generals had fixed the points of concentration of their armies too near the frontier for that concentration to be effected in season to oppose to his army an overwhelming force; he thought it very likely also, for the reasons above stated, that he would have only the Prussian army to deal with in the first encounter of the campaign.

There were, to be sure, other courses open to him. He might direct his army upon the communications of the Prussians by passing to the eastward of them and turning their left flank. But this operation involved a wide *détour* over a difficult country, and in the battle which was certain to result, the Prussian and the English armies would, beyond a doubt, both be united against him. On the other hand he could turn Wellington's right by moving *via* Lille, Valenciennes or Mons upon Ghent or Brussels. An advance in this direction presented, to be sure, fewer difficulties than the one just spoken of, and promised greater advantages. The Duke himself always maintained that this would have been Napoleon's best move. It probably would have cut the English communications with Ostend, and would very likely have forced Wellington to evacuate Brussels without a battle, that is, unless he cared to risk an engagement without the aid of his ally. But the Prussians in the meantime would have concentrated without molestation their whole army of 120,000 men, and if Wellington had been successful in avoiding a battle with the French superior force, the two allied generals ought to have been able either to manœuvre Napoleon out of Belgium or to force him to battle on disadvantageous terms. It is probable that in neither of these flanking movements would there be an opportunity afforded for a direct, immediate, crushing blow upon one of the allied armies, such as that which Napoleon thought it very possible that the temerity of Marshal Blücher was going to present to him, if he advanced by way of Charleroi.

We have seen that Napoleon seems to have thought it very likely that Blücher would fight, but, of course, Napoleon could but conjecture what Blücher would do; he could not certainly know that he would not now, as he had done in Germany in 1813, avoid a direct conflict with him, and retire on his base of operations. If Blücher should do this, the two armies, it is true, would be separated and could be dealt with accordingly; but the difficulties of the campaign would be vastly greater than if the Prussian army should be practically disposed of by a decisive victory at the outset. For if the Prussians should fall back without hazarding a battle, they would have to be pursued, certainly far enough to ascertain their real intentions, and to become assured that they were, for the time being at least, definitely separated from the army of Wellington. If this should appear to be the case the question would then arise, which of the two armies should be followed up; and in considering this question, the importance of the occupation of Brussels, at that time the capital of the Netherlands, would naturally influence Napoleon in favor of throwing the bulk of his forces against the Anglo-Dutch. Napoleon, however, as we have already said, seems to have thought it on the whole probable, knowing, as he did, the daring and resolute character of the man, that Blücher would fight, with or without the assistance of the English army, and he also thought that the situation of the English army was such that Blücher would not be likely to get much assistance from it. Napoleon, therefore, hoped to open the campaign with a signal victory, crippling, perhaps destroying, the Prussian army, and he knew that the result of such a victory must be the retreat of the beaten Prussians in a direction certain to separate them entirely and definitely from their English and Dutch allies. The French Emperor would then be free to carry the great bulk of his forces against the English and Dutch. If Wellington stood, he expected to beat him; if he retreated, he would leave Belgium and perhaps Holland at the disposal of the French.

Such, in brief, were Napoleon's calculations and expectations.

NOTE TO CHAPTER I.

THE view given above of Napoleon's plan has been by no means universally accepted. It is often stated that he intended to separate the two armies and attack them in detail, but if this expression is to be understood as meaning that the former operation was to precede the latter in point of time, it is not in our judgment a correct statement. There never was, we believe, any expectation on Napoleon's part that he could, by throwing his army between those of Wellington and Blücher, or by merely occupying strategic points, separate the allied armies definitely from one another. What he did expect, was, as we have seen,[1] to encounter one of these armies, that commanded by Marshal Blücher, alone and unsupported by its ally. If it should decline an engagement, or should fight and be beaten, he calculated on its retiring towards its own base of operations, and so separating itself by every march taken in that direction from its ally.

But several writers on the campaign present us with quite other ideas of Napoleon's intended operations. And as it is obviously of the first importance that we should start with a correct idea of Napoleon's plan, if we would follow the events of the campaign intelligently, we will examine these other theories somewhat in detail.

Take first the view that Napoleon's intention was to throw his army between those of Wellington and Blücher.

---

[1] *Ante*, pp. 4 *et seq.*

This is Alison's view. We cite him, not because his name carries any weight as a military authority, but because his error has been so clearly pointed out by no less a person than the Duke of Wellington, in a criticism[2] of Alison's History of Europe written by the Earl of Ellesmere, who wrote, as is well known, under the Duke's inspiration. In the following passage a quotation is made from the work of the famous German military critic, Clausewitz:—

"Mr. Alison (Hist. of Europe,[3] etc., vol. x, p. 991) speaks of 'Buonaparte's favorite military manœuvre of interposing between his adversaries, and striking with a superior force first on the right hand and then on the left,' as having been attempted by him and baffled in this campaign. We doubt whether the expression of interposing between two adversaries can be correctly applied to any of Buonaparte's successful campaigns, and we almost suspect that, if he had in contemplation a manœuvre of so much hazard on this occasion, it was the first on which he can be said to have attempted it. Hear Clausewitz on this matter:—

"All writers who have treated of this campaign set out by saying that Buonaparte threw himself between the two armies, in order to separate them. This expression, however, which has become a *terminus technicus* in military phraseology, has no clear idea for its foundation. The space intervening between two armies cannot be an object of operation.[4] It would have been very unfortunate if a commander like Buonaparte, having to deal with an enemy of twice his force, instead of falling on the one half with his united strength, had lighted on the empty interval, and thus made a blow in the air, losing his time, whilst he can only double his own force by the strictest economy of that commodity.

---

[2] Ellesmere, pp. 161, 162. See Maurice, pp. 333 *et seq.*; Jan. 1891.

[3] In the edition of 1850, this passage (as we suppose it to be) is found in vol. xiii, p. 625, and reads somewhat differently, but the idea is precisely the same.

[4] Thiers; vol. xx, book lx, p. 23, says: " He had conceived the belief that the English and Prussians * * * would leave between their respective forces a space, not very strongly guarded, and he thought that, by bringing the whole strength of his army to bear upon this point, he might become master of the position."

Even the fighting the one army in a direction by which it will be pressed away from the other, even if it can be effected without loss of time, incurs the great danger of being attacked in the rear by the other. If the latter, therefore, be not far enough removed to put this risk out of the question, a commander will scarcely venture on such a line of attack. Buonaparte, therefore, chose the direction between the two armies, *not in order to separate them by wedging himself between*,[5] but because he expected to find and fall on Blücher's force in this direction, either united or in separate bodies [corps]." *Feldzug von* 1815, &c., p. 54:[6]

* * * * * * * *

His main object was evidently to find the Prussian army, and beat it."

Nevertheless we find Hooper,[7] who wrote long after Clausewitz, making the very statement which Clausewitz thought so objectionable:—

"He (Napoleon) calculated that if he struck at the centre of the two armies he should be able *to wedge himself in between them*, crushing any divisions which attempted to obstruct his progress, and, having won a position of vantage, he imagined that it would be in his power to manœuvre with rapidity from side to side and defeat each army in succession."

To the same effect writes Quinet:—

"He (Napoleon) will place himself between the two armies, at the centre of the line, that is to say, at the extreme right of the Prussian cantonments. By this move, the Duke of Wellington and Marshal Blücher will be separated from the first hour. The occasion, the moment, will decide on which of the two armies it will be best to strike the first blow."[8]

It is unnecessary to repeat what has been so well said above in opposition to this view. It is plain that these

---

[5] The italics are our own.

[6] In the edition of 1862, this passage is found in Chap. 22 on pages 46 and 47.

[7] Hooper, p. 58. See also, by the same author, Wellington, p. 207. To the same effect, see Clinton, p. 378. *Cf.* Rogniat, Considérations, p. 339, who was the first to announce this theory.

[8] Quinet, p. 75.

writers have misconceived Napoleon's plan. But we must consider this more fully.

This conception of the campaign is practically identical with the theory first put forth by Rogniat in his "Considérations de l'Art de la Guerre," and repeated in his "Réponse aux Notes critiques de Napoléon," in the form of a criticism of Napoleon's operations. He maintains that Napoleon should have aimed first at seizing the two points of Quatre Bras and Sombreffe on the Nivelles-Namur road, over which the allied armies communicated with each other.

"If, instead of six leagues, he had made eight or nine (and he had time enough, inasmuch as the Sambre was crossed at two o'clock), in pushing his left to Frasnes and his advance-guard to Quatre Bras, the centre and right to Sombreffe, with the reserves at Fleurus, he would have obtained the precious advantage he ought to have aimed at, that of separating the two opposing armies, of retarding the union of their corps, of taking a central position and of attacking them one at a time. In fact, Quatre Bras and Sombreffe are on the high-road from Namur to Brussels; master of these points, he could then have opposed the junction of the English on one side, of the Prussians on the other."[9]

This view has also received the endorsement of Jomini,[10] who evidently thinks that Napoleon must have entertained it.

"Napoleon perceived that their (the Prussian) army sought to assemble between Namur and the causeway leading from Charleroi to Brussels, as it was by this route that the English would come to their assistance: now, under this supposition, the Emperor had but one wise course to follow; the most simple glance at the map would sufficiently indicate that it was essential to seize upon Sombreffe on the one side, and the central point of Quatre Bras on the other. * * * Because, once master of these two points, he was in position to act at will on either of the opposing armies, and prevent their junction."

To the same effect is the sketch of Napoleon's plan

---

[9] Réponse, &c., pp. 261, 262.

[10] Jomini, p. 122, 123; also, pp. 213, 225, 226.

put forth by his advocate, the Prince de la Tour d'Auvergne in his "Waterloo":

"The Sambre crossed, he (Napoleon) would seize the line of communication of the Anglo-Dutch and Prussians. Two columns would be charged to establish themselves, one at Quatre Bras, the other at Sombreffe.

"The separation consummated, he would easily make an end of both the Prussians and the Anglo-Dutch. For this would only be to renew a manœuvre familiar to him, and which had so often given him the victory."[11]

Charras, one of the Emperor's hostile critics, takes the same view of his intentions:

"It requires only a glance at the map to indicate with certainty the point which it was his intention to reach in dictating his order of movement. * * *

"The French army, occupying these places [Quatre Bras and Sombreffe] in force, would find itself placed between the Anglo-Dutch and the Prussians, thenceforward really capable,— to borrow from Napoleon his own expression,— of attacking them in detail, leaving to them, if they would escape from this misfortune,— the greatest that could befall them,— only the alternative of yielding ground and of uniting their forces at Brussels or beyond it."[12]

Against this array of authority we oppose with confidence that of Napoleon himself, of Wellington, and of Clausewitz. It was Napoleon's expectation, as we have seen above, that the Prussian army would be the first to be concentrated, that it would offer battle at or near Fleurus, and that he would be able to attack and overcome it before it could be joined by the Anglo-Dutch forces.[13] If Blücher fought at all at that stage in the campaign, it stood to reason that he would fight *to the south* of Sombreffe, *for the preservation of his line of*

---

[11] La Tour D'Auvergne, pp. 41, 42: also, pp. 73 *et seq.*

[12] Charras, vol. 1, pp. 115, 116. See also Quinet, p. 101,— " Pour empêcher la réunion (of the English and Prussian armies) il était indispensable de fermer à la fois les deux passages (Sombreffe and Quatre Bras)."

[13] Siborne (vol. 1, p. 47) is perfectly clear on this point.

communication with Wellington,—the Namur-Nivelles road. Hence, the intention of occupying Sombreffe, *as a preliminary to a battle with the Prussians*, could not, as we venture to think, have entered Napoleon's mind On the contrary, he believed that the seizure of Sombreffe would inevitably necessitate the retreat of the Prussians to some point further north, as Wavre, or even to the neighborhood of Brussels, where their junction with the English could be effected without molestation.[14]

But the last thing which Napoleon wanted was that the allied armies should retire to Wavre, or to the neighborhood of Brussels, and there unite. He needed a battle, and a decisive success,[15] and he needed it at once. A war of manœuvres was not the game for him to play at this crisis. It was of vital importance for him to rout, if possible, in succession, the armies of Blücher and Wellington; a battle, therefore, was what he sought, and he expected that Blücher would fight him, and fight him alone. It was only by routing Blücher's army, or forcing it to retreat, that he expected to separate it from that of Wellington.

It must also be borne in mind, that the mere occupation of two points on the line of communication between two allied armies does not in any way prevent the unimpeded concentration of each army, and its being moved, when concentrated, in any direction that its commander may decide on. The "line of communication" seized is not to be confounded with the line of supplies or the line of retreat of either army. No doubt, the occupation of any point or points on the line by which two allied armies communicate with each other tends to embarrass them, to hinder any combined movements, and to delay their union; but to direct the march of an invading army

---

[14] Corresp.: vol. 31, p. 471.

[15] *Cf.* Clausewitz, ch. 14.

merely to compass this end, when it is possible to defeat one of these opposing armies by engaging it where it cannot be supported by its ally, is to miss the opportunity of the campaign.

CHAPTER II.

THE FRENCH ARMY.

The French army, it is hardly necessary to state, had been seriously affected by the sudden and complete change in government through which France had passed in April, 1814. Without going into particulars, it is sufficient to say that Napoleon found on his return from Elba much which needed to be undone and more which it was necessary to do. But the details of this partial reorganization do not greatly concern us. Napoleon unquestionably did his utmost to bring the troops into a state of efficiency. And he certainly was in great measure successful. The larger part of the Marshals and high officers remained in France and took command with cheerfulness, and the younger officers and the men were unanimous in their devotion to the cause of their country against the coalition. But some of the Marshals and generals high in rank had retired into Belgium with Louis XVIII.; others declined active service; and where there were so many defections, there was inevitably not a little suspicion and disquietude. In the reorganization, which was beyond a question necessary, great changes had to be made in the higher commands, and the regiments, even, were to a greater or less extent recast. The Guard was also reconstituted, a measure obviously wise, taking account of the prestige which this famous corps had always possessed, but a measure which, carried out as it had to be, in a very brief period of time, could not but injure to a considerable extent the value of the regiments of the line. It is true that France at this time was full of veteran soldiers; some 200,000 men had returned into the country from foreign prisons. There was an abundance of excellent material. But the circumstances under which the existing military force was reorganized and increased in numbers were unfavorable to the *moral* of the soldiers and of the army generally, and there was not sufficient time before the outbreak of hostilities to overcome the disturbing influences inseparable from such a state of things. The men were full of enthusiasm for and confidence in Napoleon; but they mistrusted many of their commanders. They were old soldiers, nearly or quite all of them, and understood their work perfectly; but the changes of the last eighteen months had been so utterly perplexing,—so thorough,—the new organization had been so recent and attended by so many disquieting circumstances and disturbing rumors, that the absolute confidence, which ought to exist between the officers and men of an army as strongly as between the members of a family, did not prevail.[1]

Coming now to the *personnel* of the army: Napoleon's old chief-of-staff, Berthier, who had served him in this capacity for twenty years, who had grown accustomed to his ways, and was able by reason of his long experience to supplement his defects, had retired into Belgium with the King. To supply his place the Emperor selected Marshal Soult, certainly a very singular choice.[2] Soult was a man of Napoleon's own age,—he had for several years commanded an army in Spain, and had had, of course, a chief-of-staff of his own. To place such a man at such a time of his life on staff duty when he should be

---

[1] Charras, vol. 1, pp. 69, 70: Histoire de la Garde Imperiale: Saint Hilaire, p. 654.

[2] Ib., pp. 653, 654.

commanding troops, must strike any one as strange. Such an officer is not fitted by his experience in an independent command for the duties of a chief-of-staff. Those duties he has been for years accustomed to turn over to a subordinate. The personal attention which they need he has for years expected to be given by a junior officer. It is out of the question that he can, all at once, assume the extremely laborious duties which belong to the chief-of-staff. We shall, before we get through, have more than one opportunity to see how Soult performed his new tasks. It is safe to say that there was many a younger officer in the French army who would have served with much more efficiency in this all-important place, for which the utmost vigor and alertness of mind and body are wellnigh indispensable.

For the invasion of Belgium, Napoleon destined the 1st, 2d, 3d, 4th, and 6th Corps, and the Imperial Guard, besides a large force of cavalry. The five corps-commanders, d'Erlon, Reille, Vandamme, Gérard and the Comte de Lobau were all men of experience and admitted capacity. Vandamme was known specially as a hard fighter. Gérard was a comparatively young officer of great promise. The Comte de Lobau, under his original name of Mouton, had distinguished himself in the Austrian campaign of 1809. But no one of them equalled in military talent the leading generals in the Italian or Austerlitz campaigns,—Masséna, Lannes, Davout, Desaix, and their fellows. The commander of the cavalry, Grouchy, was a veteran of twenty years' hard fighting, but was not credited with possessing any great capacity. The fact is that Napoleon himself could not do for his own army what the turmoil and chaos of the Revolution had done for the army of the republic, and that was to override seniority and all ordinary claims to promotion, and to open the door wide to youthful vigor and ambition. It was to the confusion created by the Revolution that the formidable list of warriors who served France so brilliantly for twenty years owed in great measure their rapid advancement. Napoleon himself constitutes no exception to this remark.

Napoleon[3] says of his officers at this period:—

"The character of several of the generals had been weakened by the events of 1814; they had lost something of that audacity, of that resolution, of that confidence, which had   *   *   * contributed so much to the successes of former campaigns."[4]

Charras has a passage to the same effect:[5]—

"Enriched, systematically corrupted, by the prodigality of the Empire; enervated by luxury and pleasure; fatigued by twenty years of war, several among the generals would have preferred the tranquil life of their own homes to the labors of the march and the discomforts of the bivouac. They had tasted of peace for a whole year; they looked back on that period with regret. Some among them had met with rude defeats while in independent commands, and they remembered them well. Others, shaken by the cruel recollections of 1813 and 1814, despaired of the issue of the war in view of the enormous armies of the coalition and of the feebleness of our means of defence. All remained brave, intrepid; but all had not preserved the activity, the resolution, the audacity of their early days. Their *moral* was no longer equal to sustaining a reverse."

These statements may very possibly be somewhat too highly colored, but there is little doubt that there was a good deal of truth in them. It is significant that they are made by writers who wrote of the campaign from opposite points of view. Napoleon in his narrative of the campaign sought to show that he was not the sole or even the chief cause of its failure, and claimed that his orders were not carried out with the spirit and energy which his lieutenants had once possessed. Charras on the other hand, throughout his history, is uniformly harsh in his comments on the Emperor's conduct, and insists

---

[3] Corresp., vol. 31, p. 249.

[4] *Cf.* Gourgaud, pp. 67, 68.

[5] Charras, vol. 1, p. 70.

that he was greatly lacking both in physical strength and in energy of character. That both Charras and Napoleon, therefore, state that the higher officers of the army were not up to the mark of their earlier campaigns renders it very probable that such was the actual fact.

The importance of this fact is to be seen in its true light only when we bear in mind to how great an extent Napoleon's campaigns required for their successful conduct qualities in his lieutenants by no means universally found even in respectable corps-commanders,—qualities far in excess of those commonly demanded. Napoleon was not content with mere obedience; he expected from his chief officers an intelligent comprehension of his views, and a vigorous and daring execution of the parts assigned to them,—a sort of coöperation, in fact. The movements with which the campaign of 1809 opened will best illustrate, perhaps, what is here referred to. It is not too much to say that without this hearty and intelligent work on the part of his lieutenants many of Napoleon's most brilliant and successful campaigns could never have been carried out. We shall see in the course of this narrative how much he expected from Ney and Grouchy. Hence any inability or unwillingness on the part of the leading officers to render this assistance must be fully taken into account when we are seeking to understand this campaign of Waterloo.

We have not spoken of the commander of the Guard, Marshal Mortier, because he was taken ill just before the opening of the campaign, and no one replaced him. General Drouot, an artillery officer of great merit, was the adjutant-general of the Guard, and orders were given through him.

At the last moment, on the eve of the opening of hostilities, the Emperor sent for Marshal Ney. Why the orders to this distinguished officer were not given earlier, we are not informed; it seems like an unpardonable oversight, to say the least. As such Ney certainly regarded it.[6] Ney was given no time for preparation; it was only by the exercise of great diligence that he reached the front when he did, and that was at five o'clock in the afternoon of the 15th, after the Sambre had been crossed. He was assigned to the command of the 1st and 2d Corps, commanded by the Counts d'Erlon and Reille respectively; but he was ignorant of their organization, and had even to learn the names of the division commanders. It is difficult, if not impossible, to understand this strange neglect of Napoleon. No one knew better than he how important it is that the commander of an army or of a wing of an army should have ample time to know his troops and to be known by them, and that this was especially necessary where a reorganization had recently taken place.

In the army, thus constituted, there were, then, three Marshals. Of these, one, Soult, was serving in a new capacity for him, that of chief-of-staff; another, Ney, had not been given a fair chance to get a good hold on the troops assigned to him; the third, Grouchy, was not a man of superior capacity, had never commanded an army-corps in his life, and had only just been made a Marshal. Grouchy was at first assigned to the command of the reserve cavalry, consisting of the four cavalry corps of Pajol, Exelmans, Kellermann and Milhaud, numbering in all 13,784 men. But the campaign had scarcely opened when he was relieved from this duty, and placed in command of the right wing of the army, consisting of the 3d and 4th Corps, those of Generals Vandamme and Gérard, together with a considerable force of cavalry. Here again was a singular neglect on Napoleon's part of the importance of allowing the new Marshal time to get used to his new duties; and, as we shall ultimately have occasion to see, this circumstance operated most unfavorably when Grouchy found himself in

---

[6] Ney's letter to the Duke of Otranto; Jones, p. 385.

an independent command. It looks very much as if Napoleon only decided to send for Ney at the last minute, and as if the assignment of Grouchy to the command of the two corps of Vandamme and Gérard was not determined on until the campaign had opened.

But not only was the organization of the army not as perfect as it might have been by reason of the course which Napoleon pursued in regard to Ney and Grouchy; there was an officer whom he ordered to stay behind when he might have had him with himself as well as not, a man of the highest reputation, the Duke of Auërstadt, the Prince of Eckmühl, Marshal Davout. The Emperor had made him Minister of War, but Davout begged to have a command in the field. He represented to the Emperor,—[7]

"That the defence of Paris, notwithstanding its incontestable importance, was, like all questions of interior defence, only secondary, and essentially subordinate to the result of military operations; that when it was a question of playing a decisive part on the field of battle, it was not the time to make experiments with new men; that it was necessary, on the contrary, for the Emperor to surround himself with men who had given good account of themselves and who had had long experience in high command. The Marshal did not succeed in convincing the Emperor, who contented himself with replying: 'I cannot entrust Paris to any one else.' 'But, sire,' replied Davout, 'if you are the victor, Paris will be yours; and if you are beaten, neither I nor any one else can do anything for you.'"

There can be no question that the Marshal's reasoning was sound; but Napoleon persisted in his course. What he lost by not having Davout with him in this campaign, it is not easy to estimate; it is perhaps foolish to conjecture. But it would probably not be going too far to say that Davout in the place of either Ney or Grouchy would have prevented the catastrophe of Waterloo.

---

[7] Davout, p. 540.

This sketch of the *personnel* of the French army naturally leads up to an estimate of its chief, that is, of his comparative fitness at this period of his life to undertake the tasks of such a daring, laborious and perilous campaign as this attack on Blücher and Wellington was sure to prove.

Most historians have agreed that in point of bodily activity the Emperor did not show himself in this campaign the equal of his former self; in fact, most writers have gone farther than this; they have attributed to him a lassitude of mind as well as of body, they have found a want of the mental activity and a lack of the resolute will, which had been so characteristic of him in his earlier days. The portrait of Napoleon by General Foy is one of the best we have, and is of especial value as having been drawn by a contemporary, who served throughout his wars and commanded a division at Waterloo.

"With his passions, and in spite of his errors, Napoleon is, taking him all in all, the greatest warrior of modern times. He carried into battle a stoical courage, a profoundly calculated tenacity, a mind fertile in sudden inspirations, which by unhoped-for resources disconcerted the plans of the enemy.   *   *   *   Napoleon possessed in an eminent degree the faculties requisite for the profession of arms; temperate and robust, watching and sleeping at pleasure, appearing unawares where he was least suspected, he did not disregard the details to which important results are sometimes attached.   *   *   *   He carried with him into battle a cool and impassible courage; never was a mind so deeply meditative more fertile in rapid and sudden illuminations. On becoming Emperor he ceased not to be the soldier. If his activity decreased with the progress of age, this was owing to the decrease of his physical powers." And in a note he adds: "In the latter years the Emperor had grown fat; he ate more, slept longer, and rode less; but he retained all the vigor of his mind, and his passions had lost little of their strength."[8]

---

[8]Foy's History of the War in the Peninsula; vol. 1, pp. 110-112: Histoire de la Guerre de la Peninsule; pp. 161-164.

There is in fact no reason to doubt that Napoleon's habitual activity and even his capacity for physical exertion had in 1815 sensibly diminished. Like most men of forty-five, he was not so full of energy as he had been at five and twenty. He had also grown stout, and he was furthermore a sufferer from some painful maladies which rendered it difficult for him to keep on horseback for any great length of time.[9] All these circumstances would naturally tend to diminish, more or less, the once ceaseless activity of his mind; we may, therefore, expect to find him less thoughtful, less vigilant, less careful, than he had been in his earlier campaigns. But it is plain that the standard by which the Napoleon of 1815 is tested is no ordinary standard,[10] and it may well be that although he may have failed to come up to the high mark which he formerly attained, we shall nevertheless find in this campaign of Waterloo no conspicuous lack of ordinary activity and energy.

In conclusion, we may fairly say that while we recognize that the army with which Napoleon was preparing to take the field in June, 1815, was not as well-organized a body of troops as some of the armies which he had led to victory, that its corps-commanders were not as brilliant soldiers as were many of the distinguished generals of that period, that peculiar circumstances rendered Soult, Ney and Grouchy less serviceable than they probably would have been had things been otherwise ordered, and that the Emperor himself was more or less deficient

---

[9] Thiers, vol. xx, book lx, p. 37, n.: Grouchy Mém., vol. 4, p. 44, n. 2; id. in Le Mal de G., p. 18, n. 2.

[10] Soult told Sir W. Napier: "The Emperor seemed at times to be changed; there were moments when his genius and activity seemed as powerful and fresh as ever; at other moments he seemed apathetic. For example, he fought the battle of Waterloo without having himself examined the enemy's position. He trusted to General Haxo's report. In former days he would have examined and re-examined it in person." Life of Sir W. F. W. Napier, vol. 1, p. 505.

in the never-resting activity of mind and body which he had once possessed, we must not forget that the soldiers and their officers were all veterans, that their generals had won their rank by distinguished service on many a bloody field, and that no man living surpassed their leader in military talent. It is not correct to say[11] that the army which Napoleon led into Belgium was the finest he had ever commanded, but it is quite certain that it was by far the best of the three armies then in the field.

The strength and composition of this army, was, according to Charras,[12] whom we may safely follow, as follows:—

1st Corps: d'Erlon.

Four divisions of infantry,—
Allix, Donzelot, Marcognet, Durutte 16,885   Men
One division of cavalry,—Jaquinot 1,506   "
Artillery,—46 guns,—engineers, etc. 1,548   "

Total,   19,939 "

2d Corps: Reille.

Four divisions of infantry,—
Bachelu, Jerome Napoleon,[13] Girard, Foy
   20,635   Men
One division of cavalry,—Piré   1,865   "
Artillery,—46 guns,—engineers, &c. 1,861   "

Total,   24,361 "

Carried forward   44,300 "

---

[11] As do Chesney, p. 67, and Hooper, pp. 62, 161.

[12] Charras, vol. 1, pp. 65-68.

[13] Charras, vol. 1, p. 196, n., says that Jerome's command was purely nominal, and that Guilleminot, his chief-of-staff, really commanded this division.

Brought forward		44,300 Men
3d Corps: Vandamme.		
Three divisions of infantry,—		
Lefol, Habert, Berthezène	16,851	"
One division of cavalry,—Domon	1,017	"
Artillery,—38 guns,—engineers, &c.	1,292	"
Total,		19,160 "
4th Corps: Gérard.		
Three divisions of infantry,—		
Pécheux, Vichery, Bourmont[14]	12,800	"
One division of cavalry,—		
Maurin	1,628	"
Artillery,—38 guns,—engineers, &c.,	1,567	"
Total,		15,995 "
6th Corps: Lobau.		
Three divisions of infantry,—		
Simmer, Jeannin, Teste	9,218	"
Artillery,—32 guns,—engineers, &c.,	1,247	"
Total,		10,465 "
Imperial Guard:		
Old Guard:		
One division,—Friant,—grenadiers	4,140	"
Middle [15] Guard:		
One division,—Morand,—chasseurs	4,603	"
Carried forward	8,743	89,920 "

[14] Bourmont deserted to the enemy early on the 15th June, and was succeeded by Hulot.

[15] We here follow many historians in calling Morand's command the Middle Guard, "la moyenne Garde."

Brought forward	8,743	89,920 Men

Young Guard:
One division,—Duhesme,—voltigeurs, &c.,   4,283
Two divisions of cavalry, Guyot, Lefebvre-Desnouettes   3,795
Artillery,—96 guns,—engineers, &c., 4,063

      Total,   20,884 "

Reserve Cavalry: Grouchy.

1st Cavalry Corps: Pajol.
Two divisions,—Soult, Subervie   2,717
Artillery,—12 guns,   329
                 3,046

2d Cavalry Corps: Exelmans.
Two divisions: Stroltz, Chastel 3,220
Artillery,—12 guns,   295
                 3,515

3d Cavalry Corps: Kellermann.
Two divisions,—L'Heritier, Roussel   3,360
Artillery,—12 guns,   319
                 3,679

4th Cavalry Corps: Milhaud.
Two divisions,—Wathier, Delort   3,194
Artillery,—12 guns,   350
                 3,544

      Total,   13,784 "

Workmen, waggoners, &c., about   3,500 "

      Grand Total,   128,088 "

Leaving out the last item as consisting chiefly of non-combatants, we have an army consisting of 124,588 men. Of these, the infantry numbered, 89,415 Men
the cavalry, including the horse artillery of
   the reserve cavalry, numbered, 23,595 "
the artillery (344 guns including the above)
   numbered, 11,578 "

       Total,[16] as above, 124,588 "

[16]Charras' summing up of the cavalry and artillery varies from ours, and would seem to be 500 less than the number before given by him.

NOTE TO CHAPTER II.

THE opinion expressed here in regard to the health of the Emperor is substantially that entertained by Thiers and Chesney. The former says that the Emperor's brother Jerome, and also one of the surgeons on the Emperor's staff, both told him that Napoleon was a sufferer at this time from an affection of the bladder. But this was, he says, denied by Marchand, the Emperor's valet. "Whatever may have been the health of Napoleon at this epoch, his activity was not diminished."[1]

To the same effect is Chesney's opinion,[2] opposing that of Charras.[3] Further evidence on the subject has been collected by Mr. Dorsey Gardner.[4] His conclusion is entirely opposed to that of Colonel Chesney, and in our judgment he places altogether too much reliance on that delightful, but gossipy, writer, the Comte de Ségur. Ségur's History of the Russian Campaign is the best known work on the subject, but it is essentially a romance. In it he advances with great boldness his favorite theme of the breaking down of Napoleon's health.[5] But the Emperor's health was able to endure

---

[1] Thiers, vol. xx, book lx, p. 37, n.

[2] Chesney, p. 72, n.

[3] Charras, vol. 2, p. 203, n. H.

[4] Gardner; Quatre Bras, Ligny and Waterloo; pp. 31-37; p. 220, n. 138.

[5] Histoire de Napoleon et de la Grande Armée pendant l'année 1812. Paris, 1825. Book 4, chaps. 2 and 6.

without injury that terrible strain; he certainly showed in 1813 and 1814 every evidence of physical vigor. No doubt the peculiar maladies from which he suffered occasionally impaired the activity of both mind and body; but the talk of Ségur verges at times on puerility. Gourgaud's *Examen Critique* of Ségur's work points out its defects cleverly and unsparingly. As for the conversation, referred to by Gardner, which the Earl of Albemarle[6] reports as having taken place in 1870 between his son and General Gudin, who was, in 1815, a page in waiting on the Emperor, to the effect that Napoleon secluded himself all the forenoon of the day of the battle of Waterloo, and that "it was nearly noon when the Emperor descended the ladder that led to the sleeping room and rode away," it is really impossible to accept the story. Charras, who for his own reasons (and, by the way, not for the reasons which Chesney very naturally supposes actuated him), endeavors to magnify Napoleon's inactivity throughout this campaign, represents him as, on this morning of the 18th, reconnoitring the position after eight o'clock,[7] giving his orders for the marshalling of the army, watching the deployment of the troops between nine and half-past ten, riding along the lines, and dictating the order of battle before eleven o'clock. On all such points we are quite safe in following Charras, and we must consider Gudin's story as having (to say the least) suffered greatly in its transmission. Besides, there was no "ladder that led to the sleeping room," in the house[8] in which Napoleon slept the night before Waterloo.

---

[6] *Fifty Years of my Life*: by the Earl of Albemarle, p. 98. *Cf.* Thiers, vol. xx, p. 37, note,

[7] Charras, vol. 1, pp. 270, 271. This, as will be seen later on, was the third reconnoissance since midnight.

[8] *Cf.* Fraser, Words on Wellington, p. 250. The Caillou house was set on fire by the Prussians, but the principal rooms were spared, and the house was afterwards carefully restored.

To repeat, then, once more. Napoleon in this campaign was troubled by and doubtless suffered considerably from some painful maladies; and, even apart from this fact, we cannot look for the youthful vigor and activity of 1796 or 1805 in the year 1815. He was not in these respects equal to his former self; and it was further to be expected that the deficiency of his physical energy would be accompanied by a diminished mental alertness and vigilance. All the same, we think it will be found that he showed in this campaign a very fair degree of strength and activity. But we shall know more about this as we proceed with the narrative.

CHAPTER III.

THE ALLIED ARMIES.

The army which was commanded by Field Marshal Blücher numbered about 124,000 men, and was thus composed:—[1]

Ist Corps: Zieten.

Four divisions of infantry,—Steinmetz,—Pirch II.,—Jagow,—Henckel	27,887	Men
One division of cavalry,—Röder	1,925	"
Artillery,—96 guns,—engineers, &c.	2,880	"
Total	32,692	"

IId Corps: Pirch I.

Four divisions of infantry,—Tippelskirchen,—Krafft,—Brause,—Langen	25,836	"
One division of cavalry,—Jürgass	4,468	"
Artillery,—80 guns,—engineers, &c.	2,400	"
Total	32,704	"
Carried forward	65,396	"

---

[1] Charras, vol. 1, pp. 81, 82. See vol. 2, p. 202, note G, where it is shown that the number of men in the artillery given by Wagner is much too small.

THE ALLIED ARMIES.

	Brought forward		65,396 Men

IIId Corps: Thielemann.

Four divisions of infantry,—
Borcke,—Kämpfen,—Luck,—
  Stülpnagel .... 20,611 "
One division of cavalry,—Marwitz ... 2,405 "
Artillery,—48 guns,—engineers, &c. ... 1,440 "

Total .... 24,456 "

IVth Corps: Bülow.

Four divisions of infantry,—
Hacke,—Ryssel,—Losthin,—Hiller ... 25,381
One division of cavalry,—
  Prince William of Prussia .... 3,081 "
Artillery,—88 guns,—engineers, &c. ... 2,640 "

Total .... 31,102 "
Workmen, waggoners, &c., about ...... 3,120 "

Grand total .... 124,074 "

Leaving out the last item, we have an army consisting of 120,954 men. Of these,

the infantry numbered .... 99,715 Men
" cavalry   "   11,879 "
" artillery, 312 guns, numbered   9,360 "

Total as above .... 120,954 "

The headquarters of Zieten's Corps were at Charleroi, of Pirch I. at Namur, of Thielemann at Ciney, and of Bülow at Liége. The first three of these places were near the frontier.

The Prussian army was mainly composed of veterans; even of the youngest soldiers most had seen service in 1813 or 1814. The corps-commanders were experienced officers, though only one of them, Bülow, had ever had an independent command. Bülow had in 1813 won the battle of Dennewitz against Marshal Ney. The troops were certainly not so inured to war as were those of Napoleon's army, nor were they so well led; but they knew their trade, and were prepared for battle. Blücher himself was a veteran of the Seven Years' War. He had seen more than fifty years of service. In the campaigns of 1806 and 1807 he had displayed conspicuous zeal and courage. In those of 1813 and 1814, although too old and infirm to assume all the tasks which ordinarily devolve on an army-commander, he had yet, with the assistance of his chief-of-staff, markedly increased his reputation. Nevertheless no one considered him a general of a high order of talent. His conceptions of strategy were crude and imperfect, and his blunders caused his command to be more than once badly defeated by Napoleon in the winter campaign in France in 1814. But Blücher was a thorough soldier, active, daring and resolute, and never was afraid of taking responsibility. He was moreover a great favorite with the army. He was animated by an almost insane hatred of Napoleon, and he entered on the work assigned to him by the allied powers with an eager determination that bordered upon ferocity. This spirit of his infused itself into the army;[2] every man was ready to fight, and every man expected to beat in the end. His chief-of-staff, Gneisenau, was an able administrator, and relieved the old field-marshal from all attention to details.

The army commanded by the Duke of Wellington was a very heterogeneous body of troops. Although nominally divided into corps, after the fashion of the armies of the continent, this arrangement, being one

---

[2] The view of the Prussian army presented here is that of Charras (vol. 1, p. 89); but Delbrück, the biographer of Gneisenau, states that many of the troops were inexperienced, and some were half-hearted in the cause. Gneisenau, vol. 4, pp. 381, 382. *Cf.* Siborne, vol. 1, pp. 302, 303.

which had never been adopted by the Duke before, was only imperfectly[3] practised in the campaign of 1815. We shall get a better idea of the strength of Wellington's forces if we enumerate them according to their different nationalities. Leaving out the troops employed on garrison duty at Antwerp, Ostend, Ghent and other places, estimated at 12,233 men,[4] we find the forces available for the field to have been thus composed:—

British:

Nine brigades of infantry,— Maitland (Guards),—Byng (Guards),— Adam,—Mitchell,—Halkett,—Johnstone,—Kempt,—Pack,—Lambert	20,310	Men
Three brigades of cavalry,— Somerset (Guards),—Ponsonby,— Vandeleur	3,578	"
Six regiments contained in four brigades Dörnberg,—Grant,—Vivian,—Arentsschildt,—composed of British troops and those of the King's German Legion	2,335	"
Artillery,—102 guns	5,030	"
Total British force,	31,253	"

King's German Legion:

Two brigades of infantry,— Duplat,—Ompteda	3,285		
Add men on detached service	16		
	3,301		
Carried forward		3,301	31,253 "

---

[3] For instance, at the battle of Waterloo, troops of the 1st Corps, that of the Prince of Orange, were stationed on both ends of the line.

[4] These figures are taken from Siborne.

Brought forward	3,301	31,253 Men

Cavalry:

Five regiments contained in the four brigades of Dörnberg, Grant, Vivian and Arentsschildt.	2,560	"
Artillery,—18 guns	526	"
Total King's German Legion		6,387 "

Hanoverians:

Five brigades of infantry,—Kielmansegge,—Halkett,—Best,—Vincke,—Lyon	13,788	
One brigade of cavalry,—Estorff	1,682	
Artillery,—12 guns	465	
Total Hanoverians		15,935 "

Dutch-Belgians:

Seven brigades of infantry,—Bylandt,—Prince Bernard of Saxe Weimar,[5]—Ditmers,—d'Aubremé,—Hauw,—Eerens,—Anthing	24,174	
Three brigades of cavalry,—Trip,—Ghigny—Merlen	3,405	
Artillery,—48 guns	1,635	
Total Dutch-Belgians		29,214 "
Carried forward		82,789 "

---

[5] This brigade was composed of one regiment of Nassau, in three battalions, and one regiment of Orange-Nassau, and numbered 4,300 men.

Brought forward	82,789 Men

Brunswickers:

Two brigades of infantry,—Buttlar,—Specht	5,376
Two regiments of cavalry,—	922
Artillery,—16 guns	510
Total Brunswickers	6,808 "

Nassau Contingent: Kruse.

One regiment of infantry: three battalions	2,880 "
Engineers, sappers, miners, waggon-trains and staff-corps	1,240 "
Total disposable army in the field	93,717 "

Of these the

Infantry numbered	69,829
Cavalry "	14,482
Artillery " 196 guns	8,166
Engineers, waggon-trains, &c.	1,240
	93,717 "

Or, according to nationality,

the British numbered	31,253
" King's German Legion	6,387
" Hanoverians "	15,935
" Dutch-Belgians[6] "	29,214
" Brunswickers	6,808
" Nassau contingent	2,880
" Engineers, &c.,	1,240
	93,717 "

This army was organized, as we have said above, into two corps and a reserve, in addition to which was a large

---

[6] Including 4,300 Nassauers.

body of cavalry, and a small force of reserve artillery. There were six (so-called) British divisions in the army, only one of which, the 1st, Cooke's, was composed entirely of British troops,—the Guards; the others contained troops of the King's German Legion and Hanoverians. To each of these divisions were attached two batteries. Six troops of horse-artillery were attached to the cavalry.

The 1st and 3d British divisions, those of Cooke and Alten, with the 2d and 3d Dutch-Belgian divisions of Perponcher and Chassé, composed the 1st Corps under the Prince of Orange. They covered the front of the army from Quatre Bras to and beyond Enghien, occupying the country in and around Nivelles, Roeulx, Soignies and Braine-le-Comte. They numbered 25,233 men, with 48 guns.

The 2d and 4th British divisions, those of Clinton and Colville, with the 1st Dutch-Belgian division of Stedmann, and Anthing's Indian brigade, constituted the 2d Corps under Lord Hill. They continued the line of the army to the north and west, occupying the country in and around Ath, Grammont and Audenarde. They numbered 24,033 men, with 40 guns.

The Reserve, or rather that portion of it destined for service in the field, and not counting the troops on garrison-duty, was under the immediate direction of the commander-in-chief. It was composed of the 5th and 6th British divisions, those of Picton and Cole, of the Brunswick Corps under the Duke of Brunswick, and of the Nassau contingent under General Kruse. They numbered 20,563 men, with 64 guns.

The British and King's German Legion cavalry was composed of seven brigades, the whole under Lord Uxbridge. They numbered 8,473 men. To this corps were attached, as has been stated, six horse batteries. This cavalry was stationed mainly in rear of the 2d Corps, near Ninove and Grammont; but one brigade under

General Dörnberg was at and in the neighborhood of Mons.

The Hanoverian, Brunswick and Dutch-Belgian cavalry were attached respectively to the various divisions of these troops. They numbered 6,009 men, with one horse-battery of 8 guns.

To recapitulate:—

1st Corps: Prince of Orange	25,233	Men
2d Corps: Lord Hill	24,033	"
Reserve	20,563	"
Lord Uxbridge's cavalry corps	8,473	"
Other Cavalry	6,009	"
Artillery—196 guns	8,166	"
Engineers, &c.	1,240	"
Total as above given	93,717	"

Of this miscellaneous force the Duke relied really only on his English troops and those of the King's German Legion, a corps raised originally in Hanover, which had for many years belonged to the English crown. These troops had served in the Peninsula for several years with great credit. The Hanoverian contingent, strictly so called, was composed of very raw troops, and the same was true of the Dutch-Belgians. Little was known about the Brunswickers and Nassauers. The fidelity of many of the allied troops was strongly suspected, as they had been raised in countries which had for the past few years been subject to France, and the sympathies of the soldiers were supposed to be with Napoleon.[7] The Duke's opinion of his army is well known. He considered it the poorest he had ever led.[8] Very possibly he may have underestimated its quality; but certain it

---

[7] Müffling, Passages; pp. 204, 223.

[8] Gurwood, vol. xii, pp. 358, 509,—letters to Lt. Gen. Stewart, May 8, and to Earl Bathurst, June 25, 1815.

is that the force which he commanded was a very heterogeneous collection of troops, that they had never acted in the field as an army before, and that the character and steadiness of a considerable number were, on account of either disaffection or inexperience, gravely doubted by their commander.

All this was in all probability known to Napoleon, and served as the basis of his expectations, as we shall see later on.

Of the principal officers of this motley force, it is not necessary to say much. The Prince of Orange, who commanded the 1st Corps, though an officer of experience, had not distinguished himself as a general. Lord Hill, who led the 2d Corps, was a very valuable man, whose merit had been thoroughly ascertained in the Peninsula. Sir Thomas Picton had a well-won reputation as a man of energy, courage, and capacity in all the positions in which he had served. Then there were many junior officers of great merit.

The Duke himself was in the prime of life, having just passed his forty-sixth birthday. He had never met Napoleon before, but he had often met and defeated his Marshals. His career had been one of almost uninterrupted success. His experience in the field against French soldiers had been large, and he was for this reason peculiarly fitted for the work he had now in hand. He had shown very varied ability. His military imagination, if one may use such a word, may not have been large, but he had few equals in the faculty of making up his mind what it was best to do under ascertained circumstances. His decisions were always dictated by practical reasons. He never allowed sentiment to hinder the exercise of his common sense. He could advance or retreat, fight or decline to fight, with equal ease,—with him it was a mere question of what it was best under the circumstances to do. Though esteemed a cautious officer, he had shown over and over again that he possessed not only courage and firmness, but that in daring, and in coolly taking great risks, he was equal to any emergency. His hold on his army, that is, on his own troops, was perfect. In ability, reputation, and in social rank, his preëminence among the officers of the British army and the King's German Legion was cheerfully acknowledged, and over these parts of his army he exercised a perfect and unquestioned control. And his long experience in dealing with his Spanish allies had given him an uncommon facility in administering the affairs of such a composite body of troops as he was now to command.

These three armies were curiously different in their internal economy. Napoleon, as we have said before, expected from his high officers a sort of coöperation. The "Correspondence of Napoleon" is full of long and confidential letters to his marshals, written during his campaigns, explaining the situation, stating his own intentions at length, giving them not only orders to be executed, but suggestions for their guidance in case of the happening of certain contingencies. We shall see excellent specimens of these letters in the course of this narrative. Napoleon had been for years constantly in the habit of directing complicated movements, in which the active and intelligent comprehension of his main object and purpose on the part of his lieutenants who were operating at a greater or less distance from him, was essential to success. Hence these elaborate communications, in which the style of the military order is but barely preserved, and in which the effort of the writer to impart all the information in his power to his correspondent and to give him an intelligent and precise knowledge of the objects of the campaign, is very evident.

In the English army there was nothing of this sort. Obedience, not coöperation, was what Wellington required, and it was all he needed. Operating as he did on a much smaller scale than Napoleon, his simpler methods were quite adequate to his wants. It is needless to say that such a relation as that which existed between Napoleon and his old companions in arms, who had begun their careers with him in Italy or Egypt, never existed to the least extent in the English service.

The Prussian army was managed differently from either the English or French. Baron Müffling, who was the Prussian *attaché* at the headquarters of the Duke of Wellington, says:—[9]

"I perceived that the Duke exercised far greater power in the army he commanded than Prince Blücher in the one committed to his care. The rules of the English service permitted the Duke's suspending any officer and sending him back to England. * * * Amongst all the generals, from the leaders of corps to the commanders of brigades, not one was to be found in the active army who had been known as refractory.

"It was not the custom in this army to criticise or control the commander-in-chief. Discipline was strictly enforced; every one knew his rights and his duties. The Duke, in matters of service, was very short and decided."

It is clear that Baron Müffling had seen a very different state of things prevailing in the Prussian service,[10] where it would seem that advice was sometimes thrust upon the general-in-chief, and even criticism was not silent. Perhaps the fact that the Prussian army was always organized in corps, and that the chiefs of corps and all the other high officers were men of an equal social rank, rendered it hard to conduct matters according to the far more soldierly ways prevailing in the English service. Whatever may have been the reason, however, such would seem to have been the fact in the early part of this century.

---

[9] Müffling, Passages; pp. 213, 214.

[10] See, for instances, Müffling, Passages; pp. 15-18, 83, 304, 311: See also Stanhope, p. 110, for the "great discussion" the night after the battle of Ligny, when "Blücher and Grolmann carried the day for remaining in communication with the English army" against Gneisenau. See *post*, p. 230.

NOTE TO CHAPTER III.

THE Earl of Ellesmere, who wrote, as has been before said, under the inspiration of the Duke of Wellington, has given us the following critical estimate of a portion of the Duke's army. He is speaking of the English and German infantry, some thirty thousand in all, which fought at Waterloo.[1]

"Of this very body, which bore the brunt of the whole contest, be it remembered that not above six or seven thousand had seen a shot fired before. It was composed of second battalions to so great an extent that we cannot but imagine that this disadvantage would have been felt had the Duke attacked the French army, as he would have attacked it at Quatre Bras on the 17th, if the Prussians had maintained their position at Ligny—as he would have attacked it on the 18th at Waterloo, if the army with which he entered the south of France had been at his disposal. For purposes of resistance the fact is unquestionable that these raw British battalions were found as effective as the veterans of the Peninsula; but it might have been hazardous to manœuvre under fire, and over all contingencies of ground, with some of the very regiments which, while in position, never flinched from the cannonade or the cavalry charges through the livelong day of Waterloo."

---

[1] Ellesmere, page 299.

CHAPTER IV.

THE FIFTEENTH OF JUNE. — NAPOLEON.

NAPOLEON, as we have said above,[1] "proposed to assemble his own forces with all possible secrecy in the neighborhood of Charleroi," and this step was, of course, the essential preliminary to the opening of the campaign. The five corps of which the army was to be chiefly composed, were widely separated from each other, and each was at a considerable distance from Charleroi. The 1st and 2d Corps lay to the westward of Charleroi, in the neighborhood of Lille and Valenciennes respectively, the 3d and 4th Corps to the southeastward of Charleroi, near Mezières and Metz; the 6th Corps was at Laon, about half way from Charleroi to Paris, and the Guard partly at Paris, and partly, not far off, at Compiègne. The four cavalry corps were stationed to the north of Laon, between that place and Avesnes. The larger part of these commands were placed on or near the frontier, and any movements on their part were likely to be observed by the enemy. Nevertheless the concentration of the army was safely and secretly effected. The 4th Corps, which was near Metz, broke camp as early as the 6th of June, the 1st Corps, which was near Lille, as early as the 9th, the Guard left Paris on the 8th, the other corps left their encampments at somewhat later dates. The Emperor left Paris at half-past three o'clock

---

[1] *Ante*, p. 4.

[CHAP. 4.] THE FIFTEENTH OF JUNE.—NAPOLEON. 45

on the morning of the 12th, and so well were his calculations made that, on the evening of the 14th, his headquarters were at Beaumont, not more than sixteen miles south of Charleroi, with the entire army within easy reach. And, by the expedient which he adopted, of causing demonstrations to be made at various points on the frontier, from the English Channel on the west almost to Metz on the east, he diverted the attention of the enemy's pickets and created false alarms, so that his formidable army was concentrated without arousing the serious concern of the chiefs of the allied armies.

On the evening of the 14th, at Avesnes, the Emperor issued to his soldiers one of his stirring orders;[2] he reminded them that this was the anniversary of Marengo and Friedland; he called upon them to conquer or die.

As confirming what has been said above as to his plans and expectations, he wrote to his brother Joseph the same morning, as follows:[3] "To-morrow I go to Charleroi, where the Prussian army is; that will occasion either a battle or the retreat of the enemy." To the same effect he wrote at the same time to Davout:[4] "I shall pass the Sambre to-morrow, the 15th. If the Prussians do not retire, we shall have a battle." These letters show how perfectly clear his plan lay in his own mind,—not as a project of separating the allied armies from one another by occupying any points on the line by which they communicated with each other, but as an intention of attacking and defeating the army of Blücher before it could be supported by that of Wellington, unless, indeed, it should fall back before him.

That evening at Beaumont was issued a general order[5] for the forward movement of the army, to commence at

---

[2] Corresp., vol. 28, p. 324, No. 22,052: App. C, I; *post*, p. 362.

[3] Ib., vol. 28, p. 322, No. 22,050.

[4] Ib., vol. 28, p. 323, No. 22,051.

[5] Ib., vol. 28, p. 325, No. 22,053: App. C, II; *post*, p. 363.

half-past two o'clock the next morning, the 15th. For each corps special directions were given, and also for each of the three divisions of the Imperial Guard,— Marshal Mortier, its commander, having through illness been obliged to remain at Avesnes. The 2d Corps, followed by the 1st, was to advance on the left of the army; the 3d and 6th and the Guard on the centre; and the 4th Corps, which was at Philippeville, on the right. Charleroi was stated to be the general objective point of the movement: but Reille was warned that the 2d Corps would probably cross the Sambre at Marchienne, a few miles higher up, and Gérard was by a later order[6] directed to cross with the 4th Corps at Châtelet, a little lower down. The sappers were to precede each column to repair the roads and bridges, which had been in the past few months broken up by the French, in order to obstruct the march of the allies, should they cross the frontier. The centre columns were to be preceded by the cavalry of the 3d Corps and by the cavalry-corps of General Pajol. The other three cavalry-corps, under the command of Marshal Grouchy, were to follow the army. (See Map 2.)

By the carelessness of the headquarters-staff in sending but one officer to Vandamme, and in not requiring a receipt[8] from him, and by the accident of this officer being thrown from his horse and failing to deliver his message, Vandamme did not get this order in season; he consequently was not able to get the 3d Corps on the road till seven o'clock. This delay was, of course, vexatious, and operated to hinder the movement upon Charleroi, and to render it less decisive than it otherwise would have been.

---

[6] La Tour d'Auvergne, p. 62.

[7] Charras, vol. 1, pp. 101, 117: La Tour d'Auvergne, p. 57, n. *Cf.* Stanhope, pp. 65, 248.

[8] Maurice, p. 547: Sept. 1890.

An unhappy incident occurred to the 4th Corps. General Bourmont, who commanded its leading division, deserted to the enemy, accompanied by his staff. Bourmont was an old royalist, but he had apparently given in his unqualified adhesion to the imperial cause. His treason could not but have a very unfortunate effect on the soldiers, creating a feeling of distrust in their officers, particularly in those of high rank.

With these deductions, the day of the fifteenth of June was decidedly a successful one for the French. Although the Prussian General Zieten, who, with the 1st Prussian Corps, held the line of the Sambre, having advance-posts on the right or south bank, opposed at all points to the French a skilful and obstinate resistance,[9] the superiority of his adversaries was too decided for a successful stand to be made anywhere.

In the centre, the operations were under the immediate direction of the Emperor, who mounted his horse at three in the morning.[10] In the march on Charleroi the Young Guard followed the cavalry, Vandamme's Corps having been, as we have seen, delayed. Everywhere the enemy were pushed back. Pajol entered Charleroi about noon. Here a halt was made to allow Vandamme time to arrive, and the enemy took up a strong position on the heights of Gilly, a little to the north and east of Charleroi. Their firm attitude seems to have imposed somewhat[11] on Marshal Grouchy, who had come up with the cavalry-corps of Exelmans, and on Vandamme, who in the afternoon arrived and took his proper post in the advance; and it was not until about five o'clock,[12] when Napoleon assumed command in person, and with a vigor that

---

[9] For a valuable discussion of Zieten's conduct, see Col. F. Maurice's Article on Waterloo in the United Service Magazine for October, 1890.

[10] Corresp. vol. 28, p. 330, No. 22,055: Baron Fain to Prince Joseph.

[11] But see Grouchy: Observations, pp. 60 *et seq.*

[12] Charras, vol. 1, p. 111.

savored perhaps of impatience assaulted the position, putting in even the cavalry of the headquarters-guard, that the enemy gave way, and retired to Fleurus.

Vandamme and Grouchy, with Pajol's and Exelmans' cavalry, bivouacked a mile or two south of Fleurus. The Guard rested between Charleroi and Gilly; the 6th Corps on the south bank of the river, near Charleroi.

On the right, the corps of Gérard crossed the river at Châtelet, and remained for the night on the road to Fleurus.

Thus, three corps,—the 3d, 4th, and 6th,—the Guard, and the greater part of the cavalry, were concentrated near Charleroi and between that place and Fleurus, ready to attack the Prussians at Fleurus or Sombreffe the next day.

The Emperor's headquarters were fixed at Charleroi.

Coming now to the operations of the left wing,—Reille, at the head of the 2d Corps, starting from Leers, on the Sambre, at three in the morning, drove the enemy from point to point, occupying the various bridges across the river, until he reached Marchienne.[13] By the terms of an order[14] dated 8.30 A. M. he was allowed to pass the Sambre at this point, and by another order, which is not preserved, but only referred to in an order to d'Erlon,[15] he was directed to march on Gosselies, and to attack a body of the enemy which appeared to be there. In obedience to his instructions, Reille crossed the bridge at Marchienne and moved directly upon Jumet, a village on the road leading from Charleroi to Brussels. Here he encountered a Prussian rear guard, which he quickly overthrew, and at once moved upon Gosselies. It was "at this moment," when he was marching on Gosselies,

---

[13] Charras, vol. 1, pp. 99, 100.

[14] Doc. Inéd., III, p. 22; App. C, III; *post*, p. 366.

[15] Ib., V, p. 25; App. C, V; *post*, p. 367. See Napoléon à Waterloo, p. 58.

[CHAP. 4.] THE FIFTEENTH OF JUNE.—NAPOLEON. 49

he says, that Marshal Ney arrived and took command.[16] This was about five o'clock in the afternoon.[17]

Ney, who had just overtaken the army on the march, had ridden over from Charleroi, where he had seen the Emperor, and had received[18] from him the command of the 1st and 2d Corps. Napoleon had told him that Reille was marching on Gosselies, and, when he reached Reille, he found him, as we have just seen, in the very act.

On his arrival at Gosselies, Ney carried forward with himself to Frasnes the cavalry of the 2d Corps, Piré's, and the division of Bachelu. About half-past six,[19] Ney with these troops drove the enemy,—a brigade under Prince Bernard of Saxe Weimar,—from Frasnes. They fell back to Quatre Bras. The division of Girard was sent in pursuit of the Prussians, who had retired from Gosselies on Fleurus. The other two divisions,—those of Jerome and Foy,—remained at Gosselies. A division of cavalry of the Guard, under Lefebvre-Desnouettes, about 2000 strong, which had been lent temporarily to Ney, was placed by him in support of the troops at Frasnes.[20] Ney remained at Frasnes till a late hour in the evening.

---

[16] Doc. Inéd., p. 56: Statement of General Reille.

[17] Charras, vol. 1, p. 123.

[18] Doc. Inéd., p. 4, statement of Colonel Heymès. The hour given by Heymès, seven o'clock, is much too late. We can fix the time of this conversation from a statement of Marshal Grouchy's. That officer (Observations, p. 61) tells us that on going to Charleroi to take his orders from the Emperor just before the attack on Gilly, he found him giving instructions to Ney. The attack on Gilly was ordered, as we have seen above, at five o'clock, so that Ney must have joined the Emperor some time before five, and probably reached Reille about half or three-quarters of an hour later. *Cf.* Van Loben Sels, p. 140.

[19] Report of Prince Bernard, given in full in Van Loben Sels, p. 134, n. Heymès' statement is all wrong as to the hours. He says Ney met the Emperor at seven, put himself at the head of the 2d Corps at eight, and occupied Frasnes at ten. Doc. Inéd., p. 4.

[20] Doc. Inéd., pp. 4, 5. Col. Heymès' Statement.

Thus the 2d Corps had accomplished its tasks for the day. Its commander had shown himself energetic and capable. The advance at Frasnes observed the enemy's post at Quatre Bras. The troops had had a very exhausting day and needed a good night's rest.

The 1st Corps, under the Count d'Erlon, did not do so well by any means. To begin with, d'Erlon did not start at 3 A. M., as he was ordered to do, but at 4 o'clock.[21] His troops had no fighting to do; they simply followed in the rear of the 2d Corps.[22] They had, to be sure,[23] five miles farther to go, having bivouacked at Solre-sur-Sambre, and they were, no doubt, affected by that tendency to delay which seems always to attend the last half of a long marching column; it is well known that the last half never keeps up, relatively, with the first half. D'Erlon had also been required to detach part of his troops at the various crossings of the Sambre.[24] But these facts afford no adequate explanation of the tardiness of this corps. At night d'Erlon's headquarters were at Marchienne; his leading division, Durutte's, had reached Jumet;[25] but at least one-fourth of his troops had not crossed the river. Nevertheless, by an order[26] dated 3 P. M., d'Erlon had been informed that Reille had

---

[21] See Napoléon à Waterloo, p. 53, where d'Erlon's order to his troops to break camp at 4 A. M., instead of at 3 A. M., as had been directed, is given in full, and severely commented on.

[22] Charras, vol. 1, p. 98. *Cf.* the 10 A. M. order to d'Erlon: Doc. Inéd., IV, p. 24; App. C., iv; *post*, p. 367. This directed d'Erlon to cross the Sambre at Marchiennes or Ham, and take up a position close to that of Reille.

[23] Ib., p. 98, n.

[24] Charras, vol. 2, pp. 207, 208.

[25] Durutte's statement, Doc. Inéd., p. 71, that this Corps camped at night beyond Gosselies, is wholly unsupported. Durutte probably meant Jumet, not Gosselies. The divisions of Foy and Jerome, of the 2d Corps, occupied Gosselies.

[26] Doc. Inéd., V., p. 25; App. C, v; *post*, p. 367.

[CHAP. 4.] THE FIFTEENTH OF JUNE.—NAPOLEON.   51

been ordered to march on Gosselies and to attack the enemy there, and that the Emperor wished him, d'Erlon, also to march on Gosselies and to support this operation. Later in the day, or perhaps in the evening,[27] after Marshal Ney had assumed command of the two corps, d'Erlon was informed[28] that it was the Emperor's intention that he should join the 2d Corps at Gosselies, and that Ney would also give him orders to that effect.[29] This last sentence must imply that Napoleon had enjoined on Ney to bring up these troops. It is true that Charras[30] says that, on the evening of the 15th, the 1st Corps was in echelon from Marchienne to Jumet, implying that all the troops had crossed the river; and this is the generally accepted belief.[31] But we find a despatch,[32] dated at Marchienne at 3 A.M. of the 16th, from the chief-of-staff of the 3d division of the 1st corps, Marcognet's, to General Noguès, who commanded the 1st brigade of that division, informing him that the 2d brigade would remain at Marchienne until the arrival of the 1st division, that of General Allix. This shows beyond a doubt that, notwithstanding the order of three o'clock in the afternoon for the 1st Corps to reach Gosselies and support Reille in attacking the enemy, and the subsequent order to the same effect, yet,

---

[27] At six or seven o'clock, Charras thinks. Charras, vol. 2, p. 224.

[28] Doc. Inéd., VI., p. 25; App. C, vi; *post*, p. 368.

[29] In some unaccountable way Chesney (Waterloo, pp. 118, 119) has overlooked these orders that Napoleon gave to d'Erlon to close up on Reille at Gosselies. The *Documents Inédits* are not among the authorities given in the List which follows his Table of Contents, although they are referred to on page 119, and this may account for this regrettable oversight. His blame of Napoleon, which is very severe, is, therefore, entirely undeserved.

[30] Charras, vol. 1, p. 110.

[31] La Tour d'Auvergne, p. 91; Siborne, vol. 1, p. 82; Quinet, p. 90; Hooper, p. 76: The author of "Napoléon à Waterloo" alone states (p. 34) that a part of the 1st Corps had not crossed at night. See also p. 60.

[32] Napoléon à Waterloo, p. 144; App. C, vii; *post*, p. 368.

at three o'clock in the morning of the 16th, twelve hours afterwards, one division had not arrived at the river, and another division (two brigades) was still at Marchienne. This state of facts, it must be recollected, existed when the whole 2d Corps had been at and beyond Gosselies for more than eight hours! It is impossible not to blame d'Erlon for this excessive tardiness in the movements of his corps,—not only for not having executed the order of three o'clock in the afternoon to proceed at once to Gosselies, but generally, for not having seen to it that his troops were, during the entire march, within a short distance[33] of the 2d Corps, a measure certainly, when all the circumstances are taken into account,—and especially that the advance of Reille was to be made in an enemy's country and was actually stoutly resisted,—of the most obvious necessity. And it must not be forgotten that in Belgium in the middle of June, it is light until nine o'clock in the evening, and the sun rises before four.

It may be remarked that the controversies which have been waged in regard to the truth of Napoleon's statement that he, on the 15th, gave Ney verbal orders to seize and occupy Quatre Bras, have deflected the attention of historians from the subject now under consideration,—the conduct of d'Erlon in regard to the march of the 1st Corps on the 15th,—a subject closely connected, as we shall hereafter see, with the operations of the army on the succeeding day.

In regard to the much vexed question referred to above, we shall say nothing here. It is not pretended that Napoleon gave to Ney on the 15th any written orders to go to Quatre Bras. Napoleon's statement[34] that he gave him verbal orders to that effect has been

---

[33]Charras, vol. 1, p. 98.

[34]Corresp. vol. 31, p. 199: Gourgaud, p. 47.

denied, and is widely disbelieved. We prefer, for many reasons, to confine our narrative to generally admitted facts, or to those which admit of definite proof. What we have to say about this matter will be found in the Notes to this chapter.

In summing up the situation, we may fairly conclude, that, with the exception of the backwardness of the 1st Corps, the progress made during the day had been satisfactory to the Emperor. He says himself:—

"All the Emperor's manœuvres had succeeded to his wishes; he had it thenceforth in his power to attack the armies of the enemy in detail. To avoid this misfortune, the greatest that could befall them, the only means they had left was to abandon the ground, and assemble at Brussels or beyond that city."[35]

Napoleon had in fact concentrated in front of Fleurus a sufficient force wherewith to fight the Prussians, if, as he thought it not unlikely, they should risk a battle on the next day. He was not apprehensive of the Anglo-Dutch army joining their allies in this battle, for Wellington, as he calculated, could not concentrate in season a sufficient force to overcome the two corps which, under Ney, he intended should occupy Quatre Bras the next forenoon. He had purposely abstained from occupying Sombreffe, for he feared that if he did this, Blücher, finding his communications with Wellington blocked at this point, would retire without a battle, and endeavor to effect a junction with the English at Wavre, or elsewhere to the northward; whereas, so long as the road which connected his army with that of Wellington remained free, Blücher might with confidence be expected to risk a battle for the preservation of that line of communication, that is, at or near Fleurus, with the expectation of being reinforced by his ally. But if he ventured upon this course, Napoleon expected to beat him, for Napoleon calculated that, by the occupation

---

[35] Corresp. vol. 31; p. 202.

of Quatre Bras the next morning, he could prevent Blücher's receiving any assistance from his Anglo-Dutch allies.

A letter[36] written by Baron Fain, one of the Emperor's secretaries, to Joseph Bonaparte, dated Charleroi, June 15th, at 9 o'clock in the evening, states that the Emperor has just returned, very much fatigued, having been on horseback since three in the morning, and has thrown himself on his bed for a few hours' repose; but that he will mount his horse again at midnight. This, however, as we shall see hereafter, he did not do, as at midnight Marshal Ney came to confer with him, having just ridden back from his extreme front at Frasnes.

---

[36] Corresp. vol. 28; p. 330, No. 22,055.

NOTES TO CHAPTER IV.

1. MARSHAL NEY was acting under considerable disadvantage during this afternoon and evening. We have spoken of this subject before. His difficulties are well pointed out by Colonel Maurice in a recent paper,[1] in which much stress is laid, and very justly, on the fact that Ney had not with him a proper staff. It is true that Ney was no neophyte in the practice of war, and that he was perfectly well known to his corps-commanders, and in fact to his entire command. But he arrived at the front late in the day,—at nearly five o'clock in the afternoon,—and with but a single staff-officer. It was only natural and right that he should personally occupy himself with the conduct of the advance to Frasnes, that he should accompany the cavalry, and should attend to the posting of Bachelu's infantry division in support. And he may very possibly have found the leading division of the 1st Corps, Durutte's, between Jumet and Gosselies[2] on his return, late in the evening, from Frasnes to the latter place. That the 1st Corps had not fully executed its part of the programme must have been, however, only too plain to him; and the necessity of exerting himself energetically to bring it up to the

---

[1] United Service Magazine: Sept., 1890: pp. 541 *et seq.*

[2] Doc. Inéd., p. 71. Statement of General Durutte. As we have before remarked, this officer probably mistook Jumet for Gosselies. See *ante*, p. 50, note 25.

front[3] if he would have his whole command well in hand for to-morrow's work must have appeared, in view of d'Erlon's slowness, most imperative. At least, there is every reason to suppose this.

2. As to whether Napoleon accomplished as much as he had intended to accomplish, or as much as he ought to have intended to accomplish, on this day of the fifteenth of June, writers have differed. Those who, like Jomini and Charras,[4] maintain the theory that his intention was to seize both Sombreffe and Quatre Bras at once, and those who, like Rogniat, insist that this ought to have been his intention, whatever it may in reality have been, hold that the operations of this first day were incomplete. Jomini says:—[5]

"Napoleon had to renounce the idea of pushing on the 15th as far as Sombreffe and Quatre Bras, which were to be the pivots of all his after movements." "One may feel assured," says Charras,[6] "that the haste which Napoleon intended should characterize the march of the army had for its object the occupation of Quatre Bras and Sombreffe on the first day of the campaign. This occupation failed, in consequence of a considerable loss of time; the principal avenue of communication between Blücher and Wellington remained free, although menaced; it is for this reason that we hold that Napoleon told the truth in writing that 'this loss of time was very injurious' and that we add,—the day of the 15th had been incomplete."

---

[3] "An error was committed by suffering it [the 1st Corps] to remain, during the night of the 15th, echeloned between Marchienne and Jumet." Gourg. p. 66.

[4] *Ante*, pp. 12, 13.

[5] Jomini, p. 125. Jomini says (p. 123) that "Napoleon gave Grouchy a verbal order to push as far as Sombreffe that very evening, if possible"; but no evidence of such an order is cited. See Jomini's letter to the Duc d'Elchingen, pp. 225, 226. *Cf.* La Tour d'Auvergne, p. 69. That Napoleon nowhere blames Grouchy for not having pushed on to Sombreffe on the 15th,—taken in connection with his censure of Ney for not having seized Quatre Bras that evening,—is pretty good evidence that he neither ordered nor expected Grouchy to reach Sombreffe.

[6] Charras, vol. 1, p. 116: *cf.* vol. 2, p. 225, Note K.

[CHAP. 4.] JUNE 15th.—NAPOLEON.—NOTES. 57

The passage to which Charras here refers is to be found in the Memoirs,[7] and it runs thus:—

"On the same day [the 15th], the attack of the woods before Fleurus, which had been ordered to commence at four o'clock in the afternoon, did not take place until seven o'clock. Night came on before the troops could enter Fleurus, where it had been the project of the chief to place his headquarters that very day. This loss of seven [*sic*][8] hours was very injurious at the opening of a campaign."

A. Let us first consider this question so far as it affects the operations of the centre and right of the army,—that is, with reference to the non-occupation of Sombreffe on the 15th.

Rogniat's criticism, that the Emperor ought to have aimed at seizing Sombreffe on the 15th, is especially interesting, as it was answered by Napoleon himself from St. Helena.

"He [Napoleon] ought to have carried his whole army the same day as far as Fleurus, by a forced march of eight to ten leagues, and to have pushed his advance guard as far as Sombreffe; but, instead of hastening to arrive in the midst of his enemies, he stopped at Charleroi, whether because he was retarded by the bad weather or for other motives."[9]

To this Napoleon replied:—[10]

"The Emperor's intention was that his advance guard should occupy Fleurus,[11] keeping [the bulk of] his troops concealed

---

[7] Corresp., vol. 31, p. 249.

[8] Evidently a misprint for "three"; the word "seven" having obviously been carelessly repeated.

[9] Rogniat: Consid., p. 339: cited in Corresp., vol. 31, p. 471.

[10] Corresp., vol. 31, p. 471.

[11] Rogniat claims that there is a serious inconsistency between this statement, as to the occupation of Fleurus by the advance guard, and that in the Memoirs, where it is said that the Emperor intended to place his headquarters there. This seems rather hypercritical. Charras (vol. 2, p. 221) says "It stands to reason that if he had had his headquarters in that city [Fleurus], he would have occupied Sombreffe." But this is surely going too

behind the wood near this city;[12] he took good care not to let his army be seen, *and, above all, not to occupy Sombreffe*.[13] This [the occupation of Sombreffe] would of itself have caused the failure of all his manœuvres; for then Marshal Blücher would have been obliged to make Wavre the place for the concentration of his army, the battle of Ligny would not have taken place, and the Prussian army would not have been obliged to give battle [as it did] in its then not fully concentrated condition, and not supported by the English army."

In his "Réponse aux Notes critiques de Napoléon,"[14] Rogniat criticises this observation as follows:—

"In occupying Sombreffe on the 15th, Napoleon would have won, without striking a blow, the immense result of isolating the two opposing armies in order to fight them separately, a result which the victory of Ligny, so dearly purchased, did not obtain for him."[15]

While Rogniat thus condemns Napoleon for not having proposed to himself to occupy Sombreffe on the 15th, Charras[16] summarily dismisses Napoleon's statement just quoted, as unworthy of serious attention. Not to have aimed at occupying Sombreffe on the 15th, he says, would have been contrary to "the very principles of his strategy." He accordingly finds that in this re-

---

far. Headquarters might well have been in Fleurus, while the Prussians held the heights of Brye and Sombreffe, and even the villages of Ligny and St. Amand; and this actually was the case the next day,—the 16th. Fleurus, half way between Charleroi and Sombreffe, was a very natural place for the Emperor to aim at as his resting place for the night of the 15th.

[12] Clausewitz, ch. 30, p. 60. But see Rogniat, Réponse, p. 262.

[13] The italics are our own.

[14] pp. 264, 265.

[15] It is not easy to see what is meant here. It is certain that, without having occupied Sombreffe on the 15th, Napoleon did fight the Prussians separately on the 16th. That Ligny was not a more decisive victory was due to special causes.

[16] Vol. 1, p. 115, note. Quinet, p. 102, does not follow Charras here.

spect Napoleon had failed on the evening of the 15th to attain his objective point.

Jomini's view[17] of Napoleon's plan, as we have seen above, coincides with that of Charras.[18]

In respect to these criticisms, we observe in the first place that these writers have adduced no sufficient reason for distrusting Napoleon's own account of his plan and intentions. That account is perfectly clear and consistent throughout. He wanted, he tells us, to fight at the outset a decisive battle with one of the allied armies. He looked for great results from such a battle. He expected, he says, that the Prussians would be promptly concentrated, and would offer battle near Fleurus,—to the south of Sombreffe; and that owing to the unreadiness of the Anglo-allied army, and his proposed seizure of Quatre Bras on the first day of the campaign, he would be able to fight the Prussians, isolated, for the time being, from the English.[19] While he claims to have ordered the occupation of Quatre Bras on the first day, he nowhere says that he proposed to occupy Sombreffe on the first day. When he is criticised for not having attempted this, he maintains that he was right. He considered, he says, that Blücher's object in fighting a battle at this stage in the campaign must be the maintenance of his communications with his allies;[20] the Prussians would, therefore, fight, if they fought at all, to the south of the Namur-Quatre-Bras turnpike, somewhere to the south of Sombreffe. And, as he expected great and perhaps decisive results[21] from such a battle, he con-

---

[17]Jomini, pp. 123, 125.

[18]La Tour d'Auvergne, pp. 73 *et seq.* takes the same view.

[19]Vaudoncourt, vol. 3, 2d part, pp. 134, 135, states the Emperor's plan with admirable clearness. But on pp. 165, 166, he slides into the theory of Jomini.

[20]*Cf.* Clausewitz, ch. 22, p. 46. "It was certainly to be assumed that both generals would remain in communication with each other."

[21]" Bonaparte hoped, if he met Blücher's main body, to destroy it by a quick attack, before Wellington could arrive." Ib., ch. 22, p. 46.

tented himself on the 15th of June with threatening with his centre and right this turnpike, and purposely abstained from occupying Sombreffe. For if Blücher should find Sombreffe occupied and his line of communications with Wellington actually in the enemy's hands, it was probable, so Napoleon thought, that he would retire to some point further north, where a union of the two armies could easily be effected, and so this opportunity of fighting the Prussians alone and isolated from the English would be lost.

In the second place, we fail to see that the plan which Rogniat blames Napoleon for not having adopted, and which Jomini and Charras believe he really entertained, but failed to carry into effect, that is, the plan of occupying both Sombreffe and Quatre Bras on the 15th, was an improvement in any way over Napoleon's plan as described by himself, as stated above. These writers would have Napoleon begin the campaign by separating the two hostile armies by occupying two points on the road by which they communicated with each other. Napoleon says that if he had done this, while the two armies would certainly have been separated, his chances of dealing decisively with one of them, alone and unsupported by its ally, would most likely have vanished. And the probabilities are that Napoleon was right in this opinion. Blücher would naturally have retired, if he had found the Namur-Quatre-Bras road occupied at Sombreffe by the French in force; he would have tried to concert with Wellington some combined operation in the neighborhood of Wavre or Brussels; and thus the opportunity which Napoleon had at Ligny, where the Prussians were exposed to the attack of the main French army without the assistance of a single English soldier, would not have been offered by Blücher.

It seems to us that Napoleon is right in his contention, and that the great chance which he had at the battle of Ligny of defeating one of his two adversaries alone and unsupported, was in exact accordance with his expectations, and, was, as much as such things ever are, the result of his well-calculated dispositions.

We conclude, therefore, that there is no good reason to suppose that Napoleon intended on the evening of the 15th to push forward to Sombreffe and hold the Namur-Nivelles road at that point. He may very possibly have expected to fix his headquarters at Fleurus, but, although he did not succeed in doing this, his object had been substantially attained at the close of the first day of the campaign, so far as the operations of the right and centre were concerned.

B. Let us now consider the other branch of the question,— Did Napoleon intend to occupy Quatre Bras on the 15th?

(1.) If we are correct in the view taken above, namely, that Napoleon did not intend to seize Sombreffe on the 15th, because he feared that if Blücher found his line of communications with Wellington occupied in force at Sombreffe, he would retire to the northward, and there form a junction with the Anglo-Dutch army, it would seem at first blush as if Blücher might be expected to take the same course if he found the turnpike to Nivelles occupied in force by the enemy at Quatre Bras. But this seems to be pushing the argument too far. Blücher could hardly be expected to be affected by the report of the occupation of Quatre Bras so much as by the expulsion of Zieten's Corps from Sombreffe, and by the occupation of that place by the main French army. Theoretically, so to speak, the seizure of any one point on the Namur-Nivelles turnpike ought to produce the same effect on Marshal Blücher's mind, and, therefore, on his subsequent movements, as the seizure of any other. Yet one can easily see that, practically, this might not be so. On the other hand, there was certainly the risk that Blücher would not fight at or near Sombreffe unless he thought he could count on receiving aid from Wellington, and this expectation could hardly be entertained, if he knew that the French were in possession of Quatre Bras. Still, the importance of preventing Wellington, by an early occupation of Quatre Bras, from assisting the Prussians in their resistance to the attack which he hoped to make upon them the next day, may well have induced Napoleon to give on the 15th to Marshal Ney orders to occupy Quatre Bras at once, and to take the chance of the result of this step being the withdrawal of the Prussian army to Wavre or Brussels.

(2.) But the matter is really of very little consequence, so far, at least, as the successful carrying out of Napoleon's plan is concerned. Let us assume that Napoleon is correct in his statement that he gave a verbal order to Ney on the 15th to push forward to Quatre Bras. We have nevertheless just seen that the Memoirs testify to the Emperor's general satisfaction on the evening of the 15th with the progress that had been made during the day, notwithstanding the non-occupation of Quatre Bras. Napoleon has in fact nowhere said that it was *necessary* to occupy Quatre Bras on the 15th. The written orders to Ney, on the morning of the 16th, which we shall shortly have occasion to consider, imply that, at the time he wrote them, Napoleon was content with Ney's having on the 15th occupied Frasnes and threatened Quatre Bras, and that he then desired the movement on the latter point to take place on the forenoon of the 16th, while he himself was massing his troops for the advance on Sombreffe and the expected battle with the Prussians in the afternoon. In truth, when we consider that the bulk of the army under Napoleon in person could hardly have been in condition to engage the Prussians at daybreak of the 16th, we can easily comprehend that Napoleon,—whatever he might have enjoined on Ney at five o'clock in the afternoon before, when he no doubt expected that much more progress would be made before the next morning than actually was made,—should have been quite content with Ney's not having reached a point so far to the front as Quatre Bras."[21]

As for Jomini[22] and Charras,[23] they admit that, when Napoleon perceived the impossibility of seizing Sombreffe on the 15th, he ceased to desire the occupation of Quatre Bras, and was quite content with Ney's advance remaining for the night at Frasnes. In their conclusion we may, for the reasons we have just given, well agree, without committing ourselves to their theory of Napoleon's plan, which, as we have seen above, differs materially from his own account of it.

We conclude, therefore, that the result of the operations of the first day had also been satisfactory so far as the non-occupation of Quatre Bras was concerned. But Marshal Ney's command was far from being well in hand at the close of the day, as we have had occasion to point out above.[24]

3. But, it may fairly be asked, in view of what has been said, assuming that Napoleon gave Ney a verbal order at five o'clock in the afternoon of the 15th, why, if the non-occupation of Quatre Bras by Ney on that evening did not really disarrange Napoleon's plans, did Napoleon blame Marshal Ney for not having occupied it? Because, in the first place, it was a disobedience of orders; secondly, because Napoleon believed that Ney's stopping at Frasnes, this side of Quatre Bras, was dictated by an exaggerated caution, which it was equally surprising and annoying to find in a man like Ney; and, thirdly because when he came to write his narrative of the campaign, he connected this hesitation to take risks, which Ney had evinced on the 15th, with Ney's very singular management of his command on the next day,—of which

---

[21] But see La Tour d'Auvergne, pp. 75, 76.

[22] Jomini, pp. 125, 215.

[23] Charras, vol. 1, p. 124. *Cf.* Quinet, p. 102.

[24] *Ante*, pp. 51, 52. Gourg. p. 66.

we can here say nothing without anticipating our story. It was to Ney's supposed faulty arrangements on the 16th that the Emperor — who never knew all the facts of the case, by the way, — naturally attributed the failure of the 1st Corps to take part either in the battle of Quatre Bras or in that of Ligny. Hence we find Napoleon severe on Ney for not boldly pushing out to Quatre Bras on the evening of the 15th, not because it was necessary to occupy the cross-roads that night, — for the next morning would have done quite as well, — but because Ney's hesitation seemed to the Emperor to indicate in him a lack of that boldness and energy on which he had always counted hitherto with entire confidence.

4. In what has just been said, we have assumed that Napoleon gave to Ney a verbal order at five o'clock on the 15th to push forward with the two corps and seize Quatre Bras. But was this the fact?

This question has been the subject of a great deal of controversy, as every student of the campaign knows to his cost. In our view, as we have just pointed out, it is not a matter of much consequence. Napoleon nowhere claims that the failure of Marshal Ney to carry out this order was a serious matter, although he does attribute his failure to carry it out to an undue prudence and an unnecessary caution, for which he censures him. Still, the matter has been so hotly contested, that it may be best to address ourselves to it briefly.

The statements in Gourgaud's narrative [25] and the Memoirs,[26] that Napoleon ordered Ney, at their meeting near Gilly, to advance boldly to Quatre Bras with his two corps and to take up a position beyond it, with guards on the roads to Nivelles, Brussels and Namur, are exceedingly positive and explicit. These statements were written in 1818 and 1820. The only piece of strictly contempo-

---

[25] Gourgaud, p. 47.

[26] Corresp. vol. 31, p. 199.

raneous evidence that we have is the statement in the official bulletin of the army,[27] which was sent off from Charleroi on the evening of the 15th, that Ney's headquarters were that evening at Quatre Bras,—and it certainly is a very strong confirmation of Gourgaud and the Memoirs.[28]

---

[27] Corresp., vol. 28, p. 333: "L'Empereur a donné le commandement de la gauche au prince de la Moskowa, qui a eu le soir son quartier général aux Quatre Chemins, sur la route de Bruxelles." This Bulletin was printed in the "Moniteur" of the 18th. App. C, viii; *post*, pp. 369, 370. It is to be found in Jones, pp. 378, 379.

[28] Marshal Grouchy, in 1818, only three years after the battle, in the first edition of the pamphlet which he published in Philadelphia, entitled "Observations sur la Relation de la Campagne de 1815, publiée par le Général Gourgaud," in defending himself for having, on the 18th of June, as he claims, strictly obeyed his orders, instead of marching to the sound of the cannon of Waterloo, says (p. 32):—

"Besides, this way of looking at the matter was fortified in my eyes by the disapproval which Napoleon had shown in my presence of the conduct of Marshal Ney. *I had heard him blame him for having suspended the movement of his troops on the 15th at the sound of the cannonade between Gilly and Fleurus*, for having halted Reille's Corps between Gosselies and Frasnes, and for having sent a division towards Fleurus, where the fighting was going on, *in place of keeping himself to the execution, pure and simple, of his orders, which prescribed to him to march on Quatre Bras*. (The italics are ours.)

And again, when speaking of his own refusal to entertain the suggestion that he should march to the sound of the cannon, he says (p. 61):—

"Could I, moreover, so soon forget that Napoleon had censured Marshal Ney for having halted at the sound of the cannon which were being fired near Fleurus, for having sent troops in that direction, and for having permitted himself to depart from the literal execution of his orders?"

Grouchy must be referring here to the scene at the Emperor's headquarters on the night of the 15th and 16th (see *post*, p. 116).

In the edition published in Philadelphia in 1819, and in the reproduction of the pamphlet from this edition in Paris in the same year, Grouchy omits the statement that he heard the emperor blame Ney, and rests his argument on the censure on Ney's conduct contained in the Gourgaud Narrative. One may not unreasonably conjecture that, after publishing the edition of 1818, he was informed that Ney's family denied that Ney had received on the 15th any order to go to Quatre Bras, and that Grouchy was unwilling to give evidence in this controversy against this contention of the friends of the Marshal.

Captain Pringle, R. E., in an Appendix to Scott's Napoleon (Paris edition,

Again, the reason given in Gourgaud[29] and the Memoirs[30] as inducing Ney to halt this side of Quatre Bras, namely, that he deemed it unwise to advance further to the front than the main body had proceeded,—judging by the sound of the cannon, which came from the neighborhood of Fleurus and Gilly,—is a very natural[31] one. It is no doubt the reason he gave to the Emperor at their interview that very night at Charleroi.

Neither Ney nor Soult have left any statements in writing[32] about the matter. Nor is it claimed that Ney ever made any verbal statement on the subject. Thiers[33] asserts that Soult "frequently said * * * that on the afternoon of the fifteenth of June he heard Napoleon order Marshal Ney to proceed to Quatre Bras," and he cites the memoirs of General Berthezène, who commanded one of Vandamme's divisions, to the effect that Soult had told him that Napoleon gave these orders to Ney.

1828, p. 833, n.), is the only author who cites the above-quoted statements of Marshal Grouchy.

[29] Gourgaud, p. 48, n.

[30] Corresp., vol. 31, p. 200.

[31] *Cf.* Jomini, p. 214, to whom the hesitation of Ney to occupy Quatre Bras seems justifiable, "unless the order to rush headlong on Quatre Bras had been expressed in a formal manner."

[32] In his letter to the Duke of Otranto (Jones, 386), Ney says: "The Emperor [on the 15th] ordered me immediately to put myself at the head of the 1st and 2d Corps, &c., &c. With these troops * * * I pursued the enemy, and forced him to evacuate Gosselies, Frasnes, Millet, Heppignies. There they took up a position for the night. * * *

"On the 16th I received orders to attack the English in their position at Quatre Bras."

It will be observed that Ney omits to state what directions, if any, the Emperor gave him on the 15th. He confines himself to enumerating the troops placed under his orders and to stating what he accomplished with them. The remark that he was ordered on the 16th to attack Quatre Bras throws no light on the question we are examining, viz.:—what orders were given to him on the 15th.

[33] Thiers, vol. xx, p. 31, n.

[CHAP. 4.] JUNE 15th.—NAPOLEON.—NOTES. 67

On the other hand we have a statement of Ney's son, then Duke of Elchingen, that Colonel Heymès, Ney's aide-de-camp, said in 1841 to him,[34] that the name of Quatre Bras was not pronounced in the conversation between the Emperor and Marshal Ney on the afternoon of the 15th. The Duke furthermore tells us [35] that in 1829, Marshal Soult told him and Colonel Heymès that the Emperor had no idea of having Quatre Bras occupied on the evening of the 15th, and gave no orders to that effect.

But how is it possible to reconcile this hearsay evidence, with the undeniable fact that the official bulletin states Ney's headquarters on the evening of the 15th to be at Quatre Bras? It is surely much more likely that these reports by Marshal Ney's son, of statements by Heymès and Soult, of their recollections, given respectively fourteen and twenty-six years after the occurrence, are defective in some way, than that the bulletin made up on the very evening should have contained a statement that Ney was at Quatre Bras when he had never been directed to go there. The contents of the bulletin must have been known to Soult, the chief-of-staff of the army; in fact, the bulletin itself must have been either actually composed by him or under his immediate direction; and it is simply incredible that he should have inserted a statement that Ney's headquarters were, on the evening of the 15th, at Quatre Bras if he knew that the Emperor had no intention of having Quatre Bras occupied that evening, and had given no orders to that effect. It is to be noted also that Charras makes but an incidental mention of the bulletin,[36] which is the only bit of contempo-

---

[34] Letter from the Duke of Elchingen to General Jomini, 16 October, 1841, published in the "Spectateur Militaire," Dec. 15, 1841, as cited in Charras, vol. 1, p. 119, n. *Cf.* Heymès' Statement, Doc. Inéd., p. 4.

[35] Doc. Inéd., p. 30.

[36] See *post;* p. 69, n. 38.

raneous evidence that we have, and confines his discussion of the testimony to an examination of these reported sayings of Soult and Heymès. When we take also into account that, in his carefully drawn Narrative,[37] Heymès does not explicitly state that Quatre Bras was not mentioned, that there is nothing whatever from Soult over his own signature, that these sayings of Soult and Heymès rest on mere hearsay evidence, and that they were spoken, if spoken at all, many years after the campaign, it is evident that the statement in the bulletin is by far the best evidence that we have. The mention of Quatre Bras in the bulletin was made at the time,—before any controversy had arisen,—it was moreover a mere incidental mention, and cannot be supposed to have been intended to serve a purpose of any kind.

Where the evidence is so conflicting, it is impossible for many persons to make up their minds. As we remarked before, the matter is not one of any great importance in its bearing on the fortunes of the campaign. The question, whether Ney received at five in the afternoon of the 15th of June verbal orders to seize Quatre Bras that evening, is of consequence mainly with reference to the scope of Napoleon's plan at that moment, and also with respect to his reproach of unwarrantable hesitation on the part of Marshal Ney. It seems to us, we frankly say, on the whole, almost certain that the order was given. At any rate, we can hardly doubt that, when the bulletin was sent off that evening to Paris, it was believed at the headquarters of the army that Marshal Ney was at Quatre Bras; we must admit this, unless we gratuitously invent an intention to deceive the public on a point of this kind. And as Ney could hardly have been supposed to occupy Quatre Bras without orders, he must have been supposed by those who drew up the bulletin,—that is, Soult, the chief-of-staff of the

---

[37] Doc. Inéd., p. 4.

army, and the Emperor himself, — to have proceeded to Quatre Bras in conformity with the verbal order given him that afternoon.[38]

The fact that the subsequent written orders to proceed to Quatre Bras, issued on the morning of the 16th, make no mention either of this verbal order, or of Ney's failure to comply with it, does not seem to us to tend in any way to show that the verbal order had not been given. There would not only be no need of referring to such a fact in a subsequent written order, but such a mention of it would be unusual and unmilitary.[39] What light, if any, the contents of the written orders throw on the question of the previous giving of a verbal order, is a matter that will be considered hereafter.

---

[38] We cannot find any allusion to the evidence furnished by this bulletin in any of the authorities, except in the "Waterloo" of La Tour d'Auvergne (p. 75), in Mr. William O'Connor Morris's "Campaign of 1815" (Great Commanders of Modern Times, p. 327, note), and in the work entitled "Napoléon à Waterloo," p. 24, n., where the proper weight is given to the matter. Hence the elaborate discussions of Charras and Chesney, failing as they do, to meet this important piece of evidence, do not greatly assist in arriving at a decision. The bulletin is not alluded to in the Duke of Elchingen's notes to the despatches collected in his "*Documents Inédits.*"

The probability is that the existence of this Bulletin escaped Chesney's attention. Charras, however, cites the Bulletin (vol. 1, pp. 113, 114, notes). The fact that "Napoléon à Waterloo" was a reply to the work of Charras, and that the "Waterloo" of La Tour d'Auvergne was a reply to Chesney, accounts for our not finding the subject discussed by Chesney and Charras. It is, however, difficult to understand why Charras in his elaborate work should have overlooked the inference to be drawn from the statement in the bulletin.

[39] *Cf.* Charras, vol. 1, p. 120.

CHAPTER V.

THE FIFTEENTH OF JUNE: BLÜCHER AND WELLINGTON.

MARSHAL BLÜCHER had long since fixed upon Sombreffe as the point of concentration for his army, in the event of the French crossing the Sambre at or near Charleroi, and he had even chosen the line of the brook of Ligny, which borders the villages of St. Amand, Ligny, and Balâtre, as a possible battlefield.[1]

On the night of the 13th of June, Zieten, who commanded the Ist Prussian Corps, and whose headquarters were at Charleroi, saw the French bivouac fires at Beaumont and Solre;[2] and, on the evening of the 14th, Blücher ordered the IId, IIId and IVth Corps to concentrate at or near Sombreffe. Zieten with the Ist Corps was to make as obstinate resistance as possible and fall back to and hold the village of Fleurus, thus gaining time for the concentration of the whole army.[3]

These measures, it is admitted by all writers, were taken without any consultation being had with the Duke of Wellington at the moment. But it is claimed that there existed a definite understanding between the two commanders, in pursuance of which Blücher acted.[4]

There had been a meeting between Wellington and

---

[1] Clausewitz, ch. 15, ch. 16. Sib., vol. 1, p. 39.
[2] Chesney, p. 71: Siborne, vol. 1, p. 54.
[3] Clausewitz, ch. 23, p. 48: Chesney, p. 71.
[4] Charras, vol. 1, p. 127, states this to be the fact, but cites no authority.

Blücher at Tirlemont on May 3d, which the Duke[5] in a letter to the Prince of Orange pronounces "very satisfactory." Baron Müffling, who was the Prussian military *attaché* at the Duke's headquarters, states[6] that the lines of march which the English and Prussian armies should respectively pursue *in case France should be invaded*, were definitely agreed upon and laid down in writing. This agreement may have been arrived at at that interview, though Müffling does not say so. He then goes on to say:—[7]

"The junction of the English and Prussian armies for a *defensive*[8] battle * * * was so distinctly *prescribed by circumstances and by the locality* that no doubt whatever could be raised on the point."

He then proceeds to give his views, and ends by saying:—

"The point of concentration for the Prussian army was accordingly marked out between Sombreffe and Charleroi, and for the English, *en dernier lieu*, between Gosselies and Marchiennes."

We do not think[9] that Müffling intends here to state that Blücher and Wellington had made any agreement

---

[5]Gurwood, vol. xii, p. 345. Clausewitz, ch. 11, p. 28, probably refers to this meeting, though he locates it at St. Trond. *Cf.* Chesney, p. 77.

[6]Passages, p. 231.

[7]Ib. p. 232.

[8]The italics are ours.

[9]As does Chesney, for instance (p. 77), who says that the English and Prussian chiefs agreed to assemble their armies respectively at the points given in the above citation from Müffling. Maurice also (pp. 145, 146, May, 1890) makes the same statement. Both these writers evidently rest on the statement of Müffling, cited above, which does not seem to us to sustain them. They are, however, careful to confine the agreement to the measures to be taken in case the French advanced by way of Charleroi. *Cf.* La Tour D'Auvergne, p. 107.

Siborne (vol. I, pp. 39 and 40) says that Blücher and Wellington had agreed in the above-mentioned event to concentrate respectively at Sombreffe and Quatre Bras, but he gives no authority for the statement. Jomini (p. 122) says substantially the same thing. Charras (vol. I, p. 84) makes the same statement, also without citing any authority for it. Very possibly he took it from Siborne. *Cf.* Chesney, p. 93.

as to their respective action in case Napoleon should be the invader; he only tells us what in his judgment was the true course for them to take,— the course marked out, as he thought, by the circumstances and the locality. That we are right in this, will appear when the likelihood of Wellington's having definitely agreed to advance his army to the very borders of the Sambre and the immediate vicinity of Charleroi, in view of his well-known anxiety for his communications, is considered for a moment.[10] We believe that the Duke, although doubtless informed of Marshal Blücher's intention to concentrate his army at Sombreffe in case the enemy advanced by way of Charleroi, made no agreement whatever with him as to his own movements. The two commanders no doubt fully intended to act in concert, and expected and relied upon the hearty support of each other, but there was not, as we believe, any definite agreement as to the particular steps to be taken in the event of a French invasion.

This matter is an important one to settle, because some Prussian historians claim that Blücher gave battle at Ligny relying on Wellington's agreement to support him. We cannot decide on this question at the present stage of our narrative; but we have already seen that Blücher gave orders for his four corps to concentrate at Sombreffe without any definite agreement or understanding with Wellington that he was to be assisted by the English in the battle that was almost certain to occur as a consequence of this concentration. All he had a right to expect was, that the Duke, as soon as he was informed of the situation, would at once assemble his forces, and, if he could safely and wisely do so, would march to the assistance of his ally.[11] But

---

[10] *Cf.* Supp. Desp., vol. x, p. 521 : Memorandum on the Battle of Waterloo. App. C, xv ; *post*, pp. 374, 375, 376.

[11] " Naturally, then, Prince Blücher * * * would expect to be

the Prussian Marshal took the risk of the English general's not coming to his support in the next day's battle; for, in the first place, he knew the scattered situation of the Anglo-Dutch troops, and that it would take a couple of days or so to get them together; and, secondly, he could not be sure that Napoleon might not, by operating with a part of his army by way of Mons and Hal, induce the Duke to concentrate his forces so far to the westward as to put it out of his power to render any help to an army that was fighting in front of Sombreffe.

We have stated that, on the evening of the 14th, Blücher ordered the IId, IIId and IVth Corps to concentrate at or near Sombreffe. In compliance with these directions the IId and IIId Corps respectively concentrated, and marched rapidly towards Sombreffe. But Bülow, whose headquarters were at Liége, and who had, in obedience to his first orders, concentrated his corps, took it upon himself to disobey a subsequent order which he received about eleven o'clock in the morning of the 15th, directing him to march at once upon Hannut, and to put off the execution of this order until the next day. It is hardly worth while to undertake to decide how far Gneisenau, Blücher's chief-of-staff, was, as has been often asserted, partly to blame for this mischance, by not inserting in the order a statement to the effect that hostilities were imminent. The matter has been often discussed;[12] it would seem that Bülow ought to bear the largest share of the blame; but why Gneisenau, upon whose shoulders lay the burden of effecting a concentration of the entire army by the morning of the 16th, should have omitted, when a

---

supported by Wellington, so far as the existing situation would make this support possible to the Duke." Ollech, p. 124.

[12]Clausewitz, ch. 20; Chesney, pp. 82, 101; Siborne, vol. 1, pp. 70, 71, n. Charras, vol. 1, p. 128, n.; Gneisenau, vol. 4, pp. 360 *et seq.*; Ollech, pp. 90 *et seq. Cf.* Maurice, p. 259: June, 1890; also, p. 546: Sept., 1890.

battle was imminent, to put the commander of his most distant corps in possession of the facts of the situation and of Marshal Blücher's intentions, it is certainly not easy to see. In such an exigency, the chief-of-staff must be held to the duty of omitting nothing that would tend to accomplish his task.

The Duke of Wellington had been, as had Marshal Blücher, aware for the last few days of the movement of large masses of French troops near the frontier, but he had not deemed it necessary or desirable in any way to alter his dispositions. He felt that his army was the force relied upon to protect Brussels, where the King of the Netherlands was, and Ghent, where the King of France was, and that it was of the utmost importance that Napoleon should not be allowed to gain the political advantage of putting those newly made sovereigns to flight,[13] and repossessing himself of Belgium and Holland. Moreover, of the importance of preserving his own communications with Antwerp and Ostend the Duke was well aware. He believed that Napoleon's best move would be against his communications;[14] and he felt that, under this belief, he ought to hesitate before concentrating his army and moving it by its left to gain a union with that of Marshal Blücher.[15]

Hence he retained his own headquarters at Brussels, thirty-four miles[16] from Charleroi. His army, as has been already stated, lay in cantonments to the westward of the Charleroi-Brussels turnpike. It is well known that Wellington looked for a movement of the French either on the road from Mons to Brussels or to the westward of that road. He had repaired the fortifica-

---

[13] Supp. Desp., vol. x, p. 521; Memorandum on the Battle of Waterloo; App. C, xv; *post*, pp. 374, 375, 376; Ellesmere, p. 171.

[14] Supp. Desp., vol. x, p. 530. App. C, xv; *post*, pp. 374, 375, 376.

[15] Maurice, pp. 148, 149: May, 1890.

[16] Chesney, p. 76.

tions of Mons, Ypres, Tournay and other places, and put them in a state of defence.[17] It is also to be observed that for the last three days before the opening of hostilities the information that came to him of the enemy's movements indicated a probable concentration of their forces near Mons.[18] Wellington's troops, if they remained in the positions which they occupied on June 12th, for instance, could be concentrated at Braine-le-Comte or Hal,— towns on the road from Mons to Brussels,— much more readily than at Quatre Bras or Gosselies,— that is, they were well situated to oppose such a movement of the French as that which the Duke thought it most likely Napoleon would make. They were, it is true, still in their cantonments, scattered about in the towns and villages, but the Duke evidently thought that he would have time enough to assemble his various detachments and concentrate his army after the movements of his adversary should have been clearly ascertained. For holding this opinion he has been sharply criticised, but this we will consider in another place.

We must, therefore, bear in mind, first, that Wellington thought it likely that Napoleon would advance, if he advanced at all, by way of Mons, or to the westward of it, and, secondly, that he thought his own army was well placed to meet such an advance. In fact we may go further, and say that Wellington having this opinion about the line which the French would probably take, felt it all the more necessary to retain his troops in their existing positions, from which they could, as he judged, easily be assembled to meet such an attack, because he saw clearly that no assistance, certainly no

---

[17] Siborne, vol. 1, p. 33.

[18] See this information collated in Maurice, pp. 147, 148: May, 1890. He is also inclined to think that Napoleon ordered the temporary occupation of Binche, with the intention of creating the belief that a part, at least, of the French army was moving on Mons.

immediate assistance, could be expected from the Prussians, in such an emergency, so remote were they from the Mons-Brussels route. If Napoleon was to be met or baffled in such a movement it must be by the Anglo-Dutch army. And the Duke also saw with equal clearness that nothing could serve the purpose of the French, if they were making their main attack by way of Mons, better than a premature movement of the Anglo-Dutch army towards Quatre Bras and Sombreffe, by which the communications of that army would be exposed throughout their whole length. Hence it was to be expected that the Duke would be most careful not to make such a premature movement, and, therefore, that he would insist on being convinced that the main French attack was by way of Charleroi before doing more than effecting the assembling of his scattered troops at their respective places of rendezvous.

It so happened that the Prince of Orange, who commanded, as we have said, the 1st Corps, left his headquarters at Braine-le-Comte early on the morning of the 15th, rode to the outposts, heard some firing in the direction of Thuin, a village some ten miles west of Charleroi, and then rode straight to Brussels[19] without stopping on his way at his own headquarters. During his absence[20] reports had been forwarded to him from Generals Dörnberg and Behr, who were at Mons, to the effect that all was quiet in their front, and from Van Merlen, whose command lay a little to the eastward of Mons, that Steinmetz's Prussian brigade had been attacked early in the morning[21] and that the enemy's movements seemed to be directed on Charleroi. These reports remained some hours at the Prince's headquarters, and were then

---

[19]Ollech, p. 115.

[20]Ib., pp. 114, 115. Maurice, p. 540: Sept., 1890.

[21]Steinmetz sent this message to Van Merlen at 8 A. M. Van Loben Sels, p. 125, note. Chesney, p. 94, note.

forwarded to the Duke at Brussels, where they arrived in the evening. But before that time, in fact by or before 3 o'clock in the afternoon, the Prince himself had arrived, bringing his own report, which was a very indefinite one, and which was to the effect that the enemy had attacked the Prussian outposts near Thuin. This was the first information which the Duke received of the outbreak of hostilities.[22] About the same time, also, a despatch[23] sent by Zieten to Müffling arrived, announcing that he had been attacked before Charleroi.

Wellington gave sufficient credence to these reports to issue orders[24] for the immediate concentration of the different divisions[25] at the points designated for them respectively, and for their being in readiness to march at a moment's notice, but waited till further reports from Mons should come in before doing more.[26] These orders were despatched between five and seven o'clock.[27]

They provided simply, as we have said above, for the

[22]Charras, who says, vol. 1, p. 130, that Wellington received at nine o'clock in the morning a despatch from Zieten, announcing that his advance posts had been attacked, is clearly in error. Hooper, p. 83, points out that the expression on which Charras bases his conclusion really means that 9 A. M. was the date of the latest intelligence from Charleroi.

Siborne, vol. 1, p. 164, n., severely criticises the arrangements of the Prince of Orange for the transmission of intelligence.

[23]Müffling, Passages, p. 228.

[24]Gurwood, vol. xii, p. 472. App. C, ix; *post*, p. 370. We rely mainly on the " Memorandum for the Deputy Quartermaster General," from which he drafted the orders. In some cases we know that the orders actually sent varied somewhat from the terms of the Memorandum; this was no doubt true in all cases; but the differences were not material. See Van Loben Sels, p. 177, note (1).

[25]Ollech (p. 116) says Cooke's division was not mentioned in these orders. He is in error; it is Clinton's division that is not mentioned. Cooke's was ordered to collect at Ath, not Clinton's, as Ollech has it.

[26]Müffling, Passages, p. 229.

[27]Chesney, p. 83, n. Müffling, p. 229. Maurice, p. 69: April, 1890. Charras, vol. 1, p. 132, n., says between eight and half-past nine.

assembling of the various divisions of the army at certain convenient places. There is, however, one passage in these orders that requires attention. Alten's division — the third British division — had been directed in the first part of the order to assemble at Braine-le-Comte, but it was further ordered to march to Nivelles (where the two Dutch-Belgian divisions of Chassé and Perponcher had been directed to assemble), if Nivelles had been attacked during the 15th, yet not until it should be found "quite certain that the enemy's attack is upon the right of the Prussian army and the left of the British army."[28] This concentration of three divisions of infantry with cavalry and artillery, say about 25,000 men, at Nivelles, seven miles west of Quatre Bras, was thus the only provision made in this first order or set of orders for the contingency of the French attack being made on the lines on which it actually was made; and it would seem to be a legitimate inference from this arrangement that Nivelles, and not Quatre Bras, had been selected by Wellington as the point of concentration for his army in case Napoleon advanced by way of Charleroi. In this connection it is important to note that in a letter dated 7 P. M., but probably not sent off till midnight, Müffling wrote to Blücher that the Duke would be in the morning in the region of Nivelles with his whole force.[29]

Later in the evening, a despatch from Blücher to Müffling, sent from Namur, arrived,[30] announcing the concentration of the Prussian army at Sombreffe, and requesting Müffling

"To give him speedy intelligence of the concentration of Wellington's army. I immediately," says Müffling, "communicated this to the Duke, who quite acquiesced

---

[28] Gurwood, vol. xii, p. 473; App. C, ix; *post*, p. 370.
[29] Gneisenau, vol. 4, p. 365, note.
[30] Müffling, Passages, p. 229.

in Blücher's dispositions. However, he could not resolve on fixing his point of concentration before receiving the expected news from Mons."

This information from Blücher, however, induced the Duke to issue, about ten o'clock in the evening,[31] a second set of orders, having for their object a general movement of the army towards the east.[32] Alten's division was now positively ordered to Nivelles; Cooke's division of guards, which had been ordered to collect at Ath, some thirteen miles south-west of its headquarters at Enghien, was now ordered on Braine-le-Comte, eight miles south-east of Enghien; and the second and fourth divisions, and the cavalry of Lord Uxbridge, which constituted the extreme right of the army and had been cantoned between Ath and Audenarde on the Scheldt, were now ordered to Enghien. Enghien is about eight miles north-west of Braine-le-Comte, which is about nine miles west of Nivelles, which in its turn is about seven miles west of Quatre Bras. No orders were issued to the reserves.

Up to this point we can go by the records. But here we encounter serious difficulties in the evidence. Everybody knows that, somehow or other, the Duke of Wellington collected the next day at Quatre Bras a considerable part of his army. We also know that it has been claimed that during the night of the 15th and 16th the Duke ordered the whole army to Quatre Bras. We shall presently have occasion to describe how the Dutch-Belgian troops got there without his orders; but our task now is to examine the orders which Wellington gave after the despatch of those the substance of which

---

[31] At 10 o'clock, however, it was not known at Brussels that Charleroi had been taken. In a letter to the Duc de Feltre, dated 10 P. M., the Duke says that the enemy " appears to menace " Charleroi. Gurwood, vol. xii, p. 473; App. C, x; *post*, p. 371.

[32] Gurwood, vol. xii, p. 474; App. C, xi; *post*, p. 371.

has just been given, and his Report of the campaign, and also his own doings on the morning of the 16th, and see what light these documents and doings throw upon the statements and claims which have been made and set up in his behalf.

The Duke's official report,[33] dated Waterloo, June 19th, seems to contain express reference to three sets of orders.

"I did not hear," he says, "of these events [the French attack on the Prussian posts on the Sambre] till in the evening of the 15th; and I immediately ordered the troops to prepare to march," that is, by the orders which were sent off between 5 and 7 o'clock P. M., "and afterwards," that is, by the orders issued at 10 o'clock, "to march to their left, as soon as I had intelligence from other quarters to prove that the enemy's movement upon Charleroi was the real attack."

Then, after stating how the Prince of Orange reinforced the brigade of Prince Bernhard at Quatre Bras, and had, early in the morning of the 16th, regained part of the ground which had been lost the evening before, he goes on to say:—

"In the meantime," — that is to say, before the "early morning,"— "I had directed the whole army to march upon Les Quatre Bras."[34]

Müffling says[35] that, towards midnight,[36] the Duke entered his room, and said:

"I have got news from Mons, from General Dörnberg, who reports that Napoleon has turned towards Charleroi with all his

---

[33] Gurwood, vol. xii, pp. 478, *et seq*. App. C, xii; *post*, p. 372.

[34] It is remarkable that this distinct and unequivocal statement, made in an official report the day after the battle, should have received so slight attention. It is hardly, if at all, alluded to either by those who believe that Wellington did order his army to concentrate at Quatre Bras, or by those who do not believe this. There is no mention of it in Siborne, Chesney, Hooper, Kennedy, Maurice, O'Connor Morris.

[35] Passages, p. 230. *Cf.* Maurice, p. 261: June, 1890.

[36] Siborne (vol. 1, pp. 79, 80) says this information arrived about 10 P. M. Charras (vol. 1, p. 134) says it was "towards eleven o'clock."

forces, and that there is no longer any enemy in front of him; therefore orders for the concentration of my army at Nivelles and Quatre Bras are already despatched.   *   *   *   Let us, therefore, go[37]   *   *   *   to the ball."

In spite of this evidence, there is no little difficulty in arriving at the conclusion that orders for a general concentration of the Anglo-Dutch army at Quatre Bras were issued by the Duke of Wellington either during the night of the 15th and 16th, or on the morning of the 16th. It is not only that no such orders as Müffling says the Duke told him he had despatched,[38] that no orders directing (to use the Duke's own words) "the whole army to march upon Les Quatre Bras,"— have ever been produced,— that, in fact, not a single order of Wellington's, directing any troops, except those belonging to the reserves, upon Quatre Bras, has ever been brought to light. This, though true, is not conclusive. It is stated by Colonel Gurwood[39] that the original instructions issued to Colonel De Lancey[40] were lost with that

---

[37] *Cf.* Letters of the First Earl of Malmesbury, vol. 2, p. 445 (London, Bentley, 1870,), where a similar statement is said to have been made by Wellington to the Duke of Richmond just before the former left the ball-room. See App. C, xiii; *post*, p. 373.

[38] Müffling's letter to Gneisenau, dated 7 P. M. but no doubt sent off about midnight (Passages, pp. 229, 230) says that "as soon as the moon rises, the reserves will march; and, in case the enemy should not attack Nivelles, the Duke will be in the region of Nivelles with his whole force in the morning in order to support your Highness." Gneisenau, vol. 4, p. 365, note. The letter does not mention Quatre Bras. Delbrück, in his Life of Gneisenau, vol. 4, p. 367, says that "Müffling also reported about midnight to the Prussian commander-in-chief that the allied army would be concentrated in twelve hours, and that at ten o'clock on the following morning 20,000 men would be at Quatre Bras, and the cavalry corps would be at Nivelles." But he cites neither Müffling nor any other authority for this amazing statement. Müffling tells us himself that in his judgment the cavalry could not reach Quatre Bras before nightfall,— hence they could reach Nivelles only two or three hours before nightfall. Müffling, Passages, p. 235.

[39] Gurwood, vol. xii, p. 474.   *Cf.* Maurice, p. 144: May, 1890.   Van Loben Sels, p. 181. Ellesmere, pp. 173, 174.

[40] The Deputy Quarter Master General, or chief-of-staff.

officer's[41] papers; and it is of course possible that there may have been instructions for him to issue orders for the different corps or divisions to concentrate at Quatre Bras which were thus lost.[42] But the real difficulty in holding the theory that, at some time during the night, or in the early morning of the 16th, the Duke issued such instructions, is, that such a theory is apparently inconsistent with the only orders[43] given on the early morning of the 16th, of which we have copies, and also, with the Duke's actions during the same period.

Let us consider these points in their order. The orders to which we have just referred are two in number; they are said to have been signed by Colonel Sir W. DeLancey, the Deputy Quarter Master General (or chief-of-staff). They are simply dated 16th June, 1815; neither the place nor the hour is given, but they must have been written at Brussels;[45] and in the early morning. They are both addressed to Lord Hill. The first directs him to move the second division of infantry upon Braine-le-Comte, and informs him that the cavalry have also been ordered to the same place. Now, although to move from Enghien, to which place these divisions had been directed in the preceding order, to Braine-le-Comte, is to approach Quatre Bras; it certainly is not the same thing as to march to Quatre Bras. Braine-le-Comte is in fact sixteen miles west of Quatre Bras. This despatch closes by saying:—"His Grace is going to Waterloo." This would seem to indicate that the Duke had not made up his mind at that time whether he would personally go to Nivelles or to Quatre Bras, the roads to

---

[41] He was killed at Waterloo.

[42] The orders themselves, however, would be received at the headquarters of the different corps or divisions, and might, possibly, be even now in existence.

[43] Gurwood, vol. xii, p. 474; App. C, xiv; *post*, p. 374.

[45] "Previously to starting from Brussels for" Quatre Bras,—says Siborne, vol. 1, p. 88.

which points branch off at Waterloo.⁴⁶

The next despatch orders the troops at Sotteghem,— Stedmann's 1st Dutch-Belgian Division and Anthing's brigade,—to proceed to Enghien, a place some twenty-five miles to the west of Quatre Bras.

Here, then, are orders issued on the 16th, in the early morning, to be sure, as we may suppose, but still some hours after the Duke had heard from General Dörnberg at Mons that the French had turned off towards Charleroi, and there is no word in them indicating any intention or expectation of a concentration at Quatre Bras.⁴⁷ It is inconceivable that these orders, or at least the first of them, should have been worded as they were, if the Duke, at the time of giving them, had the intention of concentrating his army at Quatre Bras. They are evidently based on the leading idea of the first two sets of orders, namely, of a general movement of the army towards the east, so that a concentration at Nivelles could be easily made.

The facts in regard to Picton's division also seem to show that not only at the time when the orders to that division were given, say at 2 A. M., but even when the Duke left Brussels at about 7.30 A. M., he had not made up his mind to concentrate his army at Quatre Bras. Picton was ordered to halt at Waterloo, where, as we have said, the roads to Nivelles and Quatre Bras branch off. He arrived there about ten, halted a couple of hours,⁴⁸ and, "about twelve o'clock, an order reached him for the continuation of the march of his division

---

⁴⁶ Maurice, p. 344 : July, 1890. This is Colonel Maurice's conclusion. So, Ollech, p. 118.

⁴⁷ Siborne, vol. 1, p. 88, says: "With the early dawn of the 16th of June, the whole of the Duke of Wellington's forces were in movement towards Nivelles and Quatre Bras." And then he gives the substance of the orders to Hill. It is not easy to follow Siborne's train of thought here.

⁴⁸ Gomm, p. 352; Waterloo Letters, p. 23. Gomm says the march was resumed at 1 P. M.

upon Quatre Bras."[49] It would certainly seem that when the Duke was riding to Quatre Bras that morning, — passing Picton's division on the road, — he had not decided whether to order Picton to Nivelles or to Quatre Bras.[50] He knew that the latter place was occupied by a brigade or more of Dutch-Belgian troops, but he had not ordered them there himself, — he had on the previous evening ordered them to Nivelles; they had, in fact, come to Quatre Bras and stayed there contrary to the orders which he had given; and apparently he had not yet fully decided whether he would withdraw them or reinforce them.

If, therefore, we are to make up our minds solely from Wellington's acts in the morning of the 16th, and from the only orders issued that morning of which we have copies, taken in connection with the previous orders of which we have cognizance, it would seem, that the Duke from the first intended to occupy Nivelles strongly, as a good thing to do in any event; and that he finally determined on concentrating his army in the neighborhood of that town. It is a fair inference from these acts and orders that he had not, before he left Brussels, contemplated concentrating his army further to the eastward; and that it was not until he had ridden to Quatre Bras, and seen, as he supposed, a very small force[51] in front of him, that he, bearing in mind, no doubt, that the reserves on the Brussels road and the troops at Nivelles were not far off, decided to hold the place, and take the risk of the enemy's overwhelming him by a superior force; and that he then, — just as soon as he had made

---

[49] Siborne, vol. 1, p. 102, note.

[50] So Maurice, p. 344: July, 1890. It is curious that the contradiction between these facts and the Duke's statement in his Report should not have been commented on.

[51] Wellington's letter to Blücher: Ollech, p. 125; Maurice, p. 257: June 1890; *post*, p. 106: App. C, xvi; *post*, pp. 376, 377.

up his mind to this,—sent his aides to Picton and the rest on the Brussels road, and to Nivelles; but that not even then was a general concentration of the whole army at Quatre Bras ordered, in the strict sense of the word, though, no doubt, every effort was made to collect there all the troops that could be reached.

But there are two pieces of evidence which remain to be considered, which contradict this inference, and warrant the conclusion that before he left Brussels Wellington changed his mind, and did order a concentration of his whole army at Quatre Bras, as he says in his Report he did. The first is the letter[52] which the Duke wrote to Marshal Blücher on the morning of the 16th, and the second is the "Disposition[53] of the British Army at 7 o'clock A. M., 16th June," "written out for the information of the Commander of the Forces by Colonel Sir W. DeLancey."

The letter in question never, we believe, saw the light until it was published at Berlin, in 1876, in Von Ollech's History of the Campaign of 1815. We shall give a full translation of it later on; the original is in French. The "Disposition," of which we give below an exact copy,[54] is not signed by Sir W. DeLancey, but by

---

[52] Von Ollech, p. 125. Maurice, p. 257: June, 1890; *post*, p. 106; App. C, xvi; *post*, pp. 376, 377.

[53] Supp. Desp., vol. x, p. 496.

[54] Disposition of the British Army at 7 o'clock A. M., 16th June.

1st division		Braine le Comte	marching to Nivelles and Quatre Bras.
2d "		"	marching to Nivelles.
3d "		Nivelles	" to Quatre Bras.
4th "		Audenarde	" to Braine le Comte.
5th "		beyond Waterloo	" to Genappe.
6th "		Assche	" to Genappe and Quatre Bras.
5th Hanoverian brigade		Hal	" to Genappe and Quatre Bras.
4th "		beyond Waterloo	" to Genappe and Quatre Bras.

DeLacy Evans. Evans,[55] who became afterwards a distinguished general officer, was in 1815 a Major, and was serving as an extra aide-de-camp to Major General Ponsonby, who commanded the second brigade of cavalry. His attestation to this memorandum, therefore, can hardly have been made at the time; but we have a right to suppose that the paper was in DeLancey's handwriting, or that Evans had some other sufficient grounds for thus attesting its authenticity. It purports, in our opinion,[56] to be a statement, prepared by Wellington's chief-of-staff, of the probable positions at 7 o'clock A. M. of the 16th of June, of the various divisions of the army, and of their respective destinations.

2d division	{ army of the Low Countries }		at Nivelles and Quatre Bras.	
3d "				
1st division Indian brigade	"	Sotteghem	marching to Enghien.	
Major-General Dörnberg's brigade and Cumberland Hussars		beyond Waterloo	"	to Genappe and Quatre Bras.
Remainder of the cavalry		Braine le Comte	"	to Nivelles and Quatre Bras.
Duke of Brunswick's Corps,		beyond Waterloo	"	to Genappe.
Nassau		"	"	to Genappe.

The above disposition written out for the information of the Commander of the Forces by Colonel Sir W. De Lancey. The centre column of names indicates the places at which the troops had arrived or were moving on. The column on the right of the paper indicates the places the troops were ordered to proceed to at 7 o'clock A. M., 16th June, previous to any attack on the British.   (Signed) DeLacy Evans.

By the phrase—"the places at which the troops had arrived or were moving on"—the writer means, in all probability, the places to which the troops were, in his judgment, nearest, at 7 A. M.

[55] Waterloo Roll Call, pp. 4, 19.

[56] Maurice (June, 1890, p. 261) adopts a different construction of the statement; he thinks it means that the orders to march to the various points named were issued at seven o'clock A. M. But why should it have been thought necessary to give to the Commander of the Forces information of the hour of issuing the orders? What he would want to know would be where the various divisions probably were at a given hour, and to what points they were marching.

That this "Disposition" was relied on by Wellington when he wrote his letter to Blücher, seems, by comparing the two papers, very clear. We find, for example, that the "Disposition" states that, of the four divisions of the 1st Corps, Cooke's was at 7 A. M. at Braine-le-Comte, marching to Nivelles and Quatre Bras, Alten's was at Nivelles, and marching to Quatre Bras, and those of Chassé and Perponcher were at Nivelles and Quatre Bras. We then find the Duke writing to Blücher, that, at 10.30 A. M., one division of this corps was at Quatre Bras and the rest at Nivelles. It cannot be denied that, so far as this corps is concerned, certainly, the two papers hang together perfectly well. Wellington had a perfect right to suppose that Cooke could get from Braine-le-Comte to Nivelles, or nearly there, between seven and half-past ten; and as for the positions of the other divisions, he simply follows the memorandum which his chief-of-staff has prepared for his information, and on which he had an undoubted right to rely. We shall give, later on, other instances of this agreement between these two papers. They seem to us to demonstrate the authenticity of the "Disposition."

Assuming now the authenticity of this memorandum, we wish to point out that its statements necessarily imply that orders had been issued to the army other than those of which we have copies,—that is, other than those of which we have given abstracts above. Thus, all we have hitherto been able to ascertain in regard to the orders to Cooke's division is, that it was by the 10 P. M. order of June 15, directed to march from Enghien on Braine-le-Comte. It would appear from the DeLancey Memorandum that it had been subsequently ordered to Nivelles and Quatre Bras. And the Duke does not hesitate to tell Marshal Blücher—on the strength of DeLancey's statement, that, at 7 A. M., Cooke was at Braine-le-Comte,—that Cooke must have arrived at Nivelles by half-past ten,—he being, according to

De Lancey's memorandum, under orders to proceed there.

So with the cavalry. We have seen above that in an early morning order of the 16th, it is said that the cavalry had been directed on Braine-le-Comte. Yet there must have been some subsequently issued order to Lord Uxbridge, for we find the "Disposition" stating that the cavalry is, at 7 A. M., at Braine-le-Comte, and is marching to Nivelles and Quatre Bras; and Wellington, relying on this statement of his chief-of-staff, that a subsequent order had been sent out ordering the cavalry to continue their march to Nivelles, does not hesitate to tell Marshal Blücher, that his cavalry will be at Nivelles at noon.

We shall have occasion hereafter to examine both papers in detail; but what we have just pointed out will suffice for the purpose now in hand.

That is to say, the "Disposition" prepared for the Duke's information by Colonel DeLancey, and the letter of the Duke to Marshal Blücher are pieces of strictly contemporaneous evidence; and show beyond a doubt that further orders, issued subsequently to those of which we know the tenor, and directing the army on Quatre Bras, were really given in the morning of the 16th, as Wellington, in his Report of the battle, explicitly states was the case.

Thus, — to recur for a moment to the orders dated on the 16th, and to the inferences drawn from them, — although at the time when the despatch dated the 16th to Lord Hill, to move the second division on Braine-le-Comte, in which it was stated that the Duke was going to Waterloo, was issued, the Duke assuredly had not made up his mind to concentrate his army at Quatre Bras, nevertheless, he did subsequently, and probably not long afterwards, make up his mind so to do, and thereupon he issued an order for that division to march to Nivelles, as the "Disposition" states. As for Stedmann's division and

[CHAP. 5.] BLÜCHER AND WELLINGTON. 89

Anthing's brigade, which were the subjects of the other order written on the 16th, the "Disposition" simply embodies the purport of this order. And as for the halt of Picton's division at Waterloo, to which we have called attention above, if we suppose that, before he left Brussels for Quatre Bras, the Duke had issued orders for the concentration of the whole army, or, at any rate, of the bulk of the army, at Quatre Bras, he may well have passed Picton's division on its march to Waterloo, assured that, after a brief rest at that place, which would do the men no harm, an order would arrive from Brussels, where very possibly the staff [57] were writing out the orders to the army, for Picton to continue his march to Quatre Bras.

Wellington's decision to concentrate at Quatre Bras the whole army,—or the bulk of the army,—for it does not appear even from the DeLancey Memorandum that he ever expected the far distant divisions of Colville and Stedmann to arrive in season,—was reached, in all probability, while he was at the Duchess of Richmond's ball. He went to the ball at or soon after 10 P. M., and he stayed there until after 2 A. M.[58] He told the Duke of Richmond, just before he left the house, that he had "ordered the army to concentrate at Quatre Bras."[59] At some time, therefore, after the issuing of the orders to Lord Hill, which are dated the 16th,[60] and before 2 or 2.30 A. M., the Duke decided to concentrate the army at Quatre Bras.

---

[57] Major Oldfield states that the Duke rode out to Quatre Bras unattended by his Quartermaster-General, DeLancey, or by the other heads of departments. Oldfield, MSS.

[58] Lady Jane Dalrymple Hamilton, in her most interesting Journal, now in the possession of her granddaughter, Lady Manvers, says: "We found him [the Duke] there [at the ball] on our arrival at 10 o'clock. . . . We remained till past two, and, when I left, the Duke was still there."

[59] App. C, xiii; *post*, p. 373.

[60] *Ante*, p. 82.

NOTES TO CHAPTER V.

1. WE may properly devote a few words here to the Duke of Wellington's "Memorandum on the Battle of Waterloo," written in 1842, in reply to Clausewitz's History of the Campaign of 1815. There are some statements contained in this paper which fairly take one's breath away.

For instance, we learn that the Duke, "having received the intelligence of" the French "attack only at three o'clock in the afternoon of the 15th, *was at Quatre Bras before the same hour on the morning of the 16th*,[1] with a sufficient force to engage the left of the French army."[2]

The fact is, that, at 3 A. M. of the 16th only the brigade of Prince Bernhard of Saxe Weimar was at Quatre Bras, and he had taken it there entirely on his own responsibility, and not, as is implied in the above statement, in obedience to orders from the Duke of Wellington.

But it is unnecessary to set forth in detail any refutation of such statements as the above. The best English authorities do not rely[3] on this Memorandum, alleging that the Duke's memory, when he wrote it, was no longer exact.[4] We are quite within bounds when we say

---

[1] The italics are ours. But see *post*, p. 374, n. 2.
[2] Supp. Desp., vol. x, p. 523; App. C, xv; *post*, pp. 374, 376, 376.
[3] Chesney, p. 83, n.; p. 101; p, 131.
[4] Ib., p. 101; p. 131.

that this Memorandum adds nothing to our knowledge of the facts. We may add that it is a pity that this is so. Wellington wrote this Memorandum in 1842,— twenty-seven years only after the date of the battle of Waterloo. This is not so very long after the occurrence: we are now twenty-nine years after Gettysburg. Very many officers conversant with the facts must have been then alive; and the Duke had access to all the official papers. It is a pity, we repeat, that he did not set himself to the task of drawing up an exhaustive and accurate narrative of the facts of the campaign.

2. We desire to call attention again to the absence of evidence that Wellington and Blücher had formulated any definite plan of concerted action in the event of Napoleon's invading Belgium.

One thing, at any rate, is quite clear, and that is that neither of the allied commanders acted, so far as we can judge, in pursuance of any such agreement. Blücher, when he hears of Napoleon's advance to Charleroi, orders his army to assemble at Sombreffe, and then sends word to Wellington of what he has done; the latter, as we have seen, although he learns that the enemy's main attack is by way of Charleroi and therefore upon the Prussians, and although he has long known that in this event it was Blücher's intention to concentrate his army at Sombreffe, takes no instant steps to bring his army into close union with that of Blücher. His first idea, certainly, is to assemble his army at Nivelles. This difficulty, it is true, does not seem greatly to trouble the writers who have adopted the theory of a previous understanding or arrangement; it seems to be possible, for instance, for Siborne, to believe that Wellington had agreed to concentrate at Quatre Bras,[5] and yet actually to call attention[6] to the fact that he halted Picton's divis-

---

[5] Siborne, vol. 1., p. 40.
[6] Ib., p. 102, note.

ion at Waterloo, hours after he had known that Blücher was concentrating at Sombreffe, because he had not then made up his mind whether to send Picton to Nivelles or to Quatre Bras. But he and those other historians who have followed him, or have adopted the same theory, have certainly a serious difficulty to contend with. The Duke had been informed about midnight[7] that Quatre Bras was occupied by a part of Perponcher's division, and he had heard also that Blücher was concentrating his army at Sombreffe. If he had agreed with Blücher to concentrate the Anglo-Dutch army at Quatre Bras, he would assuredly have given his orders accordingly, and in season,— at least one would suppose so,— and he certainly could have had a large force there by ten o'clock in the morning. But he acted, on the other hand, as if he thought that he possessed perfect discretion as to what he would do,— as if he was bound by no agreement whatsoever. It is evident, in fact, that he did not make up his mind till shortly before he left Brussels to go to Quatre Bras himself, whether he would undertake to hold the place or not.

3. It is, however, to be noted that the action that was fought at Quatre Bras assumed at once such importance in the eyes of the world, that those historians who have been great admirers of the Duke have very generally asserted that he had, almost from the first news of the French attack, determined to concentrate his army there. This assertion has been accompanied by many eulogistic remarks, in which Wellington's prescience and power of quick decision have been held up to an undeserved admiration. "At ten the same night, however" [the 15th], says Gleig,[8] "the enemy's movements had suffi-

---

[7] By a despatch sent to the Prince of Orange at Brussels from Braine-le-Comte at 10 P. M. Van Loben Sels, p. 176, note.

[8] Gleig's Life of the Duke of Wellington, p. 308.

ciently disclosed his intentions; and the whole army, with the exception of the reserve, was put in motion. It marched by various roads upon Quatre Bras." Captain Pringle, of the Royal Engineers, upon whom Sir Walter Scott largely relied for his narrative of the campaign, says:[9] "Having obtained further intelligence about 11 o'clock [on the evening of the 15th], which confirmed the real attack of the enemy to be along the Sambre, orders were immediately given for the troops to march upon Quatre Bras."

We have just seen that no such orders were given until the early morning hours of the 16th.

4. Assuming now, as we fairly may, that the Duke did not direct a general concentration of his army at Quatre Bras until shortly before he left Brussels, say, for a guess, at 2 A. M. of the 16th, let us endeavor to get a notion, if we may, of his first intentions and expectations, as shown in his previously issued orders.

He had directed three divisions on Nivelles,—all his reserves to a point on the Charleroi-Brussels pike from which they could easily be moved to Nivelles,—and his more westerly divisions to Enghien and Braine-le-Comte, in the direction of Nivelles. Among the troops thus directed on Nivelles were some that had been stationed at Genappe and Quatre Bras. He had in fact ordered his army to concentrate at Nivelles; notwithstanding that he had been informed that the French attack was by way of Charleroi, that Blücher was concentrating at Sombreffe, that a brigade of Dutch-Belgians was at Quatre Bras, and that it had been skirmishing with the enemy. The question of the appropriateness of his action to these facts is certainly an interesting one.

Colonel Maurice, the most recent military commentator on the campaign, discusses this question, and arrives at the conclusion that Wellington's original

---

[9]Scott's Life of Napoleon, p. 833. Paris; Galignani; 1828.

intention of concentrating his army at Nivelles, was in accord with the principles of war.[10] "If there is one thing which rests on more certain experience than another," says he, "it is that an army ought not to expose itself piecemeal to the blows of a concentrated enemy. Wellington, therefore, contemplated concentrating his army out of reach of the advancing French. Napoleon, from his general knowledge of the position of the English army, assumed that they would, of course, not venture to oppose him till they had fallen back to concentrate. As the case actually happened, only the wild wandering of d'Erlon's Corps prevented Ney from overwhelming the force in his presence at Quatre Bras."

To this it may be replied:—

A. That Wellington, as we have stated above,[11] knew at 11 P. M. of the 15th that the main body of the French under Napoleon in person were concentrating in front of the Prussians, who were themselves concentrating at Sombreffe. He might, therefore, fairly reckon on being able, if he acted with promptness, to assemble at Quatre Bras during the next forenoon a force quite as large as any that might reasonably be expected to be spared from the main body of the French to oppose him. He, therefore, would not have exposed his troops "piecemeal to the blows of a concentrated enemy," if he had ordered a general concentration at Quatre Bras after making sure that the main body of the French was at or near Fleurus, and that the main body of the Prussians was ready to receive them there.

B. It is perfectly true that had d'Erlon's Corps come up in due time, the forces which Wellington had at Quatre Bras, including the several bodies of reinforcements, as they successively arrived, would have been

---

[10] Maurice, pp. 344 *et seq.* (July, 1890.) *Contra,* Charras, vol. 1, pp. 132, *et seq.*

[11] *Ante,* p. 80, n. 36.

overwhelmed in detail. But then, as we shall shortly show, Wellington did not issue his orders for his army to concentrate at Quatre Bras in season to effect his object. Had he done so, on the night of the 15th and 16th, he would have had by noon, certainly, a very much larger body of men than he actually did have, very possibly enough to oppose successfully both d'Erlon and Reille. It must be remembered that it was not until (say) 2 o'clock in the morning, or thereabouts, that he gave any orders to any troops to proceed to Quatre Bras.

We conclude, therefore, that Wellington would not have run any unwarrantable risk by ordering his army to assemble at Quatre Bras as soon as he had learnt of the French advance by way of Charleroi. And that this was the true course for him to take is virtually admitted by his own subsequent accounts of his doings,[12] on which we have commented above in our remarks on his "Memorandum on the Battle of Waterloo." (*Ante*, p. 90.) Had the instructions which he actually gave been strictly carried out, had the brigade of Prince Bernhard of Saxe Weimar been withdrawn to Nivelles in obedience to the orders of 10 P. M., Ney might have occupied Quatre Bras without opposition, in the morning of the 16th. And although it is possible, and, in fact, probable, that he would have been attacked by the English during the afternoon, and while it would have been obviously out of the question for him to have advanced on Brussels, leaving the English army at Nivelles, yet, supposing that he had had both his corps with him, as he ought to have had, he assuredly would have been able to spare a part of his forces to take the Prussians in rear while they were fighting at Ligny, as the Emperor (as we shall see) desired him to do.

C. As for Napoleon's expectations in regard to the

---

[12] Chesney, p. 101.

English occupation of Quatre Bras as given to us by Colonel Maurice, it must certainly be admitted by everybody that Napoleon considered the occupation of the cross-roads as of very great importance for himself, and that the reason why he gave Ney 45,000 men of all arms was in order to make a sure thing of it. Very possibly he did not expect that the English general would be able, scattered as his army was in its cantonments, to assemble a very large force there during the morning of the 16th. But it is evident that he thought that his adversary's getting 30,000 or 40,000 men together, and either assisting the Prussians or attacking his left flank, was a thing so likely to occur, and so dangerous a thing, if it did occur, that he gave his two largest corps to his best fighting general in order to provide fully for this contingency by seizing and occupying the cross-roads of Quatre Bras. If the emergency arose, Napoleon was bound to be prepared for it. If he had regarded it as extremely improbable that the English would be encountered in force at or near Quatre Bras, he would probably have strengthened his main army with one of the corps which he gave to Ney.

5. That Wellington and Blücher erred in allowing their armies to remain in their widely extended cantonments until Napoleon attacked them is now generally admitted. Sir James Shaw-Kennedy's remarks [13] on this point sum up the question forcibly:—

"They [the allied commanders] determined to continue in the cantonments which they occupied until they knew positively the line of attack. Now it may safely be predicted that this determination will be considered by future and dispassionate historians as a great mistake; for, in place of waiting to see where the blow actually fell, the armies should have been instantly put in motion to assemble. Nor was this the only error: the line of cantonments occupied by the Anglo-Allied and Prussian armies was greatly too

---

[13] Kennedy, pp. 168-170. See, also, Clausewitz, chaps. 11, 15, 17. Charras, vol. 1, p. 80. Corresp., vol. 31, p. 254.

extended. * * * From the time, therefore, that it became known that Napoleon's army was organized and formed into corps ready to take the field, the armies of Wellington and Blücher should have been so placed in cantonments as to be prepared to meet any of the cases supposed," — *i. e.*, an advance of the French by any one of the great Flanders roads, — * * * " and from the moment that it was known that the French army was at all in movement, the allied armies should have been withdrawn from their cantonments and placed very near to each other."

Wellington and Blücher, it will be remembered, had known for several days that Napoleon was massing his forces, and yet they put off till the last moment even the assembling their corps and divisions in their respective places of *rendezvous*.

Sir James Shaw-Kennedy then proceeds to discuss the proper "line of cantonments" of the allied armies from the time when "it was known that Napoleon had a large organized army ready to take the field,"[14] and he gives it as his opinion that Blücher should have "made Genappe his headquarters, cantoning his army between Louvain and Gosselies, occupying the line of the Sambre from Namur to the frontier by strong bodies of cavalry, &c.," and that Wellington, having his headquarters at Brussels, should have cantoned his army between Brussels and Soignies, with cavalry outposts.

Charras[15] expresses the same opinion as to the line of cantonments of Wellington's army, but he holds that by the end of May the Duke should have carried his headquarters six or eight leagues [15 or 20 miles] in advance of Brussels:[16] while Blücher ought at the same time to have removed his headquarters to Fleurus,[17] and to have concentrated his forces within a radius of six or eight

---

[14] Kennedy, p. 171.

[15] Charras, vol. 1, p. 80.

[16] This is also the opinion of Clausewitz; ch. 18.

[17] Charras, vol. 1, p. 83. Clausewitz, ch. 18, says "nearer Nivelles," *i. e.*, nearer than Namur is.

leagues (fifteen or twenty miles); having outposts on the Sambre and Meuse.

In this last opinion, as he says, he follows Napoleon.[18] The latter, it is to be noted, does not criticise Wellington, as do Charras and Clausewitz, for retaining his headquarters in Brussels, but only, — in this connection, that is, — for the excessive extent of his cantonments.[19] Napoleon's view seems to be that Brussels was the right place for the headquarters of the Anglo-Dutch army and Fleurus for those of the Prussian army; and that from the 15th of May both generals should have greatly reduced the extent of their cantonments, so that no part of their troops, except the advance-posts, should be more than twenty miles distant from the headquarters of the army. Had this course been adopted, he says the Prussians might have been assembled at Ligny at noon of the 15th,[20] ready to receive the attack of the French army. He does not, however, go on and state his view of the mode and time of the coöperation of the English army in that event. We must content ourselves with merely stating these opinions.

6. That Marshal Blücher, who had allowed his troops to remain in their widely scattered cantonments until the last moment, erred in giving Sombreffe as the point of concentration of his army, seems on principle and authority very clear. Napoleon's remarks[21] on this are as follows:—

"Marshal Blücher ought, as soon as he knew that the French were at Charleroi [that is to say, on the evening of the 15th,] to have given, as the point of assembling of his army, not Fleurus, nor

---

[18] Corresp., vol. 31, p. 253.

[19] Ib., p. 254.

[20] Ib., p. 253.

[21] Ib., p. 254. The words in brackets are in the edition of 1820, known as the "Mémoires," but are not in the "Correspondance." The "Mémoires" also substitute "the 17th" for "the evening of the 16th."

Ligny, which were already under the cannon of the enemy, but Wavre, where the French could not arrive until the evening of the 16th. By doing so, he would have had all the day of the 16th, and the night between the 16th and 17th, to effect the junction of his whole army."

He also for the same reasons censures Wellington [22] for establishing "Quatre Bras as the point of reunion" for his army. Sir James Shaw-Kennedy [23] says to the same effect:

"The determination of Wellington and Blücher to meet Napoleon's advance at Fleurus and Quatre Bras was totally inconsistent with the widely scattered positions in which they had placed their armies; their determination in this respect amounted in the fullest extent to that error which has so often been committed in war, by even great commanders, of endeavoring to assemble on a point which could only be reached by a portion of the troops intended to occupy it, while the enemy had the power of concentrating upon it his whole force."

We do not believe, as we have pointed out above, that any such determination had been arrived at by Wellington and Blücher beforehand; but, Blücher's taking the decisive step of ordering a concentration of his army at Sombreffe, instead of at Wavre, for instance, placed Wellington, as we have just pointed out, under the necessity of ordering a concentration of his army, or a part of it, at Quatre Bras, unless he was prepared to leave his ally without support. The criticisms of Napoleon and of General Shaw-Kennedy, are, therefore, we submit, really confined to Blücher's action. Napoleon is not considering what Wellington ought to have done *in view of the step which Blücher took in concentrating at Sombreffe*, but is only giving his opinion, that, on general principles, Quatre Bras was not the proper place of concentration for the English, just as Sombreffe was not the proper place of concentration for the Prussians, after the French were

---

[22] Corresp. vol. 31, p. 255.
[23] Kennedy, p. 172.

known to be advancing on Charleroi. It must be noted that Napoleon and Kennedy both assume that the two allied generals had agreed upon Sombreffe and Quatre Bras respectively.[24] If there was no such agreement, (and we think there was not any), then we cannot properly consider Wellington's decision to concentrate at Quatre Bras except in connection with the fact that Blücher had committed himself to a battle at Ligny and needed his support.

---

[24] Corresp., pp. 195, 197. Kennedy, p. 172.

CHAPTER VI.

THE FIFTEENTH OF JUNE: THE DUTCH-BELGIANS.

TURNING now from the consideration of the arrangements ordered by the allied commanders, our first attention is due to the occupation of Quatre Bras by the brigade of Prince Bernhard of Saxe Weimar, belonging to the Dutch-Belgian division of Perponcher in the corps commanded by the Prince of Orange. This brigade, which was cantonned along the turnpike from Genappe to Frasnes and in the neighboring villages,[1] was, on the first news of hostilities, concentrated by its commander at Quatre Bras, with its outposts at Frasnes, an act which, done without orders, as it was, did him great credit.[2] As a matter of fact, however, orders were on the way directing the same thing. In the absence of the Prince of Orange at Brussels, his chief-of-staff, General Constant Rebecque, having heard of the advance of the French, had already[3] sent to Perponcher an order to assemble one brigade of his division at Quatre Bras, and the other at Nivelles. Between 5 and 6 o'clock of the afternoon of the 15th Prince Bernhard's brigade was attacked near Frasnes by the advance of Reille's Corps.[4] At 9 he sent off to Nivelles a report of the action; this was immediately forwarded to Braine-le-Comte,

---

[1] Van Loben Sels, p. 130.
[2] Ib., pp. 131, 132. Chesney, p. 100.
[3] Van Loben Sels, p. 128, note.
[4] Ib., pp. 133, 134, note.

where the headquarters of the Prince of Orange were;[5] but he being at Brussels at the Duchess of Richmond's ball, Rebecque, his chief-of-staff, took it upon himself to order Perponcher to support Prince Bernhard's brigade at Quatre Bras with the other brigade of his division, Bylandt's.[6] Rebecque then, at 10 P. M., sent a despatch to the Prince of Orange at Brussels informing him what he had done.

About 11 o'clock,[7] an hour at least after this order had been expedited, arrived Wellington's 5 o'clock order to the Prince of Orange "to collect at Nivelles the 2d and 3d divisions of the army of the Low Countries." In obedience to this, a new order[8] was made out and sent to Perponcher, but he took it upon himself to carry out his earlier instructions to assemble his whole division at Quatre Bras, and in this he was supported by his corps-commander, the Prince of Orange. The greater part of Bylandt's brigade arrived in the early morning of the 16th. Perponcher arrived in person at 3 A. M.,[9] the Prince of Orange at 6 o'clock.[10] (See Map 3.)

Thus was Quatre Bras occupied on the evening and night of the 15th, not only without orders from Wellington, but contrary to his orders. Had his orders been obeyed, Ney would have found on the next morning no one to oppose him.

---

[5] Van Loben Sels, p. 175.

[6] Ib., p. 176.

[7] Ib., p. 176, note.

[8] Ib., p. 178, n. It would seem that the sending to Perponcher the order to return to Nivelles was a mere form.

[9] Ib., p. 183.

[10] Ib., p. 185.

NOTE TO CHAPTER VI.

"ALMOST all historians" says Colonel Maurice,[1] "write as if the occupation of Quatre Bras by Prince Bernhard was a step for which he not only deserves the greatest credit, but one which in itself was sure to be of vast advantage to the English army." In this opinion Colonel Maurice does not share. We have fully treated of this subject before.[2] All we need say here is to repeat, that the question of the suitableness of Quatre Bras as the point of concentration for the Anglo-Dutch army could not have been considered by the Duke of Wellington at this moment apart from the fact that Marshal Blücher was concentrating his army at Sombreffe; and that, when this fact was ascertained, the Duke must concentrate at Quatre Bras or abandon all hope of assisting his ally. We have also pointed out that the fact that the main French army was opposed to the Prussians constituted this case an exception to the general rule; for, in this instance, *ex hypothesi*, the Duke would encounter only those troops which Napoleon would feel himself strong enough to detach from his main body.

If we are right in this contention, therefore, then the Dutch-Belgian generals,—Constant Rebecque, Perponcher, and the Prince of Saxe Weimar,—having learned the situation of the French and Prussian armies before the Duke heard of it, did what Wellington, had he

---

[1] Maurice, p. 345 : July, 1890.

[2] *Ante*, pp. 94 *et seq.*

known what they knew, would have ordered to be done.[3] And it may be added, that we fully concur in the commendation which has so generally been awarded to them for their prompt and vigorous action.

[3] Chesney, p. 102; Hooper, p. 84.

CHAPTER VII.

THE MORNING OF THE SIXTEENTH OF JUNE: WELLINGTON.

The Duke of Wellington, as we have seen, did not decide on ordering a general concentration of his army at Quatre Bras until the early morning hours of the 16th of June.

We have produced above two orders, both addressed to Lord Hill, written at Brussels on the morning of the 16th of June, and we have shown that the first, at any rate, was written and sent out before the Duke had made up his mind to concentrate his army at Quatre Bras. We have also, however, shown, that before he left Brussels, he did make up his mind to do this, and that orders to this effect were, no doubt, then issued. We cannot fix the hour or hours at which this was done, but it was undoubtedly before the Duke left Brussels. This last hour has been differently fixed,[1] but it was probably about half-past seven. He, then, leaving the Deputy Quarter Master General and the other heads of departments in Brussels,—[2] presumably to attend to the issuing of the orders for the concentration of the army at Quatre

---

[1] Müffling (Passages, p. 230) says about 5. Mudford puts it at 7. Gardner, p. 58, at 8. Sir A. Frazer (Letters of Colonel Sir A. S. Frazer, London, 1859, p. 536), writes at 6 A. M., that he has "just learned that the Duke moves in half an hour." The Duke had 22 miles to ride to arrive at Quatre Bras, and he got there about 10 A. M. His letter to Blücher is dated 10.30 A. M. Oldfield (MSS.) puts the time of the Duke's departure as before that of Sir George Wood and Lieutenant Colonel Smyth, who "drove out in a calèche of the latter" "between seven and eight o'clock," and soon after the departure of the Brunswick troops, which was "at an early hour."

[2] Oldfield, MSS.

Bras,—rode to the latter place, where he arrived about 10 o'clock. Here he found only Perponcher's division of Dutch-Belgian troops, under command of the Prince of Orange.

At half-past ten, he wrote to Marshal Blücher the letter before referred to, which, as we have said above, never, as we believe, saw the light until it was published in Berlin,[3] in 1876, in Von Ollech's History[4] of the Campaign of 1815. We give a translation of it here in full.

On the Heights behind Frasnes:
June 16, 1815. 10.30 A. M.

My dear Prince:

My army is situated as follows:

The Corps d'Armée of the Prince of Orange has a division here and at Quatre Bras, and the rest at Nivelles.

The Reserve is in march from Waterloo to Genappe, where it will arrive at noon.

The English Cavalry will be at the same hour at Nivelles.

The Corps of Lord Hill is at Braine-le-Comte.

I do not see any large force of the enemy in front of us, and I await news from your Highness and the arrival of troops in order to determine my operations for the day.

Nothing has been seen on the side of Binche, nor on our right.

Your very obedient servant,

Wellington.

Let us see precisely how far this letter agrees with Colonel DeLancey's Memorandum, which he drew up — presumably before the Duke left Brussels — for the Duke's information, and of which we have before spoken,

---

[3] Von Ollech, p. 125. Maurice, June, 1890, p. 257. App. C, xvi; *post*, pp. 376, 377.

[4] Charras, vol. 1, p. 192, note, refers to it to show that Wellington was opposite Frasnes at 10.30 A. M., but he makes no other reference to it.

entitled "Disposition of the British army at 7 o'clock A. M., 16th June." (See Map 4.)

The 1st Corps, says the Duke in his letter, has a division here,—that is, in rear of Frasnes,—and at Quatre Bras. This, as we have seen above, was the 2d division of Dutch-Belgian troops,—Perponcher's. The rest of the 1st Corps, says the Duke, are at Nivelles. Now, of the three divisions,—those of Chassé (Dutch-Belgian), Alten, and Cooke, which constituted the rest of the 1st Corps,—the first two had been ordered to Nivelles the previous evening,—the last, Cooke's, is stated in the DeLancey "Disposition" to be, at 7 A. M., at Braine-le-Comte. The Duke, therefore, might well suppose that it would accomplish the greater part of the distance between Braine-le-Comte and Nivelles, nine miles, in three hours and a half.

The Duke next says "The Reserve is in march from Waterloo to Genappe, where it will arrive at noon." For this statement the Duke did not have to refer to the "Disposition." He had passed Picton's division on the road, a mile or two north of Waterloo, probably a little before 9 A. M.; and, supposing, as he did, that Picton either had then received, or shortly would receive, orders to push on to Quatre Bras, he was warranted in saying that the division would reach Genappe at noon. He did not take the trouble to except from his general statement, which he doubtless thought was sufficiently accurate for all practical purposes, the division of Sir Lowry Cole, which the "Disposition" placed at Assche, eight miles north-west of Brussels, nor the 5th Hanoverian brigade, which was at Hal.

The Duke next says that the English Cavalry will be at Nivelles at noon. The "Disposition" puts them at Braine-le-Comte at 7 A. M. Relying on this statement, the Duke says they will accomplish the nine miles between that place and Nivelles by noon.

"The Corps of Lord Hill is at Braine-le-Comte," is the next and last statement in the letter. That corps consisted of the 2d and 4th British divisions, of the 1st Dutch-Belgian division, and of Anthing's brigade. As respects the 2d division, the "Disposition" states that it was at 7 A.M. at Braine-le-Comte. The 4th division, the "Disposition" states, was at Audenarde at 7 A. M. and was marching on Braine-le-Comte; but the Duke certainly could not have supposed it possible that that division could have marched from Audenarde to Braine-le-Comte, a distance of more than thirty miles, between seven and half-past ten in the morning. And as for the 1st Dutch-Belgian division and the Indian brigade, the "Disposition" puts them at Sotteghem, a village near Audenarde, at 7 A. M., and states that they are marching on Enghien. The Duke, therefore, had not the authority of the "Disposition" for the statement made in his letter as to these portions of Lord Hill's Corps; but then these divisions had been stationed so far away, that probably he never counted on them at all in his own mind in connection with a concentration at Quatre Bras. These were the troops which he left at Hal and Tubize on the day of Waterloo to protect his right.

It is, therefore, we submit, easy to see that the Duke had the "Disposition" before him when he wrote the letter to Marshal Blücher. He seems to have taken it,— so to speak,—blindfold; it never seems to have occurred to him that it was practically impossible that his various divisions could have been at seven o'clock that morning where his chief-of-staff had said that they were. He accepted the memorandum as official, and followed it substantially—with a few deviations, to be sure, as we have pointed out—in his letter to Blücher. Not only this; the Duke acted at once on the faith of the representations contained in the "Disposition." He, about noon, rode over to Brye to confer with Marshal Blücher, and to propose to coöperate with him. It is evident from the narrative[5] of Baron Müffling, who accompanied the Duke, that Wellington was, in his opinion, laboring under grave misconceptions as to the whereabouts of his army. The conversation, according to Müffling, was mainly concerned with the manner of the promised coöperation, — Gneisenau wishing the Duke to march from Quatre Bras to Brye, and Wellington being unwilling thus to expose his communications with Brussels and Nivelles. Towards the close of the discussion, says Müffling, the Duke adopted a suggestion of his, and said " I will overthrow what is before me at Frasnes and will direct myself on Gosselies." We cite this simply to show how confident Wellington was that he would find a sufficiently large force at Quatre Bras on his return from Brye, at about half-past two o'clock. If Alten's division was at Nivelles at 7 A. M., *en route* for Quatre Bras, it should have arrived there before noon. The reserves, which marching from Brussels for Quatre Bras, had by 7 A. M. nearly reached Waterloo, ought to be at Quatre Bras, which is not over eleven miles further, by 2 or 3 P. M. If the cavalry was actually at Braine-le-Comte at 9 A. M. it might well be at Nivelles by noon, and at Quatre Bras, only seven miles further, by 3 P. M. Cooke might be expected about the same time, with his division of Guards. These expectations were no doubt in the mind of the Duke of Wellington as he rode back to Quatre Bras from his meeting with Marshal Blücher. The theory advanced, or perhaps suggested, by the Prussian biographer of Gneisenau, Delbrück,[6] that the Duke misrepresented the position of his army for the purpose of inducing Blücher to give battle at Ligny on the strength of his promise to support him, and of his ability to keep his promise, so that he, Wellington, might gain the necessary time for the concentration of his army, has

---

[5] Müffling, Passages, p. 236. Ollech, p. 126.

[6] Gneisenau, vol. 4, pp. 369, 370.

not, in our judgment, anything to support it.[7] The truth plainly is, that the Duke was himself entirely deceived by the statement drawn up for his information by his chief-of-staff. He took it for granted that the troops were where they were stated to be, and made his dispositions accordingly. He was destined thereby not only to be greatly disappointed, but to incur imminent danger of defeat. For, as a matter of fact, many of his divisions were at seven that morning nowhere near the positions assigned them in Colonel DeLancey's Memorandum. We shall refer to this matter in another place; suffice it to say now that the Duke's reinforcements came on the field very much later than he had reason to expect; that the allied troops were for a couple of hours or so in a very precarious situation, and would without doubt have been disastrously defeated had Napoleon's orders been carried out.

---

[7] At the same time, it must be said that Delbrück was quite naturally led to adopt this suggestion. It is only on the supposition that the "Disposition" is an authentic document and that the Duke followed it blindly, but honestly, in his letter to Marshal Blücher, that we can find a satisfactory answer to Delbrück's suggestion.

NOTES TO CHAPTER VII.

1. IT may be worth while to state, as nearly as we can, the actual positions at 7 A.M. of the 16th of the various bodies of troops mentioned in the "Disposition." (See Map 5.)

The 1st division was not at 7 A.M. at Braine-le-Comte. It did not reach that place from Enghien until 9 A.M.[1] Its commander, General Cooke, having received no further orders, halted the division till noon, when he took upon himself the responsibility of continuing the march to Nivelles, where he arrived at 3 P.M. Here he received orders to proceed at once to Quatre Bras.

The 2d division, Clinton's, which was also stated in the "Disposition" to have been at 7 A.M. at Braine-le-Comte, and to be marching on Nivelles, did not, in fact,[2] receive the order to march from the neighborhood of Ath, where it was stationed, to Enghien till twelve hours after it was dated,—*i. e.*, not until 10 A.M. of the 16th! The troops did not reach Enghien till 2 P.M., and missing, apparently, the direct road, did not arrive at Braine-le-Comte till midnight.

The 3d division, Alten's, is said in the "Disposition" to have been at Nivelles at 7 A.M., and marching to Quatre Bras. It did not arrive at Nivelles till noon.[3]

The 4th division, Colville's, was no doubt correctly

---

[1] Grenadier Guards, vol. 3, p. 15.

[2] Leeke, vol. 1, pp. 10, 11.

[3] Siborne, vol. 1, p. 90.

stated in the "Disposition" to have been at Audenarde at 7 A. M. The 10 P. M. orders of the 15th of June directed it on Enghien; and we must presume, for the reasons given above, that further orders to march on Braine-le-Comte had been issued.

The 5th division, Picton's, was not "beyond Waterloo" at 7 A. M., as stated in the "Disposition." In point of fact, it must have been some six miles on the Brussels side of Waterloo at that hour.[4] Included in this division was the 4th Hanoverian brigade,[5] and the Duke of Brunswick's Corps.

The 6th division, Cole's, is no doubt correctly stated in the "Disposition" to have been at 7 A. M. at Assche; but whether orders for it to march to Genappe and Quatre Bras had arrived at so early an hour, may be doubted.

Similar observations apply to the 5th Hanoverian brigade, stated in the "Disposition" to have been at 7 A. M. at Hal, and marching to Genappe and Quatre Bras, and to the 1st Dutch-Belgian Division and Anthing's Indian brigade, stated to be at Sotteghem, and marching to Enghien.

The "Disposition" states that the 2d and 3d divisions of the Army of the Low Countries were at Nivelles and Quatre Bras at 7 A. M. This was not true of the 3d division, Chassé's, which did not assemble at Nivelles till near noon.[6] The 2d division, Perponcher's, as we have seen, was at Quatre Bras at 7 A. M.

As for the statement in the "Disposition" that Major

---

[4] Siborne, vol. 1, p. 102, note. Gomm, pp. 353, 354. Waterloo Letters, pp. 23, 24. Gomm says Picton's division left Brussels at 5 A. M., marched to Waterloo (a distance of about eleven miles), and halted there two hours; and then at 1 P. M. resumed its march for Quatre Bras, where it arrived at 3.30 P. M. Siborne (vol. 1, p. 102) says that Picton arrived at a quarter before 3 P. M., having left Waterloo about noon. As the distance is about thirteen miles, the later hour of arrival given by Gomm is probably correct.

[5] Siborne, vol. 1, p. 103, n.

[6] Van Loben Sels, p. 232.

General Dörnberg's brigade and the Cumberland Hussars were "beyond Waterloo" at 7 A. M., it certainly was far from correct. Dörnberg had been directed by an order sent off from Brussels between 5 and 7 P. M. of the 15th to retire his brigade from the neighborhood of Mons to Vilvorde, a town seven miles north of Brussels. He could not have reached Vilvorde, which is a distance of forty-five miles, until late in the afternoon.

As for the "remainder of the cavalry," which was stationed in and near Ninove, it not only was not at Braine-le-Comte at 7 A. M., as stated in the "Disposition," but it did not receive the first order,—sent off from Brussels about 10 o'clock in the evening of the 15th,— until shortly before six in the morning.[7] It was therefore only an hour's march from Ninove on its way to Enghien at seven o'clock. It did not reach the field till "the evening was far advanced and the conflict had ceased."[8]

Nor could Kruse's Nassau brigade have passed Waterloo at 7 A. M., as stated in the "Disposition," *en route* for Genappe, for it did not arrive at Quatre Bras in season to take part in the action.

We have been at some pains to lay the facts in regard to this "Disposition" before the reader, because it certainly is the most misleading statement ever drawn up "for the information" of a commanding general. No thought seems to have been given either to the time at which the orders could be received, or to the time required to carry them out. An officer of sufficient experience in war to occupy the post of chief-of-staff to the Duke of Wellington ought certainly to have been quite competent to give to his commanding officer an estimate of the probable positions at any given time of the

---

[7] Historical Record of the Life Guards, p. 193: 2d Ed. London; Longmans: 1840. Bullock's Journal; English Historical Magazine, July, 1888, p. 549.

[8] Life Guards, p. 194. Bullock, p. 549, says eight o'clock.

various divisions of the army, on which it would be safe to rely.⁹

2. Whether, if such an estimate had been made, Wellington would have stayed at Quatre Bras, may be a question, but he probably would have risked it, as he evidently did not suppose the French to be in great force in his front, and it was obviously of prime importance to retain his communications with Blücher, if possible.

3. Finally, it must be said that the Duke of Wellington was not well served by his subordinates on the day of the 15th in respect to the transmission to him of information from the front.¹⁰ His first news of the attack on the Prussian lines near Thuin did not arrive till 3 P. M., although the French movement must have been pronounced some ten or eleven hours before that hour. Charleroi was occupied by the main French column at noon, but all the Duke had heard at 10 P. M. simply warranted him in writing that the enemy "appeared to menace Charleroi." Brussels is only 35 or 36 miles from Charleroi; and by a good despatch system news of such importance ought to have been transmitted in four hours. If that had been done,—if Wellington had known at four or five o'clock in the afternoon positively that the French had occupied Charleroi in force, and if his information from Mons had arrived at the same time, as certainly ought to have been the case,—there is every reason to suppose that he would at once have issued orders for the concentration of the army at Quatre Bras. The orders which he did issue to this effect were not sent out, as we have seen, till the early morning hours of

---

⁹It ought to be remembered, however, that the "Disposition" was in all probability drawn up in a great hurry. Wellington had put off the decision to concentrate at Quatre Bras so late that both the giving of the necessary orders and the preparation of this "Disposition" must have been done in the greatest haste.

¹⁰*Cf.* Siborne, vol. 1, p. 166, note.

the 16th, some nine or ten hours later than those which we may fairly suppose he would have issued, had information of the French movements been promptly transmitted to him. But how far the commander-in-chief is himself responsible for such delays as this is, of course, a question. It is and must be for him to devise efficient methods, and to put them to the test often enough beforehand to feel justified in relying on them in a sudden emergency. And the situation in which the Duke of Wellington was in the month of June, 1815, certainly would seem to have called for the utmost watchfulness and for the taking of every precaution. It is impossible not to conclude that he failed in these respects.

CHAPTER VIII.

THE MORNING OF THE SIXTEENTH OF JUNE: NEY.

MARSHAL NEY, as we have seen,[1] rode back from the front at Frasnes to report to the Emperor at Charleroi, where he arrived at midnight of the 15th. He informed the Emperor, so Colonel Heymès says,[2]

"Of the dispositions he had made. The Emperor made him stay to supper, gave him his orders, and received the Marshal with the frank confidence of the camp; he unfolded to him his projects and his hopes for the day of the 16th, which was very soon to begin. He talked with him a long time in the night of the 15th and 16th. All the officers of the Imperial headquarters can attest this."

Among these officers was, no doubt, Marshal Grouchy.

It goes without saying that at this interview Ney told the Emperor that he had not occupied Quatre Bras, and why he had not done so. With almost equal certainty may it be believed that Napoleon told him that he must occupy the place the next forenoon.

Heymès then proceeds as follows:[3]

"The 16th, at two o'clock in the morning, the Marshal returned to Gosselies (*i.e.*, from Charleroi), where he stopped some minutes in order to confer with General Reille; he gave him the order to set out, as soon as he could, with his two divisions and his artillery, and to get his troops together at Frasnes, where the Marshal himself would arrive almost as soon."

---

[1] *Ante*, p. 54.

[2] Doc. Inéd., Heymès' Rel. p. 6. See *ante*, p. 65, n. 28.

[3] Ib., pp. 6, 7.

And he adds that at 8 A. M. Reille at the head of his two divisions was *en route* for Frasnes. General Reille, however, while he says [4] that his troops were ready to march in the morning,[5] says also that at 7 A. M. he went to see Marshal Ney, to ask for orders; and that the Marshal said he was expecting them from the Emperor. One may infer from these statements, which are not perfectly consistent with each other, that Ney, on his return to Gosselies from Charleroi, told Reille that they must be ready to move at a moment's notice, and that that officer at once proceeded to get his men into marching order, and that he had them on the Charleroi-Brussels turnpike, ready to march, before seven o'clock. One may, perhaps, infer more than this; namely, that Ney, immediately on his return from seeing the Emperor, ordered Reille to proceed with his two divisions, as soon as he could, from Gosselies to Frasnes, so that, when the order to seize Quatre Bras should arrive, it might be executed promptly; but that he afterwards reconsidered the matter, and allowed Reille to remain in Gosselies till the written orders should come.

Whether this be so or not, however, it is plain that when Ney had been, as Heymès says he had been, informed by the Emperor himself of his projects for the ensuing day, he ought certainly to have ordered Reille up to Frasnes at once, with the two divisions then at Gosselies, — thereby uniting all of the 2d Corps that was under his control,[6] — and to have seen to it that the 1st Corps was ready to follow promptly in their rear. No special authority for this was needed. In fact it was obviously necessary to get these two divisions out of the way of the 1st Corps, which ought to be assembling at Gosselies in the early morning, if it was to accomplish anything

---

[4] Doc. Inéd., Reille, Not. Hist., p. 57.

[5] From the context, he would seem to mean before 7 A. M.

[6] Girard's division was with the main army under Napoleon.

of consequence during the forenoon. But Ney, whatever may have been his first intentions on returning from seeing Napoleon, did actually nothing of this kind.[7] One cannot avoid the feeling that he was unwilling to take the slightest responsibility, even that involved in uniting the three divisions of the 2d Corps at Frasnes, and supplying their place at Gosselies with the four divisions of the 1st Corps, — a step which, taking account of the situation, and of the written orders that had been issued to the 1st Corps, it was his manifest duty to take. The consideration, that, by this course, the formal order to seize Quatre Bras, which he undoubtedly expected, could be executed at once, while, by retaining Reille at Gosselies until the order should be received, the time required to march the five miles which lay between Gosselies and Frasnes would postpone the carrying out of the movement by some two hours or more, does not seem to have had any weight with him. In fact, beyond getting Reille in readiness to march, Ney really seems to have made no preparations to facilitate the execution of the important order which he fully expected to receive.

That this statement is not too strong, appears when we consider what Ney did to get the 1st Corps up and well in hand, a matter which assuredly demanded his most strenuous and active efforts at this moment. Ney arrived at Gosselies from Charleroi, as we have seen, about 2 A. M. He stayed there, apparently, till shortly after 7 A. M.[8] We know[9] that, even at 3 A. M. one division of the 1st Corps had not arrived at the river, and that another was still at Marchienne. The other two divisions had crossed the Sambre, and the leading one[10] was be-

---

[7] *Cf.* La Tour D'Auvergne, p. 189. Muquardt, pp. 145, 146.

[8] Doc. Inéd., Reille, p. 57.

[9] *Ante*, p. 51.

[10] *Ante*, p. 50, n. 25.

tween Jumet and Gosselies. Colonel Heymès, after stating the positions of the English at Quatre Bras,[11] says:[12] "In default of staff-officers, of whom the Marshal had none, officers of the chasseurs and lancers of the Guard were sent to meet the 1st Corps in the direction of Marchienne-au-Pont; they had orders to press its march to Frasnes." But we shall presently see, that it was not until 11 A. M., when Reille, with the divisions of Foy and Jerome, was ordered to advance from Gosselies to Quatre Bras, that the first three divisions of d'Erlon's Corps were ordered to Frasnes. It appears, then, from Heymès' statement, that the activity exhibited by Marshal Ney, to which he calls attention, was not shown until Ney had ordered these divisions to Frasnes, that is, until after eleven o'clock. That this conjecture is correct, appears also from the fact, stated by Colonel Heymès,[13] that the regiments of the chasseurs and lancers of the Guard, from which officers were detailed on staff duty, as above stated, were in reserve behind the village of Frasnes, and, therefore, not at Gosselies. There is, therefore, nothing to show that Marshal Ney did anything in regard to getting up the 1st Corps until after 11 o'clock A. M.[14] If he had, Colonel Heymès, who was on his staff, would doubtless have mentioned it. And it seems to be an unavoidable inference from what Colonel Heymès says, that at the time when these extemporized staff-officers were sent to find the 1st Corps and hurry it up, part of it, at any rate, was supposed by Marshal Ney to be yet in the neighborhood of Marchienne.

---

[11] Doc. Inéd., Heymès, pp. 7, 8.

[12] Ib., p. 8.

[13] Ib., pp. 5, 7. *Ante*, p. 49.

[14] Ib., Reille, p. 57.

The first written order [15] which Marshal Ney received on this morning of the 16th, was from Marshal Soult, who informed him that the Count of Valmy had been ordered to Gosselies with his corps of cavalry, and placed under his, Ney's, orders; these troops were to replace the division of cavalry of the Guard under Lefebvre-Desnouettes. [16] Marshal Soult then inquired whether the 1st Corps had executed its movement, that is, had crossed the river, and had joined the 2d Corps at Gosselies, in pursuance of the orders [17] to the Count d'Erlon of the day before. He further desired that Ney would inform him as to the exact positions of the 1st and 2d Corps, and of the two divisions of cavalry, which were attached to them. We do not know what answer Marshal Ney returned to these interrogatories, but he told Reille, [18] in the course of the conversation to which we have before referred, shortly before seven o'clock in the morning, that he had rendered to the Emperor an account of his situation. This first order, therefore, must have arrived about 6 A. M.; and from its contents, and also from the hour when it was sent, as well as from the tenor of the orders to d'Erlon of the day before, we can see how carefully the operations of the left wing were watched at the headquarters of the army.

Shortly after this conversation between Ney and Reille, the Marshal went back to Frasnes, [19] leaving word with Reille that, if any orders for the movement of troops should arrive in his absence, they were to be executed at once, and their contents communicated to the Count d'Erlon, who was at Jumet, or in rear of that place.

---

[15] Doc. Inéd., VII, pp. 26, 27; App. C, xvii; *post*, p. 377.

[16] *Ante*, p. 49.

[17] Doc. Inéd., Heymès. V, VI, p. 25; App. C, v, vi; *post*, pp. 367, 368.

[18] Ib., Reille, p. 57.

[19] Ib., p. 57.

About 9 o'clock, General Reille continues,[20] a report was received from General Girard, who commanded that division of the 2d Corps which had gone off to the right and joined the main army, to the effect that the Prussians were forming beyond Fleurus. This report Reille transmitted at once to the headquarters of the army at Charleroi; but he sent no word of it to Ney, at Frasnes, at that time.

About an hour afterwards, that is, about 10 A. M.,[21] General Flahaut of the Emperor's staff, passed through Gosselies, bringing with him an important letter[22] for Marshal Ney, written by the Emperor himself, the contents of which Flahaut communicated to Reille. Of this letter we shall speak at length in another connection. Suffice it to say here, that it treated of the occupation of Quatre Bras, the formal order for which, emanating from the chief-of-staff, it stated would arrive about the same time. This no doubt was the case.[23]

Reille's orders from Ney, it will be recollected, were imperative and precise, to execute[24] at once during Ney's absence, any instructions for the movement of troops that might arrive. Yet we find him writing[25] from Gosselies at 10.15 A. M., to Ney at Frasnes,—a distance of five miles,—to say that he has been informed by General Flahaut of the contents of the Emperor's letter, but that, in consequence of the information as to the Prussians taking up their positions near Fleurus, which

---

[20] Doc. Inéd., Reille, p. 57.

[21] Reille in his "Notice Historique" says 11 A. M. But his despatch to Ney, in which he says that he read the Flahaut order, is dated 10.15 A. M. Doc. Inéd., XI, pp. 37, 38; App. C, xix; *post*, p. 379.

[22] Ib., X, pp. 32 *et seq.* App. C, xviii; *post*, pp. 377, 378.

[23] Ib., p. 30: at least this was the opinion of Marshal Ney's son.

[24] Ib., Reille, p. 57.

[25] Ib., XI, pp. 37, 38. App. C, xix; *post*, p. 379. He does not mention in his "Notice Historique" that he delayed executing Ney's order.

he had received from Girard before 9 A. M., he has thought it best to postpone the march of his two divisions from Gosselies to Frasnes until the return of his messenger.[26] And this, too, just after he had read a letter from the Emperor himself, prescribing what dispositions Ney should make of his troops after he had executed the movement on Quatre Bras. One cannot but recall the criticisms on the generals in this army made by both Napoleon and Charras, which we have given in an earlier chapter.[27] If Reille thought the information sent by Girard was so important, why did he not send it to Ney at once, instead of waiting an hour and a half?

Marshal Ney sent back a peremptory order to Reille to move up to the front at once.[28] The march began at about a quarter before twelve o'clock,[29] the division of Foy leading.

Let us now look at the Emperor's letter and at the orders which Ney received from Soult during the morning of the 16th.

The orders which were received by Ney on the 16th prior to the commencement of the battle of Quatre Bras, were three in number. Of the first[30] we have already spoken.[31] The second,[32] which was the formal order, directed the Marshal to put the 2d and 1st Corps, and the 3d Corps[33] of cavalry, in march for Quatre Bras, where he was to take up a position, and make reconnois-

---

[26] The delay thus occasioned is estimated by Charras (vol. 2, p. 238) at an hour and a quarter. It was really an hour and three-quarters, as Reille ought to have started at ten.

[27] *Ante*, p. 19.

[28] Doc. Inéd., Reille, XII, p. 38; App. C, xx; *post*, pp. 379, 380.

[29] Charras, vol. 1, p. 189. *Cf.* vol. 2, p. 238.

[30] Doc. Inéd., VII, pp. 26, 27; App. C, xvii; *post*, p. 377.

[31] *Ante*, p. 120.

[32] Doc. Inéd., VIII, p. 27; App. C, xxi; *post*, pp. 380, 381.

[33] That of the Count of Valmy, Kellermann.

sances in the directions of Brussels and Nivelles. He was to station a division with cavalry at Genappe, and another division at or near Marbais.

The letter [34] states that the major-general (Soult) has issued the orders, but that Ney may perhaps receive this letter a little sooner, as the Emperor's aides are better mounted. The Emperor then tells Ney what his own plans are for the day,—a subject which will be more appropriately treated in another place,—and then says:—" You can then dispose of your troops in the following manner: the first division at two leagues in front of Quatre Bras;   *   *   *   six divisions of infantry at and near Quatre Bras and another at Marbais, so that I can order it to me at Sombreffe, if I have need of it.   *   *   *   The corps of the Count of Valmy   *   *   *   at the intersection of the Roman and Brussels roads, so that I may draw it to me, if I have need of it.   *   *   *   Your wing will be composed of the four divisions of the 1st Corps, of the four divisions of the 2d Corps, of the two divisions of light cavalry [those of Jaquinot and Piré], and of the two divisions of the corps of Valmy."

It has been asserted [35] that this letter restricted Ney in the employment of the cavalry of the Count of Valmy; but it seems perfectly clear that all the above-mentioned bodies of troops are put explicitly at Ney's disposal for the purpose of carrying out the orders which he would receive from the major-general; and that the dispositions of his command which Ney is requested to make, are to be made *only after the accomplishment of the main object of the movement,—the seizure of the cross-roads*.

But it is impossible that Ney could have had any doubt on the subject, inasmuch as there was a third formal order sent by Marshal Soult.

---

[34] Doc. Inéd., X, pp. 32 *et seq.*; App. C, xviii; *post*, pp. 377, 378.

[35] Charras, vol. 1, pp. 204, 205.

This order [36] informs Ney that an officer of lancers reports considerable bodies of the enemy near Quatre Bras. It then proceeds thus: "Unite the corps of the Counts Reille and d'Erlon and that of the Count of Valmy, [37] who has this instant started to join you; with these forces you ought to be able to beat and destroy any force of the enemy which you may meet." It then says that it is not very likely that Blücher has sent any troops to Quatre Bras, so that Ney will have to do only with the troops coming from Brussels. It concludes by stating that Grouchy has made the movement on Sombreffe of which Ney had been informed in the former order.

Now these orders, and certainly the last one, are as plain as plain can be. They do not admit of two constructions. Yet Ney, still unwilling to surrender his own judgment, still deeming it injudicious to push his command so far in advance of the main army, orders [38] the first three divisions of the 1st Corps to take up a position at Frasnes. Frasnes, it must be remembered, is two miles and a half from Quatre Bras,— nearly two miles from the field of battle,— an hour's march. Not only this, but he orders the two divisions of cavalry of the Count of Valmy to establish themselves at Frasnes and Liberchies,— the latter a village two miles southwest of Frasnes.

Consider this a moment. The principal formal order directed Ney, in so many words, to unite the two *corps d'armée*, and the corps of cavalry, and to take position at Quatre Bras,— not at Frasnes. Even if the Emperor's letter admitted of a construction at variance with this, so far as the cavalry of the Count of

---

[36] Doc. Inéd., IX, p. x31; App. C, xxii; *post*, p. 381.

[37] Charras (vol. 1, p. 190) says that this order differed from Soult's previous orders in authorizing Ney to employ the cavalry of the Count of Valmy. But both Soult's orders direct this in express terms.

[38] Doc. Inéd., XII, pp. 38, 39; App. C, xx; *post*, pp. 379, 380.

Valmy was concerned, the last order of Soult's was unmistakable. It left no room for latitude of construction. All the troops were to be united in the effort to get possession of the intersection of the roads, and the cavalry of the Count of Valmy is explicitly included. Instead of carrying out this order, which was both plain and peremptory, and called for the simultaneous employment of his entire command, or, at any rate, for the employment of as much of his command as he could assemble, more than half the force which had been placed at Ney's disposal was ordered by him to halt and "take position," "establish themselves," two miles and more to the south of the cross-roads. He himself, in his letter to the Duke of Otranto,[39] states that the 1st Corps "had been left by him in reserve at Frasnes." Although this statement is incorrect, inasmuch as that unlucky command never got quite so far as Frasnes, yet it shows beyond controversy what Marshal Ney *intended* to do with the 1st Corps. He furthermore says in this letter, that it was at the moment when he was about to order it up from Frasnes, that he learned that the Emperor had disposed of it. That is to say, he had actually *intended* to keep a whole corps of 20,000 men (or at least three-fourths of them) two miles from the battle-field till five o'clock in the afternoon, for (as we shall see hereafter) it was not until five o'clock that he learned that d'Erlon's Corps had wandered off.

---

[39] Jones, p. 386. Charras, vol. 1, p. 215.

NOTES TO CHAPTER VIII.

1. THE conduct of Marshal Ney on the 15th and 16th has been the subject of violent and bitter disputes. One principal cause of these disputes lies in the supposition that Napoleon in his accounts of the campaign has misrepresented the facts, so as to throw a large part of the blame for the final disaster undeservedly upon Ney. Accordingly, what Napoleon has said about Ney, and his motives in saying it, have been the subjects of discussion, rather than what Ney himself did. We have strictly confined our narrative to the consideration of Ney's acts, orders, and statements, supplemented by those of one of his corps-commanders and his chief-of-staff. From these it appears,

(a) That Ney was informed of the Emperor's intentions during the night of the 15th and 16th:

(b) That he contented himself, on his return to Gosselies at two o'clock in the morning, with ordering Reille to get his two divisions ready to move: he did not order Reille up to Frasnes as he might have done; nor did he see to it that the places of Reille's divisions at Gosselies were taken by the two divisions of d'Erlon's Corps, which, as we have seen,[1] were, at that hour well across the river:

(c) That instead of pushing right on to Quatre Bras with all his disposable force when he finally got his writ-

---

[1] *Ante*, p. 51.

ten orders, as those orders in express terms peremptorily directed him to do, he ordered three divisions of the 1st Corps to take up a position at Frasnes, two miles from the field of battle, and Kellermann's two divisions of cavalry "to establish themselves" partly there and partly at Liberchies, a village still further from the field:

(d) That he deliberately intended those three divisions of the 1st Corps and those two divisions of cavalry to stay at Frasnes and Liberchies, as his reserve, instead of having them with him for immediate use on the field of Quatre Bras:

(e) Lastly, all these things are *admitted* to be true; they are not accusations against him; they are facts, stated by himself, either in his own orders or letters, or by his own chief-of-staff, or by General Reille.

2. There is certainly one inference to be drawn from these facts. It is that Marshal Ney was not, in that night and morning, preparing for a decisive blow. So much, we presume, will be conceded. It is also plain that he was not proposing strictly to obey his orders. He evidently had his doubts about the wisdom of his orders. He was not going to embark too deep in what he evidently feared might prove a disastrous venture. He would proceed to Quatre Bras with the three divisions of the 2d Corps, but he would leave three divisions of the 1st Corps and the two divisions of Kellermann's cavalry to protect his flank and line of retreat, and also to be at hand in case the Emperor should need them. He did not dare to trust the Emperor fully. He must, he felt, in this emergency, act according to his own judgment.

3. If we are right in this conclusion, we can easily understand why Ney failed to carry out the order given to him at five o'clock on the afternoon of the 15th, to seize Quatre Bras that evening. We have left the much disputed question of the giving of this order on one side

in our narrative[2] for reasons already stated; but we have, nevertheless, expressed our opinion[3] that the order was given. Ney's conduct on the 16th is of a piece, we believe, with his conduct on the 15th.

4. No serious criticism can be passed, we think, on the tenor of the orders issued to the corps-commanders of the left wing, or to the commander of that wing, during the afternoon of the 15th and the morning of the 16th. Neither the Emperor nor Soult could well have done more than they did to arouse the energy of the officers who had charge of the operations there.[4] The orders were precise and imperative. The trouble was that the officers to whom they were addressed lacked either the disposition or the energy requisite to carry them into effect.

5. But why, it may be fairly asked, did not Napoleon, as soon as he had found out that Ney had not seized Quatre Bras on the evening of the 15th, order him forthwith to proceed to do so in the early morning of the 16th? Why this delay in sending him a formal written order?

This question will be considered in the next chapter, when we come to describe Napoleon's doings on the 16th.

---

[2] *Ante*, p. 52.

[3] *Ante*, pp. 67, 68.

[4] For an explanation of Chesney's (pp. 118, 119) severe strictures, see *ante*, p. 51, n. 29.

CHAPTER IX.

THE MORNING OF THE SIXTEENTH OF JUNE: NAPOLEON.

It is time that we returned to the headquarters of the French army.

Marshal Ney, as we have seen in the last chapter, reported in person to the Emperor at Charleroi at midnight of the 15th. "He rendered account" to him, says Colonel Heymès,[1] "of the dispositions he had made." Napoleon was thus informed that Ney had halted at Frasnes and had not occupied Quatre Bras, the evening before. Ney must have stopped at Charleroi about an hour and a half, as he reached Gosselies on his return about two in the morning. He must have told the Emperor where some, at any rate, of his troops were,—that Bachelu's infantry division and Piré's cavalry division of the 2d Corps were at Frasnes; that the divisions of Jerome and Foy were at Gosselies; that Durutte's division of the 1st Corps was between Jumet and Gosselies. So much as this Ney knew. But his arrival at the army had been so recent, and his occupations since his arrival had been so engrossing, that he could not probably have had much more information to give the Emperor as to the whereabouts of the 1st Corps. His almost total deficiency of staff officers was a grievous drawback, and prevented him from getting that hold on his entire command which otherwise he no doubt would have secured even by this time. Very possibly he had already

---

[1] Doc. Inéd., Heymès, p. 6.

sent word to d'Erlon to hurry up to the front. But he must have reported to the Emperor that a large part of the 1st Corps, perhaps half of it, was still far to the rear.

Napoleon does not mention this interview in his Memoirs, or in the Gourgaud Narrative, nor does he anywhere say that he, on the morning of the 16th, gave to Marshal Ney any other orders than the written ones of which we have in the last chapter given the substance.

It would seem from these orders that Napoleon thought it inexpedient that Ney should make any further endeavor to carry Quatre Bras by a *coup-de-main*. The situation was a different one from that which existed (as Napoleon correctly supposed) the evening before. It might now be expected that the cross-roads would be held by a respectable force from Wellington's army; or, at least, it was obviously unwise and hazardous not to make adequate preparations for this very possible state of things. It was also plain, from what Ney had stated at the midnight conference, that his command would not be, in the early morning hours, sufficiently concentrated for any decisive stroke.[2] Hence, somewhere about five o'clock, the first of the three orders of which we have spoken in the last chapter was sent off from Charleroi; the one in which Ney was informed that Kellermann's cavalry had been ordered to him to take the place of that of Lefebvre-Desnouettes, and in which he was directed to report to the Emperor whether the 1st Corps had "executed its movement," and to inform him of the exact positions of the 1st and 2d Corps. This order, as we have seen, Ney replied to before 7 A. M. His reply, which, we may assume, contained some news of the advance of the 1st Corps, and also stated that the divisions of Jerome and Foy of the 2d Corps were at Gosselies ready to march,

---

[2] *Cf.* La Tour D'Auvergne, pp. 91, 92.

must have reached headquarters shortly before 8 A. M. As soon as this reply was received, Napoleon and Soult prepared the formal order for the conduct of the left wing during the forenoon.

That order, as we have seen, directed Ney to unite the 1st and 2d Corps and the cavalry of the Count of Valmy, and to proceed at once to take possession of Quatre Bras. It was issued as soon as the Emperor had become satisfied, from Ney's report, that such a movement had become practicable,—that is, that it could be made in sufficient force to overcome any opposition it would be likely to encounter. Until he had become satisfied of this, it was deemed unadvisable to issue the order to advance beyond Frasnes.

We are able to fix the hour at which this formal order to seize Quatre Bras was prepared by Soult with quite an approach to accuracy. We know that Napoleon dictated a letter to Ney, which he sent by Count Flahaut,[3] and which arrived at Gosselies about the same time[4] with the formal order,—that is,—about 10 A. M.[5] Flahaut wrote[6] to Marshal Ney's son, then Duke of Elchingen, that, to the best of his recollection, the Emperor dictated the letter to him between 8 and 9 o'clock in the morning. Such a letter, dictated between 8 and 9, and afterwards reduced to proper form, would have reached Gosselies, a distance of about four miles and a half from Charleroi, about 10 A. M., as Reille[7] says it did. This accords perfectly with the statement made above that Napoleon waited to hear more definitely from Ney before framing his order for the morning's operations.

But the backwardness of d'Erlon's Corps not only de-

---

[3]Doc. Inéd., X, p. 32; App. C, xviii; *post*, pp. 377, 378.

[4]*Ante*, p. 121, note 23.

[5]*Ante*, p. 121, note 21.

[6]Doc. Inéd., XXI, p. 63; App. C, xxiii; *post*, p. 382.

[7]Ib., XI, pp. 37, 38; App. C, xix; *post*, p. 379.

ferred the forward moment of the left wing; it seems to have delayed the advance of the main body. Until Napoleon could be sure that Ney with the large force that had been assigned to him was in march on his left, able to give a good account of any Anglo-Dutch forces which might attempt to unite with the Prussians or to molest the left flank of the main French army, he seems to have been unwilling to move upon Blücher. It was part of his plan that Ney with the left wing should at least "contain" that part of Wellington's army which that general might reasonably be expected to get together at Quatre Bras. Hence, when Ney reported to the Emperor at midnight the very backward state of the 1st Corps, the latter not only decided to wait before giving him further orders until something more definite and satisfactory should be learned respecting that corps, and until Ney could fairly be supposed to have had time enough to get his entire command well in hand, but he also postponed his own forward movement upon Fleurus and Sombreffe until Ney could move simultaneously upon Quatre Bras. These considerations certainly go far to account for and justify the delay in the early morning hours of the 16th, which has drawn down upon the Emperor so much severe and almost contemptuous criticism. Napoleon, in truth, could have done nothing else, unless he had risked a battle with the Prussians on the chance that Ney, with the 2d Corps alone, could prevent their being assisted by the English. It is true, this is what actually happened; but it was Napoleon's intention that Ney should operate against the English with his entire command, and in deferring the giving of orders for the advance of the army until he had reason to believe that Ney could do this, he was simply carrying out his original scheme.

To finish now with Napoleon's intentions and expectations in regard to his left wing. He may well have expected that Ney had, in advance of receiving the formal order, sent Reille to Frasnes with his two divisions, which Ney's reply to his early morning inquiry had informed him were then all ready to march, thus uniting the entire 2d Corps, *minus* Girard's division; also, that the leading divisions of the 1st Corps would be gotten under arms without delay in Gosselies, so as to be ready to march at once. He must have expected his order to reach Gosselies by 10 A. M., and Frasnes by 11 A. M., and he may well have thought it quite possible,— as indeed it would have been,— that Ney, at the head of three divisions of infantry and one of cavalry, might be able to drive out of Quatre Bras the Dutch-Belgians who had been encountered the evening before, unless, indeed, they had been largely reinforced. At or about 1 P. M., however, the 1st Corps ought to be arriving at Quatre Bras, as its leading divisions would leave Gosselies — as Napoleon would have a right to suppose — between 10 and 11 A. M.; so that, by 2, or, at any rate, by 3 P. M., Marshal Ney would have his entire command at Quatre Bras, well in hand, and, pretty certain, — at least so Napoleon would be likely to think,— to be successful over any troops they might encounter. On these expectations, which, as we have seen, were quite warranted by the information he had received, he based his calculations for the day's doings.

While Napoleon was thus awaiting at Charleroi definite news of the progress and condition of the left wing of his army, he employed his time,— or a part of it, at least,— in determining on the lines of action he would pursue in view of possible emergencies. As we have already seen, he desired nothing so much as to join battle with Marshal Blücher on the 16th of June. It had been his expectation[8] that the Prussian general would assemble his army near Sombreffe, and fight a battle, somewhere to the south of that village, for the

---

[8] *Ante*, pp. 5, 13, 14.

preservation of his line of communications with the Duke of Wellington,— the Namur-Nivelles turnpike. At the same time, it was, of course, perfectly possible that the allied commanders had made other arrangements.[9] It was not impossible, for instance, that Napoleon's concentration had been such a surprise to them that they were purposing to fall back, for the present at least, either divergently towards their respective bases, or in a northerly direction by parallel lines. In any event it would be manifestly desirable to inform the commanders of the right and left wings of the army of the Emperor's probable course in any such event, so that every advantage might be promptly taken of the situation. It was certainly true, that instructions of this nature might not be required; they would assuredly not be required if Blücher should do what Napoleon had thought it likely he would do. In that case there would be no need of elaborate instructions being given to either Ney or Grouchy; the issue of the battle would settle everything. But in order to be prepared for the other state of affairs, Napoleon employed himself with preparing letters to the commanders of the wings of the army.

The letter[10] to Ney, which, as we have seen, was dictated by the Emperor to General Flahaut between 8 and 9 A. M., and was carried by that officer to Ney, whom it must have reached at Frasnes shortly before eleven o'clock,[11] informs him that Marshal Grouchy is marching on Sombreffe with the 3d and 4th Corps; that the Emperor is taking the Guard to Fleurus, where he will be before midday; that he will attack the enemy if he meets him, and will clear the road as far to the east-

---

[9] Ollech, p. 123.

[10] Corresp., vol. 28, p. 334. Doc. Inéd., X, p. 32; App. C, xviii; *post*. pp. 377, 378.

[11] Flahaut, says Reille, passed through Gosselies about 10 A. M. Doc. Inéd., XI, pp. 37, 38; App. C, xix; *post*, p. 379.

ward as Gembloux. There, at Gembloux, the Emperor will make up his mind what to do next,— perhaps at three in the afternoon, perhaps not till evening. But he tells Marshal Ney that, just as soon as he has made up his mind, he wants him to be ready to march on Brussels; that he will support him with the Guard, which will be at Fleurus or Sombreffe,[12] and that he would like to get to Brussels the next morning. He then tells him where he would like him to station his various divisions.[13] He informs him that he has divided his army into two wings and a reserve; that Ney's wing will consist of the 1st and 2d Corps, comprising eight divisions of infantry and two of light cavalry, and of the cavalry of the Count of Valmy; that Marshal Grouchy commands the right wing; that the Guard will constitute the reserve. He closes by reiterating the importance of Ney's dispositions being so well made that he can march on Brussels,— *i. e.*, from Quatre Bras,— as soon as ordered to do so.

To Grouchy the Emperor sent a similar[14] letter, giving him the command of the 3d and 4th Corps,— those of Vandamme and Gérard,— and of the three cavalry-corps of Pajol, Milhaud and Exelmans. He orders him to Sombreffe with his entire command; the cavalry are to be sent off at once, the infantry to follow without halting anywhere. The Emperor states that he is removing his headquarters from Charleroi to Fleurus, where he will arrive between 10 and 11 A. M., and that he is going to Sombreffe, leaving the Guard, unless it should be necessary to employ it, at Fleurus. "If the enemy is at Sombreffe," he goes on to say, "I propose to attack him; I propose to attack him even at Gembloux, and to pos-

---

[12] This seems to imply that the Emperor did not propose to carry the Guard to Gembloux.

[13] See *ante*, p. 123.

[14] Corresp., vol. 28, p. 336; App. C, xxiv; *post*, pp. 382, 383.

sess myself of that position; my intention being, after having explored [*connu*] these two positions, to set out this night, and operate with my left wing, which Marshal Ney commands, against the English." He then desires Grouchy to send him reports of everything he may learn, and finishes by saying:—"All my information is to the effect that the Prussians cannot oppose to us more than forty thousand men."

It is quite true, that this last remark shows, as several writers[15] have pointed out, that the Emperor was to a considerable extent mistaken on this morning of the 16th in his apprehension of the situation. But it is an error to take these letters as if they were written for the purpose of giving Napoleon's estimates of the probabilities; they are rather instructions in the event of the occurrence of not impossible contingencies. The fact in the case was just this,—the main army was about to make a forward movement against the Prussians; if they were found to be in force and offered battle, the result of this battle would of course settle everything; but if they should retire, instead of offering battle, they must be followed, and that involved the separation of the French army into two unequal portions. Hence it was very desirable to inform Ney, from whom in this event the right wing and reserves would march away, about how far the Prussians would be followed, and, especially to enjoin upon him, in case the Emperor should deem it safe to leave the care of the Prussians to Grouchy, and should himself retrace his steps, and, with his Guard, join the left wing, to be ready to march on Brussels at an instant's notice.

It must be noted, too, that these letters, especially when taken in connection with the formal orders of Soult to the two Marshals, show how absolutely Napoleon

---

[15] Ollech, pp. 112, 113: D'Auvergne, pp. 103, 104: Charras, vol. I, pp. 143, 144.

adhered to his original conception of the campaign, as we have before described it. To attack the Prussians first,— to follow them up for a considerable distance, so as to be assured of the direction which their retreat was taking,— and then, and only then, to return to the Brussels road and advance on the English,— such was the programme marked out in the two letters to Ney and Grouchy. We shall have occasion to refer to this in another place.

Lastly, while the Emperor expressly states in his letter to Grouchy that he estimates that the Prussians can not oppose to him a force of over forty thousand men, and while it may perhaps be inferred from his letter to Ney that he thought that that officer would meet with little or no opposition, it is to be observed that Napoleon acted in all respects as if he expected that the enemy would be found in force. Both Ney and Grouchy were explicitly directed to employ the whole of their respective forces. We have spoken of this before as it affected Ney. It was the same with the movement prescribed to Grouchy,—"Take your right wing to Sombreffe,"— [16] *i. e.*, the two *corps-d'armée*, and the three cavalry corps. Whatever Napoleon may have conjectured as to the force or intentions of the enemy, both of his movements this forenoon,— that of the main army on Sombreffe, and that of the left wing on Quatre Bras,— were to be made in force,— with all the force he could muster. If he did expect, as some writers think, that his enemies would retire before him, he at any rate made every preparation to fight and overcome them, should they give him battle. It was in order, as we have pointed out, that these movements might be made simultaneously, and in sufficient force, that they were deferred to such a late period in the day,— the backwardness of the

---

[16] "*Rendez-vous avec cette aile droite à Sombreffe.*"

1st Corps having postponed for several hours the concentration of the left wing.

It will be noticed that in none of these letters or formal orders is the 6th Corps under the Count of Lobau mentioned. The inference is, that, at that time, the Emperor desired to retain this body of troops as a reserve for the whole army. He wanted to get along, if he could, without employing it at all in the present stage of the campaign.

NOTES TO CHAPTER IX.

1. THE very simple explanation suggested in this chapter of the cause of the delay on the morning of the 16th in the movement of the main body of the French army under the Emperor in person, namely, that that movement was deferred because of the inability of the left wing of the army to make a simultaneous movement on Quatre Bras, does not seem to have occurred to most of the historians of this campaign.[1] But surely, when allowance is made for this fact, the severe criticisms of Jomini,[2] Charras,[3] Siborne[4] and others, must be held to be quite beside the mark. Had Ney occupied Quatre Bras on the evening of the 15th, the forward movement of the main French army would certainly not have been thus delayed. It would doubtless have been made in the early morning of the 16th, even though it might have been necessary to give Ney the 6th Corps in place of the backward 1st. But as Quatre Bras had not been occupied the evening before, and as the backward state of d'Erlon's Corps rendered it impossible for Ney to make a forward movement with the entire force which had been assigned to him until the forenoon was well advanced, the operations of the main body were postponed, and the troops were allowed what would otherwise have been an unnecessary[5] time to rest and recruit.

---

[1] It is, however, given in Du Casse's Vandamme, vol. 2, p. 562.

[2] Jomini, pp. 129, 130.

[3] Charras, vol. 1, pp. 138, 145, 182.

[4] Siborne, vol. 1, p. 85.

[5] The Duke of Wellington, however, thought the inactivity of Napoleon on the morning of the 16th was necessitated by the long marches of the past few days. Ellesmere, pp. 296, 297. So, Clausewitz, ch. 25, p. 53.

2. It is to be observed here, that for the backwardness of the 1st Corps at midnight of the 15th, Marshal Ney was in no wise responsible. His recent arrival at the army and his lack of a proper staff exonerate him completely from any blame for this unfortunate delay. For this d'Erlon alone must be held responsible.

3. It is unnecessary to repeat here what we have said above as to Ney's conduct on his return to Gosselies from his interview with Napoleon at Charleroi. It seems to us that any competent and energetic officer, bent upon getting ready to execute his orders as soon as they should be received, and to execute them to the letter when he should receive them, would have accomplished far more than Marshal Ney accomplished that morning.

4. We desire to call attention to the fact that up to this time there is no evidence whatever of indolence, or irresolution, on the part of the Emperor Napoleon. From the time when he left Paris at half-past three in the morning of the 12th to the time of which we are now writing, he seems to have been fully up even to his own high standard of military activity and capacity. His general order for the movement of the army on the 15th was as clear and full as it was possible for an order to be. His energy and dash on the 15th were noticeable. His vigor and endurance also seem to have been equal to the demands put upon them. From three in the morning to eight in the evening of the 15th he was on horseback, and in personal command of the troops. At midnight he had a long conference with Marshal Ney. Since the result of that conference was, as we have seen, to induce the postponement of the advance of the army, the Emperor may, very possibly, have taken some rest in the early morning hours of the 16th. But the despatch to Ney requesting from him an exact account of his position must have been sent off about five, and at or soon after eight we find him dictating to Count Flahaut the letters

to Ney and Grouchy. It is hardly necessary to add, that if the explanation given above of the causes of the delay in the advance-movement of the army on the morning of the 16th be correct, there is not the slightest foundation for the charges of hesitation or irresolution, which have been so often made.[6]

5. It seems to be difficult for some writers to keep steadily in mind the absolute necessity of Napoleon's either defeating the Prussians or compelling them definitely to retreat, before he undertook any movement in the direction of Brussels, either with the view of attacking the English or of occupying that city. Thus Chesney,[7] speaking of Napoleon's intentions on the morning of the 16th, says:—

"His morning orders clearly prove that he expected no serious opposition from them (the Prussians) or the English at present, and was divided only in his mind between the thought of pressing on direct to Brussels between the two allied armies, or striking at the supposed Prussian right, driven back on Fleurus the day before."

But Napoleon's letters to Ney and Grouchy, to which Chesney here refers, explicitly contradict this supposition. Napoleon says in his letter to Ney:—[8]

"I am sending Marshal Grouchy with the 3d and 4th Corps of infantry to Sombreffe. I am taking my Guard to Fleurus, and I shall be there myself before noon. I shall there attack the enemy if I meet him, and I shall clear the road as far as Gembloux. There, after what shall have passed, I shall make up my mind."

And he directs Ney to be all ready to march to Brussels, as soon as he (Napoleon) shall have arrived at a decision. But this decision, it is to be observed, was not to be taken until the Prussians should either have been attacked and

---

[6] *Ante*, pp. 132, 139.

[7] Chesney, pp. 138, 139: See also, Clinton, p. 380.

[8] Corresp., vol. 28, p. 334: Doc. Inéd., X, p. 32; App. C, xviii; *post*, pp. 377, 378.

defeated, or should have fallen back at least as far as Gembloux.

To the same effect is the letter to Grouchy:[9]

"If the enemy is at Sombreffe I am going to attack him; I am going to attack him even at Gembloux, and to carry even that position; my intention being, after having explored (*connu*) these two positions, to set out this night and to operate with my left wing, which is under the command of Marshal Ney, against the English."

It is plain from both these letters that to say that Napoleon was "divided in his mind" between "pressing on direct to Brussels between the two allied armies" and attacking the Prussians in front of him,—in other words, that he was hesitating which of these two courses he would take, is a statement utterly without foundation. In both despatches he states unequivocally his immediate intention,—namely, to attack the Prussians; and it was only after he should have attacked and driven the Prussians and forced them as far to the eastward as Gembloux, that he proposed to retrace his steps, to reinforce Ney, and march against the English. Brussels, indeed, was regarded by Napoleon as perhaps the most important result of the campaign, next to the enormous military advantage which would be secured by the defeat or dispersion of the armies of Wellington and Blücher. But this was all. For the Emperor to gain Brussels, these hostile armies must either be attacked and beaten, or else they must definitely separate, each retiring towards its own base. The idea of passing between the two armies at this stage of the campaign, and so arriving at Brussels, it is safe to say, never entered Napoleon's mind. His object, as Jomini[10] correctly states, was "not to occupy Brussels, but to destroy the opposing masses in succession."

---

[9] Corresp., vol. 28, p. 336; App. C, xxiv; *post*, pp. 382, 383.
[10] Jomini, p. 112.

CHAPTER X.

THE BATTLE OF LIGNY. BLÜCHER'S DECISION TO ACCEPT BATTLE NOT DEPENDENT ON WELLINGTON'S ASSURANCE OF SUPPORT.

MARSHAL BLÜCHER, as we have seen,[1] had on the evening of the 14th, ordered a concentration of his entire army in the neighborhood of Sombreffe. This, as has been pointed out above, was done without consultation, at the moment certainly, with the Duke of Wellington; and we have before stated that we do not find that it was done in pursuance of any previous arrangement between the two commanders. At any rate it is not disputed that Marshal Blücher took up a position in order of battle to the south of the Namur-Nivelles turnpike without having received either by letter or word of mouth any assurance whatsoever that his English ally was prepared to support him, other than that contained in Müffling's despatch, sent off from Brussels about midnight, and informing him that Wellington expected to be at Nivelles at 10 A. M. in strong force. Zieten's (Ist) Corps, about five o'clock in the morning of the 16th, withdrew[2] from the neighborhood of Fleurus, where it had passed the night of the 15th, to the north side of the brook of Ligny, and took up position in the villages of St. Amand, Brye and Ligny. Between 9 and 10 A. M. the IId Corps, commanded by Pirch I.,[3] arrived, and took

---

[1] *Ante*, p. 70.
[2] Ollech, p. 120.
[3] Pirch II. commanded a brigade in the Ist Corps.

up a position behind that occupied by the Ist Corps.[4] Between 11 A. M. and 12 M. the IIId Corps, Thielemann's, came up, and occupied the line between Sombreffe and Tongrinelle. These were the positions which were held during the battle by the three corps which had been gotten together; the IVth Corps, Bülow's, it was then known could not come up during the day. Not until noon[5] did Wellington's letter, dated "On the heights behind Frasnes, 10.30 A. M.," arrive. Not until 1 P. M.[6] did the Duke himself meet Marshal Blücher. Then a conversation took place between them. There is no doubt that Wellington expressed[7] himself as practically certain that the bulk of his army would be assembled at Quatre Bras early in the afternoon. His verbal statements to Marshal Blücher were to the same effect as the statements contained in his letter. We have seen how mistaken he was in these, and how he came to be mistaken. What he wrote and said, however, he honestly believed; and he certainly did give to Marshal Blücher some assurance that he should be supported by the Anglo-Dutch forces in his impending struggle with the bulk of the French army. According to some authorities, his assurance took the form of a positive promise of support; and these writers do not hesitate to assert that Blücher's decision to accept battle at Ligny was based upon this definite promise.[8] "Upon this assurance," says Charras, "the

---

[4] Ollech, p. 122.

[5] Gneisenau, vol. 4, p. 373.

[6] Ollech, p. 125.

[7] Müffling: Passages, 230, 231, 237.

[8] Charras, vol. 1, pp. 150, 151, and note. Damitz, p. 92. Gneisenau, vol. 4, p. 375. Charras states in the note cited above that Clausewitz "says that it was the promise of help from Wellington that decided Blücher to receive battle,"—but we have not been able to find the passage. He also says that Siborne substantially follows Damitz in this matter; but we can not find that Siborne represents Wellington as making any such promise. In his official report of the battle Blücher does not claim that such a promise was given. Jones, pp. 320, 321.

Prussian general decided to receive the battle which he could have avoided."

The principal knowledge we have of the conversation between Wellington and Blücher comes from what Müffling has told us about it.[9] According to him the last words the Duke spoke were: — "Well! I will come, provided I am not attacked myself." General Dörnberg's evidence[10] is to the same effect. The latest Prussian historian of the campaign[11] does not claim that the Duke gave Blücher any unconditional promise of support. That a different impression should have obtained currency with the Prussians is very natural. The Duke's statements of the proximity of his army, made with perfect honesty, but based, as we have seen, on very erroneous *data*, no doubt raised false hopes in the minds of the Prussian generals. That these statements afterwards assumed in the mind of General Gneisenau, the Prussian chief-of-staff, the aspect and dimensions of a positive pledge of support, seems from Delbrück's life of Gneisenau quite probable.[12] But the evidence, what there is of it, and the probabilities of the case, are all the other way. That is to say, Blücher decided to fight at Ligny, without having any such definite promise of support from Wellington, as the latter relied upon when he decided to await the attack of the French at Waterloo, two days later.

This will appear more clearly when we consider the other assertion made on behalf of the Prussian commander, of which we have made mention above,— namely, that Blücher's decision to accept battle at Ligny was

---

[9] Müffling: Passages, pp. 233-237.

[10] Ollech, p. 127, note.

[11] Ib., p. 127.

[12] Ollech (p. 142) quotes Gneisenau as writing on the 17th: "We received from the Duke of Wellington the written promise that if the enemy should attack us, he would attack them in the rear." There is no such promise in Wellington's letter to Blücher.

based upon this promise of support from Wellington.[13] Delbrück, in his Life of Gneisenau,[14] says: "Although this position [*i. e.*, at and near Ligny] had been carefully considered and taken up with all caution, it was yet not fully decided to receive battle." This decision was not arrived at, we are given to understand, until Blücher had received from Wellington a promise of support. That could not have been until between 1 and 2 o'clock P. M., for the Duke did not arrive at Brye till one o'clock. Müffling says[15] that it was "when the heads of Napoleon's attacking columns showed themselves moving upon St. Amand" that "the Duke asked the Field Marshal [Blücher] and General von Gneisenau: '*Que voulez-vous que je fasse?*'"

That is, we are asked to believe that Blücher had not fully decided to await the attack of these French columns, now seen to be advancing, in the positions which had been deliberately selected, and on which the troops had been carefully stationed, until the Duke of Wellington had stated himself able to do what Blücher and Gneisenau wished him to do. We are asked to believe that Blücher would have retreated if Wellington had told him that his situation was such that he could not bring him any aid.

We must say that such a contention seems to us hardly to deserve serious consideration. It is surely plain enough that Blücher had chosen a battle-field,— had posted his army there,— had encouraged his troops to expect a conflict with the French,— without taking counsel with the English general.[16] Had he determined to fight only if he should receive assurance of support from Wellington, would he not have taken some pains to

---

[13] La Tour D'Auvergne, p. 109, entirely disbelieves this assertion.

[14] Gneisenau, p. 372.

[15] Müffling: Passages, p. 234.

[16] Blücher's Report leaves the question open. Jones, pp. 320, 321.

obtain such assurance? Would he have left it entirely to the chance of Wellington's writing him a letter, or riding over to his headquarters? These questions answer themselves.

We conclude, then, that it is a fact beyond controversy that Marshal Blücher decided to accept battle at Ligny altogether independently of any support or assistance that might be afforded him by the Anglo-Dutch army. He deliberately ran the risk of encountering, unsupported by his allies, and with such only of his troops as he could on short notice collect close to the frontier, the bulk of the French army under Napoleon himself. How far he was wise in this we will consider in another place; what we have sought to make plain now is that such was the fact.

NOTE TO CHAPTER X.

WHAT were the reasons which induced Marshal Blücher to take up a defensive position at Ligny, and there await the attack of Napoleon? The question is certainly an important one. We have considered above and rejected the answer to this question offered by some Prussian writers, that Blücher accepted battle only on the definite promise of support from Wellington. It remains to see what other reasons have been adduced for his taking a step so perilous to the fortunes of the allies.

Neither Clausewitz nor Jomini pay any attention to the question.

Damitz'[1] explanation is as follows:—

"Marshal Blücher was free to refuse the combat; he could very well have avoided it, and have waited until the IVth Corps should have joined him. But, seeing himself at the head of 80,000 men, it was not in his firm and decided character to turn his back on an adversary. He knew that he could not vanquish Napoleon by skilful manœuvres, but only by repeated blows. The General and his army felt themselves strong enough; that was of itself a reason for not avoiding a battle."

He then goes on to show that a march to join the English army would involve a temporary renunciation of the Prussian base of operations.

These are the reasons he gives. He adds most unex-

---
[1] Damitz, p. 85.

pectedly:—[2] "It is then evident that the Prussians decided on accepting battle because the Duke of Wellington had given them his word." But of any such fact as this no mention whatever is made until the writer has occasion to speak[3] of the conversation between Wellington and Blücher between 1 and 2 P. M., when the French were deploying their columns for the attack. It is impossible to believe that Blücher had not before this made up his mind to fight, altogether independently of anything Wellington might say to him.

Ollech[4] suggests, as an answer to the question, "Why did Blücher give battle on the 16th although a whole army corps had not arrived?" that he did it in order to give the English army time to concentrate. This writer does not pretend that Wellington gave the Field Marshal any definite promise of support.[5]

Delbrück, in his Life of Gneisenau, says[6] that Blücher, relying on Wellington's promise, and still hoping that at least late in the evening a portion of the IVth Corps would arrive, concluded to give battle.

There is really not much to be said on this subject. The truth is plain enough. Blücher had, as we have said above,[7] long ago fixed upon Sombreffe as the point of concentration for his army in case the French should cross the Sambre at or near Charleroi; and he had, most likely, communicated this determination to the Duke of Wellington. In arriving at this determination he undoubtedly assumed that he would be able to collect his whole army together,—say, 120,000 men. He thought, and he had a right to think, that if Napoleon

---

[2]Damitz, p. 87.

[3]Ib., p. 92.

[4]Ollech, pp. 123, 124.

[5]Ib., p. 127.

[6]Gneisenau, vol. 4, p. 375.

[7]*Ante*, p. 70.

should advance by way of Charleroi, he would be sure to attack the Prussian army if it should be found posted at or south of Sombreffe; and that Napoleon would be obliged to employ against it the bulk of his army. Hence Blücher calculated that the Anglo-Dutch concentration could be effected without serious molestation, and that some assistance at any rate from that quarter might safely be counted on. But when the day arrived, he found that he could not reckon on the arrival of one of his corps in time for the battle. Yet he still adhered to his determination to accept the contest, partly from unwillingness to retreat at the outset of the campaign, and partly in the hope that important aid would be received from Wellington. This determination, however, was arrived at without consultation with Wellington and before his letter was received,— in which, it is to be noted, there is no promise whatever,— and, of course, before the Duke himself rode over to Brye. What Wellington said no doubt strengthened the Field Marshal in his belief in the soundness of his decision; it reinforced his judgment; it gave him hopes of victory. But to say that his decision to receive the attack of the French at Ligny was based upon any promise of support made by Wellington, is entirely contrary to the evidence.

CHAPTER XI.

THE BATTLE OF LIGNY.

MARSHAL BLÜCHER had taken up a position, which although in some respects determined by the nature of the ground, was nevertheless intended to secure two objects,—first, his line of communications with Namur, and an unobstructed march for his expected IVth Corps, Bülow's, and, secondly, his avenue of communication with the Anglo-Dutch army, from which he expected to receive at least some assistance in the course of the afternoon. It thus came about that the centre of the Prussian army was at Sombreffe,—that the line of the right wing ran through the villages of Ligny and St. Amand in a south-westerly direction, and that that of the left wing ran from Sombreffe through the hamlet of Mont Potriaux to Tongrinelle and Balâtre in a south-easterly direction. This left wing consisted entirely of the IIId Corps, Thielemann's. It contained 22,051 infantry, 2,405 cavalry, and 48 guns.[1] The Ist Corps, Zieten's held the front of the centre and right wing, and was supported by the IId Corps, that of Pirch I., throughout its whole extent. These two corps contained 56,803 infantry, 6,093 cavalry, and 176 guns.[2] The right wing was "in the air"; it was possible to turn it completely, by way of St. Amand and Wagnelée. Behind Ligny and St. Amand, and on commanding

[1] Charras, vol. 1, p. 155, n.
[2] Ib., p. 155, n.

ground, was the village of Brye. Blücher's whole force thus consisted of 87,352 men, of whom 8,498 were cavalry, — with 224 guns.

Napoleon, having finished giving his orders shortly after nine, arrived at Fleurus about 11 A. M.[3] He busied himself, while the troops were arriving, with examining the enemy's position. From the tower of an old and disused windmill in the outskirts of the town he made, it is said, his first observations. Then he went, — without his staff, as his custom was before a battle, — partly on horseback and partly on foot, along the front of the enemy's position, seeing for himself everything that could be seen. By the time the troops had arrived in the neighborhood of Fleurus, he had formed his plan. He had not, however, correctly estimated the numbers of the force opposed to him; the nature of the ground prevented his being able to see all the enemy's troops.[4]

The more natural and obvious plan for Napoleon would have been to direct his attack upon the exposed Prussian right wing, and to operate in conjunction with the column under Marshal Ney, so far as that might seem expedient. By moving upon Wagnelée and Brye, he would turn the position of St. Amand, and almost certainly secure a victory. But Napoleon did not see in this operation any chance of inflicting a decisive blow.[5] At most, he would only have defeated an exposed wing of the enemy's army. There would have been nothing to prevent its falling back upon the centre and left wing. The Prussians would no doubt be worsted, but their defeat could hardly be of a character to cripple them. Nor would their communications be in the slightest degree imperilled.

What Napoleon determined on was an operation far

---

[3] Charras, vol. 1, p. 145.

[4] Ib., p. 150.

[5] For a further discussion of this subject see the Notes to this chapter.

more decisive. He saw that that part of the Prussian army which lay in the neighborhood of Sombreffe, Tongrinelle and Balâtre, placed there, as it had been, for the purpose of protecting the communications with Namur, would in all probability not dare to move from its position, and would accordingly not be able to take any active part in the battle. He would therefore have to deal only with that portion of the enemy's army which lay between Sombreffe and St. Amand, — say, two-thirds of their entire force. He also saw that if the enemy's centre, between Ligny and Sombreffe, could be broken, the Prussian right wing would be separated from the rest of the army, and that he might hope to overwhelm it. He saw also one other thing. If, at or about the time when this success should be obtained, a strong column from Marshal Ney's command could march down the Quatre Bras-Namur turnpike and move upon Brye, that success would almost certainly be of the most decisive character.[6] Attacked in front and rear at the same time, its connection with the rest of the army severed, surrounded by superior numbers, the utter rout of that part of the Prussian army was inevitable. (See Map 6.)

At one o'clock the French army had arrived, and was in and about Fleurus. The Emperor threw the 4th Corps, Gérard's, about 16,000 strong,[7] with 38 guns, far to the right, opposite the whole front of the village of Ligny; the 3d Corps, Vandamme's, about 19,000 strong,[8] with 38 guns, connected with the left of the 4th Corps, and, assisted by Girard's division of the 2d Corps,

---

[6] "A movement that would certainly have obtained an immense victory." Jomini, p. 223.

[7] Charras, vol. 1, p. 155, n. The division of Hulot and the cavalry of Maurin were stationed opposite the bend in the enemy's line, beyond Ligny. Ib., p. 161.

[8] Ib., p. 155, n.

about 4,300 strong,[9] with 8 guns, menaced the Prussians in the village of St. Amand; while the cavalry of Pajol and Exelmans, to the number of about 6,500 men,[10] with 24 guns, supported by Hulot's division of the 4th Corps, observed the Prussian left wing, — stationed from Sombreffe to Balâtre. The Guard, with Milhaud's Cuirassiers, in all about 22,000 men, with 102 guns,[11] was kept in reserve, near Fleurus, ready to strike the final blow when the enemy in Ligny and St. Amand should have been sufficiently weakened by a continuous struggle of three or four hours. The whole force consisted of 67,787 men, of whom 13,394 were cavalry, with 210 guns.[12] These dispositions consumed perhaps an hour or more. At 2 o'clock the chief-of-staff, Soult, wrote [13] to Marshal Ney, informing him that, at half-past two Marshal Grouchy, with the 3d and 4th Corps, would commence an attack on a Prussian corps stationed between Sombreffe and Brye; that it was the Emperor's intention that Ney should also attack the enemy before him; and, after having vigorously driven them, should fall back upon the main army to join in enveloping this Prussian corps, of which mention had just been made.

Then, at half-past two precisely, the battle began;[14] Gérard vigorously attacked Ligny, — Vandamme and Girard, St. Amand. With equal vigor did the Prussians defend their positions. The engagement immediately

---

[9] Charras, vol. 1, p. 155, n.

[10] Ib., p. 155, n.

[11] Ib., p. 155, n.

[12] Ib., p. 155, n. This is exclusive of the 6th Corps, which was in reserve. It numbered 10,465 men, with 32 guns.

[13] Doc. Inéd., XIII, p. 40; App. C, xxv; *post*, pp. 383, 384.

[14] The battle of Ligny has often been described. Charras, La Tour d'Auvergne, Thiers, on the French side, Clausewitz and Ollech on the German side, give excellent descriptions. Siborne's account is also very clear and good. It is unnecessary to repeat the details here.

became very hot, and very sanguinary. Both sides fought with singular determination. In less than an hour Napoleon was convinced that he had more than a single corps to deal with, — as he had written to Ney, — it was an army. The success, therefore, could be made more decisive than he had at first thought possible, if only at the proper time Ney's coöperation could be secured. Without that coöperation, indeed, he was practically sure of victory; it was plain to him that the Prussians in the villages of Ligny and St. Amand and its neighboring hamlets, and on the heights in the rear of these villages, were becoming exhausted, and were suffering terribly from the fire of his guns, to which their position on the heights exposed them;[15] he knew that when the proper moment arrived he could defeat them; but he wanted something more than a defeat; he saw that the rout or capture of this part of the Prussian army was a certain thing if Ney could only make that movement from Quatre Bras upon their right and rear, of which he had spoken in his 2 o'clock order. Hence at a quarter-past three Soult wrote to Ney again,[16] urging him to manœuvre at once, so as to envelop the enemy's right, and to fall on his rear. He told him that the Prussian army was lost if he acted vigorously; that "the fate of France was in his hands." "Thus," the order proceeds, "do not hesitate an instant to make the movement which the Emperor orders, and direct yourself on the heights of Brye and St. Amand to assist in a victory perhaps decisive."

The officers who carried these orders had some

---

[15] Sir Henry Hardinge, speaking to the Duke of Wellington, said: "When you had examined the Prussian position, I remember you much disapproved of it, and said to me, 'if they fight here they will be damnably mauled.'"
* * * The Duke added: "They were dotted in this way — all their bodies along the slope of a hill, so that no cannon-ball missed its effect upon them." Stanhope, p. 109. *Cf.* Hooper, p. 96.

[16] Doc. Inéd., XIV, p. 42; App. C, xxvi; *post*, p. 384.

thirteen miles to ride, about six miles on cross-roads, as far as Gosselies, and the remainder on the great Brussels turnpike, on which d'Erlon's troops were marching towards Frasnes. Their errands could not have been performed in less than two hours,[17] and as a matter of fact they required three hours. Napoleon could hardly have expected the first order to reach Ney much before 5 P. M., and the second hardly before 6 P. M. The distance from Quatre Bras to Marbais, where the road branches off from the Namur turnpike in the direction of Wagnelée, is nearly four miles. If then at 5 o'clock it should be in Marshal Ney's power to execute the 2 P. M. order, his troops might be looked for or heard from in the direction of Marbais about 7 o'clock. If he should be unable to obey the 2 o'clock order, but should be able to execute the 3.15 order, his movement down the Namur road might be looked for about 8 o'clock.

The battle then went on with unabated determination and with heavy loss on both sides. Blücher reinforced his troops from time to time; in this way he exhausted his reserves; nearly all his divisions were brought under fire. Napoleon on the other hand was exceedingly chary of giving aid to the two corps engaged; he wished to keep his reserves as large as possible; at half-past five he had employed ten thousand fewer men than his adversary.[18] At this time, also, the 6th Corps was well on its way from Charleroi. The hour was approaching, too, when Ney's coöperation might be expected.

Up to this time Napoleon had remained in his position in front of Fleurus;[19] it was a central position, and nothing had called for his personal superintendence elsewhere.

---

[17] The Duke of Elchingen — Doc. Inéd., p. 41 — estimates the distance at nearly five leagues, that is, 12½ miles, and allows two hours for the time occupied. Charras, vol. 1, page 204, n., makes the distance six leagues (15 miles) and estimates the time at three hours.

[18] Charras, vol. 1, p. 166.

[19] Ib., p. 164.

But now he prepared to strike the decisive blow. He determined to put in the Guard. He proposed to send to Vandamme the infantry division known as the Young Guard, and one of the two brigades of the division known as the chasseurs of the Guard;[20] the other brigade of this division he would place at the disposal of Gérard. He himself, at the head of the infantry division of grenadiers of the Guard, known as the Old Guard, with all the artillery of the Guard, with Guyot's division of the heavy cavalry of the Guard, and Milhaud's division of cuirassiers of the line,— to take the place of Lefebvre-Desnouettes' division of light cavalry of the Guard which was with the left wing under Marshal Ney, —prepared to carry the village of Ligny, and the commanding heights above and to the right of the village, thereby breaking the centre of the enemy's line.

At this moment, however, word came from Vandamme that a column of the enemy was seen debouching from a wood some two miles away, and apparently marching on Fleurus. This was not the quarter in which the expected reinforcement from Ney was looked for. Curiously enough, Vandamme did not ascertain what this column was. Why he should not have done this it is not easy to see. Had he sent a patrol to find out who these troops were, time would have been saved, and time, at that hour in the day, was most important. The Emperor sent one of his own aides to ascertain the facts; and, pending his report, suspended the projected attack. The battle went on as before, but Blücher drew more and more from his centre and left wing to support his right at St. Amand and the neighboring villages.

In something less than two hours the aide returned.

---

[20]Sometimes classed as part of the Old Guard, as in Charras, vol. 1, p. 67 and La Tour d'Auvergne, p. 48, and sometimes as "the Middle Guard" (*la Garde moyenne*). See "Napoléon à Waterloo," p, 315, n. 1; p. 325.

The troops which Vandamme had reported advancing were those of d'Erlon's Corps.[21] All anxiety was relieved. Napoleon naturally concluded[22] that d'Erlon had been sent by Ney, and would immediately move on Brye. He instantly resumed the suspended movement.[23] Before half-past seven, Vandamme had received his reinforcements, and had renewed the fight with energy. At the same time the Emperor, at the head of the grenadiers and cavalry of the Guard and of Milhaud's cuirassiers, marched for the village of Ligny, of which the eastern portion was already in the possession of Gérard's Corps. The Prussians, though fighting desperately, were speedily overcome; the village was carried; the brook of Ligny, a serious obstacle for both cavalry and artillery, was crossed on the bridges in the town; and at half-past eight o'clock[24] the French troops, passing out of the northern end of the village, deployed on the heights lying between that village and Sombreffe, and ascended the plateau, the key to the field of battle, on which stood the windmill of Bussy. The Prussian troops which Blücher had allowed to remain on this part of the line offered a stout but ineffectual resistance. The old Marshal himself came up from St. Amand, where he had wrongly supposed that the crisis of the battle was being decided, and at the head of a body of cavalry fiercely charged the victorious French. In one of the encounters his horse was killed, he himself was badly bruised, and came very near being taken prisoner.

---

[21] We shall consider in another place how d'Erlon's Corps came to be there. Shortly after it was seen by Vandamme it retired to Frasnes.

[22] La Tour d'Auvergne, p. 135: Jomini, pp. 138, 139.

[23] There was no delay, as suggested by Siborne, vol. 1, p. 218. From where the Guard had been stationed to the northerly end of the village of Ligny, where it was put in, was at least two miles and a half. Only a small part of this distance had been traversed before the news from Vandamme caused a halt.

[24] Charras, vol. 1, p. 175, n. 2: letter from Soult to Joseph Bonaparte.

THE BATTLE OF LIGNY.

Meantime, the Prussians fell back from St. Amand and the neighboring villages, which were at once occupied by Vandamme. Brye, however, was held until midnight by Pirch I. with a strong rear guard, and Thielemann occupied Sombreffe and Point du Jour. The corps of Zieten, followed finally by that of Pirch I., retreated on Tilly, a town just north of Sombreffe, and in the direction of Wavre.

The Prussians lost[25] in this battle about 18,000 men killed and wounded; and, a day or two afterwards, about 10,000 or 12,000 more, who would seem to have done their duty in the fight, abandoned their colors, and retired towards Liége. These men belonged to provinces which had formerly been part of the French Empire, and their sympathies were with Napoleon.[26] The French captured some thousands of the Prussian wounded, and 25 or 30 guns. The French loss was between 11,000 and 12,000 men."[27]

The battle was over at about half-past nine. The 3d Corps established itself in bivouac beyond St. Amand and Wagnelée; the 6th Corps occupied the plateau of Bussy; the 4th Corps was on the right of the 6th, with one division at and near Potriaux. The Guard and Milhaud's cuirassiers occupied a line behind these troops.[28] At 11 P. M. the Emperor returned to Fleurus,[29] where he established his headquarters.

All parts of the French army on the field had taken part in this action except the 1st and 6th Corps. The 1st Corps retired towards Frasnes soon after it had been seen. As

---

[25] Charras, vol. 1, p. 179, where he discusses the Prussian authorities. *Cf.* Muquardt, p. 139, n.

[26] *Cf.* Gneisenau, vol. 4, pp. 381, 382. Müffling: Passages, pp. 204, 205, 223. Siborne, vol. 1, pp. 302, 303.

[27] Charras, vol. 1, p. 180.

[28] Ib., pp. 177, 178.

[29] Ib., p. 179.

for the 6th Corps, the order to Lobau, which was not sent until 2.30 P. M., could not have reached him in his bivouac near Charleroi till 3.30 P. M. He had eight miles to march before reaching Fleurus; he was then directed on Ligny, and he passed through Ligny, just after the successful attack of that place by the Imperial Guard, to his final position on the plateau of Bussy, between Brye and Sombreffe, where he arrived about 9.30 P. M.[30] It has been considered singular, that when Lobau arrived at Fleurus, say, about 7.30 P. M.,[31] he should have been directed on Ligny, apparently to support the movement of the Guard; whereas if he had been instructed to move on Brye by passing around St. Amand and Wagnelée it would seem that he might have struck the defeated Prussians in flank and rear, and accomplished substantially what Napoleon expected from Ney. But the withdrawal of the 1st Corps could only be explained by the supposition that Ney had encountered the English in considerable force; and under these circumstances Napoleon may have deemed it wiser to retain the 6th Corps as a reserve for the whole army.[32]

The battle of Ligny was a great victory, although it was not a decisive victory. Napoleon had diminished by one-third the strength of his opponent's army, and had also driven him from the field. He had certainly achieved a great success. But the advantage obtained was not all that he had a right to expect. Had it not been for the appearance of d'Erlon's Corps in the neighborhood of St. Amand, the attack by the Guard would have been made at half-past five o'clock, when there would have been sufficient daylight left to have made it possible to follow up the victory. On such a result as would have been

---

[30] Charras, vol. 1, p. 178.

[31] Charras (vol. 1, p. 184) thinks it was not later than 6.30 P. M. when the 6th Corps reached Fleurus.

[32] Charras (vol. 1, pp. 184, 185) severely criticises this decision.

obtained in this event Napoleon had a right to calculate, and that he did not obtain such a result was in no way his fault.[33] For the purpose therefore, of estimating the adequacy of the Emperor's measures to the task before him, and the danger which Marshal Blücher ran when he accepted battle, we should consider what would have been the result, if the attack of the Guard had been made two hours earlier than it was made, and there had been two hours of daylight in which to complete the defeat and to pursue the enemy.

As for the coöperation of Ney, that is a different matter. Napoleon could not know what resistance Ney might encounter; hence he could not calculate on his overcoming that resistance and sending a reinforcement to the main army, — he could only hope that Ney would be able to do this. If Ney should be able to keep off the English, all that Napoleon had a right to calculate on would be effected. Whether Ney could have accomplished more than he did accomplish will be considered in another place.

Owing, then, to the postponement of the attack on the Prussian centre caused by the unexpected apparition of a large body of troops (the 1st Corps), in a quarter where it threatened the French left, the victory of Ligny was by no means so complete as it otherwise would have been. Darkness came on before the Prussians, retiring from St. Amand and the neighboring hamlets, could be vigorously pressed. Nevertheless, the victory of Ligny had disposed of Blücher for thirty-six hours, at the very least. It gave Napoleon an opportunity of attacking Wellington the next day without danger of interference from the Prussians. And as this success had been achieved with no loss at all on the part of the 1st and 6th Corps and with a trifling loss on the part of the Guard, Napoleon

---

[33]Unless he erred in arresting the attack of the Guard on the appearance of the strange corps. See *post*, p. 174, note 8.

was in excellent condition to take advantage of the opportunity thus presented. That is to say, the decision of Marshal Blücher to accept battle when he had collected only three-fourths of his army, and the inability of the Duke of Wellington to render him any assistance, had produced this result at the close of the second day of the campaign, — that one of the allied armies had been badly beaten, and that Napoleon was perfectly free to attack the other the next day with superior forces, most of which consisted of fresh troops.

NOTES TO CHAPTER XI.

1. NAPOLEON has been often blamed because he did not begin the battle of Ligny till between two and three o'clock in the afternoon. We have spoken of this criticism before, and recur to it now merely to repeat that the greater part of this delay may (in all probability) be accounted for by his wish that his own advance-movement should be contemporaneous with that of the left wing, one-half of which was far in the rear. There was probably also an unusual amount of time spent in examining the position of the enemy.

Clausewitz[1] is undoubtedly right in saying that

"If the actual tactical shock of battle could have been arranged to take place in the morning of the 16th, it would have been an enormous mistake in Napoleon to have delayed it, for Blücher was collecting his troops at that time, and, as the whole force of the Prussians [including Bülow's Corps, which for anything Napoleon knew to the contrary, might arrive during the day] was far superior to the 75,000 men which he could use against it, nothing was so important as to offer battle before it was all got together."

It is also true,[2] that, had Napoleon advanced early in the morning with the main body of his army, leaving Ney to push forward with the left wing as soon as he could, he would have been able to interrupt the formation of the Prussian line of battle, and would not have been in the

---

[1] Clausewitz, ch. 25, p. 53.
[2] *Cf.* Charras, vol. 1, pp. 182, 183,

least interfered with by the Anglo-Dutch army. But Napoleon, although it is plain from his letters to Grouchy and Ney that he did not expect to find either the Prussians or the English in great force, preferred on the whole to make his own advance coincide in point of time with that of Marshal Ney. He could not estimate with any certainty the number of troops which Blücher might have on the heights of Ligny or within call; he could not know how large a part of his army Wellington had been able to collect. Hence he decided to defer his own movement until Ney was ready, or, at least, ought to have been ready, with all the troops which had been assigned to him, to protect the left flank of the main army from all danger of an attack by the Anglo-Dutch forces.

The question is one on which different opinions will always exist. The course adopted by Napoleon was unquestionably the one most in accordance with the principles of war. Whether a chance of success justifies a departure from the practice of those principles, or whether such a departure is warranted only in cases of emergency, is the real question. We have no room to discuss it further here.

2. Napoleon's plan of battle at Ligny has been severely criticised. Clausewitz,[3] Rogniat,[4] Marshal Davout,[5] are especially pronounced in their opinion that Napoleon should have manœuvred so as to turn the Prussian right, and not to pierce their centre. The question is thus stated by Rogniat:

"We arrived upon their right flank; reason counselled us to attack this wing; in this way we should have avoided in part the defiles of the brook; we should have approached our own left wing, which was fighting at Quatre Bras, so that both armies could have helped each other, and finally we should have thrown the Prussians far from the English, in forcing them to retire on Namur."

---

[3]Clausewitz, ch. 34.
[4]Cons. sur l'Art de la Guerre, p. 339, cited in Corresp., vol. 31, p. 472.
[5]Davout, p. 545.

To this Napoleon[6] replied from St. Helena:

"The question in this battle was not that of separating the English from the Prussians; we knew that the English could not be ready to act till the next day; but here the point was to hinder that part of the IIId Corps of Blücher which had not joined him by 11 A. M., and which came by way of Namur, and also the IVth Corps, which came from Liége by way of Gembloux, from uniting [with the Ist and IId Corps] on the field of battle. In cutting the enemy's line at Ligny, his whole right wing at St. Amand was turned and compromised; while by simply becoming masters of St. Amand, we should have accomplished nothing."

In other words, Napoleon defends his plan of battle by showing that it aimed at a decisive tactical success; that its accomplishment would practically have destroyed half of the Prussian army; which an attack upon the exposed right wing would not have effected. He contends that the Prussians being, as they certainly were, on this day, completely separated from the English, the best thing he could possibly do was to take advantage of their faulty formation, and cut off and destroy the two exposed corps. This he calculated he could effect with the troops he had in hand. Then he undoubtedly hoped that he would get assistance from Ney in this operation.[7] The order to Ney at 2 P. M. shows this beyond a question; and this order was reiterated at a quarter-past three. Napoleon said to Gérard during the battle,[8] "It is possible that in three hours the issue of the war may be decided. If Ney executes his orders well, not a cannon in the Prussian army can escape capture. That army is taken *en flagrant délit*." This last expression occurs also in the 3.15 P. M. order. The possibility of Ney's sending a force down the Quatre-Bras-Namur turnpike to take

---

[6]Corresp., vol. 31, p. 472.

[7]Clausewitz (ch. 34, pp. 81 *et seq.*) points out that Ney's coöperation could not have formed an essential part of Napoleon's plan of battle, for Napoleon "could not know whether Ney would be able to spare him a single man."

[8]Corresp., vol. 31, p. 206.

the exposed Prussian right wing in rear, was therefore an additional reason for inclining him to make his main attack at Ligny, and thereby isolate this wing, with the hope of surrounding and destroying it. That he had no right to count on Ney's coöperation is certainly true, as has been stated above; but then Napoleon believed that he could carry out his plan without Ney's coöperation, and that if Ney should assist him, his success would be overwhelming.

To the reasons advanced by Rogniat for making the main attack upon the right flank of the Prussians, Marshal Davout adds another:— [9]

"He ought not to have left the Prussian army between himself and Marshal Ney; because, in that case, if he should beat the Prussians, he would force them to retire in the direction of the English."

To the same effect Clausewitz [10] asks, "whether Bonaparte ought to have arranged his attack so as to drive Blücher towards Wellington, or so as to push him away from him,"—implying that the result of the battle as fought by Napoleon had the former effect.

"If," says Clausewitz, "Bonaparte had attacked St. Amand with his right wing, Wagnelée with his left, and had advanced with a third column against the road from Brussels,[11] the Prussians, if they lost the battle, would have been forced to retreat along the Roman road, that is, towards the Meuse, and a union with Wellington in the days immediately following the battle would have been very uncertain, perhaps impossible."

We can have no hesitation in admitting that if the Prussians had been driven in the direction of the Meuse as the result of the battle, they could not have afforded aid to the English on the 18th of June. But we can hardly believe that if Napoleon had destroyed their 1st

---

[9] Davout, p. 545.

[10] Clausewitz, ch. 34, p. 83.

[11] It is not quite clear in which direction this column was to advance.

and IId Corps, which he expected would be the result of his plan of battle, the Prussians could possibly have afforded any further assistance to the English. Still, while the decision of the Prussian generals after the battle to maintain their communication with the Duke of Wellington, and to come to his assistance at Waterloo with their whole army, was not arrived at merely or chiefly because the two corps which had been beaten at Ligny were able to fall back in a northerly direction instead of in an easterly direction, in retiring from the field of battle,[12] it is certainly true that this fact did make the task easier of accomplishment; it saved time, also. At the same time, it did not affect in any way the risk involved in the operation,—that of renouncing for the time being their line of supplies.

3. We have seen that Napoleon believed that Ney's intervention, which, as we have seen, might have occurred at the moment when the Prussian centre was being pierced, would have gained him a great victory. But Clausewitz[13] asks: "Why was it inevitable that 10,000 men in the rear of the strong Prussian army of 80,000 men, in an open country, where one can see on all sides, should bring about its complete overthrow?" In other words, Napoleon was not warranted (so Clausewitz contends) in expecting such a decisive success, even if Ney should send 10,000 men down the Namur road.

But Clausewitz has not in his question, above quoted, put the case quite fairly. The question which Napoleon considered was this:—What would in all probability be the effect upon two Prussian corps, numbering at the commencement of the action not over 63,000 men, attacked vigorously for three or four hours, subjected

---

[12]Maurice, pp. 350, 351: July, 1890. Maurice thinks that the beaten troops must have crossed the turnpike, even if they were intending to retreat towards the Rhine.

[13]Clausewitz, ch. 31, p. 66.

during that time to a most destructive fire of artillery, reduced by casualties to a force not greatly exceeding 50,000 men, assailed in front by over 20,000 fresh troops in addition to their opponents of the last few hours, forced to make a precipitate retreat by having their connection with the rest of their army broken, — what would be the effect upon them at this moment of an unexpected and vigorous attack in rear of 10,000 fresh troops? Napoleon thought and said, that, in his judgment, the result would be the total rout of the two corps, the capture of all their guns and perhaps half of their men. It is probable that he was right in his opinion.

4. But how far was Napoleon warranted in expecting aid from Ney?

As to Ney's whereabouts at the time when the 2 P. M. order should reach him, say, at 5 P. M., we have spoken before,[14] and have shown that, long before that hour, certainly as early as 4 P. M., the whole of the 2d Corps and the greater part of the 1st Corps ought to have arrived at Quatre Bras. In fact, it will be remembered that had Reille obeyed at once Ney's order to him he would have arrived at Quatre Bras at noon; and there was nothing to prevent d'Erlon following promptly on his traces. Napoleon, it is true, as we learn from his own narrative, had heard of this vexatious delay, caused by Reille, — which he naturally but erroneously attributed to Reille's superior, Ney,—but he still seemed to think it possible that Ney could be at Quatre Bras at noon, notwithstanding. This, to be sure, was absolutely out of Ney's power, as we have seen; but there was no reason whatever why Ney should not have had long before 5 P. M. his whole command well in hand, at or in front of Quatre Bras. Napoleon was perfectly justified in assuming this to be the case.

But though Ney might well be at Quatre Bras with

---

[14] *Ante*, p. 133.

his whole force, he might yet be entirely unable to comply with the Emperor's order to detach a force to attack the Prussians in rear.

Clausewitz [15] points out that Ney with his 40,000 men could easily encounter 50,000 to 60,000 English and Dutch. This is certainly true. It may be added that the last despatch [15] sent to Ney informed him that an officer of lancers had just informed the Emperor that large masses of the enemy were to be seen near Quatre Bras. This information was incorrect, as a matter of fact, yet it was believed to be true at the time the despatch was written. Of course the truth may have been ascertained before the 2 P. M. order was sent to Ney; but we do not know this for a fact. There was certainly no reason why Napoleon should have felt certain that Ney would find it possible to send troops to his assistance; it all depended upon the forwardness of the concentration of the Duke of Wellington's army; and as to this Napoleon could but guess,—he had no information at all.

5. If Napoleon, then, could not rely with any certainty on Ney's assistance, was he justified in adopting a plan of battle, to the full success of which Ney's coöperation was essential? Would it not have been wiser for him to have adopted the plan recommended by Rogniat, Davout and Clausewitz, and to have thrown his whole force on the exposed right wing of the Prussians?

This question cannot be properly answered without a careful examination of the tactical conditions, and this no one of Napoleon's critics has attempted with any detail. We will leave the matter, therefore, with this single observation. Napoleon, when he had completed his examination of the Prussian position, saw that there were open to him two plans of attack, each giving excellent

---

[15] Clausewitz, ch. 31, p. 65.
[16] Doc. Inéd., IX, p. 31; App. C, xxii; *post*, p. 381.

promise of success. He chose the one which in his judgment offered the greater chance of success, independent of Ney's coöperation, and promised a decisive success if Ney's coöperation could be secured. As it was, without Ney's assistance, and in spite of an unfortunate accident which caused an injurious delay in the final attack, he gained a great victory. It hardly seems worth our while to speculate on what the results would have been if he had adopted the other plan.

6. Why did not Napoleon order d'Erlon's Corps to remain and take part in the action? For not doing this he has been most severely criticised by Charras [16] and others. But Napoleon must have supposed that d'Erlon had come upon the field under orders from Marshal Ney expressly to remain and take part in the action. Why, then, should he send him any orders? Jomini, indeed, says [17] that Napoleon should have sent d'Erlon an order directing him on Brye. We can see now that this would have been wise; but it might well have appeared unnecessary at the time, inasmuch as the order of 2 P.M. by implication directs Ney's troops on Brye. It must also be remembered that at this moment Napoleon had all he could attend to in organizing the decisive movement on Ligny.

If any other explanation than the above be needed, it has been furnished by Clausewitz.[18] He says that the lateness of the hour probably prevented Napoleon from directing personally the employment of the 1st Corps.

"Napoleon seems to have received information of the approach of this corps somewhere in the neighborhood of half-past five; it took till seven before the news that it was d'Erlon was brought him; it would have taken an hour before d'Erlon could have received the order, and another hour would have passed before he could have

---

[16] Charras, vol. 1, pp. 170, 171, 183, 184.

[17] Jomini, p. 138.

[18] Clausewitz, ch. 34, p. 84.

[CHAP. II.] THE BATTLE OF LIGNY.—NOTES. 171

appeared in the neighborhood of Brye," *i. e.*, in obedience to such an order.

The inference is that Napoleon may well have thought it better to let d'Erlon proceed in obedience to the orders under which he was acting when he came upon the field.

7. We may fairly say that Napoleon fought few battles in his whole career more carefully and more skilfully than the battle of Ligny. The difference between a brave and zealous general of ordinary capacity and a master in the art was well illustrated on this field. Clausewitz's remarks on this battle are very clear and instructive. We give them in full,—premising that the figures vary more or less from those which we have adopted.

[19] "If we get a picture of the whole battle, it is like all modern battles, a slow destruction of the opposing forces in the first line, where they touch each other, in a fire lasting many hours, subjected to only slight oscillations, till, at last, one part obtains a clear superiority in reserves, *i. e.*, in fresh bodies, and then with these gives the deciding blow to the already wavering forces of the enemy.

"Bonaparte advances with about 75,000 men[20] against Blücher, whose three united corps form a force of 78,000 men,[21] that is of equal strength.

"With about 30,000 men he combats, from 3 o'clock till 8, the two chief points of Blücher's position, St. Amand and Ligny. He employs some 6,000 men to occupy the IIId Prussian army corps, and with 33,000 he remains far behind the fighting line, quietly in reserve. Of these he employs 6,000 men finally to sustain the battle at St. Amand.

"As early as 6 o'clock he determines to give the deciding blow at Ligny with the Guard: at that moment he receives the information that a considerable corps has appeared on his left flank, about one hour's march distant. Bonaparte stops his movement, for it might be a corps coming from the enemy at Brussels. The fact is, it was

---

[19] Clausewitz, ch. 32, pp. 73 *et seq.*

[20] This includes the 6th Corps.

[21] Charras makes the Prussian army about 87,000 strong.

d'Erlon who was marching, it is not yet known for what cause, from Frasnes against St. Amand. A troop of cavalry is sent in haste to reconnoitre this corps, but nearly two hours go by before the news comes back that it is the 1st French army corps. On this account the attack on Ligny does not take place till 8 o'clock.

"Even this blow Bonaparte does not give with the whole mass of his reserves, but only with about half of them, that is, with the Guard; the 6th Corps remains behind as a reserve.

"Blücher has in the beginning of the battle employed the Ist army corps of 27,000 men in the positions of Ligny and St. Amand, and the IIId, of 22,000 men, in that extending from Sombreffe to Balâtre, and has kept back only the IId, with 29,000 men, as a reserve. It is true that the IIId army corps could have been concentrated, since the enemy did not attack it in earnest, and it may have been looked upon as a reserve. Blücher, it is true, counted still on Bülow's arrival; but it did not take place, and so the situation of the Prussian reserves remained always unfavorable. The IId army corps, that is, the reserves, were gradually, as we have seen, employed to sustain the battle. Nothing therefore remained to decide the battle even if the state of the battle had remained perfectly balanced, or even had turned out favorably for us.

"As the day ended, the situation of the opposing forces was somewhat as follows: Blücher had used up in the villages 38,000 infantry, who had suffered considerably, had in great part expended their ammunition, and must be looked upon as useless, in which there was not much more force. 6,000 infantry were stationed behind the villages, scattered in single battalions which had however not yet fought. The rest of the 56,000 men of the Ist and IId army corps were cavalry and artillery, of which only a small part was fresh.

"If the IIId army corps had been collected, or if it had been sufficiently provided for, it would have been a reserve of about 18,000 men; it could therefore have been said that Blücher had still 24,000 men in reserve.

"Bonaparte, although originally some few thousand men weaker than Blücher, had now, however, several thousand more fresh troops than that general: the cause of this was his keeping back more men, a greater economy of forces in the firing.

"This small [22] superiority of reserves would naturally not have

---

[22] Unless we include the IIId Corps among the Prussian reserves, the French superiority in reserves was very large; and Blücher, as Clausewitz goes on to state, did not have the IIId Corps at his disposal.

decided much, but it must nevertheless be looked on as the first cause of the victory.

"The second reason was the unequal result which the firing had up to that time produced.

"It is true that when Bonaparte advanced against Ligny we still occupied part of this village, but we had then lost the rest; it is true that we still occupied a position between Wagnelée and St. Amand, but here, too, we had lost villages and ground; the engagement had therefore turned out everywhere a little to our disadvantage, and in such a case the preparations for the deciding blow are already made.

"The third and most important reason was, however, without doubt, the fact that Blücher did not have at his disposal the troops which had not yet fought, namely, the IIId Corps. It is true that the XIIth brigade was very near him, but that was too little: the IXth was also not far away; but of this, as well as of the whole of Thielemann's Corps, there had been no thought; and the IIId Corps, therefore, as regards a decisive blow to be given by it, was as good as out of reach and could be used only for the retreat. Perhaps and very probably, this scattered disposition of Thielemann is to be looked upon as on the whole an actual advantage. If the IIId Corps had been at hand, it would have been employed also, without increasing the chances for a successful result, which, considering the turn which the whole affair had taken, could have been secured only by a decided superiority, such, in fact, as the arrival of Bülow's Corps would have procured. And if the IIId Corps had been used, the loss in battle would probably have been greater by 10,000 men."

We cannot leave this subject without calling attention to a remark[23] of Marshal Davout's in his criticism of the Emperor's conduct of this campaign. He speaks of him in connection with this battle as

"The Napoleon of the Moskowa, who, to make use of a vulgar expression, takes the bull by the horns; this was the reason why this battle was so bloody and so hotly fought, etc."

How much justification there is for this remark appears from Clausewitz's review of Napoleon's tactics, which we have cited above. But Davout had a case to

---

[23]Davout, p. 547.

make out, apparently, and he desired to score a point at every stage of his criticism; an extremely common temptation, by the way, to which very many critics yield. As for the losses suffered by the French to which Davout refers, it must be remembered that Napoleon would have brought the action to a close two hours sooner, had it not been for the unexpected apparition of d'Erlon's Corps; and that a good part of the French loss was suffered in those two hours. The same cause also operated to render the victory much less decisive than it otherwise would have been, as darkness came on before anything like pursuit could be attempted. Any fair criticism, therefore, of Napoleon's conduct of the battle of Ligny ought to proceed on the supposition that this unlucky incident, for which a superserviceable staff-officer was solely responsible, had not occurred. On this supposition, then, the Prussian centre at Ligny would have been broken between 6 and 7 P. M., the losses of the French would have been much less, and their victory would necessarily have been much more complete.

8. The wisdom of Napoleon's course in arresting the attack on the Prussian centre when the news of the appearance of a strange corps which might possibly consist of hostile troops was brought to him, has perhaps not received the attention it deserves. When Napoleon decided to wait till he should learn what this body of troops might be, he was all ready to give the finishing blow to the Prussian army. He was pretty certain to break up a large part of that army. If the unknown corps should turn out to have come from Ney, it was certainly in a position where it could play a most important part in the attack. If, on the other hand, it should turn out to have come from Wellington, Napoleon, provided only that he should have time enough to complete his contemplated stroke against Blücher, would probably be in a much better situation to deal with his antagonists than he could otherwise hope to occupy. It would seem, there-

fore, as if it was by no means clear that Napoleon took the wisest course when he deferred the main attack on the Prussians on the appearance of d'Erlon's Corps.

9. It is not easy to see why Napoleon, certainly when he found that he would have to fight a battle at Ligny, should not have ordered the 6th Corps up to Fleurus at once, so that he might have it close at hand in case he needed it. The extreme importance of inflicting, if possible, a crushing defeat on the Prussians was so clearly seen by him, as his orders to Ney on the afternoon of the 16th and morning of the 17th abundantly show, that we cannot understand why he should not have availed himself of the aid of Lobau's command. Lobau, even if he were not sent for until 11 A.M., could have been at Fleurus at or before 4 P.M.; and had he then been directed to march in rear of the troops of Vandamme and Girard which were fighting at and near St. Amand, he could have fallen upon the Prussian right and rear near Brye at or about half-past five o'clock, which was the moment when Napoleon was preparing for the decisive stroke at Ligny. Lobau could undoubtedly have accomplished all that Napoleon expected from Ney. And the coöperation of Lobau could have been arranged for without any chance of failure, while that of Ney was necessarily dependent on the situation in which he might find himself at Quatre Bras.

CHAPTER XII.

THE BATTLE OF QUATRE BRAS.

MARSHAL NEY, as we have seen, took no steps what ever, on his return to Gosselies from his midnight interview with the Emperor, to get his command in readiness for the work of the coming day. Frasnes, in any event, he must have known, would have to be occupied in force, whether an advance from that place to Quatre Bras should be decided on or not.[1] Yet, instead of getting the divisions of Foy and Jerome up to Frasnes at once, where Bachelu and Piré already were, and supplying their place at Gosselies by the divisions of the 1st Corps, one of which, we know (Durutte's), had bivouacked between Jumet and Gosselies, he suffered them to remain at Gosselies; and, so far as appears, sent officers to hurry up d'Erlon only after he had ordered him to Frasnes (*ante*, p. 119), that is, after 11 A. M. Then there was a delay of an hour and three-quarters, for which Ney was not directly responsible, which was caused by Reille,[2] who, instead of obeying Ney's order to march promptly from Gosselies to the front on receipt of any orders of movement from the headquarters of the army, delayed doing so until he had informed Ney, who was at Frasnes, that he had heard from Girard that the Prussians were concentrating near St. Amand, and had thereupon received fresh orders. But this delay could never have occurred had Reille been at

---

[1] *Cf.* Jomini, p. 221.

[2] Jomini, p. 226, defends Reille's course. We shall discuss this question in the Notes to this chapter.

Frasnes himself, to which place he ought to have been ordered by Ney hours before.

It is, therefore, perfectly correct to say, that if Reille's two divisions at Gosselies had been, early in the morning, ordered to Frasnes, where Bachelu and Piré had been since the previous evening, Marshal Ney could have commenced the battle of Quatre Bras with all the 2d Corps, except Girard's division, which was with the main army, at eleven o'clock, the hour when he received his orders from Soult and his letter from the Emperor. Or, if he had thought best to defer the attack until he should have communicated to the Emperor the information as to the concentration of the Prussian army near St. Amand conveyed by Girard,[3] he would have been able to obey his orders, whatever they were, the moment his messenger returned. There was also no reason why d'Erlon should not have been likewise ordered up from Gosselies to Frasnes to support Reille, certainly with Durutte's division, leaving the other divisions to come along as fast as they could. And it is not going too far to say that the measures above suggested were simply those which common sense would dictate, to an officer in Ney's position.[4]

However, as a matter of fact, Ney did not take these measures, nor did he, even on the receipt of his orders, which, as we have seen, peremptorily directed him to assemble the 1st and 2d Corps and Kellermann's two divisions of cavalry, and with this force to carry Quatre Bras, proceed to comply with them. He ordered d'Erlon to halt at Frasnes; he ordered Kellermann[5] to station

---

[3] *Cf.* Jomini, pp. 221, 226.

[4] La Tour d'Auvergne, pp. 91, 92, 145; Muquardt, pp. 145, 146, 149, n. Charras, though discussing Ney's conduct at considerable length (vol. 2, pp. 236 *et seq.*), does not touch upon this part of it.

[5] Kellermann, Charras says, vol. 1, p. 188, had at 10.30 A. M. passed Gosselies. His two divisions were, therefore, long before 2 P. M., at Frasnes and Liberchies.

one division at Frasnes and one at Liberchies; and he assailed the enemy's position at Quatre Bras about 2 P. M. with the infantry divisions of Bachelu and Foy, and the cavalry division of Piré. It was not until nearly 3 o'clock[6] that the division of Jerome[7] arrived, and took its place in the line of battle. With the 2d Corps alone, then, did Marshal Ney attempt the task which he had been directed to undertake with all the troops which had been assigned to him. The 1st Corps and the cavalry he ordered to stay behind to protect his flanks and line of retreat.

When such are the preparations, nothing but extraordinary luck can give success in battle; and at first it seemed as if this luck was in store for Marshal Ney. When he began the action, Perponcher's Dutch-Belgian division constituted the sole force of the enemy at Quatre Bras; and Wellington not having yet returned from Brye, where he had been to see Blücher, the Prince of Orange, a gallant young officer, but possessing no remarkable abilities, was in command. Ney's two divisions gave him a slight superiority in infantry, which was augmented by the arrival of the third, and his soldiers were much the better fighters. He easily gained ground, and success seemed assured.

The Duke of Wellington reached the field about half-past two; and of course assumed control. He now had occasion to see how far the statements of the "Disposition" were from the actual facts; he found himself obliged to sustain a vigorous and well-conducted attack by superior forces, as best he might. Fortunately, about 3.30 P. M.,[8] Picton's British division arrived, followed immediately by the Duke of Brunswick's Corps, and Ney

---

[6] "*Vers 3 heures.*" Reille's statement, Doc. Inéd, p. 59.

[7] Or that of Guilleminot, as Charras prefers to call it. Charras, vol. 1, pp. 195, 196, n.

[8] Gomm, p. 353; Waterloo Letters. p., 23.

[CHAP. 12.] THE BATTLE OF QUATRE BRAS. 179

found himself slightly outnumbered.[9] Nevertheless, the quality of his troops, both officers and men, was so good, and his superiority to his antagonists in cavalry and artillery was so great, that he continued the fight with the expectation of success and with the chances in his favor.[10] But no efforts of his could overcome the steadiness and courage of the British infantry. The Dutch-Belgians retired after a couple of hours' fighting; the Brunswickers were broken, and the Duke of Brunswick was killed; but the British and Hanoverian troops, though outmatched at this stage of the action, stubbornly maintained the fight.

At five or soon after, two brigades of Alten's 3d British division arrived, and gave Wellington an equality, perhaps even a slight superiority in force. Ney, on the other hand, had not been reinforced either by d'Erlon or by Kellermann's two divisions of cavalry, all which troops had been placed at his disposal by the Emperor, and all which he had been, by the last order which he had received from Marshal Soult, expressly directed to employ in the movement upon Quatre Bras. That is to say, as late as five o'clock, when the battle had been in progress for three hours, Ney had not got his command together, had not, in fact, assembled one-half of it on the field. Where were these missing troops? (See Map 7.)

Take, first, the case of the 1st Corps. We have seen that the division of the 2d Corps, which was the last to arrive, arrived on the field of battle at or shortly before 3 P. M. Quatre Bras is distant from Frasnes about two miles and a half, and the field of battle, therefore, was about two miles beyond Frasnes. Since Jerome arrived on the field at 3 o'clock, he must have left Frasnes about or soon after 2 o'clock. If Durutte, who commanded the

---

[9] Siborne, vol. 1, p 108.
[10] We shall not attempt a tactical account of the battle. It is well described by Siborne and Charras, and there is much of value in other writers. But it is not worth while at this late day to go into detail.

leading division of the 1st Corps, had followed Jerome promptly from Jumet, which is not over a mile and a half to the south of Gosselies, he would have reached Frasnes before 3 o'clock. The other two divisions, which were ordered to Frasnes, should have arrived certainly in the course of the next hour and a half; so that by 4 or 4.30 P. M. Ney should have had the three divisions of the 1st Corps which he had ordered to Frasnes, ready for use there.

What actually happened was this. Durutte, who commanded the leading division of the 1st Corps, when in march from Jumet for Frasnes,[11] received orders from Ney to continue his march to Quatre Bras. But, as he was reaching Frasnes,[12] he was ordered by one of the Emperor's aides, on his own responsibility,[13] to direct his march towards Brye. This order Durutte obeyed, and, on arriving at Frasnes, turned the head of the column to the right. D'Erlon, who, had he been present, might have stopped this unauthorized proceeding, had unfortunately ridden in advance of his corps. The aide, who, according to d'Erlon's statement, was carrying a pencil note to Marshal Ney, came up with d'Erlon just beyond Frasnes, and told him what he had done. D'Erlon then rode back to join his command, sending his chief-of-staff to Marshal Ney to inform him what had happened. The 1st Corps then proceeded by way of Villers-Peruin towards St. Amand for possibly a couple of miles,[14] when it was seen by Vandamme, who between 5.30 and 6 o'clock reported to the Emperor the appearance of this unexpected body of troops.[15] The corps must have

---

[11] Doc. Inéd., p. 71, Durutte's statement.

[12] Drouet, p. 95.

[13] Ib., p. 95; Doc. Inéd., p. 65; d'Erlon's statement.

[14] As it would seem from the map. But the distance is a matter of conjecture only.

[15] Corresp., vol. 31, p. 207.

[CHAP. 12.] THE BATTLE OF QUATRE BRAS. 181

been seen, therefore, shortly after 5 o'clock. It must, therefore, have left the Charleroi road at Frasnes somewhere about 4.30 P.M. That is, the head of d'Erlon's column did not reach Frasnes till two hours and a half after the rear of the 2d Corps had left it. For, as we have seen, the last division of the 2d Corps, Jerome's, had passed through Frasnes by 2 o'clock.

This fact, that there was a march of two hours and a half between the two corps which constituted the principal part of Marshal Ney's command, has not received due attention.[16] It is impossible to account for it without laying a grave responsibility on the shoulders of both Marshal Ney and the Comte d'Erlon. There is no need of dwelling on the importance of the matter. That there was no sufficient effort to obey the orders of the Emperor,—vigorously and energetically to carry out the duty assigned to this wing of the army,—is too plain for argument. It needs hardly to be remarked, that if Durutte had followed closely on the traces of Jerome,— even if he had started from Jumet at the moment when Jerome started from Gosselies, and had not (as would have been natural and proper) moved up nearer to Gosselies before the order to march to Quatre Bras arrived,—he could not have been turned off the main road by the Emperor's staff-officer, for, long before half-past four o'clock, which was the hour when the staff-officer reached Frasnes, Durutte would have been fighting the English at Quatre Bras. One cannot avoid the conclusion that Marshal Ney's measures for getting his command together on the field of battle this day were singularly ineffective.

For d'Erlon's marching off towards St. Amand, Ney, of course, was in no wise responsible. When he heard of it, he sent him a peremptory order to return at once. For this he has been severely, and, in our opinion,

---

[16] But see "Napoléon à Waterloo," pp. 132 *et seq.*

unjustly blamed by many critics who have approached the question in the belief that d'Erlon was ordered to leave Ney's immediate command by the Emperor himself. But this was not so. Napoleon addressed no order to d'Erlon. The only orders which the Emperor sent on this afternoon of the 16th of June of which we have any knowledge were sent to Marshal Ney. Napoleon cannot be imagined to have sent a direct order to one of Ney's corps-commanders, for they, the Emperor must have supposed, were acting under the Marshal's immediate supervision. Napoleon himself always denied having sent any order to d'Erlon, and even Charras believes him to be correct in this statement. We shall recur to this subject later; suffice it to say here that we are inclined to think that it was the 2 P. M. order that was shown, or, of which more likely, the supposed purport or intent was stated, to Durutte.[17] The time at which Durutte's column was perceived heading for St. Amand indicates approximately when he must have left the turnpike at Frasnes; and this, as we shall hereafter see, was about the hour when the officer who carried the 2 P. M. order must have reached Frasnes.

D'Erlon, on receiving Ney's order to return, retraced his steps, leaving Durutte's division on his right in the neighborhood of Marbais, but he did not reach Frasnes till after 9 P. M. Thus the 1st Corps was of no use either to Ney or Napoleon that afternoon.

Take next the case of Kellermann's cavalry. The last order which Ney received was, as we have seen, perfectly explicit in terms.[18] It directed him to "unite the corps of Counts Reille and d'Erlon, and that of the Count of Valmy [Kellermann]," and stated that "with these forces he ought to be able to beat and destroy any force of the enemy which might present itself." Yet Ney ordered one of

---

[17] So, Hooper, pp. 136, 137.

[18] Doc. Inéd., IX, p. 31; App. C, xxii; *post*, p. 381.

THE BATTLE OF QUATRE BRAS. 183

Kellermann's divisions to halt at Frasnes and the other at Liberchies,—two miles, and two miles and a half, respectively, from the field of battle. It is not going too far to say that there is no excuse for such flat disobedience of orders. Cavalry, as respects the use to which they were put in those days, must be on the spot, ready to take advantage in an instant of a weak place in the enemy's line of battle. No one knew this better than Marshal Ney. The disposition he made of his cavalry was deliberately made, from the same reason which induced him to order the 1st Corps to take up position at Frasnes,—probably because he deemed it unwise and even dangerous that the left wing should be advanced so far in front of the main army; and he did not send for Kellermann till six o'clock, and then he only employed one brigade.[19]

To return now to the battle. The arrival of Alten's division gave Wellington the advantage, certainly in point of numerical force; still, the three infantry-divisions of the 2d Corps were superior in numbers to the two divisions of Picton and Alten; and the Dutch-Belgian and Brunswick troops had suffered so much that there was very little fight left in them. The cavalry of Piré was easily superior to that of the Brunswickers and Dutch-Belgians; none of the English cavalry had arrived; and the French were decidedly superior in artillery.

About 5 P. M.[20] the 2 o'clock order from Napoleon was received, but it was impossible for Ney, situated as he was, to execute it. At 6 P. M.[21] the 3.15 P. M. order arrived. Then, according to Charras,[22] Ney for the first time sent to Kellermann to bring up L'Heritier's division. The

---

[19] Charras, vol. 1, p. 206.

[20] Ib., p. 204, n.

[21] Ib., p. 206.

[22] Ib., p. 206. Charras says that Roussel's division remained where it was. He is probably correct. But see Siborne, vol. 1, p. 136, and Hooper, p. 127.

veteran of Marengo made a gallant and at first a successful charge[23] at the head of the cuirassier brigade of this division, but, finally, the galling fire from the British in the farm-enclosures near the intersection of the roads, received when the horses were blown and the impetus of the charge was exhausted, brought about a panic, and the troops retired in great disorder. Soon after this, which was the last offensive move made by the French, Cooke's division of the English Guards came up from Nivelles, and the French were forced to retire to Frasnes, which they did in good order.

At the close of the action, the Duke of Wellington had employed his 1st, 3d and 5th British divisions, the 2d Dutch-Belgian division, and the Brunswick contingent, numbering in all over 31,000[24] men; Marshal Ney, of the 43,000 men which had been entrusted to him and with which he was to "beat and destroy any enemy's force" in his front, had brought to the encounter less than 22,000 men. The casualties of the Anglo-Dutch army were nearly or quite 4,500,— those of the French over 4,000.

It cannot be seriously questioned that the result of the action would have been a victory for the French if the 1st Corps, d'Erlon's, had not been diverted from the turnpike.[25] The head of his column reached Frasnes, as we have seen, about half-past four o'clock, and the leading division could have been put in line before half-past five, that is, shortly after the arrival of Alten's division. Wellington at this moment was deeply involved in the

---

[23] Siborne is in error in supposing that there were two charges. Only one brigade was put in, the cuirassiers, and this was towards the end of the action.

[24] Siborne, vol. 1, p. 153. Charras, vol. 1, p. 210, rates Wellington's force as high as 37,000 men.

[25] Even Hooper admits (p. 137) that the "timely presence" of these troops would have "placed Wellington in an extremity of peril." *Cf.* Siborne, vol. 1, pp. 162, 163.

battle. He was expecting reinforcements hourly. He probably would not have thought of retiring. In fact his deficiency in cavalry and artillery would have made it a difficult matter to bring off his command in good order, and it is not likely that any of his troops save his (so called) British divisions could have sustained with firmness the strain of a retreat before an enemy fired with the success of the first battle of the campaign. The chances are that if d'Erlon's Corps had marched straight on to Quatre Bras, the result would have been a severe defeat for the Duke of Wellington. Distrust and even demoralization would almost certainly have appeared in most of his foreign contingents; and with only his English regiments and those of the King's German Legion he could not have mustered a sufficient force to justify him in accepting battle at Waterloo, even if he had been otherwise disposed to do so. In fact, one may safely conclude, that the battle of Waterloo would not have been fought had not d'Erlon's Corps been turned aside by the unauthorized act of the staff-officer. We may, and in fact we must, even go further. It is altogether improbable that if Blücher had found that Wellington was in no condition to receive battle on the 18th, he would have deviated from his natural course of action after losing the battle of Ligny; he would without doubt, in such case, have retired on either Liége or Namur. These consequences are assuredly not too remote. The immediate and palpable results of an action, or of a failure to act, are within the legitimate field of inquiry; in fact, unless this be permitted, history can yield no lessons at all; it is only when we carry our speculation into the region of remote results, or vary too much from the conditions which actually existed, that we are going beyond the line of legitimate inference and useful deduction. It may be added that it is, and in the nature of things must be, for each person to draw the line in each case.

If, now, we ask what would probably have happened if

Ney had collected his troops at Frasnes during the forenoon, in order that he might be able promptly to obey his orders as soon as they should be received, as we have above maintained he ought to have done, we are inclined to think that the simultaneous movement upon Quatre Bras between twelve and two o'clock of 40,000 men would have brought about the prompt retirement by the Prince of Orange[26] of Perponcher's division. It would probably have fallen back on Nivelles, where Chassé was assembling the other Dutch-Belgian division. Whether the Duke on his return from Brye could have effected a concerted attack on the French by combining a movement on the Brussels road by Picton and the Brunswickers with one on the Nivelles road by Perponcher and Alten, it is not easy to say. The advantage of position would have clearly been with the French, and in fact they would have been considerably superior in numbers. There would certainly have existed no reason why in this case Ney could not have sent 10,000 or even 20,000 men down the Namur road in compliance with the orders of 2 and 3.15 P. M."[27]

Neither of the above-described advantages was gained by Marshal Ney. By leaving the divisions of Jerome and Foy at Gosselies instead of bringing them up to Frasnes early in the morning,—by leaving that of Durutte at Jumet, and the other three of d'Erlon's divisions still further in rear until long after the last regiments of the 2d Corps had left Gosselies,—he rendered a prompt and bloodless occupation of Quatre Bras almost

---

[26] The Duke of Wellington did not get back from Brye, where he had gone to confer with Marshal Blücher, until half-past two o'clock.

[27] Jomini, however, says (p. 227) that all that could have been expected of Ney even in this case would have been to maintain his position. But he says this in a letter to Marshal Ney's son, and his statement cannot be taken seriously. The events of the day demonstrated that one corps would have been amply sufficient to hold the place, had it been once occupied by the French.

impossible. Exactly how far he was responsible for the gap between his two corps, we do not know. But we can certainly say that a diligent and experienced officer in Ney's place would have known to a half an hour just how long after the arrival of the last division of the 2d Corps, the van of the 1st Corps might be expected. The whole management of Marshal Ney on this day shows distrust of the Emperor's judgment, unwillingness to take the most obvious steps, finally, disobedience of orders. As the natural consequence of his wilfulness and perverseness he failed to reap the enormous successes which the Emperor's sagacity had placed within his power. All he did was to prevent Wellington from giving any aid to Blücher. This he certainly accomplished; and an important service it was. He also showed himself as he always did, a brave, resolute, capable officer on the field of battle. Probably he did as much as any one could have done with the force actually under his hand. But had he taken the necessary steps to get the large and powerful body of troops which Napoleon had entrusted to his care well in hand in due season, he could not have failed, so far as we can see, to achieve a striking success, which might very possibly have had a decisive effect on the fortunes of the war. If each of the two allied generals had been defeated at the outset of the campaign, the chances of Napoleon for final victory would have been greatly in his favor.

In regard to the conduct of this battle by the Duke of Wellington nothing new can be said. He has always received the credit which he certainly fully merited, of maintaining most skilfully and with great spirit and tenacity a fight in which he was outmatched until nearly the close of the day. He had been gravely misled by his chief-of-staff as to the situation of the various bodies which composed his army; and in fact it must be admitted that his own calculations were very far from being worthy of his reputation. Hence he ran the risk of encountering a largely superior force; and that he had actually to deal with only half of this force was due to no strategy of his. He found himself in a most perplexing and dangerous situation, in which he displayed undoubtedly great skill and courage, but for the successful result of the day he was largely indebted to the "fortune of war."[28]

---

[28] *Cf.* Chesney, p. 137.

NOTES TO CHAPTER XII.

1. CHARRAS' references to the orders to Marshal Ney as respects Kellermann's cavalry, are disingenuous and very misleading. They are evidently intended to throw the blame for the non-employment of this body of troops upon the shoulders of Napoleon.

It will be remembered that in his letter[1] to Ney, which the Emperor said might arrive a little before the formal order signed by Marshal Soult, the Emperor told Ney what his wishes were as to the disposition of his troops after he should have occupied Quatre Bras. One division was to be stationed two leagues in front of Quatre Bras, — six divisions around Quatre Bras, — and Kellermann's cavalry at the intersection of the Roman road with the Charleroi turnpike, so that the Emperor might recall it, if he desired so to do. In the same letter he tells Ney to be careful of Lefebvre-Desnouettes' division, which belonged to the Guard.

It seems plain enough that this letter must be taken in connection with Soult's definite order,[2] to which the letter refers, which ordered Ney to direct the 1st and 2d *corps d'armée* and the 3d corps of cavalry, — Kellermann's, — upon Quatre Bras, and there take up his position.

But the latest order[3] of Soult positively instructs Ney to unite the two corps of Counts Reille and d'Erlon and

---

[1] Doc. Inéd., X, p. 32; App. C, xviii; *post*, pp. 377, 378.

[2] Ib., VIII, p. 27; App. C, xxi; *post*, pp. 380, 381.

[3] Ib., IX, p. 31; App. xxii; *post*, p. 381. This refers to the prior order in distinct terms.

also that of the Count of Valmy, and says in so many words that with these forces he ought to be able "to beat and destroy" the enemy.

There is not either in the letter or in these orders a single word limiting the employment of Kellermann's cavalry to "a case of necessity." Yet this is what Charras states[4] was contained in Soult's order. He even says that Ney did not dare[5] to employ but one out of the four brigades of which Kellermann's Corps consisted,— meaning that he was so hampered by his orders.

Hooper[6] also says that Ney used Kellermann's cavalry "sparingly, in obedience to the instructions of Napoleon."

The orders speak for themselves. Ney was not only permitted to use Kellermann's Corps, but was positively directed to do so. It was only in his use of the cavalry of the Guard—the division of Lefebvre-Desnouettes[7]— that he was restricted.

2. Napoleon in his account of the campaign labored under a mistake as to the time when he gave Ney his orders on the 16th. He says it was in the night. This involved him in another mistake, namely, that the orders directed Ney "to push on at daybreak beyond Quatre Bras." It is true that he rendered it possible for the readers of his book to rectify these errors, for he says that Flahaut was the bearer of these orders, and he survived the campaign. Doubtless if the Emperor could have had access to him, these mistakes would have been rectified; as it is, they render much of what Napoleon says of no value. Then, Napoleon never learned the truth about the wanderings of d'Erlon's Corps; and this of course, invalidates his criticisms as to that matter.

---

[4]Charras, vol. 1, p. 205.

[5]Ib., p. 206.

[6]Hooper, p. 127.

[7]Even in regard to this division, Soult's order plainly implies that Ney might make use of it. Doc. Inéd., VIII, p. 28; App. C, xxi.; *post*, pp. 380, 381.

[CHAP. 12.] THE BATTLE OF QUATRE BRAS.—NOTES. 191

But in regard to the main point made in this chapter, the Emperor's opinion is given explicitly. He blames Ney[8] *for not having* "executed his orders and *marched on Quatre Bras with his* 43,000 *men.*" That Ney should concentrate his entire command was in reality, the burden of his orders.

That this neglect to keep his command together was in Napoleon's eyes Ney's principal fault in his conduct on the 16th, appears unmistakably from the following passages in Soult's despatch[9] to Ney of the next day:—

"The Emperor has seen with pain that you did not yesterday unite your divisions; they acted independently of each other; hence they experienced losses.

"If the corps of the Counts d'Erlon and Reille had been together, not an Englishman of the troops which attacked you would have escaped. If the Count d'Erlon had executed the movement upon St. Amand which the Emperor had ordered, the Prussian army would have been totally destroyed, and we should have taken perhaps 30,000 prisoners.

"The corps of Generals Gérard and Vandamme and the Imperial Guard have always been united: one exposes one's self to reverses when detachments are put in peril.

"The Emperor hopes and desires that your seven divisions of infantry and your cavalry shall be well united and organized, and that together they shall not occupy more than one league of ground, so that you may have them under your hand and may be able to employ them at need."

What Soult told Sir William Napier,[10] years afterwards, is without question the truth:—"Ney neglected his orders at Quatre Bras."

3. It may be worth while to correct a curious error into which Siborne has fallen in his anxiety to show that Ney was not ordered to seize Quatre Bras early in the morning. He[11] calls attention to the fact that the 2 P. M.

---

[8]Corresp., vol. 31, p. 209.
[9]Doc. Inéd., XVII, p. 46; App. C, xxvii; *post*, pp. 384, 385.
[10]Life of General Sir W. Napier, vol. 1, p. 505.
[11]Siborne, vol. 1, p. 146, n.

order to Ney was addressed on the back of the letter to the Marshal at Gosselies. "This circumstance," he says, "proves that Napoleon was under the impression that Ney had not at that time (two o'clock) commenced his attack, but was still at Gosselies." But this argument, if it is good for anything, shows that Napoleon supposed that Ney and, of course, the bulk of his command also, would be at Gosselies when the bearer of the letter arrived there, say at 3 o'clock, which is simply absurd. The fact is that, Ney having the previous night had his headquarters at Gosselies, all orders to him were naturally and properly sent there first.

4. Jomini,[12] in a letter to the Duke of Elchingen, suggests that Napoleon might well have left Reille's corps and Lefebvre-Desnouettes' cavalry at Frasnes to watch the enemy at Quatre Bras, and thrown d'Erlon's Corps and Kellermann's cavalry on the rear of the Prussians at Brye, a manœuvre which, he says, "could be executed from Frasnes as well as from Quatre Bras." Into the merits of this suggestion we do not propose to enter; there is certainly much to recommend it. But in a postscript General Jomini takes special pains to express his opinion that General Reille is not "deserving of the least censure" for having deferred putting his corps in motion from Gosselies for Frasnes, on the morning of the 16th, until he had communicated Girard's information to Marshal Ney.

"We must not forget that General Reille had just sent — nine o'clock — positive information of the presence of the entire Prussian army towards Ligny: he must have concluded from this that the left would be called upon to take part in the attack of this army, and that it would be unfortunate if, after such information, he took the Genappe [Quatre Bras] route when it would be necessary to turn to the right towards Brye. This reasoning was more than logical, it was based on the laws of *la grande tactique*."[13]

---

[12] Jomini, pp. 219, 221.
[13] Ib., p. 226.

[CHAP. 12.] THE BATTLE OF QUATRE BRAS.—NOTES. 193

In this passage Jomini seems to overlook what he has just before said about Frasnes. Even if the left should be called upon to take part in the attack of the Prussians instead of being concentrated for the attack of Quatre Bras, it would still be necessary for a large force to establish itself at Frasnes, in order to observe the enemy at Quatre Bras; to proceed then to Frasnes, with the two divisions of Foy and Jerome, from Gosselies, where he was when the Emperor's order reached him, was the right thing for Reille to do in any event. Jomini in fact suggests this very thing as in his judgment the correct course, viz.: to leave the 2d Corps at Frasnes and to throw the 1st Corps on Brye. This attempt, therefore, to justify Reille's delay in marching to Frasnes, fails.

5. Other theories than the one we have adopted as to the cause of the wanderings of d'Erlon's Corps have been broached. Thiers thinks that Napoleon sent d'Erlon a direct order; Charras[14] has combated this view in a careful examination of the evidence, and we agree with him. There is, however, considerable conflict of testimony. Lieutenant-Colonel de Baudus, who was on the staff of Marshal Soult in this campaign, in his "Études sur Napoléon,"[15] tells this story: —

"At the moment when the affair [the battle of Ligny] was at its height, Napoleon called me and said to me: 'I have sent an order to the Comte d'Erlon to direct his whole corps in the rear of the right of the Prussian army; go and carry to Marshal Ney a duplicate of this order, which ought to be communicated to him. You will tell him that, whatever may be the situation in which he finds himself, it is absolutely necessary that this disposition should be executed; that I do not attach any great importance to what is passing to-day on his wing; that the important affair is here, where I am, because I want to finish with the Prussian army. As for him, he must, if he cannot do better, confine himself to keeping the English army in

---

[14]Charras, vol. 2, pp. 242 *et seq.*

[15]Vol. 1, pp. 210 *et seq.* Paris: 1841.

check.'[16] When the Emperor had finished giving me his instructions, the major-general [Soult] recommended me in the most energetic terms to insist most forcibly on the Duke of Elchingen that, on his part, nothing should hinder the execution of the movement prescribed to the Comte d'Erlon."

Notwithstanding this circumstantial narrative, we do not believe that Napoleon sent d'Erlon a direct order. Napoleon had in all his communications with Ney placed d'Erlon under him; the letter written to Ney that morning by the Emperor said :—" The major-general has given the most precise instructions, so that there shall be no difficulty about obedience to your orders when you are detached from the main army; when I am present, the corps-commanders will take their orders from me." Now Napoleon must have supposed that d'Erlon would be with Ney at 5 P. M.

Baudus' book was published twenty-six years after the battle. His recollection of the fact that he was sent on such a mission was no doubt clear; very likely he remembered with approximate accuracy what Napoleon and Soult said to him; but he may easily have been mistaken as to the order itself. It would be very natural that an order to Ney directing him to send the 1st Corps to attack the Prussian right might be mistaken for an order to d'Erlon, who commanded the 1st Corps, to do this. And what to our mind settles the matter is, that if the order had really been one directed to d'Erlon, neither the Emperor nor Soult would have wasted their time in asking Baudus to ask Ney not to interfere with its execution. If, on the other hand, it was an order to Ney,

---

[16] This is exactly what was enjoined on Ney by the 3.15 P. M. order. It is to be noted that, while the 2 P. M. order expressly directed Ney to attack the English, and only after having vigorously pushed them, to turn back and operate against the Prussians, the 3.15 P. M. order directed him to manœuvre *at once*,—that is, without waiting until he should have driven the English,— so as to surround the Prussian right wing. This is precisely what Baudus says the Emperor and Soult desired him so strongly to urge upon Marshal Ney.

[CHAP. 12.] THE BATTLE OF QUATRE BRAS.—NOTES.   195

urging on him to detach a part of his command to take the Prussians in rear, such remarks as Napoleon and Soult made to Baudus were directly apposite, and were made, no doubt, in order that they might be repeated to Ney, so that he might enter more fully into the Emperor's view of the situation. Lastly, although no specific mention might be made in the written order of the troops which Ney was to detach, it is extremely probable that both Napoleon and Soult spoke of the 1st Corps in this connection, as it was of course known that d'Erlon was to come up in rear of Reille, who might very probably be actively engaged, and that d'Erlon's Corps, therefore, would probably be sent, if any was sent.

We have little doubt that Baudus carried the duplicate of the 3.15 P. M. order to Marshal Ney. Everything that he says about it points to this; the statement that the battle was at its height when the order was given to him would be true at a quarter-past three; the strong language of the Emperor and Soult as to the importance of persuading Ney to comply with their request has the same ring as the language of the order.[17] Baudus tells us that when he was nearing Quatre Bras he was nearly run down by Kellermann's cuirassiers, who were, as we have seen,[18] routed between 6 and 7 P. M.[19] Charras says that the 3.15 P. M. order[20] arrived at 6 o'clock.[21] This

---

[17] See note 16, on page 194.

[18] Charras, vol. 1, pp. 206-208.

[19] Heymès, Ney's aide-de-camp, says (Doc. Inéd., pp. 9, 10) that it was just when Kellermann's cuirassiers had been routed that Colonel Laurent arrived and told Marshal Ney that he had ordered d'Erlon to turn off the main road in the direction of St. Amand. Baudus came up a little later, evidently, as he met the cuirassiers some distance from the field of battle. But as Baudus saw nothing of the troops of the 1st Corps, we think Heymès must be mistaken, as to Laurent's having just turned off the head of the column to the right. If so, Baudus must have passed at least half the corps on the road.

[20] According to Gourgaud, p. 57, Colonel Forbin-Janson carried this order.

[21] Charras, vol. 1, p. 206.

duplicate of it, dated 3.30 P. M.[22] the transmission of which was delayed, as we have seen, by the verbal messages to Ney, may very possibly not have reached the Marshal till half-past six. Baudus found Ney in a state of great exasperation against the Emperor, who had, as he had been told, ordered the 1st Corps to march upon St. Amand without informing him of this change of plan. The fact that Baudus saw nothing of the 1st Corps on the road confirms our hypothesis that that corps had been turned off by the bearer of the 2 P. M. despatch.

In conclusion, we may say that the evidence as to this matter is not entirely satisfactory. D'Erlon says the order he saw was addressed to Marshal Ney. Reille says the same. D'Erlon says the order was brought by General Labedoyère; Heymès, by Colonel Laurent. Heymès says that Colonel Laurent, after turning the 1st Corps off the turnpike, informed Ney what he had done;[23] Baudus says that Ney told him[24] that he never received any advice of the sort at all, and that he only learned that the corps had gone off by sending to Frasnes for it, and there being no troops there. It is idle to seek to reconcile these minor contradictions. They are not important.

---

[22]Doc. Inéd., p. 42.

[23]Ib., pp. 9, 10.

[24]Baudus, vol. 1, p. 212.

CHAPTER XIII.

THE SEVENTEENTH OF JUNE: NAPOLEON.

NAPOLEON had, thus far, as we have seen, in the main, accomplished his programme. Things had turned out, so far as the enemy were concerned, very much as he had originally expected. He had found Blücher determined to fight; he had found Wellington wholly unprepared to assist his ally. He had encountered the Prussians, therefore, alone; and he had beaten them. He had, in the main, as we have said, done what he expected to do. It now only remained to complete the original plan marked out in the letters to Ney and Grouchy of the morning before; and, leaving the latter with the 3d and 4th Corps and plenty of cavalry to ascertain the direction in which the Prussians had retreated, to march himself at the head of the 6th Corps and the Guard to join Ney, and move promptly against the English. (See Map 8.)

There was no reason in the world for delay. As has been pointed out above, Napoleon had not been obliged to employ all his troops in obtaining the victory of Ligny. The troops which he intended to take with him were fresh, or substantially so. The 6th Corps had not fired a shot; the Guard, though it had lost perhaps a thousand men, had certainly done no very hard fighting, and it had been brilliantly successful. The cavalry, also, had suffered but little. Ney, too, had plenty of fresh troops. The 1st Corps, d'Erlon's, had not been engaged; nor had the light cavalry division of Lefebvre-Desnouettes; only one of the four brigades of Kellermann's heavy cavalry had been in action at Quatre Bras. Thus a formidable army, almost entirely composed of fresh troops, could be led at once against the Duke of Wellington's heterogeneous forces. The weather, in the morning of the 17th, was fine; the Prussians, wherever they had gone, were, at any rate, for the time being, out of the way; there was no reason, we repeat, why advantage should not have been promptly taken of the fortunate situation in which the victory of Ligny had temporarily placed the French,—why there should have been any hesitation whatever in dealing with the Anglo-Dutch army, separated, as it now was, from its ally.

But we may go farther than this. Fortunate as the situation of the French was on the morning after the battle of Ligny, there were grave reasons for deeming this advantage to be very brief in its duration. Napoleon had, indeed, won a victory over Blücher. But the tardiness of d'Erlon and the disobedience of Ney had prevented Napoleon from getting from his left wing the assistance on which he had counted; and he himself had not seen fit to modify his operations so as to conform to this different state of facts. He had not attacked the Prussians while they were taking position on the heights of Ligny, because at that early hour the forward movement of the main army could not have been covered by the advance of the whole of the left wing. He had not been able to win the crushing victory over the Prussians when concentrated which he would undoubtedly have won if Ney had obeyed his orders intelligently and boldly, and had been able, as he then would have been able, to send a large force down the Namur road to take the Prussians in rear. Lastly, Napoleon had not achieved the success on which he had a right to count without the aid of Ney, for, on the unexpected appearance of the 1st Corps, he had delayed the final stroke until it was too dark to take full advantage of it. Napoleon had not in the battle of Ligny, as he very well knew, destroyed the

Prussian army. He understood perfectly the difference between the victory he had actually won and the victory which he would have won had he received from Ney the assistance of d'Erlon's Corps, or even of 10,000 men.[1] Hence it is remarkable that he should not have exerted himself to use his incomplete success to the best advantage, and this required, of course, the utmost energy and activity on his part.

There was also, had he only known it, a magnificent opportunity before him on this morning of the 17th. For, owing to the carelessness of the Prussian staff, Wellington had not been promptly informed of the result of the battle of Ligny, and he was still at Quatre Bras, only six miles from Brye, where he could be assailed in front and flank. He had not yet succeeded in collecting his entire army. It was perfectly practicable to attack him in this condition before the Prussians could possibly reorganize their beaten forces, and come to his assistance. For such an attack Napoleon had ample means, and of the best quality, as we have just seen. Ney's movements could easily be coördinated with his own; Ney could attack the English in front, while the Emperor brought up the 6th Corps and the Guard over the Namur-Quatre-Bras turnpike directly upon their flank. The march from Brye could be begun at sunrise,—at 4 A. M.; Quatre Bras could be reached before 7 o'clock. Had Napoleon, then, acted with energy in accordance with his own plan, he would have stood a very good chance of crushing this portion of Wellington's army,—so far from its ally, so open to attack.[2] But, apart from this, this was not one of those cases where time is required to come to a decision; nothing was risked by marching against the English at once. And, as it hap-

---

[1] See his despatch to Ney, of the 17th, cited above; p. 191.
[2] Siborne, vol. 1, p. 255.

pened, fortune had put in Napoleon's way the opportunity of striking a decisive blow.

Napoleon allowed this opportunity to escape him. Up to this moment we have seen him as active, as sagacious, as energetic as ever. But it would certainly seem that on this morning of the 17th he was not up to the mark. He probably was greatly fatigued, and we need not wonder at it. From half-past three on the morning of the 12th, when he left Paris, to eleven o'clock at night of the 16th, when, having fought and won the battle of Ligny, he sought rest at Fleurus, he had been subjected to a tremendous strain. Neither Wellington nor Blücher had had anything like it. He had been on the move and at work, night and day. He had had to decide at the moment the most important questions, he had had to take the gravest responsibilities. There was a natural reaction. The Emperor yielded to the sense of fatigue. He put off the execution of the next part of his plan. He moreover neglected to ascertain the facts of the situation, and hence was unaware, until too late, of the great opportunity then presented to him. General Jomini considerately remarks: — [3] "Undoubtedly the Emperor had powerful motives for resigning himself to such inactivity; but these motives have never reached us."

Napoleon wasted most of the morning. He expected, he says, to hear from Ney what the result of his operations had been; but that officer, furious with the Emperor for having, as he supposed, withdrawn the 1st Corps without notice from his command,[4] vouchsafed no report to headquarters. Finally, about 8 A. M., General Flahaut, the Emperor's aide, who had carried the letter to Ney the previous morning and had remained with him during the day, returned to Napoleon and brought him the first information of the battle of Quatre Bras.

---

[3] Jomini, p. 148.

[4] See Ney's letter to the Duke of Otranto; Jones, 386.

He also brought word that Ney had received no news of the result of the battle of Ligny.[5] Thereupon Soult wrote a despatch[6] to Ney informing him that the Prussians had been "put to rout," and that Pajol was pursuing them on the roads to Namur and Liége. Ney was then told that the Emperor was going to Brye; that it did not seem possible for the English to do anything against him, Ney, but that if they should undertake anything, the Emperor would march directly upon them. Then the Emperor comments on the fact that Ney did not act on the preceding day with his entire force.[7] Lastly, Ney is ordered to take up position at Quatre Bras; but if that should not be possible, then he was at once to state the facts in detail, and the Emperor would immediately march on Quatre Bras himself, while Ney should assail the enemy in front. If, on the contrary, there should be only a rear-guard there, Ney was to attack it and take up position there. Ney was also directed to inform the Emperor of the exact situation of his divisions, and of all that was going on in his front.

That no move of importance was then under contemplation at headquarters appears from this sentence:—

"To-day will be needed to terminate this operation, to supply ammunition, bring in stragglers, and call in detachments. Give your orders accordingly; and see to it that all the wounded are cared for and transported to the rear; we hear complaints that the ambulances have not done their duty."

This despatch was probably written about 8 A. M.[8] It is clear from reading it that Napoleon presumed, as a matter of course, that Wellington had long before heard of the defeat of Blücher, and had fallen back towards Brussels, leaving only a rear-guard at Quatre Bras. Had

---

[5] See Charras' very apposite remarks on this: vol. 1, p. 234.

[6] Doc. Inéd., XVII, pp. 45, 47; App. C, xxvii.; *post* pp. 384, 385.

[7] See *ante*, p. 191.

[8] Charras, vol. 1, p. 235, n.

he known the truth,—which was, as we shall soon see, that the Duke did not move a man till 10 A. M.,—he would no doubt have attacked him at once. It is true that Napoleon's conjecture as to Wellington's movements was a very natural one. It is true, also, that he had a perfect right to expect to receive from the commander of his left wing an accurate and full account of the situation there; Ney ought, it is not necessary to say, to have prepared a report of the battle of Quatre Bras on the evening of the 16th, and sent it off to headquarters at once. Furthermore, he ought to have informed the Emperor on the morning of the 17th that the English were still at Quatre Bras in force. Napoleon's inactivity does not in the least excuse him. But Ney's neglect to make proper reports of the situation at Quatre Bras does not in any way justify Napoleon's delay in marching upon the English. The propriety of this step was not dependent on the accounts to be received from Marshal Ney. To unite the reserves to the left wing and move upon Wellington at the earliest possible moment was the thing to do, whatever might be the reports from Ney.

Marshal Soult seems to have been of no assistance to the Emperor on this morning. If he had been a competent and efficient chief-of-staff he would assuredly have had all needed information ready for the Emperor when the latter made his appearance in the morning. As it was, knowing nothing of what had happened at Quatre Bras till nearly eight o'clock, waiting till it should suit Ney to furnish him with the information requested in the 8 A. M. despatch, assuming that Wellington must have heard of the defeat of Blücher and fallen back in consequence, the Emperor amused himself with going over the field of battle, and talking politics to the generals.[9] He did not exert himself in the least to stimulate the energy

---

[9] La Tour d'Auvergne, p. 214. See also, pp. 208 and 233.

and activity of his subordinates; in fact, he yielded to that lassitude which is so apt to succeed unusual exertion. He deliberately postponed the execution of the next step in his campaign, notwithstanding that the incomplete result of his encounter with the Prussians rendered it all the more imperative that no time should be lost and no opportunity neglected.

During the forenoon, however, the troops intended to join Ney were ordered to Marbais on the turnpike,— Lobau[10] at ten o'clock,— the Guard and Milhaud's cuirassiers at eleven. At noon, it having been reported that the English were still at Quatre Bras, another order[11] was sent to Ney, directing him to attack the enemy there, and informing him that the Emperor was leading the troops now at Marbais to support his operations. Thus the execution of the plan of campaign marked out in the letters to Ney and Grouchy was at last resumed; the reserves under Napoleon marched to join the left wing under Ney; the right wing under Grouchy was assigned to take care of the defeated Prussians. Girard's division of the 2d Corps, which had suffered severely in the battle,— Girard himself having been mortally hurt,— was left on the field to take care of the wounded.

Napoleon had undoubtedly assumed that the Prussian army, if beaten, would retire on its base of operations, towards Namur and Liége. This assumption was strengthened by the circumstances of the battle of Ligny. He had not failed to note the strong force retained by Marshal Blücher to protect his communications with Namur as well as the road to Gembloux, by which the IVth Corps was expected to arrive. He was perfectly justified in inferring that if Blücher had established a new or secondary base at Wavre, for instance, or

---

[10] One division of the 6th Corps, that of Teste, was detached, and added to Grouchy's command.

[11] Doc. Inéd., XVI, p. 44; App. C, xxviii; *post*, pp. 385, 386.

Louvain, or if he had had any idea whatever of renouncing his line of communications, so as to be able to coöperate with the English in subsequent operations, he would without doubt have placed his left wing in a wholly different position, where he could have made some use of it in the battle.[12] The fact that Thielemann's Corps was placed where it could not be of any assistance to those of Zieten and Pirch I., seemed to indicate that reliance was placed upon the English for any help these corps might need, and corroborated the presumption that Blücher and Gneisenau were willing to take the risk of the defeat of a part of the Prussian army by accepting battle where support could only be furnished by their allies, and had no intention whatever of renouncing their base of operations, *via* Namur and Liége. Added to these considerations was the general presumption against such a dangerous and inconvenient course as a change of base must always be.[13]

It must also be remembered that the Prussians held the villages of Brye and Sombreffe till after midnight, so that there was no obstacle whatever to the troops of the two beaten corps retiring after the battle by the Quatre-Bras-Namur turnpike towards Namur. It may well be questioned whether there was any need for these troops to cross the pike at all; or whether any of them would have crossed it, had Blücher given orders for the whole army to retire on Namur.[14]

Hence it was assumed at the headquarters of the French army that it was in the direction of Namur that

---

[12] Maurice, p. 350; July, 1890: citing Clausewitz, ch. 33, p. 76. Gneisenau, vol. 4, p. 386.

[13] Maurice, pp. 350, 354: July, 1890.

[14] But see Maurice, pp. 350, 351: July, 1890. He thinks that the troops of the two beaten corps must at first have retreated northward,— that is, across the turnpike, in the direction of Wavre.

the Prussians had retreated.¹⁵ Soult, early in the morning, sent out Pajol on the Namur road with a division of his own corps, supported by a brigade from Exelmans' Corps, to ascertain the facts; and before 8 A. M. Pajol reported the capture of a battery and prisoners at Le Mazy on that road.¹⁶ It was on this information that Soult informed Ney that Pajol was pursuing the Prussians on the road to Namur.

It is nevertheless very strange that no reconnoissance should have been ordered in the direction of Tilly and Wavre.¹⁷ This may perhaps be partly due to the fact that the cavalry divisions belonging to the 3d and 4th Corps, upon which such duties would most naturally fall, were exhausted by their efforts of the day before, that the 6th Corps, which bivouacked nearest to Brye, had no cavalry division attached to it, and that the rest of the cavalry was on the right of the position. These facts may perhaps serve to account in a way for what cannot but be considered as an inexcusable neglect. There was plenty of cavalry with the army. Exelmans could have been sent out towards Wavre, as easily as Pajol towards Namur. Both routes were equally open to the enemy. It was certainly by no means impossible that Blücher should, in spite of his defeat, endeavor to keep up his communication with Wellington, especially considering

---

[15] This mistake could not have been made, as Ollech points out (p. 172) if the battle had been decided before nightfall.

[16] As a matter of fact, these troops were not a part of a column in retreat for Namur; but, of course, this could not be known at once. See Siborne, vol. 1, pp. 286, 287. Clausewitz, ch. 37, p. 92.

[17] Jomini states (p. 150, n.) that General Monthion reconnoitred in the direction of Tilly and Mont St. Guibert in pursuance of orders given him by the Emperor on the morning of the 17th. Siborne, vol. 1, p. 317, states that Domon's cavalry division of the 3d Corps, which had been temporarily attached to the main column, reconnoitred the country between the Brussels road and the Dyle. This must have been, however, in the afternoon of the 17th.

that half his army,— the IIId and IVth Corps,— was untouched, as Napoleon very well knew. The neglect, therefore, to explore the country to the north of the turnpike cannot be excused. The blame for this neglect must fall primarily upon Napoleon, for he ought to have ordered Soult to attend to this matter in the early morning. This he certainly failed to do. Soult ought, to be sure, to have had the reconnoissance made, on his own motion; and in neglecting this, he shows that he was not a good chief-of-staff. But the Emperor seems to have been satisfied with what Soult had done; hence, the blame of not ascertaining that the two beaten Prussian Corps had retreated in the direction of Wavre, falls finally on his shoulders. Nor can Napoleon's fault in this matter be explained or excused on the ground of his fatigue; it costs no exertion to order a cavalry officer to make an exploration in a certain direction; the reason the order was not given was because the Emperor was so sure that such an exploration would result in nothing,— because in fact he was so confident that the Prussians had retired to the eastward, towards their base of operations. There was, it is true, as we have pointed out above, strong reason to believe this to be the fact; but there was also a possibility that it might not be the fact; and if it should turn out not to be the fact, the plan of Napoleon would have to be essentially modified, for a retreat of the two beaten corps in the direction of Wavre, where they could easily be united with the two unbroken corps, could hardly have any other object than a junction with the English army, retiring, as that army was sure to do, from Quatre Bras towards Brussels.

Before Napoleon left the field of battle for Marbais, shortly before twelve o'clock, he called Grouchy to him and gave him instructions by word of mouth. Up to this time no further information had been received since Pajol had reported the capture of guns and prisoners on the Namur road. The Emperor at first simply told him to take the 3d and 4th Corps and the cavalry of Pajol and Exelmans and to pursue the enemy.

"I replied to him," says Marshal Grouchy, whose account [18] we are now giving, "that the Prussians had commenced their retreat at ten o'clock the evening before; that much time must elapse before my troops, who were scattered over the plain, were cleaning their guns and making their soup, and were not expecting to be called upon to march that day, could be put in movement; that the enemy had seventeen or eighteen hours the start of the troops sent in pursuit; that although the reports of the cavalry gave no definite information as to the direction of the retreat of the mass of the Prussian army, it was apparently on Namur that they were retiring; and that thus, in following them, I should find myself isolated, separated from him, and out of the range of his movements. These observations," Marshal Grouchy goes on to say, "were not well received; the Emperor repeated his orders, adding that it was for me to discover the route taken by Marshal Blücher; that he himself was going to fight the English, 'if they will stand on this side of the Forest of Soignes' [19] that it was for me to complete the defeat of the Prussians in attacking them as soon as I should have caught up with them, and that I must communicate with him by the paved road,"[20]—the Namur-Quatre-Bras turnpike.

These objections raised by Marshal Grouchy were clearly not well taken. His two corps had done the principal part of the fighting the day before; they were unquestionably in need of repose the forenoon after the battle. The fresh troops in the army were required for the operations which were to be immediately undertaken against the English. Hence the delay in beginning the pursuit of the Prussians, of which Grouchy complained, was unavoidable, unless the whole plan of campaign was to be changed. It would have been very desirable, no doubt, had it been possible, to follow up the defeated Prussians with the greatest promptness and vigor. But

---

[18] Grouchy, Obs., p. 12 *et seq.*

[19] Fragments Hist., Lettre à MM. Méry et Barthélemy; pp. 4, 5. Grouchy Mem., vol. 4, p. 44.

[20] Grouchy, Obs. p. 13.

under the circumstances this was not practicable, unless, as we have said, Napoleon should change his plan, and should march against Blücher with the bulk of his army, consisting almost entirely of fresh troops, and should leave Grouchy with the corps of Vandamme and Gérard to watch the English. This the Emperor was not proposing to do. Moreover, if the Prussians were really retiring on their base, as both Napoleon and Grouchy at this time supposed was the case, delay in following them up could not be a very material matter.[21]

Then, as for the objection that, if he followed the Prussians towards Namur, he would "find himself isolated, separated from the Emperor, and out of the range of his movements," this was to a certain extent unavoidable. The fact that such an objection should be raised shows how unfit Grouchy was for an independent command. The slightest reflection should have convinced him that the task assigned to him could not well be assigned to any one else; and that it was a task which some one must perform. It was, therefore, his manifest duty to undertake it with cheerful alacrity, and not in the fault-finding spirit which he does not even attempt to conceal.

These were the only orders which Marshal Grouchy ever admitted having received on the 17th; he denied, over and over again, in his pamphlets written about the battle, ever having received any written order, whether from Napoleon or Soult, until the next day.[22] In consequence of these formal and explicit denials, which were very generally credited, the statements made by Napoleon in his St. Helena narratives, which, though anything but exact, nevertheless conveyed the truth substantially, were generally disbelieved. For nearly thirty years after the battle of Waterloo a wholly false notion was

---

[21] Ollech, p. 171. *Cf.* Clausewitz, ch. 51.

[22] This subject will be treated of in Appendix B; *post*, p. 355.

prevalent as to the task assigned by Napoleon to Marshal Grouchy. Neither Siborne, who wrote in 1844, nor Van Loben Sels, who wrote in 1849, was aware of the existence of the written order which we are now about to give. The mischievous influence which this deliberate concealment of his orders by Marshal Grouchy has exerted upon the general opinion of Napoleon's conduct of this campaign can hardly be exaggerated.

Shortly after giving these verbal orders to Grouchy, which were plainly based on the theory that Blücher had fallen back on Namur, Napoleon received [23] a report from Berton, who commanded the brigade which was sent out in support of Pajol, to the effect that he had been led by the statements of the inhabitants to proceed to Gembloux, where he had seen, at 9 A. M., a Prussian corps of some 20,000 men.[24] This certainly looked as if the Prussians were not retiring on Namur. The first thing to be done, therefore, was to find out where they were going, and what they were proposing to do. At Gembloux, so it now appeared, one would be sure to get on the track of the Prussians, and obtain news of their movements and designs. Accordingly the Emperor, in the temporary absence of Marshal Soult, dictated to General Bertrand the following order [25] to Grouchy:—

"Proceed to Gembloux with the cavalry corps of General Pajol, the light cavalry of the 4th Corps, the cavalry corps of General Exelmans, the division of General Teste, of which you will take particular care, it being detached from its own corps,[26] and the 3d and 4th corps of infantry.

"You will explore in the directions of Namur and of Maestricht,[27]

---

[23] Charras, vol. 1, p. 240.

[24] Berton, pp. 47, 48. Berton supposed it to be the corps of Bülow, but it was really that of Thielemann. Ollech, p. 157.

[25] Pascallet, p. 79. Charras, vol. 1, p. 241. Appendix B; *post*, p. 358.

[26] This division belonged to the 6th Corps.

[27] Namur lay nearly south-east and Maestricht nearly north-east from Sombreffe.

and you will pursue the enemy. Explore his march, and instruct me respecting his manœuvres, *so that I may be able to penetrate what he is intending to do.* [28]

"I am carrying my headquarters to Quatre Bras, where the English still were this morning. Our communication will then be direct by the paved road of Namur. If the enemy has evacuated Namur, write to the general commanding the second military division at Charlemont to cause Namur to be occupied by some battalions of the national guard and some batteries which he will organize at Charlemont. He will give the command to a brigadier-general.

"*It is important to penetrate what the enemy is intending to do; whether they are separating themselves from the English, or whether they are intending still to unite, to cover Brussels or* [29] *Liége, in trying the fate of another battle.* [30] In all cases, keep constantly your two corps of infantry united in a league of ground, and occupy every evening a good military position, having several avenues of retreat. Post intermediate detachments of cavalry, so as to communicate with headquarters.

Dictated by the Emperor,
in the absence of the major-general, to the

Ligny, 17 June, 1815.   Grand-marshal Bertrand." [31]

Not only is the tone of this letter altogether different from that of the verbal orders previously given, but the duty assigned to Grouchy is a wholly different one.

There is in the letter no trace of that certainty as to the position of affairs so plainly exhibited in the verbal orders. The news that a Prussian corps has been seen at Gembloux has evidently made a strong impression on the Emperor. It may very possibly indicate that Blücher is not falling back to Namur. The statement is twice made in the letter that the Emperor is in doubt as to the

---

[28] The italics are ours.

[29] The original is "*et*," but this is plainly an error, very possibly caused by the fact that the letter was dictated.

[30] The italics are ours.

[31] There are other readings varying in unimportant points from the above.

intentions of the Prussians, and the chief task now imposed upon Grouchy is to ascertain those intentions. *The precise danger to be anticipated is stated explicitly.* Grouchy is warned in so many words that the Prussians may be intending to unite with the English to try the fate of another battle for the defence of Brussels, — which was exactly what they were intending to do, and what they succeeded in doing. Whether they are or are not intending to do this, is the principal thing for Grouchy to find out. As the Emperor had previously informed Grouchy of his determination to fight the English " if they will stand on this side of the Forest of Soignes,"— which meant of course that he looked upon a battle with them the next day as very possible, — this question of the Prussians uniting with the English in fighting this battle was of vital importance to him.[32] *What Grouchy was to do if he found the Prussians directing their movements so as to compass this end, it was left to him to determine for himself.* It might be that he could hinder the accomplishment of their design most effectually by attacking them; it might be that his best course would be to rejoin the main army as soon as he could, or to manœuvre so as to act in conjunction with it. It was impossible for Napoleon to tell beforehand how things would turn out. Full discretion was therefore left to Grouchy to take whatever course might seem best to him.

Marshal Grouchy was making his arrangements to get his command under way when he received this letter. He experienced great delay in beginning his march to Gembloux. Vandamme did not get started till two o'clock. Gérard left Ligny an hour later. It came on to rain hard about two o'clock, and the roads soon became

---

[32]Whether it was wise under these circumstances for Napoleon to detach such a large force as that which he intrusted to Grouchy, is a question which will be discussed in the notes to Chapter XV.

very bad. Grouchy did not succeed in getting farther with his two infantry corps that night than Gembloux, which is rather less than eight miles from St. Amand.[33] The cavalry of Exelmans was, however, stationed at Sauvenières, to gather information. Grouchy had with him a force of 33,319 men of all arms, of whom 4,446 were the cavalry belonging to the two corps of Pajol and Exelmans.[34] Napoleon took with himself Domon's light cavalry division of the 3d Corps, but Grouchy retained that of Maurin, belonging to the 4th Corps, — say, 1,500 men. That is, he had 6,000 cavalry in all.

At ten o'clock that evening Grouchy wrote to the Emperor from Gembloux a letter[35] which seemed to indicate that he comprehended, at least to a certain extent, the nature of his task. He says that it appeared to him that the Prussians had passed through Sauvenières, where his (Grouchy's) cavalry now have arrived, and that, at Sauvenières, they had divided into two columns, one taking the road to Wavre, by Sart-à-Walhain, and the other that to Perwez, a town on the way to Maestricht. Grouchy then goes on to say: —

"One may perhaps infer that a part is going to join Wellington, and that the centre, which is the army of Blücher, is retiring on Liége; another column with artillery has effected its retreat on Namur. Exelmans has been ordered to send this evening six squadrons to Sart-à-Walhain and three to Perwez.

"According to their reports, *if the mass of the Prussians is retiring on Wavre, I shall follow them in that direction, in order that they may not be able to gain Brussels, and to separate them from Wellington.*[36]

---

[33]Charras, vol. 1, p. 242.

[34]Ib., vol. 1, p. 238.

[35]Gérard: Dernières Obs., p. 15; Charras, vol. 1, p. 244; Siborne, vol. 1, p. 297. Of the mutilations in the text affecting the significance of this letter, contained in the Grouchy Memoirs, notice will be taken in Appendix B, *post*, p. 359, where a full copy of it will be given.

[36]The italics are ours.

"If, on the contrary, my information proves that the principal Prussian force has marched on Perwez, I shall direct myself on that city in pursuit of the enemy."

That Marshal Grouchy understood something of the nature of the task before him is apparent from this despatch. But when he says that his object in following the mass of the Prussians in the direction of Wavre is to prevent their gaining Brussels, he is plainly beside the mark. No movement of his from Gembloux to Wavre or in the direction of Wavre could possibly hinder a force at Wavre from marching on Brussels. When he declares that his object in proceeding in the direction of Wavre would be to separate the Prussians from Wellington, he must be understood to mean the direction of Wavre, as contradistinguished from the direction of Perwez,— that is, in other words, if the Prussians go north instead of east he will also go north instead of east. And as he had abundance of cavalry, there was certainly no reason, now that he had cause, as he says he had, to suspect that a part of the Prussians had gone to Wavre, with the intention of uniting with Wellington, why he should not have reconnoitred to his left the next morning and ascertained the facts.

Leaving Marshal Grouchy at Gembloux with the right wing, we now return to Napoleon, who, when we left him, was about to lead the reserves, consisting of the 6th Corps and the Guard, and some cavalry, to Quatre Bras. Orders, repeated orders, had been sent, as we have seen, to Marshal Ney, to get him to move upon Quatre Bras. But Ney had not moved a man.[37] Charras thinks he must have informed the Emperor, in obedience to the 8 A. M. order, that the English were still in force in his front. But there is no evidence whatever of this. Charras himself,[38] after censuring the Emperor for his delays on

---

[37] Charras, vol. 1, p. 249.

[38] Ib., pp. 236, 237.

this morning, does not assign as the cause of the second and more peremptory despatch to Ney, dated at noon, any reply of Ney's to the 8 A. M. despatch, but the return of a reconnoitring party sent out by Napoleon himself, which reported the English at Quatre Bras. If anything further were needed to show that Ney vouchsafed no reply to the 8 A. M. despatch, it is found in the fact that this noon order refers to no such reply. In fact it was not until Ney saw the column under the Emperor in person advancing on the Namur road that he put his cavalry in motion, and it was the Emperor's own staff officers[39] that ordered d'Erlon forward in pursuit of the English. This was about 1 P. M.

Wellington had collected at Quatre Bras about 45,000 men. The rest of his army was at Nivelles and Braine-le-Comte. Since 10 A. M. he had been quietly withdrawing his forces, and Ney had not offered an interruption.[40] Probably he did not know what Wellington was doing. Yet Ney must have had at his disposal about 40,000 men, 25,000 of whom had not fired a shot or drawn a sword. There is no saying what loss the English might not have been obliged to suffer, if he had vigorously pressed them. His conduct on this day is even more culpable than on the day before. There was not only not any of that intelligent coöperation which, as has been remarked, Napoleon always counted upon in his lieutenants, — there was positive disobedience of orders.

At Quatre Bras, the Emperor, who had ridden from Ligny in his carriage, mounted his horse,[41] and led the pursuit in person. He now saw, and no doubt with mortification, what an opportunity he had missed. He

---

[39]Charras, vol. 1, p. 250.

[40]*Cf.* Napoléon à Waterloo, p. 181.

[41]Charras, vol. 1, p. 250.

was also, and with reason, indignant[42] with Ney for not having obeyed his orders, ascertained that Wellington was withdrawing his forces, sent him word at once, and energetically pressed the enemy. His fatigue seems to have wholly disappeared, and he showed, this afternoon of the 17th as he had on the afternoon of the 15th,[43] how he could infuse his own activity and energy into his troops. We have two pictures of Napoleon on this afternoon, by eye witnesses. The Count d'Erlon, in his autobiography,[44] says: —

"The Emperor found me in advance of this position (Quatre Bras), and said to me in a tone of profound chagrin these words, which have been always graven on my memory: —

"'They have ruined France; come, my dear general, put yourself at the head of this cavalry, and vigorously push the English rearguard.'

"The Emperor never quitted the head of column of the advance-guard, and was even engaged in a charge of cavalry in debouching from Genappe."

Says the author of "Napoléon à Waterloo," — an officer of artillery of the Guard, who was near the Emperor throughout the campaign: — [45]

"One must needs have been a witness of the rapid march of this army on the day of the 17th, — a march which resembled a steeple-chase rather than the pursuit of an enemy in retreat, — to get an idea of the activity which Napoleon knew how to impress upon his troops when placed under his immediate command. Six pieces of the horse-artillery of the Guard, supported by the headquarters squadrons, marched in the first line, and vomited forth grape upon the masses of the enemy's cavalry, as often as, profiting by some accident of ground, they endeavored to halt, to take position, and retard our pursuit. The Emperor, mounted on a small and very

---

[42] Gourgaud, pp. 77, 78; Corresp., vol. 31, p. 214.

[43] *Ante*, p. 47.

[44] Le Maréchal Drouet, p. 96.

[45] Napoléon à Waterloo, pp. 185, 186.

active Arab horse, galloped at the head of the column;[46] he was constantly near the pieces, exciting the gunners by his presence and by his words, and more than once in the midst of the shells and bullets which the enemy's artillery showered upon us."

There was a smart skirmish at Genappe. The 7th English regiment of hussars was injudiciously ordered to charge the French lancers, and was beaten back. Then the pursuing French, in mounting the hill behind the town of Genappe, were ridden down by the 1st Life Guards.

During the whole afternoon the rain fell in torrents, and there was a severe storm of thunder and lightning. Very possibly the bad weather may have favored the retiring army. The retreat of the English was continued to the position to the south of the hamlet of Mont St. Jean, where the battle of the next day was fought.

---

[46] *Cf.* Gourgaud, pp. 78, 79. *Cf.* Mercer's Diary, vol. 1, p. 269.

NOTES TO CHAPTER XIII.

1. IN regard to Napoleon's action with reference to the defeated Prussians, it is necessary to distinguish between instituting a prompt and vigorous pursuit of them, and taking immediate measures for ascertaining in which direction they had retreated. The first was under the circumstances impossible, that is, without an entire change of plan, but the second was not only possible, but of prime necessity.

Charras,[1] however, complains bitterly of Napoleon for not following up the Prussians. "Not to pursue the vanquished, sword in hand, to leave him time to collect himself, to reform his forces, to gather in his reinforcements, was so strange a thing for troops accustomed to the tactics of Napoleon."

But Clausewitz[2] with better judgment says:—

"If we seem here to find so great a difference from the earlier methods of procedure adopted by the French, we must get a true picture of the changed conditions. The extraordinary energy in pursuit to which the brilliant results of Bonaparte's former campaigns were due, was simply pushing very superior forces after an enemy who had been completely vanquished. Now, however, Napoleon had to turn with his main force, and above all with his freshest troops, against a new enemy, over whom victory had yet to be gained. The pursuit [of the Prussians] had to be carried out by the 3d and 4th Corps, the very two who had been engaged in the bloodiest fight till ten in the evening, and now necessarily needed time to get into order again, to recover themselves, and to provide themselves with ammunition."

---

[1]Charras, vol. 1, p. 233.
[2]Clausewitz, ch. 37, p. 95.

Napoleon, therefore, while censurable for not having ascertained as early as possible the direction of the retreat of the Prussians, and for not having moved promptly with his main body against the English, can not be blamed for having allowed Grouchy's troops to remain on the field till noon, to recover from their fatigues.

2. It hardly needs to be said that if Napoleon had known that the Ist and IId Prussian Corps were retiring on Wavre, he would not have ordered Grouchy on Gembloux. Exactly what he would have done, it is needless to conjecture, but in all probability he would have kept the whole army together, or within easy reach, so as to have concentrated an overwhelming force against Wellington the next morning, if not on that afternoon.

3. To illustrate the effect which the concealment of the Bertrand order by Marshal Grouchy has produced on the mind of an able critic, take the following passages from Clausewitz,[3] who wrote his narrative before the order came to light:—

"Bonaparte, it is claimed, ordered Grouchy to keep between Blücher and the road from Namur (Charleroi) to Brussels, for the second battle would have to be fought on this road, and only thus was there a possibility of Grouchy's coöperating in it. But of such an order nothing can be found except in the untrustworthy account[4] of Bonaparte and of the men who have copied him. The account which Grouchy gives of the movements of the 17th bears too much the character of the simple truth[5] not to gain credence; and, according to this, Bonaparte's instruction was directed in very general terms towards pursuing Blücher, and was drawn up in very uncertain expressions."

---

[3] Clausewitz, ch. 37, p. 93.

[4] The Memoirs are exceedingly unsatisfactory in regard to this part of the campaign. Napoleon evidently had no exact recollection of the order which he dictated to Bertrand. He was only sure that he gave Grouchy an intimation that he might need him. See App. A; *post*, p. 351.

[5] Very possibly Grouchy did tell "the simple truth" in his account of the interview between himself and the Emperor. The trouble with Grouchy was, that he did not tell "the whole truth." He denied having received any written order.

[CHAP. 13.] NAPOLEON.—NOTES. • 219

⁶ " As we read Marshal Grouchy's account of the events which took place with Bonaparte on the morning of the 17th, we see: —

(1) That this Marshal in all probability actually received no other direction for his action on the 17th besides a very general instruction to pursue the Prussians:

(2) That Bonaparte had no idea of the retreat of the Prussians towards the Dyle, and considered the opinion that they had gone towards Namur not unreasonable, and therefore did not give the Marshal the direction of Wavre."

Clausewitz concludes by surmising that Napoleon was "affected by a sort of lethargy and carelessness." Had Clausewitz known the truth, namely, that Grouchy was sent off with a letter of instructions, telling him in so many words that the Prussians might be intending to unite with the English to fight a battle for the defence of Brussels on the turnpike on which Napoleon was now marching with the intention of encountering the English, we should have had a very different criticism from this, we may be sure.

4. But it is a curious thing, that, even with those historians who wrote after the Bertrand letter came to light, the influence of Grouchy's misrepresentations has induced a sort of ignoring of the letter, and an acquiescence in the erroneous judgment of Napoleon's conduct formed when the existence of the letter was unknown, and when the verbal instructions, as given by Grouchy, were all the orders which it was believed that Napoleon ever gave to Grouchy. Thus Chesney,[7] after giving the substance of the document, says: —

" Such was the whole tenor of this important letter, which serves to show two things only: that Napoleon was uncertain of the line of Blücher's retreat, and that he judged Gembloux a good point to move Grouchy on in any case."

The injunction to Grouchy, though given by Chesney almost textually, to ascertain whether or not the Prussians

---

⁶Clausewitz, ch. 48, p. 130.
⁷Chesney, p. 152.

were intending to unite with the English and fight a battle for the defence of Brussels, — the very thing which they actually were intending to do, — has evidently made no impression whatever on his mind.

The same determination, — for we know not what other word indicates more correctly the temper of mind which must possess a historian of this campaign who shuts his eyes to the contents of the Bertrand letter, — the same determination, we say, not to recognize the fact that the Bertrand letter shows beyond a question that Napoleon was alive to the danger that the Prussians might be intending to do exactly what they were intending to do, that is, unite with the English and fight another battle, — this time on the Brussels road, — is shown also by the latest English critic, Colonel Maurice. He says: — [8]

" He (Napoleon) gave orders to Grouchy, with a force of 33,000 men and 96 guns, to pursue the Prussians, complete their defeat, and communicate with him by the Namur road. [9] Written orders were subsequently given to Grouchy *directing him to move on Gembloux.*" [10]

Here, the warning contained in the written order, the injunction to ascertain whether the Prussians were intending to join Wellington, is absolutely and quietly ignored. One would suppose that all that the Bertrand letter contained was an order to move on Gembloux. Colonel Maurice proceeds: —

" He (Grouchy) promised, that if, from the reports he received, he gathered that the Prussians had for the most part retired on Wavre, he would follow them there, in order to prevent them gaining Brussels, and in order to separate them from Wellington. *This is the first indication we receive, on any authentic evidence, that any one in the French army supposed that the duty of separating the Prussians from Wellington would become the task of Grouchy's force. Up till then, all the French supposed that*

---

[8] Maurice, pp. 73, 74: April, 1890.
[9] These are the verbal orders.

there was no prospect of Blücher's attempting to unite with Wellington." [10]

Yet in the body of the Bertrand letter, of which Colonel Maurice quotes the first line, are these words:—

"*It is important to penetrate what the enemy is intending to do; whether they are separating themselves from the English, or whether they are intending still to unite, to cover Brussels, or Liége, in trying the fate of another battle.*"

We confess our inability to explain or account for criticism of this nature, unless by the hypothesis that to a mind preoccupied with a certain view, firmly held, it is often possible that the plainest evidence should be, so to speak, invisible. It is as plain as anything can be that Grouchy's letter, from which Maurice makes his quotation, *is a reply to that part of the Bertrand letter* which we have given above; but Maurice, his mind full of the verbal orders only, wholly overlooks this.

But Colonel Maurice and Colonel Chesney are not alone in their views.

General Hamley,[11] in his account of the campaign, says of Grouchy: "His orders were to follow them [the Prussians], complete their rout, and never lose sight of them." Hamley does not seem even to have heard of the Bertrand order. Hence his elaborate criticism on Grouchy's conduct,[12]—leaving out, as it does, the two most important *data*, viz.:—Napoleon's explicit warning to Grouchy of the possibility of the Prussians uniting with the English to fight a battle for the defence of Brussels, and his equally explicit statement to Grouchy (as reported by the latter), that he was going that very afternoon to attack the English "if they will stand on this side of the Forest of Soignes,"—is entirely beside the mark, and cannot be considered as possessing any

---
[10] The italics are our own.
[11] Hamley, Op. of War, p. 190. He also cites the verbal orders.
[12] Ib., pp. 196-198.

practical value whatever. He has addressed himself to a case which never really existed.[13]

Hooper, also, omits entirely the information which the Emperor gave of his own intention, and of his conjecture that the English might fight "on this side of the forest of Soignes,"— where they actually did fight,— and dismisses the explicit injunction for Grouchy to ascertain the facts in these words:—[14]

"Yet some doubts of the correctness of his views had entered the mind of the Emperor before he quitted Ligny, and he remarked (*sic*) to Grouchy that it was important to learn whether the Prussians were separating themselves from the English, etc."

These instances suffice to show how seriously the concealment of the Bertrand letter by Marshal Grouchy has affected the historians of the campaign. The prominence assigned to the verbal orders to Grouchy, so common in most of the narratives, is not only utterly useless,— but most misleading.

5. But was the Bertrand letter sufficiently explicit?

Charras,[15] who, unlike the English historians cited above, fully admits that the letter shows that Napoleon saw "the possibility of the union of the allied armies to cover Brussels," observes that this involved the necessity of reconnoitring in the directions of Mont St. Guibert and Wavre. "Nevertheless," he goes on to say,

---

[13]Hamley contends that the injunction to Grouchy—which, by the way, is contained in both the written and the verbal orders,— to communicate with Napoleon by the Namur-Quatre Bras turnpike, is not consistent with a movement towards Wavre. But why should not this arrangement have been prescribed for the sake of greater safety? If the Prussians were moving towards Wavre and the Dyle, their cavalry might be expected to make all communication across the country very hazardous for couriers or staff-officers. And, as a matter of fact, it was by the Brussels turnpike to Quatre Bras, thence by the Namur turnpike to Sombreffe, and thence *via* Gembloux to Grouchy's position in front of Wavre, that Napoleon sent Grouchy the two orders on the day of the battle. Napoléon à Waterloo, pp. 277, 278.

[14]Hooper, p. 153.

[15]Charras, vol. 1, pp. 241, 242.

"Napoleon did not make this the subject of a special recommendation to Grouchy; * * * and the latter, given over to his own inspirations, did not repair the inconceivable fault of the commander-in-chief. He had an order to proceed to Gembloux; he did not trouble his head about anything else."

If Napoleon had entertained as low an opinion of Marshal Grouchy's capacity as Charras evidently did, it certainly would have been a terrible mistake to have omitted to tell him to explore the region between Gembloux and Wavre. But questions of this kind hardly bear discussing; every one has his own opinions on such matters, based on his own estimate of other men's ability, his own experience, his own notions of what is fitting. The suggestion of danger to the main army, if it should find the Prussians as well as the English opposed to it on the Brussels turnpike, would have amply sufficed for many generals. It was not, however, sufficient, as we shall soon see, for Marshal Grouchy.

6. We cannot agree with those who contend that it was an error to direct Grouchy on Gembloux in the first instance.[16] Up to the moment when the order was dictated to Bertrand no other considerable force of the enemy had been discovered; at Gembloux, Berton had found a whole corps. Here, therefore, one could not help getting at the direction of the Prussian retreat. And, owing to the lack of an early morning reconnoissance in all directions, this was, at noon, obviously the most promising direction for the pursuing force to take.

7. We owe to Colonel Maurice some valuable suggestions which serve to explain Napoleon's neglect to take adequate measures to ascertain the direction of the

---

[16] Assuming, that is, that it was wise in Napoleon to detach Grouchy with his two corps from the main army after he had reason to apprehend that the Prussians might be intending to unite with the English. See the Notes to Chapter XV; *post*, pp. 273 *et seq.*

Prussian retreat. He points out in the first place[17] the folly of such writers as Quinet, who would have Napoleon sleep in the midst of his Guard,— who expect the commander of an army to do the work of a sentry on the outer picket-line. It may be remarked in this connection, by the way, that as the French were not able to push up to the Namur turnpike on the evening of the 16th, their advanced posts could not possibly have heard anything more than the withdrawal of the enemy towards the pike, down which they might have marched without let or hindrance towards Namur. Colonel Maurice in the next place quotes an able criticism[18] by an officer whom he does not name, to the effect that Napoleon's vast experience enabled him in his later years to dispense with much of that personal attention to the facts which in his earlier campaigns it had been absolutely necessary for him to give.

Colonel Maurice also calls attention to the circumstances which we have detailed above, which very naturally induced Napoleon to adopt the opinion that the Prussians had fallen back towards the Rhine.[19]

8. In conclusion, we may admit, fully, with Colonel Maurice, to whom we owe a great deal for setting this matter of the probabilities of the case in its true light, that Napoleon's estimate of the probabilities was a correct one. He was quite warranted under all the circumstances in believing that the Prussians had retired towards their base. Nevertheless, this belief does not justify him for having neglected to ascertain the facts by a prompt exploration of the whole region through which the Prussians could have retreated.

The lesson which this neglect teaches, is a plain one. It is, that where there is any chance at all of the occur-

---

[17] Maurice, p. 348: July, 1890.
[18] Ib., p. 353.
[19] Ib., pp. 350-355.

rence of an event, which, if it does happen, will be fatal, it is folly to trust to the probabilities of the case; every precaution should be taken; nothing that can avert a fatal calamity should be neglected, no matter how small may appear to be the chance of its happening. In this case, we find Napoleon, at one o'clock in the afternoon of the day after the battle of Ligny, entirely ignorant of the whereabouts and intentions of the Prussians, and, in fact, alarmed lest they should be intending to unite with the English, whom he is expecting to fight the next day; obliged to go off himself to join his left wing, and to leave the all-important task of preventing the union of his adversaries to a newly-made Marshal, in whose abilities he cannot place very great confidence. And all this, because he did not have the facts as to the Prussian retreat ascertained at day-break.

CHAPTER XIV.

THE SEVENTEENTH OF JUNE: BLÜCHER AND WELLINGTON.

ZIETEN and Pirch I. fell back after the battle of Ligny, as has been above stated,[1] in the direction of Wavre. Gneisenau, the chief-of-staff of the Prussian army, on whom, in the absence of Marshal Blücher, who was unhorsed and quite seriously bruised in a cavalry encounter at the end of the day, and was supposed to have been taken prisoner,[2] the command devolved, gave the order at first for the two beaten corps[3] to retire on Tilly, and then, as one of his staff-officers called his attention to the fact that Tilly was not on all the maps, he substituted Wavre for Tilly as the point to be reached.[4]

This step involved obviously the renunciation of the line of Namur. It implied also that the IIId and IVth Corps, those of Thielemann and Bülow, would be ordered to retire in the general direction of Wavre, so that a union of the whole army might be effected somewhere to the northward. But it did not necessarily imply that this union of the army would be effected at Wavre; or even that, if effected at Wavre, it would be followed by an attempt to unite with the Anglo-Dutch army. It was quite possible that the two beaten corps might, after

---

[1]*Ante*, p. 159.

[2]Ollech, p. 157.

[3]He could not at this time communicate with Thielemann and Bülow.

[4]Gneisenau, vol. 4, p. 385; Ollech, p. 156.

reforming at Wavre, be ordered in the direction of Maestricht, towards which place the IIId and IVth Corps might also be ordered to retire. In fact, this was the interpretation put by General Thielemann on the facts as he first learned them. He wrote to Bülow,[5] that he had heard nothing from the Marshal, but supposed that the intention was that the Ist and IId Corps were to fall back from Wavre towards St. Trond, which is a town in the direction of Maestricht, some 35 miles from Wavre.

At the same time it is clear that Gneisenau, in ordering Zieten and Pirch I. to Wavre, had taken the necessary preliminary steps to effect a concentration of the whole army at that place, from which a movement for the assistance of Wellington, if he should be willing to accept battle at Waterloo, could be made. This union with the Anglo-Dutch army was, therefore, naturally regarded by the Prussian officers and soldiers as the real object of the movement to Wavre.[6] It may be that Gneisenau himself gave his orders with the sole intention of bringing about a union of the two allied armies.[7] But this is doubtful. It is more likely that he ordered a retreat on Wavre, knowing that this alone could render such a union possible, and leaving its practicability and advisability to be determined afterwards.

It must be remembered that the step which Gneisenau had taken involved a temporary change of base, with all

---

[5]Ollech, p. 157. Maurice (pp. 354, 355 : July, 1890) points out that this serves, as far as it goes, to show that Napoleon might have known of the retreat of Zieten and Pirch I. to Wavre without changing his opinion that the whole Prussian army was intending to fall back to the eastward.

[6]Damitz, p. 143.

[7]This is Ollech's opinion (p. 156): "Thus had Gneisenau broken all bridges behind him, given up all communication with the Rhine, that he might once again offer the hand to the English for a common blow which should forever overthrow the French forces." But this is surely going too far. Communication with the Rhine could be maintained as well by way of Maestricht as by way of Liége.

the many inconveniences and risks therefrom resulting. The communications with Namur must be abandoned. No such course as this had been thought of when Marshal Blücher decided on accepting battle at Ligny; if it had been, he would have posted his troops very differently, as we have had occasion to observe.[8] Gneisenau, however, though disappointed at not receiving help from the English during the battle, yet influenced, very possibly, by the fact that Wellington had successfully held his ground against the attack of the French left wing,[9] was extremely unwilling to renounce, by retiring on Namur, all hopes of another battle to be fought in coöperation with the English. Hence he determined to take at any rate the first steps to make it possible to fight such a battle; and in the absence of his chief, and in the confusion and turmoil which followed the successful charge of the Imperial Guard, he did not hesitate to take the responsibility of ordering the beaten corps to retire on Wavre.[10]

But whether it would be wise to concentrate the whole army on Wavre was a question that could not be settled in an instant. It was in truth dependent on many things. The question of supplies of ammunition was perhaps the most serious problem; but there were others, each presenting more or less difficulty. Then, besides these, there was the question of the amount of confidence to be placed in the Duke of Wellington. The whole object, the sole justification, of the manœuvre now in contemplation was the fighting another battle in coöperation with the English. Here, of course, it had to be assumed that the Duke would be desirous of fighting such a battle. But could Wellington be relied upon to fulfil the expectations which would be entertained

---

[8] *Ante*, pp. 151, 204. *Cf.* Gneisenau, vol. 4, p. 38.
[9] Gneisenau, vol. 4, p. 386.
[10] Ollech, p. 156; Gneisenau, vol. 4, p. 385.

in regard to his willingness and ability to fight such a battle? Gneisenau had been gravely disappointed by the non-arrival of support from the English army during the battle of Ligny. He never had had,—so we learn from Müffling,"—entire confidence in the Duke's trustworthiness. The letter[12] received on the morning of the battle,—so far from accurate,—the confident statements[13] made by the Duke at Brye early in the afternoon, on which such expectations had been formed, and which had proved so utterly unreliable,—must have seriously shaken Gneisenau's belief in Wellington. He feared lest the danger to the Prussian army involved in its concentration at Wavre might be incurred only to see the Anglo-Dutch army marching off to Antwerp or Ostend.

During the night Marshal Blücher had been carried, badly bruised and suffering a good deal,—a man, too, it must be remembered, seventy-two years of age,'[14]—to the little village of Mellery,— or Melioreux, as the older maps have it,—a mile or two north of Tilly.[15] Here, in a little house, filled with wounded men, he passed the night. Here Gneisenau, his chief-of-staff, and Grolmann, his quartermaster-general, joined him. Here also was brought Lieutenant-Colonel Hardinge, the English military *attaché* at Blücher's headquarters, who had lost his left hand in the battle.[16] He gave to the Duke of Wellington, twenty-two years after, an account of his experience during that night, making the mistake,—natural enough under the circumstances, and considering how

---

[11]Müffling: Passages, p. 212.

[12]*Ante*, p. 106.

[13]*Ante*, p. 144.

[14]He was exactly seventy-two years and six months old on the day of the battle of Ligny.

[15]Ollech, p. 157.

[16]Siborne, vol. 1, p. 241, n.

long a time had elapsed,—of locating the scene at Wavre, and not at Mellery. The story is thus reported by Earl Stanhope:—[17]

"Yes," said Hardinge, "Blücher himself had gone back as far as Wavre. I passed that night, with my amputated arm, lying with some straw in his ante-room, Gneisenau and other generals constantly passing to and fro. Next morning Blücher sent for me. * * * He said to me that he should be quite satisfied if, in conjunction with the Duke of Wellington, he was able now to defeat his old enemy. I was told that there had been a great discussion that night in his rooms, and that Blücher and Grolmann had carried the day for remaining in communication with the English army, but that Gneisenau had great doubts as to whether they ought not to fall back to Liége and secure their own communication with Luxembourg. They thought that if the English should be defeated, they themselves would be utterly destroyed."

Colonel Maurice tells us in confirmation of this story that General Hardinge "records that, as he was, on the 17th, lying on his bed, Blücher burst into his room, triumphantly announcing: 'Gneisenau has given way. We are to march to join Wellington.'"[18]

If these statements are to be accepted literally, and there is, perhaps, no sufficient reason why they should not be, the credit of the decision remains wholly with Marshal Blücher. Still, it may, not impossibly, be that Gneisenau, to whose action alone it was due that the original intention of retreating on Namur, in case it should be found necessary to retreat at all, had been departed from, felt himself morally bound to pre-

---

[17]Stanhope, p. 110.

[18]Maurice, p. 355: July, 1890. Colonel Maurice is inclined to believe that the above incident "must have taken place in Wavre, after the receipt of Wellington's offer to remain and fight at Waterloo, if Blücher would join him with one or two corps." This is certainly very possible. The incident reported in Stanhope's work, however, is stated to have occurred the night after the battle, which, as we know from the Prussian historians, Blücher spent at Mellery. Ollech, p. 157. Very possibly there may have been a second discussion at Wavre on the 17th.

sent to his impetuous and unthinking chief the more cautious and conservative course; and that in reality he was not averse to find that the movement which he had ordered in Blücher's absence should receive from his chief and his advisers such hearty approval and be prosecuted to its natural result.

While the Ist and IId Corps were making their way towards Tilly and Mont St. Guibert, Thielemann, in ignorance of the dispositions of the commander-in-chief, retired from Tongrinelle and Balâtre to Sombreffe, and thence continued his retreat to Gembloux, so as to approach the IVth Corps, which had arrived late in the evening in the neighborhood of Baudeset and Sauvenières. Thielemann reached Gembloux at 6 A. M. of the 17th. Here he wrote a letter to Bülow, to which reference has been already made. Bülow in reply requested him to retire to the neighborhood of Corbaix, half way between Gembloux and Wavre, and informed him that he himself was directing his corps on Wavre. In these movements, which were to be nearly parallel, the corps of Bülow was to keep to the eastward of that of Thielemann.

Thus the temporary separation of the four corps composing the Prussian army worked no harm. The corps-commanders acted with cheerful and zealous coöperation in the absence of orders from the commander-in-chief. In fact nothing can be finer than the spirit displayed by the Prussians after the loss of the battle of Ligny,—whether we look at their willingness to take risks and make sacrifices to ensure the success of the combined movement now in process of execution, or at the harmony which prevailed among the chief officers, which it is evident neither the loss of the battle nor the non-arrival of Bülow's Corps had disturbed in the least.

Orders were now issued for the retreat of the whole army on Wavre. It was conducted as follows:— [19]

---

[19] Ollech, pp. 166 *et seq.*

The Ist Corps marched from its position between Tilly and Mellery early in the morning of the 17th, and proceeded through Gentinnes and Mont St. Guibert towards Wavre, where it crossed the Dyle, and took up position at Bierges.

The IId Corps followed by the same route somewhat later, and halted at Aisemont, a village on the south side of the Dyle, opposite Wavre.

The IIId Corps rested at Gembloux till 1 or 2 o'clock P. M., and then marched by way of Corbaix to Wavre, the head of the column passing through the town in the evening, but the rear guard not arriving till the morning of the 18th.

The IVth Corps marched in two columns, by way of Walhain and Tourinnes to Dion-le-Mont, a village about two miles east of Wavre, where it arrived about 10 P. M of the 17th.

One brigade of infantry belonging to the IId Corps and some cavalry were stationed for a time at Mont St. Guibert for purposes of observation,[20] and General Groeben, of Blücher's staff, who accompanied these troops, witnessed from a high hill near Tilly[21] the march of the troops which Napoleon carried with him to Quatre Bras, and the movement of a smaller body, estimated by him at about 12,000 or 15,000 men, in the direction of Gembloux. He supposed, naturally, that this was all the force which had been detached for the pursuit of the Prussians.[22] The march of the rest of Grouchy's command was concealed by the inequalities of the ground.

The artillery trains, containing the needful ammunition for the coming battle, for the arrival of which Gneisenau

---

[20] Ollech, p. 166. These troops were afterwards replaced by two battalions of infantry, a regiment of cavalry, and two batteries, under Lieutenant-Colonel Ledebur. See *post*, p. 260; Ollech, p. 168; Siborne, vol. 1, p. 285.

[21] Ollech, p. 168.

[22] Ib., p. 169.

had felt great anxiety, arrived safely at Wavre about 5 P. M. of the 17th.

Thus the retreat of the Prussians on Wavre had been successfully and quickly accomplished, and, what is almost as important, it had escaped the observation of the French. Marshal Blücher had collected at Wavre somewhere about 90,000 men, and both the army and its leaders were animated by the best spirit, impatient to encounter the enemy again, and confident of success in another battle.

The Duke of Wellington spent the night after the battle of Quatre Bras at Genappe, but returned to the front "at daybreak, or soon after."[23] A detachment of cavalry was soon afterwards sent out, which ascertained that the Prussians had been beaten the day before, and were now retreating on Wavre. This information reached Wellington about 7.30 A. M.[24]

Blücher had sent an officer, Major Winterfeldt, from the field of battle the evening before to inform General Müffling of his intended retreat, but he had been wounded,[25] and the information had not reached the Duke.

At 9 o'clock another officer arrived from Blücher,[26] Lieutenant Massow.[27] The Duke told him that he would fall back to the position of Mont St. Jean where he would give battle, if he were supported by one Prussian corps. This answer Massow carried to Blücher. He arrived at Wavre at noon. At this hour, as we are told by the latest Prussian historian,[28] it was not known

---

[23] Waterloo Letters: Vivian, p. 153.

[24] Ollech, p. 179.

[25] Müffling: Passages, pp. 238, 239.

[26] For a capital story connected with this incident, see the "Letters of the First Earl of Malmesbury," vol. 2, p. 447. London, 1870. App. C, xxix; *post*, p. 386. See also Waterloo Letters, pp. 154, 167.

[27] Müffling Passages, p. 241; Ollech, p. 180.

[28] Ollech, p. 187.

where the IIId or IVth Corps was, and the reserve ammunition had not arrived.[29] No decided assurance could, therefore, be given during the day. Finally, about 11.30 P. M., news arrived from Bülow of the arrival of his corps at Dion-le-Mont, and about the same time a despatch from Müffling arrived, stating that the Anglo-Dutch army had taken position for battle at Mont St. Jean. Then Grolmann wrote to Müffling Blücher's answer. It was sent off about midnight of the 17th.

This despatch stated that Bülow would move at break of day by way of St. Lambert to attack the right flank of the enemy, and that the IId Corps would support the IVth Corps in this operation. The Ist and IIId Corps were to hold themselves in readiness to do the like.

This despatch, which could not have reached Wellington until the morning of the battle of Waterloo, seems actually to have contained the first definite promise of support from Blücher.[30] Long before its arrival the Duke had taken up his position at Waterloo in the hope — in fact, in the expectation, — of receiving some such promise of assistance and support. Messages were doubtless exchanged, as we are told,[31] between the English and Prussian headquarters during the whole day. But the Duke received no positive assurance until the early morning of the 18th that the Prussian army, or any part of it, would come to his assistance. It is true that he was aware that the Prussians were concentrating at Wavre; and he knew that their object in so doing could be nothing else than to tender him their support in the battle that was sure to occur the next day. But it must have required all the resolution and courage which he possessed to have decided him to take up position for

---

[29]It arrived about 5 P. M. See *ante*, p. 232.

[30]*Contra*: Siborne, vol. 1, p. 279. This subject will be considered in the Notes to this chapter.

[31]Gneisenau, vol. 4, p. 393.

battle without having received any definite assurance that the necessary support would be furnished.

For it was a perfectly possible thing that he might the next morning be assailed by a hundred thousand men. Blücher had, no doubt, sent him the information obtained by Groeben, that Napoleon had detached only 12,000 or 15,000 men to follow the Prussians, and was bringing against the Anglo-Dutch army all his remaining troops.[32] As we see it now, that would have been Napoleon's best course. If he had known the facts at the time, as he might easily have done had he not neglected to take the proper measures to ascertain them, that is what he probably would have done. At any rate, Wellington had no assurance from any quarter whatever that Napoleon would not do exactly that thing. If Napoleon had done it, and if the weather had been fine and the ground hard, what chance would Wellington have stood? The question is asked simply to define the situation in which the Duke placed himself on the night of the 17th and 18th. That is, we desire to bring out the fact that Wellington in taking up position at Waterloo, instead of continuing his retreat to Brussels and arranging with Blücher to do the like from Wavre, ran a very great risk of being beaten before he could get help from the Prussians, whereas if both commanders had proceeded to Brussels, where the roads from Waterloo and Wavre converge, they would have greatly outnumbered the French. This course was the one which Napoleon maintained would have been the safer and wiser.[33]

Still, it must be remembered that both Wellington and Blücher were anxious to close the campaign with a great battle, which was certain to take place if Wellington stood at Waterloo, and that it was by no means certain

---

[32] In point of fact Wellington supposed that only the 3d Corps had been detached for the pursuit of the Prussians. See his Official Report, Jones, p. 307.

[33] See *post*, p. 243.

that Napoleon would push through the forest of Soignes only to find the combined armies confronting him. They also thought that there was a very fair chance that they would succeed in effecting the union of their armies at Waterloo.

NOTES TO CHAPTER XIV.

1. COLONEL MAURICE has recently examined the evidence in reference to the communications which passed between the Duke of Wellington and Marshal Blücher on the subject of the support to be given to the English army by the Prussians.[1] We think he has shown that the account given in Siborne is not altogether correct, and we have followed Colonel Maurice in preferring the statements of Müffling and Ollech.

Siborne says[2] that the Duke, on the morning of the 17th, sent back the Prussian officer[3] who first brought him the news of Blücher's defeat, with a letter to the Field Marshal, "proposing to accept a battle on the following day in the position in front of Waterloo, provided the Prince would detach two corps to his assistance"; and that, in the course of the evening[4] he received from Blücher a reply in these terms: —

"I shall not come with two corps only, but with my whole army; upon this understanding, however, that, should the French not attack us on the 18th, we shall attack them on the 19th."

Colonel Maurice is inclined to the opinion that the letter which is quoted by Siborne is really one written to

---
[1] Maurice, pp. 534 *et seq.*: Sept., 1890.
[2] Siborne, vol. 1, p. 251, following Damitz, p. 212.
[3] Lieutenant Massow.
[4] Siborne, vol. 1, pp. 278, 279, following Damitz, p. 213.

Müffling at Blücher's dictation on the following morning, after nine o'clock, in which Müffling is desired to inform the Duke of Blücher's intentions, and in which some of the words given above are employed. If this be so, and it seems very likely, the Duke not only took up his position for battle before he had received any definite assurance of support from his ally, but he did not get any until the arrival at the Duke's headquarters at Waterloo of the letter sent off from Wavre between 11 and 12 P. M.,[5] which could hardly be before 2 A. M. of the 18th. How much longer the Duke would have remained in his position waiting for the promise of Prussian support, no one, of course, can say. He certainly did not propose to stay and fight single-handed. He had sent word to Blücher by Massow that without Prussian support he would be obliged to fall back to Brussels.[6] Yet according to Siborne, he waited till evening,[7] according to Ollech, he must have waited till two o'clock in the morning, before receiving any definite assurance of assistance.

2. But there is a story, which rests on testimony which it is impossible to disregard, to the effect that the Duke, after having caused his army to take up its position on the field of battle, rode over to Wavre in the evening to ascertain for himself whether or not he was to be supported by Marshal Blücher in the battle of the ensuing day. This story has been carefully investigated by Colonel Maurice,[8] and we shall state, as briefly as we can, the evidence collected by him.

We first find the story in print in the year 1835, in Lockhart's Life of Napoleon.[9] It reads as follows:—

---

[5] Ollech, p. 187; Gneisenau, vol. 4, pp. 393, 394.
[6] Ib., p. 180.
[7] Siborne, vol. 1, p. 278.
[8] Maurice, pp. 533-538: Sept., 1890; and pp. 330 *et seq.*, January, 1891.
[9] Vol. 2, p. 313. The History of Napoleon Buonaparte. By J. G. Lockhart. 3d ed., 2 vols. John Murray: 1835. See also the same work, p. 594; London: William Tegg: 1867.

"All his arrangements having been effected early in the evening of the 17th, the Duke of Wellington rode across the country to Blücher, to inform him personally that he had thus far effected the plan agreed on at Brye, and express his hope to be supported on the morrow by two Prussian divisions. The veteran replied that he would leave a single corps to hold Grouchy at bay as well as they could, and march himself with the rest of his army upon Waterloo; and Wellington immediately returned to his post."

To this the following note is appended:—

"The fact of Wellington and Blücher having met between the battles of Ligny and Waterloo is well known to many of the superior officers in the Netherlands; but the writer of this compendium has never happened to see it mentioned in print. The horse that carried the Duke of Wellington through this long night journey, so important to the decisive battle of the 18th, remained till lately, it is understood, if he does not still remain, a free pensioner in the best paddock at Strathfieldsaye."

Lord Ellesmere, however, writing, as we have before had occasion to remark, under the inspiration of the Duke of Wellington, states in a review of a biography of Blücher that Lockhart is mistaken.[10] But it is curious that no statement whatever is given by him of the manner in which the Duke passed the evening of the 17th. His actions are accounted for only till dark.

The story is most circumstantially told in the journal of the Rev. Julian Charles Young:—[11]

"In the year 1833, while living in Hampshire, no one showed my wife and myself more constant hospitality than the late Right Honorable Henry Pierrepont, the father of the present Lady Charles Wellesley. * * * On one of our many delightful visits to Conholt, Mr. Pierrepont had but just returned from Strathfieldsaye as we arrived. He had been there to meet the judges, whom the Duke was accustomed to receive annually, previously to the opening

---

[10] Ellesmere, p. 157; Quarterly Review, vol. 70, p. 464.

[11] A Memoir of Charles Mayne Young, Tragedian: With extracts from his son's journal. By Julian Charles Young, M. A., Rector of Ilmington. London and New York: Macmillan & Co.: 1871; pp. 158 et seq.

of the assizes. After dinner, Mr. Pierrepont was asked by the Duke of Beaufort, who, with the Duchess, was in the house, if he had had an agreeable visit. 'Particularly so,' was the answer. 'The Duke was in great force and, for him, unusually communicative. The two judges and myself having arrived before the rest of the guests, who lived nearer Strathfieldsaye than we did, the Duke asked us if we were disposed to take a walk, see the paddocks, and get an appetite for dinner. We all three gladly assented to the proposition. As we were stumping along, talking of Assheton Smith's stud and hounds, one of the judges asked the Duke if we might see Copenhagen, his celebrated charger. 'God bless you,' replied the Duke, 'he has been long dead; and half the fine ladies of my acquaintance have got bracelets or lockets made from his mane or tail.' 'Pray, Duke, apart from his being so closely associated with your Grace in the glories of Waterloo, was he a very remarkable — I mean a particularly clever horse?'

"*Duke* — 'Many faster horses, no doubt, many handsomer; but for bottom and endurance, never saw his fellow. I'll give you a proof of it. On the 17th, early in the day, I had a horse shot under me. Few know it, but it was so. Before ten o'clock I got on Copenhagen's back. There was so much to do and to see to, that neither he nor I were still for many minutes together. I never drew bit, and he never had a morsel in his mouth till eight P. M., when Fitzroy Somerset came to tell me dinner was ready in the little neighbouring village, Waterloo. The poor beast I saw myself stabled and fed. I told my groom to give him no hay, but, after a few go-downs of chilled water, as much corn and beans as he had a mind for, impressing on him the necessity of his strewing them well over the manger first. Somerset and I despatched a hasty meal, and as soon as we had done so, I sent off Somerset on an errand. This I did, I confess, on purpose that I might get him out of the way; for I knew that if he had had the slightest inkling of what I was up to, he would have done his best to dissuade me from my purpose, and want to accompany me.

"'The fact was, I wanted to see Blücher, that I might learn from his own lips at what hour it was probable he would be able to join forces with us the next day. Therefore, the moment Fitzroy's back was turned, I ordered Copenhagen to be resaddled, and told my man to get his own horse and accompany me to Wavre, where I had reason to believe old 'Forwards' was encamped. Now, Wavre being some twelve miles from Waterloo, I was not a little disgusted, on getting there, to find that the old fellow's tent was two miles still farther off.

"'However, I saw him, got the information I wanted from him, and made the best of my way homewards. Bad, however, was the best, for, by Jove, it was so dark that I fell into a deepish dyke by the roadside; and if it had not been for my orderly's assistance, I doubt if I should ever have got out. Thank God, there was no harm done, either to horse or man!

"'Well, on reaching headquarters, and thinking how bravely my old horse had carried me all day, I could not help going up to his head to tell him so by a few caresses. But hang me, if, when I was giving him a slap of approbation on his hind-quarters, he did not fling out one of his hind legs with as much vigour as if he had been in stable for a couple of days. Remember, gentlemen, he had been out with me on his back for upwards of ten hours, and had carried me eight and twenty miles besides. I call that bottom! ey?'"

Then there is another piece of evidence. Colonel Maurice says:—[12]

"Mr. Coltman — a well-known barrister now alive — remembers to have distinctly heard his father, then Mr. Justice Coltman of the Common Pleas, tell the story, and say that he had heard it from the Duke's own mouth during a particular visit to the Duke at Strathfieldsaye in a named year, 1838. He wrote to me, giving the story substantially, though not with quite as much detail, and making the horse's kicking out in reply to the caress take place on the 18th instead of on the 17th, as it appears in Young's narrative. He had at the time never seen Young's book. Obviously, the difference as to the day of the kick is just such a lapse as would naturally occur in a narrative not written down at the time. Either may be right."

Notwithstanding the improbable features in these accounts,— and there are many,[13]— it is at first sight

---

[12] Maurice, p. 337 : January, 1891.

[13] Mere improbability, however, is not a sufficient reason for rejecting a story supported by credible evidence. It is always impossible to place one's self precisely in the position of those of whom the story is told. And some, at any rate, of the improbable features may be mere accretions on the original story.

difficult to account for the existence of this evidence, except on the supposition that the story is true. But a close examination of the so-called Diary of the Rev. Mr. Young shows that it is not, strictly speaking, a diary at all, for the stories and remarks contained in it were not set down at the time, as in an ordinary journal. Thus, this very story, the date of which is given as 1833, is entered under the date of October 7, 1832. (Diary, p. 153.) Take another instance. The writer is speaking of Mr. John Wilson Croker, and he says, under date of March, 1832 (pp. 144, 145), that "for forty years he [Croker] filled a prominent position in the world of letters." Now forty years before 1832, Croker was only twelve years old. Again, in this very story of the ride to Wavre, which is said to have been told in 1833, the Duke is made to say of his horse Copenhagen that he had then "been long dead." But, in fact, Copenhagen did not die till 1836; the date of his death is given on the grave-stone erected over his remains at Strathfieldsaye.

As for the letter of Mr. Coltman to Colonel Maurice, which is a statement recently made of the former's recollection of what he had heard his father say that the Duke of Wellington told him in 1838, it clearly cannot have much weight, unless corroborated.

There is, moreover, some newly-discovered evidence. It consists of notes taken by the late Baron Gurney, of the Court of the Exchequer, of conversations with the Duke of Wellington. In one of these, the Duke was asked "whether a story was true of his having ridden over to Blücher the night before the battle of Waterloo and returned on the same horse. He said: 'No; that was not so. I did not see Blücher the day before Waterloo.'" This seems to settle the question.

[CHAP. 14.] BLÜCHER AND WELLINGTON.—NOTES.   243

3. We have spoken briefly of Napoleon's opinion, that the Duke of Wellington and Marshal Blücher ought to have retired on Brussels. The passage to which we referred reads as follows: — [14]

"One may ask,— What ought the English general to have done after the battle of Ligny and the combat of Quatre Bras? There cannot be two opinions on this subject. He ought on the night of the 17th and 18th to have traversed the Forest of Soignes by the Charleroi pike, while the Prussian army was traversing it by the Wavre pike; the two armies could then unite at daybreak before Brussels, leaving rearguards to defend the forest,— gain some days to give those of the Prussians who had been dispersed by the battle of Ligny time to rejoin the army,— obtain reinforcements from the fourteen English regiments which were either in garrison in Belgium or had just landed at Ostend on their return from America,— and leave the Emperor of the French to manœuvre as he liked. Would he, with an army of 100,000 men, have traversed the forest of Soignes to attack on the other side of it the two hostile armies united, more than 200,000 strong, and in position? That would certainly have been the most advantageous thing that could happen to the allies. Would he have been contented to take up a position himself? He certainly could not have kept it long, for 300,000 Russians, Austrians, and Bavarians, already arrived at the Rhine, would in a few weeks have been on the Marne, which would have obliged him to fly to the defence of the capital. Then, the Anglo-Prussian army could have marched forward, and joined their allies under the walls of Paris."

It is plain that the course pointed out by the Emperor would have avoided all the risks incurred by Wellington in giving battle at Waterloo, with the needed support not available until afternoon. But Clausewitz[15] denies that Wellington incurred any risk.

"Wavre is distant from Wellington's field of battle about two [German, or about ten English] miles. From the moment when the Duke of Wellington saw the enemy appear in his front up to

---

[14] Corresp., vol. 31, p. 258.
[15] Clausewitz, ch. 39, pp. 99, 100.

Blücher's arrival, six or eight hours would therefore have to elapse, unless Blücher had started still earlier; but in that time a battle against 70,000 men cannot be begun, fought and decided; it was therefore not to be feared that Wellington would be defeated before Blücher arrived."

It is, perhaps, a sufficient reply to this remark to recall the fact that the battle of Ligny was begun at half-past two and was completely finished at half-past nine, and that this period of seven hours includes the delay of nearly two hours caused by the unexpected appearance of d'Erlon's Corps. It seems to us foolish to contend that Wellington did not run a great risk of being defeated before the arrival of the Prussians. Had the battle been begun five or six hours earlier, all the troops in Napoleon's army could have been employed against the Anglo-Dutch forces, and the battle could have been fought as the Emperor intended to fight it. The risk of being beaten, we repeat, was a great risk; and we believe the Duke was quite aware that it was such when he assumed it. The question then is,— recurring to Napoleon's censure on Blücher and Wellington for not having avoided this risk by continuing their retreat to the immediate neighborhood of Brussels,— whether the possibility of overthrowing Napoleon at the beginning of the campaign by effecting a union of the allied armies at Waterloo warranted the two allied commanders in taking the risk of the defeat of the Anglo-Dutch army before this union could be effected. As this question is evidently one capable of indefinite discussion, we content ourselves with stating it.

CHAPTER XV.

THE EIGHTEENTH OF JUNE: GROUCHY AND BLÜCHER.

NAPOLEON received Marshal Grouchy's letter, dated Gembloux, 10 P. M. of June 17th, about 2 A. M. of the 18th, at the Caillou House, on the Brussels turnpike, where he passed the night of the 17th. A close examination of it might have raised a suspicion in his mind that Grouchy did not thoroughly comprehend his task, and that he might possibly fail to take the right course, if the emergency, which he had in his letter represented as not unlikely to occur, should actually confront him. He had said, that, if he found that the mass of the Prussians were retiring on Wavre, he "would follow them in that direction, in order that they might not be able to gain Brussels, and to separate them from Wellington," but if they were retiring on Perwez, that he would direct himself on that city. We have pointed out above that it was clearly impossible for him to prevent the Prussians from getting to Brussels. He was thirty miles from Brussels,— the Prussians less than twenty,— and they were directly between him and Brussels. And as for separating the Prussians at Wavre from Wellington, while Grouchy must of course follow them in the direction of Wavre as distinguished from that of Perwez, yet the only thing really open to him was to cross the Dyle at once by the bridges of Moustier and Ottignies and then to act in close connection with the main French army,— to stand between it and the Prussians, and ward off the danger as best he might. This could be done; but this was all that could be done. It was not to be expected that an attack upon the Prussian rearguard at Wavre,—which was the only other thing that Grouchy could do,—however vigorously made, could have the result of detaining their whole army. But, in Grouchy's letter, a movement on his part to rejoin or to approach the main army by crossing the Dyle, in case he found that the Prussians were massing at Wavre, was not even mentioned.

Napoleon and Soult, therefore, one would suppose, might have seen by the programme which Grouchy had marked out for himself in his despatch that in all probability he was not clearly apprehending the situation, and that it was therefore possible that he might make a serious, perhaps a very serious, mistake the next day. They ought, therefore, if they suspected this to be the state of the case, to have replied at once, giving him precise instructions as to his course in the event of the retreat of the Prussians on Wavre. They should have told him, that, if he should find this to be the fact, he must at once march to cross the Dyle above Wavre, at Moustier and Ottignies, approach the main army, and act in conjunction with it. Yet although Grouchy told the officer who carried the 10 P. M. despatch to wait for an answer, none was returned.[1] Grouchy was not even informed where the army was, and that it was confronted by the English army in position. Nor was he advised, as he surely should have been, that Domon's reconnoissance had proved that a strong Prussian column,—consisting, as we have seen, of the two beaten corps, those of Zieten and Pirch I.,—had retired on Wavre by way of Gery and Gentinnes.[2] It is impossible to account for these omissions.[3]

---

[1] Mém. du Duc de Raguse, vol. 7, pp. 124, 125.
[2] Soult's despatch to Grouchy: June 18th, 10 A. M.
[3] Even if the Emperor had been asleep when Grouchy's aide arrived, or

Now this last-mentioned fact, that "a pretty strong (Prussian) column" had "passed by Gery and Gentinnes, directed on Wavre," was the most important fact that could be ascertained, both for Napoleon and Grouchy. Napoleon had in fact, at 2 A. M. of the 18th, when Grouchy's letter arrived, strong reason to apprehend that Grouchy might, during the night, ascertain that the whole of Blücher's army had retired on Wavre. It certainly would seem that this was one of those cases where nothing should be omitted that could assist the mind of a subordinate in arriving at a correct conclusion.[4]

Napoleon, however, seems to have thought it unnecessary to send Grouchy any precise directions. We know that he expected Grouchy to arrive the next afternoon by the bridge of Moustier. Marbot, whose Memoirs have just been published, states,[5] that, towards 11 A. M. of the day of the battle, he was sent with his own regiment of hussars and a battalion of infantry to and beyond the extreme right of the army, with instructions, brought to him by one of the Emperor's aides, to push reconnoissances to the bridges of Moustier and Ottignies. He says that these detachments were connected by cavalry-posts, "so that they could quickly inform him of their junction with the advance guard of the troops of Marshal Grouchy, which were to arrive on the Dyle."

It may perhaps be, that Grouchy's expressed intention that he would try to prevent Blücher from joining Wellington was held by both the Emperor and his chief-of-

---

had been at the front, where he was between one and two o'clock in the morning, to see if the English army was still in position, a competent chief-of-staff should, of his own motion, have sent back at once to Grouchy the information possessed at headquarters.

[4] Especially when, according to Marshal Marmont, the subordinate was a man like Grouchy: Mém., vol. 4, p. 125. See, also, Napoléon à Waterloo, p. 226, n.

[5] Marbot, vol. 3, pp. 404 *et seq.*; Gérard: Dern. Obs. p. 44.

staff as indicating with sufficient certainty that, if he found that the Prussians were retiring on Wavre, he would proceed at once to cross the Dyle at Moustier or Limale, and operate on the left bank of that river, on the right of the main army.[6] This course was almost necessarily implied in an attempt to prevent the Prussians at Wavre from joining the English, as we have just pointed out; it may be, therefore, that the Emperor thought another order needless. But whatever the reason, no order was sent to Grouchy till 10 A. M. the next morning. This did not reach him till 4 P. M.[7] that afternoon, when he was fighting in front of Wavre.

Marshal Grouchy, then, acted up till 4 o'clock of the 18th of June under the order dictated the previous day by the Emperor to Count Bertrand. This fact we desire distinctly to bring out, so that there shall be no possibility of further mistake on this subject. The history of this day, from the very first narratives down to the very last, has been illustrated by the mistakes of historians and critics as to the orders under which Marshal Grouchy acted. Not only did Grouchy himself deliberately deny for nearly thirty years that he received any written order on the 17th, thereby misleading the most sagacious critics and rendering their criticisms on this part of the campaign in great part valueless, but even long after the fact was universally acknowledged that he did get a written order in the shape of the Bertrand letter, a certain unwillingness or inability to take in the meaning of this written order, to recognize that it imposed a different task on Marshal Grouchy from that laid upon him by the verbal orders which had previously been given him, has, nevertheless, strangely enough existed. We have pointed this out in the Notes to Chapter XIII; but we will add one or two more instances here.

---

[6] *Cf.* La Tour d'Auvergne, pp. 232, 233, 245.

[7] Grouchy Mém., vol. 4, pp. 70, 87, 131, n.

The Bertrand order, as we have seen, instructed Grouchy to find out what the Prussians were intending to do,—*whether they were intending to separate themselves from the English, or to unite with them for the purpose of trying the fate of another battle for the defence of Brussels or Liége,*—and the order closed without giving him any directions whatever in case either of these emergencies should arise. The thing which Grouchy was to do, therefore, was to ascertain whether the Prussians were intending to unite with the English, *and then to act in accordance with his best judgment.* No directions whatever, we repeat, were given to him for his conduct if he should find that the Prussians were intending to unite with the English. We have just adverted to this omission of the Emperor to give Grouchy precise instructions in this emergency. There is no question that he did not give any. Grouchy was entirely untrammelled. If he found that the Prussians were intending to unite with the English to fight another battle for the defence of Brussels, he was absolutely free to adopt whatever course might seem to him best.

Yet we find the latest American historian of this campaign, in speaking of Grouchy's rejection of the advice given by Gérard, when the cannon of Waterloo was heard, saying, that the question was, "whether to turn the army to its left on reaching Corbaix, and, crossing the Dyle by the bridges of Moustier and Ottignies, to take the road to Maransart and Planchenoit, *or to adhere to the Emperor's orders to follow the Prussians* whom they now knew to be at Wavre,"—[8] and, again, that Grouchy "*persisted in adhering to the orders the Emperor had given him.*"[9]

In the same way we find the latest English commentator on the campaign saying, "Whether Grouchy can

---

[8] Gardner, pp. 160, 161. The italics are our own.
[9] Ib., pp. 161, 162.

be held responsible for not having" marched to the sound of the guns "*when Napoleon's instructions directed him on Wavre*, will always be a subject for endless, and, I think, not very profitable, debate." [10]

It is quite time that an end should be put to misunderstandings on this subject. Until 4 P. M., we repeat, Grouchy acted under the Bertrand order only.

To return to the narrative.

Marshal Grouchy had written to the Emperor at 10 P. M. of the 17th, as we have seen, telling him that, "arrived at Sauvenières, the Prussians had divided into two columns, one taking the road for Wavre in passing by Sart-à-Walhain, and the other appearing to be directed on Perwez." He then went on to say that he would operate in the direction in which he found that the mass of their forces had gone.

Being thus in doubt as to the direction of the retreat of the enemy, he determined to move at first on Sart-à-Walhain, from which point he could march either on Wavre or on Perwez according to the information he might there receive. Inclining probably at this time to the opinion that the Prussians had retreated by way of Perwez, in which case there would be no necessity for unusual haste, he determined to give his troops a good night's rest. Of the absolute necessity of gaining time in case he should find that the Prussians had retreated on Wavre with the intention of joining Wellington, he seems to have been utterly unmindful.

Hence, at or soon after 10 P. M., he issued his orders to his corps-commanders to march in the morning to Sart-à-Walhain. Vandamme,[11] whose corps had biv-

---

[10] Maurice, p. 550: Sept. 1890., The italics are our own. It is possible that Colonel Maurice may have had in mind the language of Soult's order dated 10 A. M., in which Grouchy's movement on Wavre is approved. But this did not reach Grouchy till 4 P. M., as we have just stated. See, also, Kennedy, p. 159.

[11] La Tour d'Auvergne, p. 315, n. 1. The hour of starting is given in the

ouacked somewhat in advance of Gembloux, was to start at 6 A. M. It was to be preceded in the march by Exelmans' cavalry, the bulk of which was at Sauvenières. Gérard,[12] whose troops were in and about Gembloux, was to follow with his corps at 8 A. M. Pajol[13] was ordered from Mazy on the Namur road, where he then was, taking with him the division of Teste, to Grand Leez, where he would receive further orders.

Then, at 2 A. M., Grouchy writes to the Emperor to inform him that he was intending to march on Sart-à-Walhain,[14] but without indicating his ulterior course.

During the early morning hours, however, information was received[15] which removed his doubts as to the direction of the Prussian retreat, for we find him writing to Pajol[16] "at daybreak," as follows:—

"The movement of retreat of Blücher's army appears to me very clearly to be upon Brussels."[17]

Marshal Grouchy, therefore, at daybreak,— which in Belgium at that season of the year is at least as early as 3.30 A. M.,— for the sun rises at 3.48 A. M.,— had come

---

Grouchy Memoirs (vol. 4, p. 56) as "before four o'clock." But this is a gross and manifest error. *Cf.* Charras, vol. 2, p. 33, where the hour is given as 6 A. M.

[12]La Tour d'Auvergne, p. 316, n. 1 ; Grouchy Mém., vol. 4. p. 55.

[13]La Tour d'Auvergne, p. 316, n. 2 ; Grouchy Mém., vol. 4, p. 57.

[14]This despatch is not in existence, but its receipt was acknowledged and the above statement in it was referred to in Soult's despatch to Grouchy, dated 1 P. M., June 18th. From Grouchy's statement that he was going to Sart-à-Walhain, Soult drew the inference that he was going to Corbaix or to Wavre.

[15] Gérard : Dern. Obs., pp. 13, 14 ; Letter of General Exelmans.

[16]Grouchy Mém., vol. 4, pp. 62, 63.

[17]There is in the Grouchy Mémoires, vol. 4, pp. 65, 66, what purports to be a copy of a despatch to the Emperor dated Gembloux, 3 A. M. But its authenticity is more than doubtful. *Cf.* La Tour d'Auvergne, p. 318, n. It begins with the statement that all Grouchy's reports and information confirm the idea that the Prussians are retiring on Brussels, to concentrate there, or to deliver battle after being united to the English.

to the conclusion that Blücher was retiring on Brussels by way of Wavre. Yet he still adhered to his plan of marching on Sart-à-Walhain, although that place had been chosen the evening before as the first stage in the next day's march because he had then been in doubt as to whether his ultimate movement would be in the direction of Wavre or in that of Perwez.[18] Moreover, although he had come to the conclusion that the Prussians were retiring on Wavre, towards the English, which made promptness and celerity on his part of the very first importance, he did not change the very late hours he had fixed for the march of the next morning. In fact, even these hours were not adhered to. Exelmans,[19] who preceded the column, did not start till 7.30 A. M.; Vandamme,[20] who came next, did not move until 8 A. M.; and it was not until 9 A. M. that Gérard's[21] corps got through the town of Gembloux, and was in full march for Sart-à-Walhain. And yet no one knew better than Marshal Grouchy that the Prussians had many hours the start of him, and that if he was going to do anything that day to prevent them from joining Wellington, there was no time to be lost.

There is no difference of opinion among the Continental[22] authorities as to Marshal Grouchy's true course on this morning. As soon as he had arrived at the conclusion that the Prussians were retiring on Wavre, which was, as we have seen, between 3 and 4 A. M., he should have changed his evening orders entirely; he should

---

[18] Charras, vol. 2, pp. 33, 55. Charras seems to us to be in error in supposing that Grouchy's uncertainty still existed on the morning of the 18th. He has, perhaps, overlooked the statement in Grouchy's order to Pajol, dated at daybreak, quoted in the text.

[19] Gérard: Dernières Obs., p. 24; Letter of General Exelmans.

[20] Ib., p. 25; Letter of General Berthezène.

[21] Gérard: Quelques Doc., p. 12.

[22] We shall examine the English authorities in the Notes to this chapter. See *post*, p. 280.

have begun his march at once, and should have directed it to the bridge of Moustier. (See Map 9.)

Says Jomini:—[23]

"The Marshal should not, then, have hesitated; he should at daybreak on the 18th have marched with all speed on Moustier with Exelmans, Vandamme and Gérard, directing Pajol's cavalry and Teste's division on Wavre, in pursuit of the enemy's rearguard.

"Being able to reach Moustier by ten o'clock,[24] he could have then forwarded his infantry on Wavre by Limale, pushing Exelmans' dragoons on St. Lambert, or else have marched to Lasne himself."

Says Clausewitz:—[25]

"But the moment he learnt that Blücher had turned towards the Dyle, which must have happened in Gembloux in the night between the 17th and 18th, the idea must have shot at once into his mind that this could only be in order to join Wellington, for one does not leave one's natural line of retreat without reason. From that moment he had to consider it his duty, not to lie at the heels of Blücher's rear-guard, but to get between him and Bonaparte, in order to be able to throw himself in front of Blücher in case he wanted to march off to his right. According to this, he would have to turn from Gembloux to the Dyle by the shortest road, &c."

Says Charras:—[26]

"Everything indicated that the most advantageous manœuvre for Blücher was that which would bring him the most quickly near Wellington,—would unite the Prussians to the Anglo-Dutch. Since the opening of hostilities the two allied generals had manœuvred to bring about this union; and it was evident that they were not going to renounce this idea after the defeat of one of their armies; the activity, energy, audacity,—so well known,—of Blücher—the tenacity,—equally well known,—of Wellington,

---

[23] Jomini, pp. 175 *et seq.*

[24] 10.30 A. M., according to Charras, vol. 2, p. 62.

[25] Clausewitz, ch. 50, p. 146.

[26] Charras, vol. 2, pp. 57, 58.

sufficed to guarantee that they would not easily renounce this intention.

"If they should succeed in this, Napoleon would find himself exposed to being crushed under the weight of the two allied armies.

"This catastrophe, the greatest of all misfortunes, Grouchy ought, before everything, to put himself in position to avert, so far as he could do so. Hence it was imperative that he should come as speedily as possible within the sphere of Napoleon's operations; and hence, also, he must march on Moustier.

"From this point, in fact, better than from any other, he would be equally in position to diminish the consequences of the union of the Prussians and the Anglo-Dutch, if it should already have been effected, or to hinder it, if it should not yet have taken place."

With these authorities we entirely concur. Marshal Grouchy, as soon as he had made up his mind that Blücher was retiring on Brussels by way of Wavre, should have marched for the bridge of Moustier, and should have started at daybreak.[27] Instead of this, he adhered to the direction of Sart-à-Walhain, although, even if he were proposing to follow Blücher straight to Wavre, Sart-à-Walhain was out of the direct route. It had in fact been selected *because* it lay to the eastward of the Wavre road. He might have saved from two to four hours by starting at daybreak, but of this he was utterly unmindful. He did not thoroughly reconnoitre with his cavalry towards the Dyle, to see if the enemy were not marching towards the English, although it was certainly his manifest duty to do so.[28] All he did in this direction was to send [29] a staff-officer with a small escort at daybreak or soon after to the bridge of Moustier, to see, apparently, if any Prussian troops had crossed there, but

---

[27] We reserve for the Notes to this chapter the consideration of the various opinions on the consequences of this movement, had it been made.

[28] See Siborne's excellent remarks on this subject, — vol. 1, pp. 318 *et seq.*

[29] Declaration of M. Leguest, in the Grouchy Mém., vol. 4, pp. 141, 142. The staff-officer, by name Pont-Bellanger, must have left Moustier several hours before Marbot's officer, Captain Eloy, got there. See Marbot, vol. 3, p. 407.

he rejoined Grouchy before Grouchy had arrived at Sart-à-Walhain, that is, before 11 A. M. With this exception the Marshal made absolutely no reconnoissances to his left until he had arrived in front of Wavre.

Somewhere between 10 and 11 A. M. he reached Sart-à-Walhain. Thence he proceeded to Walhain, or, as it is sometimes called, Walhain St. Paul.[30] He alighted at the house of a M. Hollert, the notary of the neighboring village of Nil St. Vincent, who lived in a large house in Walhain known as the Chateau Marette. Here he stopped to write a despatch to the Emperor and to get his breakfast. The cavalry of Exelmans and the 3d Corps under Vandamme had passed this point on the road to Wavre, and had reached or perhaps passed Nil St. Vincent.

The despatch, which is dated Sart-à-Walhain, by an error for Walhain,—11 A. M.,—begins by stating that the Ist, IId and IIId Corps of Blücher's army are marching in the direction of Brussels. Grouchy subsequently says:—[31]

"This evening I expect to be concentrated at Wavre, and thus to find myself between Wellington, whom I presume to be in retreat before your majesty, and the Prussian army."

He also states that some of the Prussians are proceeding towards the plain of the Chyse, near the Louvain road, with the design of concentrating there, or of fighting any troops which may pursue them there, or of uniting themselves to Wellington. This part of the despatch looks as if Grouchy thought that a part of the Prussians intended to concentrate to his right. Still, as he distinctly states that the Ist, IId and IIId Corps are marching in the direction of Brussels, we must suppose that he is not referring to these three corps when he

---

[30] See the Notes to this chapter.

[31] Grouchy Mém., vol. 4, pp. 71, 72. This despatch is given in full in Appendix C, xxx; *post*, pp. 386, 387.

speaks of those Prussians who are proceeding towards the plain of the Chyse. So that, when he says that at Wavre he expects to be between Wellington, who he supposes is retiring on Brussels by the Charleroi turnpike, and the Prussian army, three of whose corps are, he says, also retiring on Brussels, it is difficult, if not impossible, to know what he means. He seems to have been completely bewildered.

This despatch had hardly been handed to the staff-officer[32] who was to carry it to the Emperor, when the cannon of Waterloo was heard. Then, at any rate, Marshal Grouchy knew that the English were not retreating before Napoleon, but were standing "on this side of the Forest of Soignes," as the Emperor had, the afternoon before, conjectured they might. Three Prussian corps had gone towards Brussels, as Grouchy had just written to the Emperor. It was very possible that they might at that moment be marching across the country to join the Anglo-Dutch army. Perhaps nothing could prevent this. But it was plainly Grouchy's duty to march towards the Emperor as fast as he could. If he could not prevent the Prussians from joining the English, he might at any rate be able to prevent them from attacking the French. If he should cross the Dyle at Moustier and Ottignies, and move directly towards the line of march which they must take in order to attack the French, their march would, if he arrived in time, assuredly be suspended. This was at any rate the thing to try to do. It was to be feared that a terrible disaster was impending over Napoleon and his army; but there was a chance of averting it. There was only one thing to do, — and that was, promptly and gallantly to make the attempt to avert it. (See Map 10.)

Gérard, who had arrived at Walhain with his corps, strenuously urged Grouchy to march to the sound of the

---

[32]Grouchy Mém., vol. 4, p. 75.

cannon. He pressed this on Grouchy with perhaps undue heat; but the occasion was one that admitted of no delay. The son of Marshal Grouchy, who may be supposed to have heard his father's account of the interview, says: —[33]

"The commander of the 4th Corps uttered haughtily, and in a fashion little in harmony with the respect due to his chief and with military discipline, the advice that the right wing ought to march to the sound of the cannon in order to effectuate a junction with the Emperor.

"Grouchy did not find the advice bad in itself, but the form employed to present it. At the same time he consented to discuss Gérard's opinion with him."

That personal feelings had some influence on Marshal Grouchy's decision would seem from the above statement very probable.[34]

We do not reproduce the arguments of Marshal Grouchy here, because they are based mainly upon his statement, which we have found to be erroneous, that "his instructions, from which he was not permitted to depart, enjoined formally upon him not to lose sight of the Prussians when he should have joined them."

A discussion where one of the parties concealed the existence of a written order, which prescribed no such instructions as those stated above, cannot enlighten us much.

The difficulties of marching across the country by way of Mont St. Guibert to the Dyle were also dwelt upon,— the chief-of-artillery of the 4th Corps, Baltus, having great doubts as to the possibility of such a march, and the chief-of-engineers, Valazé, offering to remove the obstacles.

Grouchy finally decided to resume the march towards Wavre. His army marched in a single column by the

---

[33] Le Mal. de Grouchy, p. 15, n. 2: p. 59; Grouchy Mém., vol. 4, p. 75.
[34] La Tour d'Auvergne, p. 328. *Cf.* Grouchy Mém., vol. 4, p. 295.

road which, passing through Nil St. Vincent and just to the north of Corbaix, reaches La Baraque, and thence leads to Wavre by a line, almost straight. Not a half a mile beyond La Baraque there is a road which leads to the bridge of Moustier, less than three miles off; three-quarters of a mile farther on is another road, which, with its branches, leads to the bridges of Limelette and Limale, at a distance of only two miles. Half a mile north of the bridge of Moustier is another bridge, that of Ottignies. These bridges had not been destroyed, and they were all unguarded.[35] Then there were convenient woods able to conceal any movement of the troops towards the river.

There was a slight affair in a wood a short distance beyond La Baraque, in which the cavalry of Ledebur,[36] assisted by two battalions of infantry, skirmished for an hour or so. While this was going on, two divisions of the IId Corps, which had been making their way through the town of Wavre, were brought back, and took up position, facing south, about a mile south of the town. But there was no resistance to speak of. When the French advanced, the Prussians retired on Wavre.

In its march, which was made to the sound of the cannon of Waterloo,[37] the army of Marshal Grouchy had then abundant opportunity to cross the Dyle at Moustier and Ottignies, at Limelette and Limale.[38] La Baraque, on the main road to Wavre, from near which the roads to these bridges diverge, was reached about two o'clock.[39]

---

[35] The one of these bridges which was nearest Wavre, that at Limale, was passed at six o'clock by Valin's cavalry, without experiencing any serious resistance. Siborne, vol. 2, p. 286. Berton, pp. 66, 67. Marbot's cavalry-picket occupied the bridge of Moustier all the afternoon. Marbot, vol. 3, p. 407. *Cf.* Charras, vol. 2, p. 69.

[36] Ollech, pp. 208, 209.

[37] Berthezène, in Gérard, Dern. Obs., p. 25.

[38] Berton, p. 66, n.

[39] Charras, vol. 2, p. 44.

From this point on to Wavre, the Prussians were clearly to be seen marching to the field of Waterloo.[40] If Grouchy had in season recalled Pajol and the division of Teste from the extreme right of the column, in order to mask the movement by threatening Wavre, it would certainly seem that Vandamme's Corps might have crossed at Limale and Limelette, and Gérard's at Ottignies and Moustier, and that, before 4 P. M., the whole force could have been *en route* for St. Lambert.[41]

The fact is, the whole question of Grouchy's flank march at noon has been unnecessarily confused by three very general misconceptions, namely: —

(1) That it was at Sart-à-Walhain where the sound of the cannon was heard. It was at Walhain, a good mile nearer to the bridges.

(2) That it was necessary, in order to go to the bridges, for Grouchy's column to cut across the marshy and difficult country between Walhain and Moustier,[42] by way of Mont St. Guibert. Instead of this, the main road could be kept until the army had arrived at La Baraque; or, possibly, the 4th Corps could have taken a somewhat long cross-road which leads to Moustier from Neuf Sart, a village on the main road about a mile to the south-east of La Baraque, while the 3d Corps could have marched on the roads which branch off to the bridges just beyond La Baraque.

No doubt, if Grouchy had started at daybreak from Gembloux, as he ought to have done, he would have passed through Mont St. Guibert, and over very bad and miry roads; but to gain the bridge of Moustier from Walhain, the route he actually pursued, by way of La Baraque, was nearly as short as the other, and was, up to

---

[40] Berthezène, in Gérard, Dern. Obs., p. 25.

[41] Charras' discussion of this movement will be considered in the Notes to this chapter: *post*, p. 284, n. 6.

[42] Charras, vol. 2, p. 69, n.

that point, so far as we know, a tolerable road.⁴³   At least there were no such complaints of it as were made of the roads from Ligny to Gembloux.

Now, from the point just beyond La Baraque, where the first road branches off, it is nearer to Moustier than it is to Wavre. From where the other road branches off to Limale and Limelette, the distance is about the same as to Wavre. Making allowance, then, for the badness of the river roads, on the one hand, and for the time saved by passing the army over several instead of over one single road on the other hand, and assuming that there had been no fighting, the whole force could have successfully crossed the river by 4 P. M., which was the hour at which Grouchy's force arrived in front of Wavre.

(3) That there would have been any serious resistance experienced at the bridges.

Not one of these bridges, as has been above pointed out,⁴⁴ was occupied in force by the Prussians. Only one, that at Limale, was occupied at all, and that only by a small detachment. They had had also some cavalry and two battalions of infantry in observation at Mont St. Guibert, but these retreated to La Baraque on finding that the cavalry of Exelmans had got in their rear by way of Corbaix.

Had Marshal Grouchy, therefore, pursued his march to the neighborhood of La Baraque, which place his head of column reached about 2 P. M., and had he then promptly availed himself of the roads which lead to the bridges, directing Pajol, who was a very able and experienced officer, to cover and conceal the movement with his cavalry and the division of Teste, he could, as it seems to us, in all probability, have been across the Dyle at 4 o'clock, ready to march towards Lasne and St. Lambert.

---

⁴³The paved *chaussée* which now runs straight from Gembloux to Wavre was not built in 1815. Nor was the *chaussée* from Sombreffe to Gembloux.

⁴⁴*Ante*, p. 258.

Now at 4 o'clock only two brigades [45] of Bülow's (IVth) Corps had passed through Lasne. They, with the artillery and cavalry which accompanied them, were at that moment resting and reforming in the Wood of Paris,[46] a little wood just west of the town of Lasne, after an exhausting march.[47] The other two brigades were between St. Lambert and Lasne. The IId Corps was stretched along the road between Wavre and St. Lambert. It had not yet reached the latter place.[48] The Ist Corps was a mile and a half from Ohain, on the northerly road. The IIId Corps was in and about Wavre. (See Map 11.)

If, then, Marshal Grouchy had succeeded in the operation of crossing the Dyle at the four bridges or any of them while Thielemann's Corps was detained in Wavre by Pajol and Teste, and if he had boldly advanced towards Lasne and St. Lambert, he would certainly have arrested the march of Bülow and Pirch I. Although the Prussians would have been superior in numbers, they yet would have been compelled to halt and form line of battle on observing the advance of Grouchy's 30,000 men. The chances are that Grouchy would ultimately have been forced to retire; he could hardly have been a match for the 50,000 men opposed to him; and his retreat could at any time have been precipitated by an attack on his right flank by Thielemann, if that officer had felt himself at liberty to leave Wavre. Yet these operations would without question have consumed the rest of the afternoon; it would almost certainly have been impossible for the corps of Bülow and Pirch I. to have attacked the French at Planchenoit that day. Zieten certainly might have pursued his march unmolested if

---

[45] The Prussian brigade corresponded then to the French or English division.

[46] Sometimes called the Wood of Frischermont.

[47] Siborne, vol. 2, pp. 127, 128.

[48] See Siborne's Map of the Field of Wavre, 4 o'clock P. M., 18th June.

he had thought it wise to do so. How these movements would have affected the result of the battle of Waterloo, we will consider when we come to the account of the battle. All we want to show at this stage of the narrative is, that, had Gérard's counsel been taken, Marshal Grouchy's command might have been across the Dyle at Moustier and the other bridges by 4 P. M., and that at that moment the van of the IVth Corps had only just passed through Lasne.

It is time that we returned to the Prussians.

Bülow, whose corps (the IVth) had not been engaged at Ligny, was ordered to march at daybreak from Dion-le-Mont, where he had passed the night, for St. Lambert, with the view of attacking the French right.[49] He had a long distance to go, and was, moreover, detained by a fire which broke out in the streets of Wavre, and his main body did not reach St. Lambert till noon.[50] Here there was a long halt.[51]

The IId Corps was to follow the IVth, but for some reason or other it did not begin to leave Wavre till nearly noon,[52] and it was not until 4 P. M. that the whole corps had got through the town and had taken the road for St. Lambert.[53]

The Ist Corps,— Zieten's,— which was to march by the northerly road, by way of Ohain, to join the army of Wellington, also did not start until nearly noon.[54] The IIId Corps, which was to be the last to leave Wavre, was to march by way of Couture towards Planchenoit, in support of the IVth and IId Corps. But it was to remain

---

[49] Ollech, p. 187.

[50] Clausewitz, ch. 42, p. 107.

[51] Maurice, p. 549: Sept., 1890.

[52] Charras, vol. 2, p. 43.

[53] Ib., p. 45. *Cf.* Siborne's Map of the Field of Wavre, 4 o'clock P. M., June 18th.

[54] Ib., p. 43.

in Wavre, if the enemy should show himself there in force.

These arrangements, it must be confessed, do not indicate that determination to march with all possible speed to the support of an ally in danger of being defeated before the promised support arrives, which has usually been attributed to Marshal Blücher. They are so deliberate, so tardy even, that we must seek an explanation of them. Bülow, it is true, moved out promptly enough; but the delay of the IId Corps in leaving Wavre is most extraordinary, under the circumstances, considering that its commander had been informed at midnight that the IVth Corps had been ordered to march at break of day, and that he himself had been ordered to join that corps immediately, and follow its line of march.[55]

It appears now, from the recent history of Von Ollech, that about 9.30 A. M. Marshal Blücher dictated a note to General Müffling, stating that he would place himself, ill as he was, at the head of his troops in order to attack at once the right of Napoleon's army; and that Gneisenau, still disposed to be cautious in trusting to the assurances of the English general that he would accept battle at Waterloo, added a postscript in these words: —[56]

"General Gneisenau has been informed of the contents of this letter, but asks your Excellency to ascertain definitely whether the Duke really has a fixed determination to fight in his present position, or whether perhaps it is a mere demonstration, which at the best would be very unfortunate for our army. Your Excellency will have the kindness to obtain for me full information on this matter, as it is of the highest importance to be thoroughly assured of what the Duke is going to do, in order to determine our course of action."

Ollech[57] goes on to tell us that Gneisenau was, even

---

[55] Ollech, p. 188.
[56] Ib., p. 189; Maurice, p. 537: Sept., 1890.
[57] Ollech, p. 190.

at this late hour, not without his misgivings. He says that Gneisenau believed that the Duke had left him in the lurch at Ligny. He also says that he fully took in the exposed situation of the Prussian army, if the Anglo-Dutch forces should fall back to Brussels, — a retreat by way of Louvain being probably then the only thing open to the Prussians. He says, indeed, that before an answer was received to this communication, Gneisenau had determined to go ahead, and carry out the plan, and that between 11 and 12 in the morning Zieten had been ordered to Ohain.

But may we not fairly infer, that, under the impression of these feelings, — of this doubt whether Wellington really intended to fight, — a doubt, it must be remembered, which no sound of cannon until half-past eleven in the morning came to dispel, — Bülow had been ordered to be very cautious, and to proceed with all deliberation, — and that the departure of Pirch I. and Zieten had been delayed? It would certainly seem as if this were the case.

The welcome sound of the cannon of Waterloo, however, shortly before noon, dispelled all doubts and all hesitations; and there can be no question that every one in the Prussian army from the old Field Marshal down to the privates in the ranks did their best for the success of the day. The roads were frightful; it was almost impossible to get the artillery and waggons over them; but every exertion was made.

Grouchy's obstinate determination to operate on the right bank of the Dyle brought him in front of Wavre. He displayed more troops than the Prussian generals had supposed that he had with him. But their plan was not altered. To Thielemann's Corps alone was it left to defend the town.

It is not necessary to go into the details of this action. It was not fought by Marshal Grouchy with any skill. The troops of Vandamme entangled themselves in the vain endeavor to carry the lower bridges in the town. The 4th Corps repeatedly but ineffectually endeavored to get possession of the Mill of Bierges, just above the town. Here Gérard was wounded. Between 6 and 7 P. M. Pajol carried the bridge of Limale, and this position was held, despite an attempt of the Prussians to repossess themselves of it. The attack on Wavre was conducted in the most gallant manner by the French, but without any well-arranged plan. Their efforts were in the main uselessly directed against an enemy behind walls and in houses, when nothing would have been easier than to have turned the whole position by crossing the river at Limale. The resistance of the Prussians was worthy of all praise.

During the action Marshal Grouchy received two despatches from Marshal Soult. These demand our careful consideration, not because they can in any way explain the motives which actuated Marshal Grouchy in directing his command upon Wavre instead of upon Lasne and St. Lambert, for they were received too late to have influenced him at all, but because they throw light on the expectations entertained by Napoleon in regard to Grouchy's movements and especially in regard to his coöperation with the main army.

These orders were both signed by Marshal Soult, the chief-of-staff, and were no doubt drafted by him.

The first, dated at 10 A. M., reads as follows: — [58]

In front of the Farm of Caillou,
June 18, 1815, 10 A. M.

Marshal:
The Emperor has received your last report, dated from Gembloux.[59]

You speak to his Majesty of only two Prussian columns, which have passed at Sauvenières and Sart-à-Walhain. Nevertheless,

---

[58] Grouchy Mém., vol. 4, p. 79; Charras, vol. 1, pp. 283, 284; App. C, xxxiii; *post*, p. 388.

[59] *Ante*, p. 212; also App. B, *post*, p. 358.

reports say that a third column, which was a pretty strong one, has passed by Gery and Gentinnes, directed on Wavre.[60]

The Emperor instructs me to tell you that at this moment his Majesty is going to attack the English army, which has taken position at Waterloo, near the Forest of Soignes. Thus his Majesty desires that you will direct your movements on Wavre, in order to approach us, to put yourself in the sphere of our operations, and to keep up your communications with us, pushing before you those portions[61] of the Prussian army which have taken this direction, and which may have stopped at Wavre, where you ought to arrive as soon as possible.

You will follow the enemy's columns which are on your right by some light troops, in order to observe their movements and pick up their stragglers. Instruct me immediately as to your dispositions and your march, as also as to the news which you have of the enemy; and do not neglect to keep up your communications with us. The Emperor desires to have news from you very often.

The Marshal, Duke of Dalmatia.

To understand this despatch one must refer to that to which it professes to be an answer, namely, that dated Gembloux, at ten o'clock the night before. In that despatch Grouchy says, as will be remembered,[62] that, at Sauvenières, the Prussians apparently divided into two columns, one directed on Wavre and the other on Perwez; and that he will follow the principal force of the enemy in either direction as his information may indicate. Now Soult, having this before his eyes when he is writing the 10 A. M. despatch, simply says,— Do not take the Perwez direction,— take the Wavre direction,— for that will bring you nearer to us. We, also, have heard of a pretty strong Prussian column which has retreated on Wavre; that is an additional reason why you should take that direction. We want you to approach us, — to get within the sphere (*en rapport*) of our opera-

---

[60] This must have been the Ist and IId Corps.

[61] The original has "corps"; but army-corps are not meant. The same word is used below, — "quelques corps légers."

[62] *Ante* p. 212; App. B, *post*, p. 358.

tions; to keep up your communications with us; therefore you ought to get to Wavre as soon as possible.

The object of directing Grouchy on Wavre was therefore that he might approach the main army; that he might keep in strict communication with it,—might be within the sphere of its operations. There is no strategical or other object even hinted at in directing Grouchy on Wavre, save that of approaching the main army.[63] Nor is there any difficulty whatever in discerning the meaning of the writer.

It is also perfectly plain that no opposition to Marshal Grouchy's occupation of Wavre was apprehended. It is therefore fairly to be inferred that the writer intended, that, if the situation should be such from any cause that the occupation of Wavre or the attempt to occupy it, would not subserve the purpose of enabling Grouchy to draw nearer to the main army, he should carry out this purpose in some other way. It seems to us foolish to say that this despatch would have justified Grouchy in taking the course which he did take, supposing, that is, that he had received it in time for it to affect his action. If, for example, a gentleman on a walking tour should order his servant to bring his baggage to a certain town, so that he might easily get at it from the place where he was himself expecting to be the next day, and the servant should find that all communication between this town and the region where his master expected to be had been interrupted by some accident, like the destruction of a railway-bridge, for instance, and he should nevertheless bring his master's baggage to that town, instead of

---

[63]Gérard (Dern. Obs. p. 19) remarks:—"If one analyzes separately the text of these two despatches, * * * one perceives that the Emperor has spoken of the direction of Wavre only because he finds it indicated in the reports of the commander of the right wing. The principal object of both of them was to insist upon movements which would bring the troops of the right wing near the main body." Gérard is here referring to the order sent to Grouchy at 1 P. M. (*post*, p. 270), as well as to that dated 10 A. M.

bringing it within his master's reach by carrying it to some other place, justifying himself by the terms of the letter, he would generally be regarded as having acted like a fool. Yet this is very nearly a parallel case to that of Marshal Grouchy, supposing that he had received the despatch in time to have acted on it, and had then acted as he did. The only thing needed to make it absolutely parallel is, that the servant in the case supposed should be in possession of information, of which his master was ignorant, making the carrying of the baggage to him at the earliest possible moment a matter of the utmost importance. Then the cases would be on all fours with each other.

But we have delayed perhaps too long to show that this order cannot justify Grouchy's action. Our excuse is that it has been so used by more than one authority.[64] Nor does the order show that Napoleon would have made the same mistake that Grouchy did, as has sometimes been thoughtlessly said; for Napoleon, at the time the despatch was sent off, knew nothing, as has just been pointed out, of the circumstances then under Grouchy's observation.

It cannot, of course, be contended that Napoleon was not responsible for this order of 10 A. M. A commander-in-chief must be supposed to know what orders are issued in his name. Yet it is certainly true that the directions given to Marbot do not tally at all with this order to Grouchy. According to the latter, Grouchy would be looked for in the direction of Wavre, — that is, of Lasne and St. Lambert; but Marbot was given to understand that the Emperor expected Grouchy to cross the Dyle at the bridges of Moustier and Ottignies. Colonel Marbot, in a letter written to Marshal Grouchy in 1830, says: —[65]

---

[64] Chesney, p. 206; Kennedy, p. 162; Gardner, p. 161, n.; Grouchy Mém., vol. 4, pp. 78, 80, 87.

[65] Marbot, vol. 3, pp. 404 *et seq.* This letter is chiefly made up from his

"At the commencement of the action, towards 11 A. M., I was detached from the division with my own regiment and a battalion of infantry, which had been placed under my command. These troops were posted on our extreme right, behind Frischermont, facing the Dyle.

"Particular instructions were given to me on the part of the Emperor by his aide-de-camp, Labedoyère, and by a staff officer whose name I do not recall. They prescribed to me to leave the bulk of my command always in view of the field of battle, to post 200 infantry in the Wood of Frischermont,[66] one squadron at Lasne, having outposts as far as St. Lambert; another squadron, half at Couture, half at Beaumont, sending reconnoissances as far as the Dyle, to the bridges of Moustier and Ottignies."

He then describes the arrangements for the speedy transmission of intelligence, and proceeds:—

"A note from Captain Eloy,[67] which the intermediate posts promptly transmitted to me, informed me that he had found no force at Moustier, nor at Ottignies, and that the inhabitants assured him that the French on the right bank of the Dyle would pass the river at Limale, Limelette and Wavre."

He sent this word to the Emperor, who ordered him to push reconnoissances in those directions. Then, half a mile beyond St. Lambert, they captured some Prussians, who informed him that they were followed by a large part of the Prussian army. He then says:—

"I proceeded to St. Lambert with a squadron to reinforce the troops there. I saw in the distance a strong column, approaching St. Lambert. I sent an officer in all haste to forewarn the Emperor, who replied, telling me to advance boldly, that this body of troops could be nothing else than the corps of Marshal Grouchy, coming from Limale, and pushing before it some stray Prussians, of whom the prisoners I had just taken were a part."

---

report, which is to be found in "Napoléon à Waterloo," pp. 344 *et seq.* The editors of Marbot's Memoirs say (vol. 3, p. 408) that the steps they have taken to find the report at the War Office have been unsuccessful.

[66]Sometimes called the Wood of Paris.

[67]He commanded the picket at Moustier.

Soon after, the fact that the approaching column was composed of Prussian troops was manifest. The Emperor was now sure that Grouchy would come by the upper bridges: —

"My adjutant, whom I had ordered to go and inform the Emperor of the positive arrival of the Prussians at St. Lambert, returned, saying to me that the Emperor ordered me to inform the head of Marshal Grouchy's column, which ought at this moment to be debouching by the bridges of Moustier and Ottignies, since it had not come by Limale and Limelette, of the fact that the Prussians were advancing by way of St. Lambert."

It is plain from the above narrative that the Emperor, when he sent Marbot off, shortly before 11 A. M., expected Marshal Grouchy to arrive during the afternoon,[68] and that his first idea was that he would arrive by the bridges of Moustier and Ottignies. This seems to show that the Emperor did not revise the 10 A. M. despatch sent off by Soult, which indicated that they expected Grouchy to arrive from Wavre. Napoleon must have been at this hour, — 10–11 A. M., — making his final preparations for the battle.

Then there was another despatch to Grouchy, which we also give here in full: —[69]

Field of Battle of Waterloo,
the 18th of June: 1 P. M.

Marshal:

You wrote to the Emperor at 2 o'clock[70] this morning, that you would march on Sart-lez-Walhain; your plan then is to proceed to Corbaix or[71] to Wavre. This movement is conformable to his Majesty's arrangements which have been communicated to

---

[68] This was Marbot's own conviction; vol. 3, p. 408.

[69] La Tour d'Auvergne, pp. 270, 271; Charras, vol. 1, pp. 286, 287; Siborne, vol. 1, pp. 400, 401; Napoléon à Waterloo, pp. 279, 280; App. C, xxxiv; *post*, p. 389.

[70] The Grouchy Memoirs (vol. 4, p. 82) give this as 3 o'clock.

[71] The text given in the Grouchy Memoirs, vol. 4, p. 82, replaces this "or" by an "and." This is not followed in any other work.

you. Nevertheless, the Emperor directs me to tell you that you ought always to manœuvre in our direction.[72] It is for you to see the place where we are, to govern yourself accordingly, and to connect our communications, so as to be always prepared to fall upon any of the enemy's troops which may endeavor to annoy our right, and to destroy them.

"At this moment the battle is in progress[73] on the line of Waterloo. The enemy's centre is at Mont St. Jean; manœuvre, therefore, to join our right.
The Marshal, Duke of Dalmatia.

"P. S. A letter, which has just been intercepted, says that General Bülow is about to attack our right flank; we believe that we see this corps on the height of St. Lambert. So lose not an instant in drawing near us and joining us, in order to crush Bülow, whom you will take in the very act."

In this letter the Emperor's desire that Grouchy would manœuvre in his direction is expressed again and again, and even in the body of the letter it is plain that some apprehension is entertained at headquarters of an attack upon the right of the army by the Prussians. The postscript, of course, speaks for itself.

Grouchy did not receive this letter till between 6 and 7 P. M.,[74] when it was too late for him to accomplish much. He, however, carried the bridge of Limale, and established himself on the left bank of the Dyle for the night.

---

[72] The text of the Grouchy Memoirs inserts here the following:—"and to seek to come near to our army, in order that you may join us before any body of troops can put itself between us. I do not indicate to you the direction you should take."

[73] The original is "engagée." "This letter," says Marshal Grouchy (Fragm. Hist., Lettre à MM. Méry et Barthélemy; p. 14), "was in a hand writing so difficult to decipher that I read it, as did also my chief-of-staff, and my senior aide-de-camp, 'gagnée.'" The chief-of-staff, General Le Sénécal, says that the Marshal closely questioned the officer who was the bearer of the despatch, but he was so intoxicated that they could not get anything from him. Grouchy Mém., vol. 4, pp. 132, 133. *Cf.* Gérard, Dern. Obs., p. 20, n.

[74] Grouchy Mém., vol. 4, p. 87.

Taking the two letters together,—and leaving out of view for the moment the postscript of the second,—we see that Napoleon was expecting that Grouchy would approach him. He had learned of the "pretty strong column" which had passed by Gery and Gentinnes, directed on Wavre. He, no doubt, supposed that Grouchy had also learned of it; and he knew from Grouchy's despatches of 10 P. M. of the 17th and 2 A. M. of the 18th, that Grouchy had recognized the necessity of manœuvring in the direction of Wavre, if the mass of the Prussian army should have taken that course. Hence he expected to see him. He thought it likely that he would come by the bridges of Moustier and Ottignies, and strike in on his right and keep off any of the enemy's troops who might seek to molest him.

Of any apprehension of a serious attack by the Prussians in force there is no trace till we come to the postscript to the second letter. Up to the time when this postscript was written, Napoleon would seem to have felt pretty sure (though perhaps with some misgivings), either that Grouchy would prevent the Prussians from attacking him, or would himself join, or connect with, the main army. But the appearance of the Prussians at St. Lambert and the absence of any information from Grouchy evidently alarmed him.

NOTES TO CHAPTER XV.

1. THE first question that demands consideration in connection with the matters narrated in this chapter is this: —

Was it wise in Napoleon to detach from his main army such a large force as that which he gave to Grouchy? Or, — to state the question more carefully, — Napoleon, being, at 1 P. M. of the 17th (through his own neglect, but the cause is not important in this connection), in ignorance of the direction of the retreat of the Prussians, but having in mind that they might be intending to unite with the English and fight another battle for the defence of Brussels,[1] — was it wise in him to detach 33,000 men from his main army to find out about and take care of the Prussians?

This question, it must be observed, is quite a different one from that presented to Napoleon in the forenoon of the 17th, when he and Grouchy and every one else believed that the Prussians had fallen back on Namur. If the Prussians had retreated on Namur, they had assuredly given up all idea of further coöperation with the English, at any rate for the present. The two corps entrusted to Marshal Grouchy might perhaps accelerate their retreat, and ought to be able to prevent an offensive return on their part against the communications of the French. For this purpose they could perfectly well be spared; for the army which Napoleon was taking with

---

[1] See the Bertrand order, *ante*, p. 210.

him to Waterloo was able alone to defeat the army of Wellington. It was a somewhat larger army,² — it was composed throughout of excellent troops, — it was full of enthusiasm, — and it was commanded by the greatest general of the day. Nor was it a matter of any great importance that Grouchy could not well be detached till after twelve o'clock, owing to the necessity of giving his troops time to recover from the fatigues of the battle of the day before, the stress of which had fallen almost wholly on them, for, if the Prussians had retreated on Namur and Liége, there was no special and imminent danger to be apprehended.³ To detach Marshal Grouchy with 33,000 men under these circumstances, which were then believed to exist, was one thing. But the question we are now considering is, — whether Napoleon's adhering to the plan of sending Grouchy off with two corps is to be justified after he had seen reason to be apprehensive of the possibility of the Prussians uniting with the English to fight another battle for the defence of Brussels.

This danger of the union of the two allied armies was, as the Bertrand order shows, distinctly recognized as a possible danger by Napoleon when he dictated the order to Bertrand. It is true that Napoleon did not think it likely that this union would be made, but he knew perfectly well that if it should be made, it would place him in the greatest peril. He, therefore, expressly warned Grouchy that the Prussians might be intending to unite with the English to fight another battle for the defence of Brussels; and we have seen that, in the event of

---

² This statement is true only of the army which the Duke had in line of battle at Waterloo. There were besides some 18,000 men, stationed at Hal and Tubize, of whom he did not avail himself.

³ "Napoleon would not have lost his line of communication with France had Blücher immediately reoccupied the position of Ligny upon Napoleon's leaving it; for his advance upon Wellington necessarily opened to him both the Mons and Lille great lines to France." Kennedy, pp. 154, 155.

Grouchy's finding this to be the case, Napoleon expected him to cross the Dyle and act in conjunction with the main army. If this was, in Napoleon's opinion, to be his true course in the not impossible event of Blücher's falling back on Wavre, why send him off at all? What was there to be gained by sending him off which made it worth while to run the risks inseparable from detaching such a large force from the main army when such a terrible danger as the union of the Prussian and English armies was even remotely apprehended? For there certainly was a chance of Grouchy's not coming back in time to prevent the catastrophe; Napoleon ran the risk of Grouchy's not receiving accurate or trustworthy information as to the doings of the enemy,—of his not acting on the information which he might obtain in accordance with sound military principles,—of his being delayed by the destruction of the bridges, and by the manœuvres of the enemy.

But this is not all. If the Prussians had fallen back on Wavre with the intention of uniting with the English and fighting another battle for the defence of Brussels, as Napoleon in the Bertrand order warns Grouchy they might be intending to do, they must have carried out their project in great part at the time when Napoleon was dictating his order to Bertrand. On this hypothesis, they had certainly already obtained a great advantage over any force sent to pursue them or to interrupt the execution of their scheme. Was it not therefore much wiser to keep the whole army together, well in hand, and under the Emperor's immediate direction?

These risks and chances, and others, Napoleon took, when he sent Grouchy off with his 33,000 men; and for what?

The fact probably is this; that Grouchy was originally ordered to follow up and observe the Prussians when every one supposed them to be retreating towards the Rhine, and especially to prevent or check any offensive return upon the French communications; and that when Napoleon, between 12 and 1, received information which awakened in his mind doubts of the correctness of this supposition, and even some apprehension that Blücher might be intending to unite with Wellington and fight another battle for the defence of Brussels, he adhered to his original disposition of Grouchy's force, contenting himself with giving him an express warning of the danger to be apprehended.

The question then comes down to this:—

If the Prussians were going to separate themselves from the English, there was no great risk in making such a large detachment from the main army, and there might very possibly be occasions in which a force of 33,000 men might accomplish more than a smaller one. It may, however, well be questioned whether half the number would not have answered every end, and allowed the Emperor the use of 15,000 more men in his contest with Wellington, who certainly could have brought to the encounter 18,000 more men than he actually had on the field.

On the other hand, if the Prussians were intending to unite with the English, as Napoleon had some reason at any rate to believe, and if Grouchy did not rejoin the main army, or at least act in connection with it, or defeat the Prussians while marching to the field of battle, Napoleon was ruined. There was then the risk of his not doing either of these things,—whether through the Prussians having so many hours the start of him,—or through ignorance of the facts,—bad roads,—broken bridges,—unsound judgment,—it matters not,—and that risk was assumed by Napoleon when he detached him, without, as it seems to us, any compensating advantage.

Our conclusion, then, is this: if Napoleon had sent off Grouchy with his 33,000 men in the full belief that the Prussians had fallen back on Namur, he would be chargeable only with neglect in not having found out where they had gone; but his sending off this large force after he had so much reason to apprehend that the Prussians were intending to unite with the English that he expressly warned Grouchy to that effect, was to take a wholly unnecessary and very dangerous risk. It was to persist in carrying out a plan which new information had rendered entirely inapplicable to the circumstances as now understood to exist.

Had Napoleon, when he had come to entertain the apprehension that the Prussians might be intending to unite with the English, followed on the 17th the same general plan which he had adopted on the 15th, and, leaving, say, Pajol with the division of Teste, to find out where the Prussians had gone and what they were proposing to do, had taken the rest of the army with him, sending Grouchy at daybreak of the 18th with one, or perhaps both, of his corps to St. Lambert, with instructions to delay the Prussians in every way possible should they come from Wavre either to attack the main army or to reinforce Wellington, he would have taken no serious risk, and he would have had his whole army under his own eye and subject to his immediate control on the day of the great battle. In this case Grouchy would have performed at St. Lambert the task which Ney performed at Quatre Bras,—of preventing the intervention of the other allied army in the battle then in progress. There is not the least reason to suppose that this course would have affected the decision either of Wellington to accept battle or of Blücher to support him. But the chances in favor of Napoleon's success in the battle would have been vastly greater than they actually were.

2. We have expressed the doubt whether, even if the Prussians were known to be separating from the English, it would not have been wiser if Napoleon had given Grouchy only one corps wherewith to pursue them. But while this may be true, we cannot agree with Sir James

Shaw-Kennedy in his reasons for criticising the detachment of Grouchy's force from the main army. He says:—[4]

"His (Napoleon's) great difficulty — as he ought well to have known from the experience of a whole succession of disastrous campaigns to his armies in Spain — was the overthrow of the Anglo-Allied army; and against it he should have led his last man and horse, even had the risk been great in the highest degree; which, as has been seen,[5] it clearly was not. Had Napoleon attacked the Anglo-Allied army with his whole force, and succeeded in defeating it, there could be little question of his being able to defeat afterwards the Prussian army when separated from Wellington."

And again:—[6]

"If Grouchy's proper place was on the field of battle at Waterloo, then Napoleon should have sent for him at daylight on the morning of the 18th, when he saw the Anglo-Allied army in position and determined to attack it."

The difficulty with this reasoning, as it seems to us, lies in the fact that it was not that he might be strong enough to defeat Wellington that Napoleon needed to have all his army on the field of Waterloo, but in order to prevent his being overwhelmed by the union of the army of Blücher to that of Wellington. With the army of Wellington the force Napoleon had at Waterloo was abundantly able to cope; but against the two armies of Wellington and Blücher united, he was certain to succumb. Hence, inasmuch as he, at 1 P. M. of the 17th, had changed his mind as to the Prussian retreat, had come to regard as very questionable the view which until after 12 o'clock of that day he certainly had entertained, that the Prussians were separating themselves definitely from the English, and had recognized the possibility of their uniting with the English and even joining with

---

[4] Kennedy, p. 157.

[5] *Ante*, p. 274, n. 3.

[6] Kennedy, p. 160; Chesney, pp. 206, 207.

them in a battle to be fought for the defence of Brussels, he should have changed his dispositions accordingly. He should have left a comparatively small force,—perhaps of cavalry only,—to follow up and find out about the Prussians, and should have taken all his army-corps with him, because if the Prussians should attempt to take part in the battle he would be sure to need every man he could muster.[7]

3. It seems for many writers to be well-nigh impossible to treat separately of the conduct of Marshal Grouchy. This may require some effort of mind; but it surely is worth while to make it.[8] Suppose we are of opinion that Napoleon made a mistake in the first place in detaching him with his 33,000 men; that he was furthermore inexcusable in not advising him on the night of the 17th and 18th of the most important fact that the two armies were confronting each other at Mont St. Jean,—in not sending him the information which Domon had picked up as to the retreat of a part of the Prussians towards Wavre,—and, finally, in not directing him in precise terms, that, if he should find that the Prussians were retiring on Wavre, he should cross the Dyle at Moustier and Ottignies, and operate in connection with the main army. Suppose, we say, we find all this to be true. We have yet to pass upon Grouchy's conduct.

---

[7] Marshal Soult, according to Baudus (vol. 1, pp. 222, 223), was opposed to detaching Grouchy with the large body of troops assigned to him. He said to one of his aides that it was a great fault to detach so considerable a force from the army which was going to march against the Anglo-Belgian troops; that in the condition in which the defeat of the evening before had put the Prussian army, a feeble force, with the cavalry of General Exelmans, would suffice to follow and observe it in its retreat. We concur in Marshal Soult's conclusion, but not with his reasons. It was not because the Prussian army was so weak, but because it was still so formidable, that Napoleon should have kept all his army together.

[8] See the admirable observations of Siborne (vol. 1, pp. 318 *et seq.*); and of Van Loben Sels, pp. 319 *et seq.* With many writers, to blame Napoleon is to exonerate Grouchy; with others, again, to blame Grouchy is to exonerate Napoleon.

The Emperor's faults cannot excuse Grouchy's faults, nor can his faults excuse those of the Emperor.[9] The object of military criticism is not to see which officer made the most mistakes.

4. As to the proper course for Marshal Grouchy to take after he became satisfied (as he did about daybreak of the 18th) that the Prussians were retreating on Wavre, we have seen that the principal continental critics,— Jomini, Clausewitz and Charras,— are of opinion that he should at once have manœuvred to his left and crossed the Dyle, so as to get in communication with the main army under the Emperor.

But General Hamley[10] is of a different opinion. He approves of Grouchy's direct movement on Wavre. After remarking that Grouchy did not know that Wellington would stop to fight at Waterloo, he says:—

"He thought the Prussians, if they were really moving on Wavre, intended to join Wellington at Brussels. * * * And were they so moving, he, by marching to Wavre, would threaten decisively their communications with their base by Louvain, and so either prevent the execution of their project, or render it disastrous."

It is unnecessary to say anything in regard to this observation, except that, if Grouchy thought as Hamley thinks he did,— and as he very likely did,— he was wholly mistaken as to the intention of Marshal Blücher. Very possibly he might have injured the Prussians a good deal had they been intending to go to Brussels; but, as they were, on the contrary, intending to join Wellington, who had taken up a position for battle to the south of the Forest of Soignes, Grouchy's calculations, as given us by Hamley, were beside the mark, and his movements were entirely useless.

---

[9] *Cf.* Kennedy, pp. 160, 161; Chesney, pp. 206, 207. On the other hand see Van Loben Sels, pp. 323, 324.

[10] Operations of War, p. 196 *et seq.*

[CHAP. 15.] GROUCHY AND BLÜCHER.—NOTES. 281

It is certainly true, as Hamley says,[11] that Grouchy did not know that "Wellington would stop to fight at Waterloo." But Grouchy expressly says that Napoleon told him[12] that he was going "to march upon the English, and fight them, if they stood this side [*i. e.,* south of] the Forest of Soignes," *i. e.,* at Waterloo. This indicated that Napoleon thought it quite possible that the English might take their stand there and fight. And the Bertrand order warned Grouchy that the Prussians might be intending to unite with them to fight a battle for the defence of Brussels. But this order, as we have observed before, is utterly ignored by General Hamley.

5. We have pointed out in the text that the three principal Continental critics,—Jomini, Clausewitz and Charras,—unite in the opinion that Marshal Grouchy should have marched at daybreak for the bridge of Moustier,—covering the movement by his cavalry. What would have been the result of this manœuvre? (See Map 9.)

Let us suppose that the Prussian detachment of Ledebur, which was stationed at Mont St. Guibert to observe the movements of Marshal Grouchy's column, had been driven out of their position, or flanked out of it (as they finally were), before six in the morning, by the French cavalry, and had been compelled to retire to the neighborhood of Wavre. The movements of the main body of Grouchy's command might, therefore, without much difficulty, have been concealed from observation. At least this seems to be assumed by Jomini,[13] who says that Grouchy could have been at the bridge of Moustier at 10 A. M.,—and then have moved "on Wavre by Limale, pushing Exelmans' dragoons on St. Lambert, or else have marched to Lasne himself."

---

[11] Hamley, p. 196.

[12] Frag. Hist.; Lettre à MM. Méry et Barthélemy, p. 5; Grouchy Mém., vol. 4, p. 44.

[13] Jomini, p. 176.

But Charras[14] thinks that the movement to Moustier would have been at once perceived by Ledebur's cavalry, and that Grouchy would probably, on arriving at Moustier and Ottignies, have found himself in face of 40,000 men and 150 pieces of cannon, in position behind the Dyle, and that it could only have been by a very unlikely concurrence of circumstances that Grouchy could have seized these bridges before the Prussians would have been in sufficient force to oppose him.

These conclusions seem to us very strained. Grouchy had 6,000 excellent cavalry. Ledebur's detachment consisted of two battalions of infantry, four squadrons of cavalry and two guns,—possibly 1,500 men in all.[15] A movement on Corbaix would have compelled him to fall back to La Baraque as surely at five in the morning as at one in the afternoon, when, as we have seen, it had this effect. Certainly, Ledebur could have been got out of the way, and could only have reported that the French were very active, and were manœuvring apparently on Wavre by way of Corbaix and La Baraque. We see no reason to doubt that Jomini is perfectly correct in supposing that the column of Marshal Grouchy, with the exception of one of his cavalry divisions, say, that of Pajol, supported, perhaps, by the infantry division of Teste, could have crossed the bridges of Moustier and Ottignies, without any molestation whatever, by or soon after 10 A. M., and that they might have been well on their way towards Lasne and St. Lambert before the Prussians were aware what they were about.

---

[14] Charras, vol. 2, pp. 62, 63. Hooper's view [pp. 342 *et seq.*] is substantially that of Charras. He also seems to think that unless Grouchy could succeed in defeating the Prussian troops opposed to him, his intervention would be useless. It seems to us, on the other hand, that all that it was needful for Grouchy to do was to engage, and so to detain, the corps of Bülow and Pirch I.; and by marching from the Dyle upon their line of march from Wavre to St. Lambert, he was, it seems to us, certain to accomplish this. This view is well presented by Quinet, pp. 301-304.

[15] Charras, vol. 2, p. 42.

In speculations of this kind, it is very easy, of course, to omit by accident some of the *data* of the problem. But when it is remembered that the principal subject which the Prussians were contemplating that morning was not the movements of the 12,000 or 15,000 men, who were (as they supposed) [16] all the troops which Napoleon had detached against them, but the very serious question whether the whole army, or three-fourths of it, should march across the country to attack Napoleon and succor Wellington, we can hardly believe that any reports which Ledebur could have brought in would have brought 40,000 men to the bridges of Moustier and Ottignies by 10 or 10.30 A. M.

It seems to us, then, altogether probable that Marshal Grouchy could have crossed the Dyle at Moustier and Ottignies with the bulk of his forces before 11 A. M. [17]

At this hour, only "the advanced guard of Bülow's corps had * * * reached St. Lambert. The 16th, and then the 13th, brigade arrived much later, and the 14th brigade, which formed the rear-guard was a long way behind." [18] At this hour the Ist, IId and IIId Corps were still in and about Wavre. It would have been at this moment, when the IVth Corps was thus strung out, toiling through the bad roads, that Grouchy would have made his appearance, and have commenced his march from Moustier and Ottignies to Lasne and St. Lambert. Can it be believed that he would not have stopped Bülow? What else could Bülow have done but halt, and concentrate his command, and await the reinforcements which were expected from Wavre? But this would have involved him in an engagement with

---

[16] *Ante*, p. 232.

[17] Siborne (vol. 1, p. 320) thinks that Grouchy could have successfully crossed the Dyle even if he had not started from Gembloux earlier than he did.

[18] Siborne, vol. 1, p. 311; Charras, vol. 2, pp. 72, 73.

Grouchy's force, from which he could be released only by the arrival of those reinforcements. When would they have arrived? (See Map 10.)

If Grouchy's movement on Moustier had not been observed and promptly reported to Blücher,—which is the assumption on which we are proceeding, as being on the whole the most probable,—there is no reason to suppose that the Ist and IId Prussian Corps would have moved out of Wavre earlier than they did,—that is, about noon.[19] The IId Corps followed the IVth, and would of course have become engaged with Grouchy. The IIId would in time very likely have followed the IId; but it probably would not have left Wavre till much later. These three corps would have been Grouchy's opponents; they would have outnumbered him considerably, and would, no doubt, ultimately have worsted him. But he probably would have prevented any portion of their troops from attacking the main army under Napoleon.

As for the Ist Corps, there would have been nothing to prevent its marching along the northerly road by way of Ohain to join Wellington, if Zieten had thought it safe to run the chance of the Anglo-Dutch army holding out until his arrival.

What effect these operations would have had on the issue of the battle of Waterloo will be considered later.

6. We have stated above [20] that Grouchy, once arrived at La Baraque, might have crossed the Dyle by the four bridges of Moustier and Ottignies, Limale and Limelette, without, as it seems probable to us, encountering serious opposition.[21] This view is strongly maintained by Thiers, and as strongly contested by Charras. The

---

[19] Charras, vol. 2, p. 43; Siborne, vol. 1, pp. 311, 312. Kennedy (p. 163) seems to suppose that Pirch I. and Zieten followed Bülow without any interval.

[20] *Ante*, p. 259.

[21] Van Loben Sels (pp. 322, 323, 340) is very positive as to this.

latter's principal reason for doubting the feasibility of this movement is the supposed presence in the woods of Sarats and Warlombrout, which line the road from La Baraque to Wavre on the east and west sides respectively, just after passing the former place, of the two divisions of Reckow and Brause of the IId Corps, some 11,000 or 12,000 men.[22] The wood of Warlombrout lies between the road leading to Moustier and that leading to Limelette.

We think Charras in error as to the advanced position of these two brigades, or divisions, as they may more properly be called.

Siborne makes no mention at all of the occupation of the wood of Warlombrout, and says that that of Sarats was occupied by some battalions of the 8th brigade, Reckow's,[23] and that the rest of the brigade was in rear of the wood. He says that the 7th brigade, that of Brause, was in reserve. Ollech[24] says that Reckow's brigade sent two battalions into this wood of Sarats,[25] and that the brigade took up position between Manil and St. Anne, which is nearly a mile in rear of the wood; and that the other brigade was in rear of this. He says nothing about the occupation of the wood of Warlombrout.

We do not know where Charras obtained his information; but it seems quite clear that the movement to the bridges would not have met with the amount of opposition which he claims. These brigades of Reckow and Brause were portions of the IId Corps, and were expecting to cross the Dyle at Wavre, and march to support Bülow. No one, of course, can say what these troops would have done had Grouchy attempted to cross the

---

[22] Charras, vol. 2, p. 376; also, p. 44.

[23] Siborne, vol. 1, p. 313. He strictly follows Damitz, p. 247.

[24] Ollech, pp. 208, 209.

[25] Called by him Lautelle. It is sometimes called the wood of Lauzel, as it adjoins a farm of that name.

Dyle by the bridges or any of them; but it is certain that these troops were not then expecting any such movement, nor were they stationed where they could at once or easily have interfered with it.

7. Where was Grouchy when he heard the sound of the cannon of Waterloo, and rejected the advice of Gérard to march to the support of the Emperor?

That it was at Sart-à-Walhain where Marshal Grouchy heard the sound of the cannon of Waterloo, is the universally accepted belief. But it is an error. It may be interesting to see how it originated.

Berton, who wrote in 1818, says [26] that Grouchy's column "was still at the village of Walhain when it heard the first cannon-shots of Mont St. Jean," and that it was there that Gérard gave his advice. [27]

Grouchy, writing his "Observations" the same year in Philadelphia, which were reprinted in Paris in 1819, states [28] that the cannon was heard while they were skirmishing in the wood of Limelette, between 1 and 2 P. M.

Gérard, in a letter also written in 1819, states [29] that it was "at Wallin, or Sart-à-Wallin." He says he found the Marshal eating some strawberries. It was about 11 A. M., a little more, or a little less. He gives an account of the interview, and then says "We quitted Wallin, &c."

His acting chief-of-staff, Colonel Simon Lorière, says in his report:— [30]

"At 11 o'clock the Third [Fourth] Corps was entirely assembled at Walin.

"The Count Gérard, who preceded the march of his corps, learnt that Marshal Grouchy had stopped at a house in the village

---

[26] Berton, p. 55.

[27] Berton, pp. 55, 59.

[28] Grouchy, Obs., p. 16.

[29] Quelques Doc., p. 7. He means Walhain and Sart-à-Walhain.

[30] Ib., 12. By "Walin," he means Walhain.

belonging to a M. Hollaert; he went there with the officers of his staff; he told me to follow; we found his Excellency at breakfast."

Colonel Denniée of Gérard's staff locates the incident at Sarra-Walin, and speaks of Gérard's having found the Marshal at breakfast.[31]

Gérard wrote to a friend of his at Brussels to look up M. Hollaert; he did so, and wrote[32] to Gérard to say that he had been to see him at Sarra-Walin.

This seems to have decided Gérard that the place was Sart-à-Walhain; for he writes in 1820 to Colonel Grouchy, a son of the Marshal, as follows:—[33]

"It was not at 3 o'clock in the afternoon that I rejoined the commander-in-chief of the right wing, but towards 11 o'clock in the morning; he was at Sarra-Walin, at the house of a M. Hollaert, a notary, where he was breakfasting."

Grouchy finally conceded to Gérard that it was long before they were skirmishing in the wood of Limelette, that the sound of the cannon of Waterloo was heard. He admitted in a letter[34] published in 1829, that it was at Sart-à-Walhain, and at 11.30 A. M. This is also the statement made in the Grouchy Memoirs.[35]

Nevertheless it was at Walhain and not at Sart-à-Walhain where Marshal Grouchy was when he heard the sound of the cannon, and Gérard proffered his advice to march toward the field of battle. It is certain that the incident took place at the house of a notary—a M. Hollaert (or Hollert, as it should be spelled),—for many of the officers who give their recollections mention his name; and it is in no wise remarkable that the name of the village in which his house stood should have made no

---

[31] Quelques Doc., pp. 17, 18. By "Sarra-Walin," he means Sart-à-Walhain.

[32] Ib., p. 19. His letter was dated September 30, 1819.

[33] Ib., p. 24. See also Gérard's "Lettre à MM. Germain-Sarrut et B. Saint Edme," pp. 10, 11; and his "Dernières Observations," pp. 8, 29.

[34] Fragm. Hist.; Lettre à MM. Méry and Barthélemy, p. 9.

[35] Grouchy Mém., vol. 4, pp. 71, 75.

distinct impression on their memories. Now there was at that time no notary at Sart-à-Walhain. There is none now. It is a very small village. There was not in fact a notary's office at Walhain in 1815; there was none until 1818. But M. Joseph Hollert was in 1815 the notary of the neighboring town of Nil St. Vincent, and he lived in a large house in Walhain known as the Chateau Marette. It was here that he received Marshal Grouchy in the forenoon of the 18th of June, 1815, and it was into his garden that the officers went out from the house to catch the direction of the firing.[36]

The matter is of no very great importance. Still, Walhain was certainly a good mile nearer than Sart-à-Walhain to the bridges, whether Grouchy marched by way of Mont St. Guibert or La Baraque. (See Map 11.)

---

[36] The writer has abundant proof of the above statements. He has also visited the house. M. Wenseleers, who is referred to in the Preface, obtained for him this information in 1888 and 1889.

CHAPTER XVI.

THE BATTLE OF WATERLOO.

NAPOLEON, as we have seen, took up his headquarters on the evening of the 17th at the Caillou house on the Brussels road, about a mile and a half south of the little tavern known then and now as La Belle Alliance. All the afternoon and night it rained hard. We may suppose that, as his custom was, he slept during the evening. At 1 A. M. of the 18th, he mounted his horse, and, with Bertrand, rode out to the front.[1] Here he rode or walked along the line of the pickets until he had satisfied himself that Wellington's army was in position, awaiting battle. The fires at which the soldiers of the English and Dutch army were drying and warming themselves left no doubt of this. He must have been occupied in this way more than two hours, as he was near the wood of Hougomont at half-past two in the morning.

After returning, various reports came in. Between 7 and 8 A. M. he received from an officer who had been sent to the advanced posts, word that the enemy were retiring. This information he at once communicated to d'Erlon,[2] whose corps was in the first line,— that of Reille not having got fully up,— and ordered him to put his troops in march and to pursue the enemy with vigor. But d'Erlon having judged the enemy's movement quite differently, sent his chief-of-staff to the Emperor to tell

---

[1] Corresp., vol. 31, p. 219; Charras, vol. 1, p. 263.
[2] Drouet, pp. 96, 97; Vaudoncourt, vol. 4, p. 24.

him that he, d'Erlon, thought that the English were making their dispositions to receive battle. D'Erlon proceeds:—

"The Emperor came immediately to the advanced posts. I accompanied him; we dismounted in order to get near the enemy's vedettes, and to examine more closely the movements of the English army. He perceived that I was right, and being convinced that the English army was taking position, he said to me:—

"Order the men to make their soup, to get their pieces in order, and we will determine what is to be done towards noon.'"

Napoleon seems in fact not to have spared himself any trouble, and there evidently was no very conspicuous deficiency in the physical energy of a man who, after a good afternoon's work in the saddle in directing the march of an army, was able to go out twice in the deep mud during a rainy night and morning to visit the outer pickets of his line of battle, nearly two miles from the house where he had established his headquarters.

The reason of this apparently rather unnecessary solicitude is really not far to seek. Napoleon felt as confident of beating Wellington's army that day as he had felt of beating Blücher's army on the day but one before, provided only that it would accept battle. He believed, and he was justified in believing, that his army was superior to that opposed to him, in fighting capacity certainly, and even, possibly, in numbers. He trusted to Grouchy to keep the Prussians off, as he had on the day of Ligny trusted to Ney to protect him against the English, and he may also have thought it possible that Grouchy would arrive on the field in time to make the victory more crushing,— playing, in this way, much the same *rôle* which Napoleon had marked out for Ney at Ligny. He accordingly feared nothing so much as the retreat of the English.

That he supposed that Grouchy would cross the Dyle at Moustier is certainly a fair inference from Marbot's report and letter, from which we have made extracts above.³ That he should have been so certain about it, however, is remarkable, as he had given Grouchy no instructions⁴ of any kind whatsoever since he had sent him the Bertrand order, and that left him entire freedom of action.

Another very remarkable thing is that Napoleon should not have drawn from the fact that Wellington was awaiting battle the inference that he was expecting the assistance, and the powerful assistance, of Blücher.⁵ At least it would seem pretty certain that he did not draw this inference, for he took neither of the steps which, if he had come to that conclusion, would seem to be dictated by common sense,— he neither attacked Wellington as early as he possibly could, nor did he do anything to make sure of Grouchy's intervention until 10 A. M., when he sent him the order which we have given above.⁶ If, on his return to the Caillou house at half-past three or thereabouts in the morning, he had sent an officer to order Grouchy to march towards the main army by the bridges of Moustier and Ottignies, he would have done only what the fact of Wellington's confronting him, which he had just ascertained with his own eyes, should have led him to do.

The rain ceased, according to Charras,⁷ at 6 A. M.; Vaudoncourt,⁸ a much earlier authority, puts it at 8 o'clock; Van Loben Sels⁹ says that the rain had diminished at break of day, but it was not until 10 o'clock that the atmosphere became clear; Baudus,¹⁰ who was at the

---

³*Ante*, pp. 268 *et seq.*
⁴The question of the alleged orders sent to Grouchy during this night will be treated of in Appendix A; *post*, p. 353.
⁵Van Loben Sels, p. 319.
⁶*Ante*, p. 265.
⁷Charras, vol. 1, p. 265.
⁸Vaudoncourt, vol. 4, 24.
⁹Van Loben Sels, p. 270.
¹⁰Baudus, vol. 1, p. 225.

battle on Soult's staff, says the rain ceased towards 9 o'clock. We may probably assume that the rain had ceased by 8 o'clock, and that in another hour, had Napoleon so chosen, he might have begun the battle.

This, in point of fact, he originally intended to do. He had issued an order in good season to the corps-commanders, that they should see that the soldiers cleaned their guns and got their breakfasts, so that at 9 o'clock precisely they should be ready to commence the battle.[11] Drouot, who was a distinguished artillery-officer, and was then acting as adjutant-general of the Guard, tells us[12] that Napoleon intended to begin the battle by 8 or 9 at the latest. But Drouot advised a delay of two to three hours on account of the condition of the ground, which the heavy rain of the past afternoon and night had rendered too soft for the rapid and effective movements of artillery; and Napoleon, who was himself an artillery officer, and always made great use of this arm, yielded to the suggestion, and determined to put off the main attack till towards one o'clock P. M.

About 8 A. M. the Emperor rode along the lines,[13] examining the enemy's position, which he had already, as we have seen, inspected twice since midnight. He then dictated an order of battle, or, rather, an order of movement, the result of which would be that the army would be arranged in three lines, ready for the attack. This marshalling of the army was, according to all accounts, a magnificent and imposing spectacle; the bands played; the men shouted "Vive l'Empereur!"; the movement was skilfully designed and beautifully executed; but, except as a way of occupying the time, it would probably never have been thought of. It began shortly before

---

[11]Doc. Inéd., XVIII, p. 52; App. C, xxxi; *post*, p. 387.

[12]Thiers, vol. xx, p. 157, n.

[13]Charras, vol. 1, p. 270.

nine and was over by half-past ten."[14] It showed at any rate that had it been thought advisable, the battle might have been begun at 9 A. M.

After this pageant "Napoleon passed before the lines and was received by immense, by enthusiastic acclamations."[15] He then, shortly before eleven o'clock, dictated his plan of attack. Of this we shall speak later on.

One cannot but be struck with a recurrence here of the same error to which we have had occasion to call attention before,—namely, the error of acting on the probabilities of the situation when it is admitted that a different state of things may nevertheless, in spite of the probabilities, exist, and that, if it does exist, a wholly different course of action must be taken, or a fatal result will inevitably follow. Napoleon was, very likely, warranted in thinking it probable that morning that, what with the loss and demoralization consequent on their defeat at Ligny, and what with the interference with their plans which Grouchy with his 33,000 men could reasonably be expected to make, he himself was safe against any intervention on the part of the Prussians. But he did not and could not know where the Prussians were; in fact, he had great reason to believe that a large part of them had gone to Wavre; and at that very moment he thought it very likely that their action in going to Wavre would induce Grouchy to come to him by way of Moustier. If, then, the exigency called in the Emperor's mind for this course on the part of Grouchy, why did it not equally demand from Napoleon the promptest action against Wellington, and the exertion of every means to make sure of Grouchy's intervention? This criticism is, in fact, only an extension of that made in reference to the step taken by Napoleon in detaching Grouchy's large force when he felt it necessary at the same time to warn Grouchy

---

[14]Charras, vol. 1, p. 274.

[15]Ib., p. 275.

expressly that the Prussians might be intending to unite with the English.

However we may explain these apparent contradictions, they certainly existed in Napoleon's mind and also in his actions. He was so sure of having only the Anglo-Dutch army to fight that he deliberately postponed attacking it until he could do so in the most approved style; he was confident that if the Prussians had gone in the direction of Wavre with the intention of joining the English or of attacking the French, Grouchy would return to him by the bridge of Moustier. And yet, from 1 P.M. of the afternoon of the 17th to 10 A.M. of the 18th, he sent Grouchy no orders, and no information. Where such is the lack of ordinary care on the part of the commanding general, a great deal surely must depend upon the energy and capacity of the subordinate.

While this was the general situation at the French headquarters, the Duke of Wellington, having with his customary carefulness set his army in battle array, was quietly waiting until it should suit his adversary to assault his lines. Every hour's delay was a distinct gain to him; and he knew it. He knew, what Napoleon of course could not know, that the Prussians were on their way to attack the French and to join the English.

At the same time, it must not be supposed that the Duke had no cause for anxiety. Of the defects of his army he was well aware. No one knew better than he that such a conglomerate mass of troops as that which he commanded, consisting, too, in great part of raw and untried soldiers, could not possibly be equal to the well-appointed army of Napoleon's veterans whose blows he was soon to receive. His only reliance, therefore, was on Blücher's promised support. As Sir James Shaw-Kennedy well says:—[16]

---

[16] Kennedy, p. 131.

"In order at all to understand the views of the Duke of Wellington as to accepting battle on the field of Waterloo, it is essential to keep this arrangement [*i. e.*, with Blücher] fully in view; otherwise the Duke might justly be accused of the utmost temerity and folly in accepting battle, as much the greater portion of his army consisted of mere Landwehr and of Dutch-Belgian troops. The latter, from political and other causes, could not be depended upon; which, in fact, had been already proved on the 16th. It would be an error to suppose that it was from any want of courage that the Dutch-Belgian troops could not be depended upon; proof enough exists that the people of those countries are capable of the most heroic and persevering exertions when engaged in a cause that they care to support; but under the circumstances in which they were placed on this occasion, they were without confidence, were not acting in a cause which they cordially supported, and showed that it was not one in which they wished to oppose themselves seriously to French troops."

But Wellington felt that he could rely on Blücher's promise, and he took his chance that Blücher would be able to fulfil his promise, and that he himself would be able to hold out until the promise should be fulfilled. These risks, however, were by no means small.

In the first place, the Duke not only did not know that Napoleon had given Grouchy two whole corps; he even supposed that he had given him but one, and that Napoleon was confronting him on the morning of the battle with his whole army, "with the exception of the 3d Corps, which had been sent to observe Marshal Blücher."[17] This risk, fortunately for the Duke of Wellington, was not actually incurred. But, all the same, Wellington is entitled to the credit of having faced it with his eyes open.

Secondly, there was the chance that Grouchy might intervene, and prevent the Prussians from fulfilling their promise. We have already shown what Grouchy could have done in this way had he either acted of his own

---

[17] Wellington's Official Report: Gurwood, vol. xii, p. 481.

motion in accordance with the demands of the situation by marching at daybreak for the bridge of Moustier, or had followed the counsel of Gérard at noon.

The issue of the battle of Waterloo, in fact, might have been entirely changed if the movements of troops not under the control of either of the commanding generals had been other than they were; it is this fact among others which gives the battle a peculiar interest.

The position to the south of the villages of Mont St. Jean and Waterloo, known as the field of Waterloo, had been, some time before the campaign opened, reconnoitred by the English engineers; "the several sketches of the officers had been put together, and one fair copy made for the Prince of Orange; a second had been commenced for the Duke."[18] The chief-of-engineers, Lieutenant-Colonel Smyth, who was present at the action of Quatre Bras, sent back to Brussels during the afternoon, presumably by the Duke's direction, for a plan of this position; and the original sketches, which, together, constituted a plan, were forwarded to him by Captain Oldfield, the brigade-major of engineers.[19] The next morning, "upon the receipt of a communication from Blücher,"[20] the Duke obtained from Colonel Smyth these sketches, and gave them to Sir William De Lancey, his Deputy-Quartermaster-General, or chief-of-staff, "with orders" (as Major Oldfield states)[21] "to take up the ground on which we fought the next day. Colonel Smyth was at the same time desired to take the

---

[18] Oldfield MSS.; Porter's Hist. Royal Engineers, vol. 1, p. 380. A copy of this sketch is inserted opposite page 565 of C. D. Yonge's "Life of Wellington"; London: Chapman and Hall; 1860. See, also, p. 616 of the same work.

[19] Curiously enough they were very nearly lost in the action; the officer who had them in his keeping, Lieutenant Waters, being unhorsed in the *melée*.

[20] Probably the information brought by Lieutenant Massow; *ante*, p. 233.

[21] Oldfield MSS.

necessary measures for entrenching the village of Braine-la-Leud."

To this position, then, well understood and mapped out, the Duke of Wellington fell back on the afternoon of the 17th from Quatre Bras with that part of his army which was under his immediate command, and to it also he directed the greater part of the troops which were at Nivelles and other places. (See Map 13.)

The position was a strong one. The first or main line of battle crossed the Charleroi-Brussels pike at right angles where the road from Ohain and Wavre strikes into it, nearly three-quarters of a mile south of the hamlet of Mont St. Jean, where the *chaussée* to Nivelles branches off from the pike. To the east of this pike the English left extended for a mile or so,—for more than half this distance on the crest of a gentle slope; but the little villages of Smohain, Papelotte and La Haye, lying from a quarter to a half a mile in front, were occupied. To the west of the pike the line ran along the same ridge for nearly a third of a mile, when it turned somewhat towards the southwest, but still ran along the crest of the ridge, and so continued for nearly a half a mile farther. Here the line was covered by a garden and a considerable wood enclosing a solid old building, known as the Chateau of Hougomont. This building and its enclosures lay about 350 yards in front of the main line of battle, at its extreme right, and they were occupied in force. The ridge was admirably suited for defensive purposes. The reverse slope offered excellent protection for infantry lying behind it; and in front, there were no trees or other impediments; every movement of the enemy was plainly to be seen, and was exposed to fire. Moreover the ground over which the enemy must advance for the attack was so moist and muddy, that all rapidity of movement, even of cavalry, was out of the question.

Wellington had on the field the whole of the 1st, 2d, 3d, 5th and 6th British divisions, one brigade (Mitchell's) of the 4th division, the 2d and 3d Dutch-Belgian divisions, and the contingents from Brunswick and Nassau,— numbering in all 49,608 infantry, 12,408 cavalry and 5,645 artillery, with 156 guns,— a total of 67,661 men.[22]

These troops, as we have before observed,[23] were stationed on the field without reference to the corps to which they belonged. The reason for this probably was that the Duke desired to distribute his foreign troops, on some, at any rate, of whom he placed no great reliance, among his British troops and those of the King's German Legion, which were his main dependence. Then, inasmuch as the army had never before acted by corps, or, in fact, at all, in the field, no special inconvenience was to be apprehended from this arrangement.

The army of the Duke was composed as follows:—[24]

British troops:—

Infantry	15,181	
Cavalry	5,843	
Artillery	2,967	
		23,991

King's German Legion:—

Infantry	3,301	
Cavalry	1,997	
Artillery	526	
		5,824

Total British and King's German Legion — 29,815 Men

Hanoverians:—

Infantry	10,258	
Cavalry	497	
Artillery	465	
		11,220 "

Carried forward — 41,035 "

---

[22] Siborne, vol. 1, pp. 460, 461; App. xxx. Charras, vol. 1, p. 269, n. 2, raises the total to 70,187 men of all arms, of whom 13,432 were cavalry. He gives the number of guns as 159.

[23] *Ante*, p. 35, n. 3.

[24] Siborne, vol. 1, pp. 460, 461: App. xxx.

Brought forward	41,035	Men
Brunswickers:—		
Infantry	4,586	
Cavalry	866	
Artillery	510	
	5,962	"
Nassauers:—		
Infantry	2,880	"
Dutch-Belgians:—		
Infantry	13,402	
Cavalry	3,205	
Artillery	1,177	
	17,784	"
Total as above.	67,661	"

To the eastward, or English left, of the turnpike, were stationed in the first line the 5th and 6th British divisions, the 2d Dutch-Belgian division, and the British cavalry brigades of Vivian and Vandeleur. This part of the line seems to have been commanded by Sir Thomas Picton,[25] although it is not clear whether he had any authority except over his own division, the 5th. Of these troops the cavalry were stationed on the extreme left. One brigade of Dutch-Belgians, that of Prince Bernhard of Saxe Weimar, occupied the villages of Smohain, Papelotte and La Haye. The English infantry were placed on the reverse of the slope of the ridge, so as to be sheltered from the enemy's fire. But the other Dutch-Belgian brigade, Bylandt's, was, as Sir James Shaw-Kennedy says,[26] "posted, most unaccountably, in front of the Wavre road, on the slope. * * * In this position, it was jutted forward in front of the real line of battle, which was mainly the Wavre road. It was directly exposed to the fire of the greatest French battery

---

[25] Sir Lowry Cole, commanding the 6th British division, was not in the action.

[26] Kennedy, p. 61; Waterloo Letters, pp. 30, 31, Sir W. Gomm.

that was on the field, and singly exposed to the first onset of the French attacking columns." Who was responsible for this inconsiderate and dangerous measure we do not know. In rear of the left wing, and protected from the French fire, stood the Union brigade, so called, of Major General Sir William Ponsonby, composed of the Royal Dragoons, the Scots Greys, and the Inniskilling Dragoons.

The right of the left wing rested on the Charleroi turnpike. The 3d British division, Alten's, continued the line to the west of the turnpike. On the westerly side of the pike, and about 300 yards to the south of the point where the Wavre road crosses it, was the farmhouse of La Haye Sainte, which was strongly occupied by a battalion of the King's German Legion under Major Baring. An *abatis* was formed across the road at the south end of the boundary wall of the house,[27] but it was broken up during the course of the battle.

Beyond the third division, on the allied right, were stationed the two brigades constituting the 1st division, Cooke's, — a part of the 2d brigade, Byng's, occupying, with some Nassau and other foreign troops, the Chateau and enclosures of Hougomont.

The 2d division, Clinton's, was in reserve near Merbe Braine, as was also the Brunswick contingent. The 3d Dutch-Belgian division, Chassé's, was on the extreme right, and partly in the village of Braine-la-Leud. The heavy cavalry brigade of Lord Edward Somerset was stationed in the rear, near the Charleroi pike; the Dutch-Belgian cavalry were farther to the right.

It is plain from the foregoing that, with the exception of the unfortunate brigade of Bylandt, the army was skilfully arranged so as to escape as far as was possible the fire of the enemy's artillery, which was known to be extremely formidable. The occupation of Hougomont was most carefully attended to; the walls were loop-

---

[27] Waterloo Letters, pp. 403, 404.

[CHAP. 16.] THE BATTLE OF WATERLOO. 301

holed, — not only of the house, but of the garden; and, surrounded, as it was, on the sides nearest the French by a considerable wood, it was a really strong place. So long as it was held, the right of Wellington's line was practically unassailable.[28] The farmhouse of La Haye Sainte on the Brussels road was also made very strong, although, owing to some oversight, no adequate mode of reinforcing the defenders, or of supplying them with ammunition, was provided. No earth-works had been thrown up anywhere.[29] An *abatis* had, as has been observed, been placed across the Charleroi road, and another was thrown across the Nivelles road in rear of Hougomont.

Napoleon brought to the field of Waterloo the 1st, 2d, and 6th Corps (*minus* the division of Teste), the Imperial Guard, the heavy cavalry of Kellermann and Milhaud, the light cavalry of Domon, detached from the 3d Corps, and of Subervie, detached from the cavalry-corps of Pajol, — a total of 71,947 men, of whom 48,950 were infantry, 15,765 cavalry, and 7,232 artillery. There were 246 guns.[30]

The 1st Corps constituted the right of the first line. Its left rested on the Charleroi turnpike near the inn of La Belle Alliance, and its light cavalry observed the villages of La Haye and Papelotte on the extreme right. The 2d Corps continued the first line to the west, the cavalry of Piré being stationed beyond the Nivelles road. The 6th Corps and the Guard, with the cavalry of Kellermann and Milhaud, were in reserve.

Of the three divisions of the 2d Corps present at the battle, — that of Girard having been left at Ligny, — the division of Jerome was on the left, that of Foy in the

---

[28] Kennedy, p. 65.

[29] Oldfield MSS.

[30] Siborne, vol. 1, p. 461: App. xxxi. Charras (vol. 1. p. 238, n.) gives the total as 72,447 men and 240 guns.

centre, and that of Bachelu on the right,—its right resting on the Charleroi road.

Of the four divisions of the 1st Corps, that of Donzelot was the left, and its left rested on the Charleroi road; then came that of Allix, commanded by Quiot; then that of Marcognet, and then that of Durutte. This last was opposite Papelotte and La Haye.

The two armies were nearly equal in numbers; and had that of the Duke of Wellington been equal in point of material to that of the Emperor, the advantage of position which it possessed would have fully made up for the slight superiority in numbers possessed by the French. As it was, however, the superiority of the French, not only in artillery and cavalry, but so far as a large part of the Anglo-Dutch army was concerned, in *moral*, was unquestionable, and Wellington's only justification for receiving battle lay, as Kennedy points out above, in his expectation of receiving help from Blücher.

Napoleon, as we have seen, dictated his plan of battle before eleven o'clock. It provided that,[31] as soon as the whole army should be ranged in order of battle, about 1 P. M., and the Emperor should give the order to Marshal Ney, the attack should commence, having for its object to get possession of the village of Mont St. Jean, where the road from Nivelles strikes into the Charleroi turnpike. This attack was to be made by the 1st Corps, supported on the left by the 2d Corps. To aid this attack a formidable battery of seventy-eight guns, many of them twelve-pounders, was to be moved forward on the east side of the road to a ridge which ran in front of and parallel to the French line of battle, and only 600 yards from the English position.

The Emperor had then definitely decided before eleven o'clock to defer the principal move of the day till about one in the afternoon. In this decision he was mainly, if

---

[30] Doc. Inéd., XIX, pp. 53, 54; App. C, xxxii; *post*, p. 388.

not wholly, influenced by the difficulties which he saw would be caused by the deep mud of the fields over which his troops would have to manœuvre.

The determination of Napoleon to make his main effort against the village of Mont St. Jean, so as to possess himself of the principal avenue of retreat open to the enemy, — the road to Brussels, — has always elicited the commendation of military men. The Emperor undoubtedly intended to aid the attack of the 1st Corps by advancing the 6th Corps in its support; but this, as we shall see, owing to the intervention of the Prussians, he did not attempt. Whether, in case the attack had succeeded, so far as to give to the French the possession of the Brussels road, the Forest of Soignes would have afforded cover to Wellington's retreating army, as English writers have always maintained, or would have necessitated the abandonment of the greater part of their artillery, as Napoleon contended, is a question which we will not undertake to discuss here.

At 11.30 A.M., before the time arrived for beginning the main operation of the day, Napoleon ordered Reille to attack Hougomont with his left division, that of Prince Jerome.[32] This movement, intended only as a diversion, was undertaken without any sufficient examination of the enemy's position, and in the most inconsiderate manner.[33] Neither Jerome, who commanded the division, nor

---

[32] We shall not attempt to give a complete tactical description of the battle of Waterloo. The narratives of Siborne, Charras, Hooper, La Tour d'Auvergne, and others give all the facts. With the exception of two or three points, their accounts do not differ materially.

[33] The following extract from a letter by Baron Müffling written on June 24, 1815, is directly in point here : —

"Before we arrived there I said to the Duke, ' If only there were an apparently weak point in the right flank of your position, so that Bonaparte might assail it right furiously, and neglect his own right wing to such an extent that he should fail to discover the march of the Prussians !'

"And see! when we arrived there, there lay the advanced post of Hougomont, upon which he (B.) indeed fell." Militär Wochenblatt, Nov. 14, 1891.

Guilleminot, who, Charras maintains, really controlled its operations, took the pains to direct the boiling courage and superfluous energy of the men, which, skilfully used, might have resulted in obtaining at least partial success. For example, the western entrance of the Chateau was perfectly open to artillery fire, and, had a few heavy guns been employed, the doors and adjacent wall would have been demolished, and the building would probably have been taken,[34] although it is doubtful if it could have been held. Bags of powder, also, would have destroyed the garden wall, but no one thought of supplying them to the men.[35] In consequence of these neglects, the soldiers of Jerome's division, after possessing themselves of the wood and orchard, were shot down by their opponents from behind the garden wall, and from the loopholes in the house and its outbuildings, and could make no further progress. This, of itself, was, perhaps, of no great consequence; but Reille, impatient of being thwarted, and still neglecting to ascertain the precise reasons of the ill-success of the attack, sent in the division of Foy to support that of Jerome. In fact, later in the day, the division of Bachelu was also employed in this useless and most costly attempt to get possession of Hougomont. When it is considered that the 2d Corps contained on this morning not far from 12,000 foot soldiers, and that very few of them assisted in the attacks on the main line of the English army, one gets an idea of the wasteful, and, in fact, inexcusable mismanagement of the resources of the French army on this day. Not more than half the above number of men were employed to maintain the position.

The main operation of the day was to be, as we have said, an advance by the 1st Corps under d'Erlon to break the centre of the English line at and near the junction of

---

[34] La Tour d'Auvergne, p. 266; Charras, vol. 1, p. 281.
[35] Charras, vol. 2, p. 18.

the Wavre road with the turnpike. The great battery of seventy-eight pieces of cannon continued firing for an hour and a half at a distance of less than a third of a mile from the crest in front of which lay the brigade of Bylandt, and behind which lay the brigades of Kempt and Pack and Best of Picton's division. At half-past one Napoleon ordered d'Erlon forward.

His attack was to be made in four columns, marching in *échelon*, the left in advance. The formation of these columns was so extraordinary, and so ill-suited for the work to be done, that it has always excited the comment of military men. We owe to Charras [36] a clear explanation of this formation. The first, or left, column consisted of the brigade of Bourgeois of the division of Allix, — the other brigade of this division, that of Quiot, being assigned to the special task of capturing La Haye Sainte. This brigade of Bourgeois contained four battalions, one behind another; each battalion stood in three ranks, one behind the other; and there was a distance of five paces between the battalions. The front of this column, therefore, consisted of one-third of the number of men in the leading battalion; and there being four battalions in the brigade, there were of course twelve ranks in the column. It was the same, *mutatis mutandis*, with the other columns. Donzelot's division, which contained nine battalions, had, therefore, twenty-seven ranks in its column; the divisions of Marcognet and Durutte, which had only eight battalions each, had each twenty-four ranks. This formation was quite an exceptional one. A column very generally in use at that day consisted of a battalion in the centre, in line, — that is, in three ranks, — flanked on either side, by battalions in column of divisions, capable of promptly forming line or square. And then there were other convenient formations in frequent use. But these formations of d'Erlon's divis-

---

[36] Charras, vol. 1, p. 288, and note 2.

ions were unwieldy, — they lacked mobility. Why Ney and d'Erlon should have departed from the usual practice on this occasion, no one knows.[37]

The story of d'Erlon's charge has been often told.[38] How the soldiers of the unfortunate brigade of Bylandt, utterly unable, as they were, after having been exposed to the fire of the great battery for an hour and a half, to resist alone the impact of such an enormous force, broke in confusion and fell to the rear amid the undeserved curses of their English allies;[39] how the French in their unwieldy masses pressed forward to the crest of the ridge to receive the fire at short range of the brigades of Pack and Kempt, which only the leading battalions were able, owing to the faulty formation of the columns, to return at all; and how, when staggered by the fire, and while endeavoring to disengage their closely following ranks, Ponsonby's brigade of heavy cavalry charged them furiously, riding down between the columns, throwing them into confusion, cutting down the exposed foot-soldiers, capturing two eagles, and many prisoners, disabling some 15 guns, and forcing the three left columns to fall back in disorder, — all this is familiar to all readers of the story of Waterloo. It is difficult to find a parallel to this clumsily executed movement of d'Erlon's. At the same time, faulty as the formation of the columns was, the troops got actually on the crest of the British position; and had there been any timidity or hesitation on the part of their adversaries, the columns would undoubtedly have forced their way through the British line. But the necessary time was not allowed them. Sir Thomas Picton was alive to the danger; he was prompt to seize the opportunity; his troops by their close and

---

[37] Charras, vol. 1, p. 288; La Tour d'Auvergne, p. 274. D'Erlon in his autobiography throws no light on the matter; Drouet, p. 97.

[38] Nowhere better, perhaps, than in Erckmann-Chatrian's "Waterloo."

[39] Siborne, vol. 2, pp. 5, 6.

deadly fire threw the heads of the columns into confusion, and then charged them with the bayonet. Lord Uxbridge, who commanded the cavalry, rode over from his own position on the other side of the turnpike, and ordered Ponsonby to charge. He then returned to lead Somerset's cavalry brigade in a successful charge on the west of the pike. The whole affair was a great and deserved success for the English. Their cavalry, however, was very severely handled on returning to its original positions.

Shortly before d'Erlon moved out, Napoleon had seen a body of troops on the heights of St. Lambert, far off on his right. It was soon ascertained that they were Prussians. He then sent off the 1 P. M. order to Grouchy.[40] By the time that the unfortunate charge of the 1st Corps had resulted in the repulse narrated above, certainly before 3 P. M., Napoleon had decided that he must employ the 6th Corps in resisting the Prussians, and not in supporting the 1st Corps in further operations against the English, as he had originally intended to do. But whatever shape the next movement might assume, the first thing to be done was evidently to carry the farm-house of La Haye Sainte, which had just been unsuccessfully attempted.

This was undertaken in the same reckless and careless manner which had characterized the assault on Hougomont. Although the French had an abundance of heavy guns, none were used to batter down the doors and walls, in front of which the bravest officers and men could accomplish but little, and were sacrificed to no purpose.[41] The place was finally taken shortly before 4 P. M.[42]

---

[40] *Ante*, p. 270.

[41] Charras, vol. 2, p. 18. Colonel Heymès of Ney's staff says that more than 2,000 men were killed in endeavoring to get possession of La Haye Sainte. Doc. Inéd., p. 17. This, however, must be an excessive estimate.

[42] Charras, vol. 1, pp. 302, 303; vol. 2, p. 18; Hooper, p. 213, n.; O'Connor

But the capture of La Haye Sainte was only a necessary preliminary to a serious attack on the enemy's main line. Napoleon (or perhaps Ney) seems to have thought that the troops of d'Erlon had been too severely handled to warrant the expectation of any immediate aid from them. They would require an hour or two, perhaps, to recover. At any rate, it was determined to assail the English centre to the west of the Charleroi road, and as the infantry of the 1st Corps were not for the moment available, and as that of the 2d Corps, or at least, the greater part of it, was engaged in attacking Hougomont, it was decided to make the assault this time with cavalry alone.

The troops on this portion of Wellington's line,— between the Charleroi road and Hougomont,— had been subjected only to artillery fire, and even that had not been anything like as severe as that sustained by the troops exposed to the great French battery on the opposite side of the road. They consequently were in good condition to resist cavalry,[43] especially considering that the bad ground over which the cavalry must pass would be certain to diminish the force of their assaults. Sir James Shaw-Kennedy, who was on this part of the line, tells us that the opinion at the time among the English officers was that the attack was premature.

This was also Napoleon's own opinion; he seems to have yielded to Ney's solicitations against his own judgment. But at this time, shortly after 4 P. M., the advance of Bülow's Corps occupied the constant attention of the Emperor; he was constrained to leave the conduct of the

---

Morris, p. 352. Other authorities put the capture of La Haye Sainte two hours later. Colonel Heymès of Ney's staff places the hour between 6 and 7 P. M. Doc. Inéd., pp. 18, 19.

[43] Kennedy, pp. 114–116. Kennedy's account of this part of the battle, as indeed of all parts of it, is most valuable; but we think he is in error in supposing that La Haye Sainte had not fallen before these cavalry attacks were made.

battle against Wellington to Marshal Ney, in whose tactical skill and management he had great confidence, and to devote himself mainly to the task of directing the movements of the 6th Corps and of those portions of the Guard, which from time to time he was obliged to detach for its support, so as to prevent the Prussians from seizing the village of Planchenoit and thus menacing the communications of the army. Napoleon's neglect of the conduct of the operations against the English has often been the subject of comment and severe criticism; but we imagine that he was far more anxious to hinder the Prussians, who were aiming, so to speak, at a vital part, from succeeding, than even to defeat the English. To fend off the Prussians was an absolute necessity; to drive the English from the field, a thing no doubt very desirable; but as there was no fear that they would take the offensive, and as, if they did, the army, or, at least, the great bulk of it, was in line of battle opposed to them, no great danger was to be apprehended from them. Whereas the Prussians were striking at the flank and rear, aiming to get control of the Charleroi road, and thus of the line of communications and retreat of the army. To prevent their succeeding in this was, therefore, of vital importance. Hence Napoleon attended to this himself, and left to Ney the conduct of the fight against Wellington's army.

Marshal Ney, then, determined to carry the allied centre by charges of cavalry. He seems to have made no effort to support this attack by the infantry of the 2d Corps, although it would certainly have been quite possible to have withdrawn at least Bachelu's division from the wood of Hougomont and to have used it with good effect. But Ney was originally an officer of cavalry; this fact may have made him think it possible to accomplish more with cavalry alone than to others would seem practicable. At any rate, from 4 to 6 P. M. the splendid divisions of Milhaud, Lefebvre-Desnouettes, Kellermann and Guyot were successively launched against the English lines. Every one has heard of the magnificent gallantry of these fine troops; every one knows the indomitable steadiness with which their repeated onsets were borne. At the close of these assaults the French cavalry had become wellnigh exhausted; and they had not broken a single square. Nevertheless, the English, Hanoverian, Nassau and Brunswick troops had suffered severely; obliged to remain in squares for fear of the repeated irruptions of the French cavalry, they presented an easy mark to the French infantry skirmishers of Donzelot's division, which with a portion of Quiot's was finally brought over from the east side of the turnpike, as well as to the artillery from the French main position, which, necessarily silent while the cavalry were on the plateau, constantly recommenced its fire as soon as the cavalry retired down the slope, as was done many times during these two hours. In fact this part of the allied line was finally weakened so much that it was very near giving way, as we shall shortly see. At one time, all the troops for nearly half a mile to the west of the Brussels pike had retired from exhaustion, and in disorder, and the Duke himself had to lead up fresh troops to take their places.[44]

More, however, might have been accomplished by the French. For instance, the enfilading batteries, which towards the close of the day, dismounted Mercer's guns[45] and practically destroyed several squares of infantry, might have been employed quite as easily two hours before, and more of them might well have been used.[46]

---

[44] Kennedy, pp. 127 *et seq.*; Siborne, vol. 2, pp. 152 *et seq.*

[45] Mercer, vol. 1, p. 325; Napoléon à Waterloo, p. 315; Siborne, vol. 2, pp. 154, 155. Mercer in his Diary seems to think these enfilading batteries were Prussian; but see his letter and plan in the Waterloo Letters, pp. 214 *et seq. Cf.* Waterloo Letters, p. 330.

[46] Van Loben Sels, p. 333.

But no use whatever was made, except as above stated, of the very great advantage afforded by the position of La Haye Sainte for the posting of batteries which should sweep the whole line of the allies, dismount their guns, riddle their squares, and render their infantry unable to resist the shock of cavalry. Nor was the infantry of the 1st Corps brought up in season. As for that of the 2d Corps, Ney hardly made any use of it at all; he suffered it to remain in the wood and enclosures of Hougomont.

Napoleon said, and it cannot be seriously disputed, that the heavy cavalry of the Guard, the division of Guyot, went in without his orders. Whether Ney ordered it in is, however, doubtful. His chief-of-staff, Colonel Heymès, denies that he did. He says that the cavalry of the Guard went in of its own accord. (Doc. Inéd., pp. 16, 17.) At any rate, it was a great mistake, whoever committed it, as all the authorities freely say. It destroyed the last cavalry-reserve of the army.

While these operations were going on in front, Napoleon was personally superintending the desperate and gallant fight made by the two divisions of the 6th Corps under Lobau against Bülow's advance. The two leading divisions of the IVth Corps, which moved out about 4.30 P. M., were easily checked at first; but they rallied, and were reinforced by the rest of the corps; and, between 5 and 6 P. M., Lobau was driven back, and Planchenoit itself was threatened. The Emperor was obliged to put in the Young Guard, which, with three batteries, occupied Planchenoit, while the 6th Corps extended on its left so as to connect with the right of the 1st Corps. But the Prussians drove the Young Guard out of the village; and the Emperor had to order in three battalions of the Old and Middle Guard with two batteries. These troops, gallantly supported by the Young Guard, retook the town, and the Prussians fell back some distance. Napoleon then seems to have thought that the attack of the Prussians was exhausted. It was nearly seven o'clock.[47] In this action the fighting on both sides was very obstinate. The French troops were superior in point of experience to those of Bülow,—those of the 6th Corps were led by a very able officer, Lobau, and the regiments of the Guard were the *élite* of the army. Hence, though much inferior in numbers, they obtained this success, which under other circumstances, would have been decisive. But in this case their enemies had reinforcements at hand. Pirch I., at the head of the IId Corps, was only two miles in rear.

This, however, Napoleon of course could not know. Hence, thinking that the danger from the Prussians was practically over, he hastened towards the front, where for the last hour, ever since the conclusion of the cavalry attacks, the battle had languished. It had in fact consisted during this period only of a general skirmish-firing along the centre of the English position to the west of the Brussels pike, the result of which, however, was, undoubtedly, to weaken perceptibly the strength and *moral* of the allied troops. This part of the English line was in fact in a bad way at this period of the battle.[48] As Sir James Shaw-Kennedy, who was on this part of the line on the staff of the 3d division, says:—[49]

"La Haye Sainte was in the hands of the enemy; also the knoll on the opposite side of the road; also the garden and ground on the Anglo-Allied side of it; Ompteda's brigade was nearly annihilated, and Kielmansegge's so thinned, that those two brigades could not hold their position. That part of the field of battle, therefore, which was between Halkett's [50] left and Kempt's [51] right, was

---

[47] Charras, vol. 1, p. 318.

[48] Siborne, vol. 2, pp. 152 *et seq.*; Van Loben Sels, p. 295. *Cf.* Porter's Hist. Royal Engineers, vol. 1, p. 382: Waterloo Letters, p. 339, where the hour is fixed by Lieutenant-Colonel Dawson Kelly at "about half-past six."

[49] Kennedy, p. 127.

[50] Halkett's brigade was on the main line, nearly half of a mile west of the pike.

[51] Kempt's brigade was on the east side of the Brussels pike; its right rested on it.

unprotected; and being the very centre of the Duke's line of battle, was consequently that point, above all others, which the enemy wished to gain. The danger was imminent; and at no other period of the action was the result so precarious as at this moment. Most fortunately Napoleon did not support the advantage his troops had gained at this point by bringing forward his reserve; proving that he did not exert that activity and personal energy in superintending and conforming to the progress of the action, which he ought to have done."

As to this last observation, we have just seen how the Emperor was employed during this critical period of the action. He was in truth fighting another battle with inferior forces against the Prussians, and this, too, at a distance of a mile and a half from the English line of battle.[52] The criticism on Napoleon is therefore unfounded; it is due simply to the fact that his occupation during this period of the battle was not borne in mind by General Shaw-Kennedy. But the fact remains; if there had been no other battle to fight, — no desperate action at Planchenoit, requiring the presence and personal direction of the Emperor, — if the attack upon the allied lines could have been made under the eye and direct orders of Napoleon himself, — in the opinion of Kennedy, whose account of the battle is one of the best we have, it would have gone hard with Wellington's army. Add to this, that if there had been no other battle to fight, the Emperor could have brought 16,000 fresh men to bear upon this exhausted force of Wellington's. It should be added, also, that the English heavy cavalry of Somerset and Ponsonby, which had been well nigh exhausted by their charges at the beginning of the action, and had suffered more or less during the afternoon, were not able to render efficient service at the close of the day.

---

[52] It is almost exactly a mile and a half from the point of intersection of the Brussels turnpike with the Wavre road to the church in Planchenoit.

Napoleon, as we have seen, as soon as he had, as he supposed, definitely repulsed the Prussians in the neighborhood of Planchenoit, hastened to the front, where he must have arrived somewhere about seven o'clock. His absence from the field during this time was, as we have seen, not due to any fault or neglect of his, but nevertheless it was most unfortunate for the success of his army.[53] Marshal Ney had exhausted, as he supposed,[54] all the resources available to him. Over the Imperial Guard he had no authority; and the only infantry in the army that had not been put in belonged to the Guard. Meanwhile Wellington had exerted himself to the utmost to restore at least a semblance of strength to his line of battle west of the turnpike; he had rallied the men of Alten's division, who had been shaken by the fall of that officer, who was severely wounded; he had brought forward some Brunswick troops; he had ordered Chassé's (3d) Dutch-Belgian division from its position near Merbe Braine to a position in rear of the guards; he had brought over to the centre the light cavalry brigades of Vivian and Vandeleur from the extreme left. He had, in fact, done all that could be done, and he was now awaiting the next move of his antagonist with a coolness, vigilance and alertness which the discouraging aspects of the fight did not in the least affect. But his situation was a perilous one. His losses had been very great. His English troops were much exhausted; the patience and confidence of most of his foreign allies were nearly worn out; and on that part of his line lying to the west of the turnpike his artillery was mostly dismounted. He had, however, in reserve some of his best troops, and one or two batteries.

---

[53] See Napoléon à Waterloo, pp. 313, 318.

[54] The principal question as to this is in regard to the corps of Reille, a part of which, certainly, might have been more usefully employed in sustaining the cavalry attacks than in fighting in the wood of Hougomont, or on the Nivelles road on the west side of Hougomont. See Heymès' statement in Doc. Inéd., pp. 17, 18.

Maitland's brigade of guards and Adam's brigade of Clinton's division had suffered but little, and were troops of the best quality.

Ney had acquainted the Emperor with the state of things in his front, and had been informed that, as soon as he could, the Emperor would sustain him with a part of the Guard. Meantime, he was to collect as much of the cavalry, and of Reille's infantry, as he could, to support the attack which might soon be expected to be made by the Guard, supported by the infantry of the 1st Corps.

It was, as must be sufficiently apparent to the reader, out of the question at this period of the action for Napoleon to organize an attack against the English lines with the Imperial Guard, in any such fashion as that which he employed with such crushing effect on the day but one before, at Ligny. To begin with, the cavalry of the Guard, both the light and the heavy, had been shattered, and virtually ruined for the time being, by their repeated, ineffectual, and costly efforts to carry the plateau during the previous few hours. Then, but a fraction of the infantry and artillery of the Guard was disposable. The Young Guard, consisting of eight battalions, organized in four regiments, with twenty-four guns, was in Planchenoit,[55] where, also, was one of the eight battalions of the Old Guard (grenadiers), two battalions of the Middle Guard (chasseurs), and two batteries.[56] Two more battalions[57] of the Old Guard and one battery were on the road which, leading from Planchenoit to the Charleroi pike, comes out near the Maison du Roi, and one battalion of the Middle Guard was at the farm of Chantelet, in the neighborhood of the Caillou house, where were the headquarters-baggage and trains. As each of the divisions of

---

[55] Charras, vol. 1, p. 316.

[56] Ib., p. 317.

[57] Ib., p. 321, n.; correcting the statement on p. 318, which speaks of only one battalion of grenadiers being on the road to the Maison du Roi.

the Guard consisted of eight battalions, there were therefore but ten battalions left which could be employed against the English.[58] But, in addition to these detachments, for which we have the authority of Charras, we learn from Damitz,[59] who states with more minuteness than any other author the disposition made of the Imperial Guard, that one battalion of grenadiers and one of chasseurs were brought forward from Rossomme and stationed near La Belle Alliance. This left but eight battalions disposable for the projected attack.

These eight battalions[60] constituted four regiments, namely, the 3d and 4th grenadiers (Old Guard) and the 3d and 4th chasseurs (Middle Guard). The 3d and 4th regiments of grenadiers constituted the brigade of General Roguet; the 3d regiment was commanded by General Poret de Morvan, the 4th by General Harlet. The 3d and 4th regiments of chasseurs constituted the brigade of General Michel; the 3d regiment was commanded by General Mallet, the 4th by General Henrion.[61] The whole force, which could not have much exceeded 3,000 men, was under the command of General Friant, a very distinguished officer, titular colonel of the 1st regiment of foot-grenadiers of the Guard.

The Imperial Guard, which consisted of 24 battalions, organized into 12 regiments, of which 4 belonged to the

---

[58] Charras, vol. 1, p. 321.

[59] Damitz, vol. 1, p. 285. Damitz gives a complete roster of the Guard, and, in fact, of the whole army, at the end of his first volume. He also gives the numbers of the regiments and battalions detached in and around Planchenoit.

[60] Damitz, vol. 1, p. 285, states that owing to the losses suffered at Ligny these eight battalions had been consolidated into six. Batty (pp. 106, 107) also says that the 4th regiment of grenadiers consisted of but one battalion, and that the same was true of the 4th regiment of chasseurs.

[61] At least this was the fact on the 16th of June, prior to the battle of Ligny. See the Roster at the end of Damitz' first volume. All these officers, except Henrion, are mentioned by Charras (vol. 1, p. 322) as participating in this charge. Cf. Gore, p. 59. This work is an explanation, in 1817, of Craän's Map of the Field.

[CHAP. 16.]   THE BATTLE OF WATERLOO.   317

Old Guard, 4 to the Middle Guard, and 4 to the Young Guard, had been stationed at the beginning of the day just in front of the farm of Rossomme, and on either side of the Charleroi turnpike. From this point 16 battalions had been detached to various points, as we have seen. The Emperor in person now took the remaining 8 battalions [62] from this position to the front, and handed them over to Ney just to the south of La Haye Sainte. This was about 7 P. M. Here he addressed them; he encouraged them, and urged them to make their best efforts. These eight (or, probably, only six battalions) were then formed in as many columns, each of a front of two companies, and arranged in *échelon*,[63] the right battalion in front.[64] This was the 1st battalion of the 3d regiment of grenadiers, commanded by General Poret de Morvan. Two batteries of horse-artillery, placed on the left flank, accompanied the infantry. There seems to have been no arrangement for the proper support of the movement by cavalry, although a body of cuirassiers did, shortly before the main shock took place, charge Napier's battery. They were, however, easily and speedily driven off. The French cavalry was, in fact, nearly exhausted. Protection on the left of the advancing column, however, the Guard imperatively needed, as, in its march towards the enemy, its left flank would inevitably be exposed to all the troops stationed between the north end of Hougomont and the main British line. On its

---

[62] Ney: Letter to the Duke of Otranto; Jones, p. 387. But Drouot (Jones, p. 227) and Napoleon (Corresp., vol. 31, p. 238) say four battalions only, and the latter adds " of the Middle Guard." It is not unlikely that the other battalions had previously been brought up to the neighborhood of La Haye Sainte.

[63] Charras, vol. 1, p. 321.

[64] This is implied in Damitz' statement, vol. 1, p. 286, as well as from Charras' statement that the horse-batteries were on the left flank of the column. It is distinctly so stated in Van Loben Sels, p. 295.

right, the column was protected from a flank attack by the troops of the 1st Corps. (See Map 14.)

It was, according to all the accounts, Napoleon's intention that Reille should disengage at least one division of his corps from the enclosures of Hougomont, and support this charge of the Guard on the left; but this does not seem to have been even attempted. D'Erlon, on the other hand, must have exerted himself to the utmost to support the Guard; for the divisions of Donzelot and Quiot most gallantly and forcibly attacked the Anglo-Allied line for about a third of a mile to the west of the turnpike, overthrowing and driving back the Brunswick and Nassau troops, and even the Hanoverians and English, so that the personal interposition of the Duke was required to reëstablish the line. These attacks were made about the time when the Guard began its forward movement, and they had the effect of shaking the allied troops on this part of the field so much that they certainly could not have stood another serious and well-sustained assault, such as might have been delivered by the Imperial Guard.

But the movement of the column[65] of the Imperial Guard was not made in this direction, but diagonally across the field towards the enemy's right centre, where Wellington had stationed his reserves, and where he had at least one battery, Bolton's, then commanded by Napier, in good condition.

The English, as soon as they perceived the famous bearskin caps of the Imperial Guard, directed all their disposable guns upon their approaching foes; but, whether it was owing to the smoke, or to the inequalities of the ground, the Guard does not seem to have

---

[65] We call the whole mass, consisting of columns of battalions,—division (or two company) front,—arranged in *échelon*,—a column, merely for convenience' sake. It may be remarked that the French infantry were formed in three ranks.

[CHAP. 16.] THE BATTLE OF WATERLOO. 319

suffered until it got to close quarters with the 1st (Maitland's) brigade of the English guards.[66]

The leading battalion of the Guard was, as we have seen, formed in column with a front of two companies in three ranks. As each battalion had four companies,[67] and consisted of about 500 men,[68] there would be about 75 men in the front rank of the leading battalion, allowing for the file-closers. To its left and rear, marching in *échelon*, were the other battalions which constituted the attacking force, accompanied by two batteries of horse artillery of six pieces each, which kept up a destructive fire as the infantry advanced. We quote from the journal of an officer[69] in the English guards: —

"Suddenly the firing ceased, and, as the smoke cleared away, a most superb sight opened on us. A close column of Grenadiers (about seventies in front) of *la Moyenne Garde*,[70] about 6,000 strong, led, as we have since heard, by Marshal Ney, were seen ascending the rise, *au pas de charge*, shouting " *Vive l'Empereur*." They continued to advance till within fifty or sixty paces of our front, when the brigade[71] were ordered to stand up. Whether it was from the sudden and unexpected appearance of a corps so near them, which must have seemed as starting out of the ground, or the tremendously heavy fire we threw into them, *La Garde*, who had never before failed in an attack, *suddenly* stopped. Those, who from a distance and more on the flank could see the affair, tell

---

[66] Waterloo Letters, pp. 254, 257; *Contra*, Siborne, vol. 2, p. 166.

[67] St. Hilaire: Hist. de la Garde, p. 634.

[68] Charras, vol. 1, p. 67.

[69] Captain Powell, in Waterloo Letters, pp. 254, 255.

[70] This is an error. "La Moyenne Garde" consisted solely of the chasseurs of the Guard; the grenadiers constituted the Old Guard, strictly so called. It is not uncommon to find the grenadiers and chasseurs spoken of as constituting the Old Guard; this is Charras' usage. But it is an error to speak of the grenadiers of the Middle Guard. The grenadiers whom he saw were the 1st battalion of the 3d regiment, — *ante*, p. 317. See Napoléon à Waterloo, p. 315, n. 1; pp. 321, 325, 327, n. 1. *Contra*, Gore, p. 75.

[71] The 1st brigade of guards, about 1,800 strong,— Siborne, vol. 1, p. 460. App. xxx. They were formed in four ranks.

us that the effect of our fire seemed to force the head of the column bodily back.

"In less than a minute above 300 were down. They now wavered, and several of the rear divisions began to draw out as if to deploy, whilst some of the men in their rear beginning to fire over the heads of those in front was so evident a proof of their confusion that Lord Saltoun * * * holloaed out, '*Now's the time, my boys.*' Immediately the brigade sprang forward. *La Garde* turned, and gave us little opportunity of trying the steel. We charged down the hill till we had passed the end of the orchard of Hougomont, when our right flank became exposed to another heavy column (as we afterwards understood, of the chasseurs of the *Garde*) who were advancing in support of the former column. This circumstance, besides that our charge was isolated, obliged the brigade to retire towards their original position."

It is plain from this account that the head of the French column consisted of some 70 (or 75) men, as we have pointed out would be the case if the leading battalion was in column with a two company front; and that the fire of Maitland's brigade, which must have had a front of about 450 men, added to that of a part of Halkett's brigade, to that of Napier's battery, and to that of the Dutch-Belgian battery of Van der Smissen,[72] which General Chassé had most opportunely brought up, destroyed this leading battalion and one or more of those in *échelon* with it on its left and rear. It is also clear from this account that the pursuing troops soon found themselves flanked by the other battalions of the Imperial Guard, which they took to be a separate column, and were obliged to fall back. It is very unlikely, by the way, that they advanced as far as the end of the orchard of Hougomont, a quarter of a mile from their position.

It may be that the rear battalions of the Guard inclined in their advance, by accident or oversight, more to their left than they should have done, and thus pre-

---

[72] Relation Belge, pp. 74 *et seq.*

sented the appearance of a separate column. General Maitland says:— [73]

"As the attacking force moved forward, it separated; the chasseurs inclined to their left. The grenadiers ascended the acclivity towards our position in a more direct course, leaving La Haye Sainte on their right, and moving towards that part of the eminence occupied by the 1st brigade of Guards."

He also speaks of the effect of the fire of the batteries which accompanied the Guard:—

"Numerous pieces of ordnance were distributed on the flanks of this column. The brigade suffered by the enemy's artillery, but it withheld its fire for the nearer approach of the column. The latter, after advancing steadily up the slope, halted about twenty paces from the front rank of the brigade.

"The diminished range of the enemy's artillery was now felt most severely in our ranks; the men fell in great numbers before the discharges of grape shot and the fire of the musketry distributed among the guns."

General Maitland goes on to describe the repulse of the French attack:—

"The smoke of the [French] artillery happily did not envelop the hostile column, or serve to conceal it from our aim.

"With what view the enemy halted in a situation so perilous, and in a position so comparatively helpless, he was not given time to evince.

"The fire of the brigade opened with terrible effect.

"The enemy's column, crippled and broken, retreated with the utmost rapidity, leaving only a heap of dead and dying men to mark the ground which it had occupied."

The attempt of some of the rear battalions to deploy, noticed by Captain Powell, is thus mentioned by Charras:— [74]

"Unhappily, whether by orders, or by the instinct of the soldier, the Guard deploys, in order to reply to the musketry which decimates it from moment to moment; and, by this movement, it masks

---

[73] Waterloo Letters, pp. 244, 245.

[74] Charras, vol. 1, pp. 325, 326.

the two batteries which have followed it, which have taken position on the crest of the plateau, and whose fire has, up to this instant, protected its flanks."

But what the leading battalions of the Guard needed at the moment when they were being destroyed by the superior fire of the brigade of English guards was not so much the continued effect of the fire of artillery upon the brigade as the prompt advance of cavalry, which would have compelled Maitland to throw his regiments into squares.

Failing this, the best thing for the Guard would have been a flank attack on Maitland's brigade by troops of the 1st Corps; but this was averted by the gallant and skilful conduct of Sir Colin Halkett and Colonel Elphinstone in bringing the remains of Halkett's brigade, which had suffered terribly during the past hour, to the left of the English guards, and thus protecting them in their contest with the Imperial Guard.[75] In fact the attack on Halkett's brigade by Donzelot's troops at this time was very sharp, and at one time caused great confusion. It was a critical moment; for, if Halkett had been beaten, Donzelot's troops would have flanked Maitland's brigade, and, attacked as it then would have been, on front and flank, it would have been forced to retire, and perhaps even routed. Donzelot's troops did their best to gain a foothold on the plateau; they did gain a temporary success; they knew the importance of the task assigned to them, and gallantly strove to support the charge of the Guard. On the other hand, the intelligent appreciation of the emergency on the part of Halkett and his subordinates, and their obstinate and courageous maintenance of their exposed position deserve the highest commendation.

If this attack of the Imperial Guard had been sup-

---

[75] See Waterloo Letters, pp. 320, 321; Siborne, vol. 11, pp. 170 171, n.; See, also, Waterloo Letters, pp. 330, 331, 339, 340.

ported on the right by cavalry, this resistance on the part of Halkett's and Maitland's commands could not have been encountered.

It seems probable that the failure of the attack of the Guard upon Maitland's brigade involved in confusion both the 3d and 4th regiments of grenadiers (Old Guard), the four (or, more probably, three) battalions of which were the leading battalions in the whole column. This, however, is by no means certain. All we know is, that those troops which were not swept off the field by the charge of Maitland's guards, among which assuredly were the 3d and 4th regiments of chasseurs (Middle Guard), ignorant, probably, of the fate which had befallen their comrades, steadily pursued their way towards the right centre of the English position. As the eight (or, more probably, six) battalions of the original column were formed in *échelon*, the right in advance, it is plain that the march of the four (or, more probably, three) rear battalions would bring them on a part of the English line to the English right of the position of Maitland's brigade,—in fact, "towards that part of" the English "position which had been vacated by the second brigade of Guards, when it moved to Hougomont."[76] In this direction, then, these remaining battalions of the Imperial Guard advanced. To all intents and purposes they now constituted a second column. As a second column they must have appeared not only to the men of Maitland's brigade, when their pursuit of the leading and defeated battalions brought them on a line with the left *échelons* of the original formation, but also to the troops of the brigade of Sir Frederick Adam, who, having been lying behind a ridge, a little to the north of Hougomont, were now advanced, and found the French guard in full march for the summit of the acclivity.

The initiative seems to have been assumed without a

---

[76]Waterloo Letters, p. 245; Maitland's narrative.

moment's hesitation by Sir John Colborne, the lieutenant-colonel of the 52d regiment, who brought his command into line parallel to the flank of the Imperial Guard, and at once opened fire. This action was approved on the spot by General Adam, who ordered the other regiments of the brigade to support the 52d. The French column was obliged to halt, and to deploy to its left, in order to return the fire, and for a few minutes the action was very heavy on both sides.[77] But the other British regiments coming up, and the French, who were acting at a manifest disadvantage in being thus compelled to halt when half way up the slope, and resist an unexpected and resolute attack on their flank while they were exposed also to the fire from the enemy's batteries in front, becoming evidently uneasy, Colborne ordered a charge, which broke the column up completely. He followed the disintegrated and demoralized battalions without an instant's hesitation even across the Charleroi turnpike.

In this attack, the Imperial Guard was supported on its left flank neither by cavalry nor by the infantry of Reille's Corps. Had either been employed, the disaster could not have happened. A charge of cavalry would have forced the 52d to form square; an advance of Bachelu's division, or a part of it, would have engaged all the attention of Adam's brigade, and permitted the Guard to pursue its way unmolested to the crest of the hill.

What would have succeeded the repulse and defeat of the Imperial Guard had the Prussians not interposed, no one of course can tell. But while these movements were going on, about 7.30 P. M., the van of Zieten's Corps reached Papelotte;[78] and the division of Steinmetz, supported by cavalry and artillery, turning at once the right

---

[77] Waterloo Letters; Colborne's narrative, pp. 284, 285; Gawler's narrative, p. 293.

[78] Charras, vol. I, p. 327, n.

of the 1st Corps and the left of the 6th, advanced upon the field of battle, spreading terror and confusion throughout the right wing of the French army. Durutte's and Marcognet's divisions abandoned their positions; Lobau retired towards Planchenoit; while the immense success which the English had obtained over the French left in routing the Imperial Guard was instantly improved by Wellington in ordering his two remaining and as yet untouched cavalry brigades, those of Vivian and Vandeleur, to charge. These bodies of horse, which had been, in the latter part of the afternoon, brought over from the English left to the rear of their centre, were now launched upon the troops of Donzelot and Quiot, and the remains of the French cavalry; and then the Duke, seeing that the battle was won, ordered the whole line to advance. (See Map 12.)

There was no resistance of any consequence made, except by the scattered regiments of the Imperial Guard, and by the 6th Corps under the Count de Lobau, which held Planchenoit against the renewed assaults of Bülow's Corps, supported now by two divisions of the corps of Pirch I. until the retreat of the army beyond that point was assured. The Emperor did what he could; he exerted himself in every way;[79] his headquarters-cavalry charged the English light horse; but the army was too much exhausted to make any extraordinary exertions; and, attacked both in front and flank as the French were, nothing but extraordinary exertions could possibly suffice to check the victorious enemy, superior in numbers as well as in position. Hence with the exception of the 6th Corps, whose task was a definite one, and undoubtedly comprehended by every soldier in it, and of which one of the most courageous and efficient officers in the French army had charge, no resistance on a large scale was offered. The 1st Corps was hopelessly disorganized,

---

[79]Charras, vol. 1, p. 331.

and necessarily so; the 2d Corps could no doubt have effected an orderly retreat on Nivelles,[80] but Reille did not see the necessity of this course, and perhaps could not have been expected to do so. Most of the battalions of the Guard preserved their organization, and resisted heroically to the last. The Emperor was finally forced to take refuge in one of the squares of the Guard, and in its midst he was safely borne off his last field of battle.[81]

The French army was routed; but its condition was made exceptionally bad because only one avenue of retreat was followed, and also because this avenue was practically blocked at Genappe by the supposed necessity of crossing the Dyle on a single bridge.[82] Had the army been able to spread itself over an open country, it is not likely that the rout would have been so complete, and it is quite certain that the captures of artillery would not have been so great. But the Prussian cavalry took up the pursuit which neither the Prussian nor the British infantry were sufficiently fresh to maintain; and in the exhausted condition of body and bewildered state of mind in which the mass of the French soldiers were when the catastrophe came, little was needed to complete their demoralization. At Genappe over a hundred pieces of cannon were abandoned, and from that point on no attempt was made to keep up even a semblance of order.

Such was the famous battle of Waterloo. It has become a synonym for hopeless and irremediable disaster. It is not, however, necessary here to review the causes of the catastrophe. What we have still to say on this head we shall put into the Notes to this chapter. But there is one subject that properly belongs here.

What would have been the effect if Grouchy had detained the corps of Bülow and Pirch I., so that they could not have taken part in the action?

---

[80] Doc. Inéd., p. 62; Reille's Statement.
[81] Hist. de l'Ex-Garde, pp. 538, 539.
[82] Charras, vol. 1, p. 334.

In this discussion we shall assume the correctness of our conclusions, reached previously, that if Grouchy had started at daybreak for the bridge of Moustier, or even if he had followed the counsel of Gérard, he would almost certainly have prevented Bülow, Pirch I. and Thielemann from taking any part in the battle.[83] We shall not reargue these questions, for they have been already fully discussed.

Let us suppose, then, that Napoleon could have utilized his whole force against the army of Wellington during the whole afternoon; that he could have given his personal direction to the conduct of the action; that he could have followed up the repulse of the 1st Corps with a new attack in which Lobau should support d'Erlon, and in which the cavalry should take its proper part; that he had been on the spot when La Haye Sainte fell, and had improved that advantage as he well knew how to do; that he had had the whole of the Imperial Guard,—infantry, cavalry, and artillery,—at his disposal for the carrying of Wellington's position; it seems to us there can be no reasonable question as to the result; the Duke would have been badly beaten, and the action would in all probability have been over, or substantially so, by six o'clock. This question is not asked to gratify the imagination, or for purposes of speculation, but simply that we may form a judgment on the adequacy of Napoleon's means to the end which he had in view; for, if military history cannot assist us in forming correct opinions on the adequacy of certain available means to the attainment of certain proposed objects, it is of no use whatever. The view we hold as to the necessity of Blücher's support to Wellington's success is the same as that which we have seen[84] put forth by Sir James Shaw-

---

[83] *Ante*, pp. 261, 283.

[84] *Ante*, pp. 294, 295.

Kennedy, where he is justifying the Duke for accepting battle at Waterloo.[85]

As for Zieten, he could not have come up till half-past seven o'clock, which would have been too late for him to be of any use to the English. The probability is that he would have joined the other corps that were fighting Grouchy. It is hardly likely that he would have pursued his intention of joining Wellington, after he had heard that the other three corps were not likely to interfere in the battle between Napoleon and Wellington. This would have been to run a great risk; and one that under the circumstances no prudent officer would run. We are supposing now that Zieten hears at Ohain, for instance, that the other corps are engaged with Grouchy at St. Lambert or Couture,—now, then, he must admit that if Grouchy shall be able, owing to obstinate or skilful fighting, or to the lateness of the hour, or to chance, to prevent Bülow, Pirch I. and Thielemann from attacking Napoleon that afternoon, the chances are that Napoleon will defeat Wellington before he, Zieten, can possibly arrive; and, therefore, for him to proceed further than Ohain will simply be to involve himself in the disaster of the Anglo-Dutch army.

But while we must state our conviction that Grouchy would have prevented the defeat of Napoleon had he crossed the Dyle, we certainly do not consider him the sole cause of the defeat.

---

[85] *Cf.* Wellington's Report (Gurwood, vol. xii, p. 484; App. C, xii; *post*, pp. 372, 373), where he says that *he attributes the successful result of the day to the assistance he received from the Prussians.*

NOTES TO CHAPTER XVI.

1. That the tactics employed by the French at the battle of Waterloo in their operations against the army of the Duke of Wellington were unworthy of the experience and reputation of their commanders is almost universally admitted. The word "commanders" is used advisedly, because Ney seems to have had the immediate direction of the 1st and 2d Corps even when the Emperor was personally superintending the battle, and when Napoleon was called off to direct the defence of Planchenoit, Ney was certainly in sole control. But this does not fully exonerate the Emperor from responsibility for the dispositions which were made.

The faulty formation of d'Erlon's Corps in its great assault on the English left was the first blunder. The employment of the whole of Reille's Corps in the attack on Hougomont was the next. Then the negligent and wasteful way in which the attacks on both Hougomont and La Haye Sainte were conducted warrant severe criticism. The employment of all the reserve cavalry of the army was a most unheard of and uncalled for proceeding; they were all put in, and kept in until they were all exhausted. One would certainly suppose that Ney, who was responsible for this proceeding, must have seen, long before the close of the afternoon, that the cavalry were being completely ruined, and that no appreciable injury was being inflicted on the enemy.

We cannot but think that if Napoleon had personally directed the battle at this period, this useless and wasteful employment of the cavalry would not have been made. And we cannot help thinking, also, that the Emperor would have brought some at least of Reille's troops out of the enclosures of Hougomont to support any attacks of cavalry which he might have ordered, either in conjunction with the divisions of Donzelot and Quiot, or with the Imperial Guard, which, but for the attack of the Prussians, he would no doubt have put in between 4 and 5 o'clock. We must bear in mind, that Napoleon was fighting the Prussians near Planchenoit during a large part of the afternoon, and, in fact during the critical period of the battle; and that he cannot fairly be held liable to the censure for the tactics used in the fight against the English, which some English writers, in forgetfulness of this fact, have undertaken to apply to him.

The 1st Corps, after its severe repulse, rallied well and did extremely good work. The persistent attacks of Quiot's and Donzelot's infantry showed great enterprise and daring, up to the very last; and these troops deserve all praise. No doubt the bravery of the men of the 2d Corps in their ineffectual attacks on Hougomont was equally commendable; but it was a great waste of material to employ the entire corps in such an operation as attacking Hougomont. Hougomont should have been attacked, undoubtedly, but only by a moderate force; very possibly it might have been carried, had proper means been employed.[1] But it was of far more importance to utilize the infantry of the 2d Corps in breaking the English lines to the eastward of Hougomont, in conjunction with cavalry or the Imperial Guard, than to persist in throwing fresh regiments against the brick walls of the house and garden. Hougomont might in

---

[1] *Ante*, pp. 303, 304.

fact have been turned; and, if the last charge had succeeded, it would have been. A notable exception to the unfavorable criticism on the French tactics on this day is made by all historians when speaking of the gallant, skilful and obstinate defence of Planchenoit against the Prussians by the 6th Corps under the Count de Lobau, assisted by the Young Guard and some regiments of grenadiers and chasseurs. No praise is too high for these troops.

2. The English tactics deserved, and have always received, the high commendation of historians. Not only was the Duke himself always watchful and alert, but his efforts were admirably seconded by his officers. The unfailing energy and enterprise shown even at the very close of this exhausting day by the Duke himself and his lieutenants is at least quite as remarkable as the obstinacy and courage displayed in resisting the repeated attacks of their antagonists. The conduct of Maitland, Halkett and Colborne in the last great emergency exhibits the tenacity, courage, presence of mind, and readiness to seize the opportunity, which are the great military virtues, existing in undiminished vigor at the close of a most bloody and doubtful contest.

3. The account given in the text of the charge of the Imperial Guard does not agree fully with any of the narratives, but will be found, on reflection, it is submitted, to harmonize most of the conflicting evidence. The subject is a large one, and the testimony is very confusing. It is impossible to reconcile all the statements. But it is believed that the view maintained in the text,— that the Imperial Guard advanced in one body, or column, not in two; that this column (as we may call it, for lack of a better term) consisted at most of eight, and probably of only six battalions, each formed in close column of grand divisions,— that is, with a front of two companies,— the usual practice in those days,— presenting about 75 men in the front rank,— that these battalions advanced in

échelon, the right in advance,— explains most of the discrepancies, and accounts for all or nearly all the important statements contained in the different narratives. It was the leading battalions of this column which were met and defeated by Maitland's guards; it was the rear battalions which were flanked and routed by the 52d and the other regiments of Adam's (light) brigade.

A. There is, in our judgment, no foundation for the hypothesis of two columns, which, introduced by Siborne, has received the indorsement of Chesney, Kennedy and Hooper. It is opposed to the contemporaneous authorities of both nations. Napoleon's report of the battle,[2]— Ney's letter to the Duke of Otranto,[3]— Drouot's speech in the chamber of Peers,[4]— speak but of one column,— of one attack,— of one repulse. Sir Digby Mackworth, who was on Lord Hill's staff, in a position where he could observe everything, wrote in his journal at eleven o'clock at night, after the battle was over, as follows:—[5]

"A black mass of the grenadiers of the Imperial Guard, with music playing and the great Napoleon at their head, came rolling onward from the farm of La Belle Alliance. * * * The point at which the enemy aimed was now evident. It was an angle formed by a brigade of guards [Maitland's] and the light brigade [Adam's] of Lord Hill's Corps."

Mackworth then goes on to describe the contest, and the rout of the enemy. There is not a word of there being two columns and two attacks.

This is true, it is believed, of all the early narratives by British officers.[6] It may fairly be deduced from this evi-

---

[2]Corresp., vol. 28, p. 343; Jones, p, 384.

[3]Jones, p. 387.

[4]Ib., p. 227.

[5]Sidney's Life of Lord Hill, p. 309.

[6]Jones (Artillery Operations), p. 177; Sharpin in the "Waterloo Letters," pp. 228 *et seq.*; Gore, pp. 58 *et seq.* See, also, Captain Batty's account (pp.

[CHAP. 16.] THE BATTLE OF WATERLOO.–NOTES. 333

dence that the repulse of the right and advanced battalions by the guards, and the attack on the left and rear ones by the light brigade were nearly synchronous,—the latter being probably a few minutes later than the former.

B. The claims put forward on behalf of the light brigade (Adam's), and specially of the 52d regiment, next demand our consideration.

Gawler, a distinguished officer of the 52d, in his "Crisis and Close of the Action at Waterloo"[7] admits that "the headmost companies of the Imperial Guard * * * crowned the very summit of the position." He says that "the fire of the brigade of guards then opened upon them, but they still pressed forward." And he claims[8] that their attack was repulsed not "by a charge of General Maitland's brigade of guards," "but * * * by a charge of the 52d, covered by the 71st regiment, without the direct coöperation of any other portion of the allied army."

Unfortunately for this claim, however, we have it from another officer of the 52d, Leeke, that Gawler was on the extreme right of the regiment.[9] In this position, as

---

106 *et seq.*,) in his "Historical Sketch of the Campaign of 1815": London, 1820. He was an ensign in the 1st regiment of foot-guards in Maitland's brigade. He speaks, it is true, of the chasseurs of the Guard "forming another attack"; but he says that it was when Maitland was advancing, that he perceived the chasseurs "so far advanced as to menace the right flank of the brigade,"—which is substantially the view maintained in the text. *Cf.* Siborne, vol. 2, p. 170, where the same statement is made. Yet Siborne (vol. 2, p. 174) says that "between the heads of the two attacking columns there was a distance during their advance of *from ten to twelve minutes' march.*" How such an interval was possible, when the contest of the Guard with Maitland's brigade was of such extremely short duration, is not apparent. See Maitland's statement in "Waterloo Letters, pp. 244, 245; also statements of Powell and Dirom; pp. 255; 257, 258.

[7]Gawler, p. 15.
[8]Ib. pp. 31, 32.
[9]Leeke, vol. 1, p. 84.

Leeke remarks, he could not have seen what took place at the head of the French column.[10] When he says, therefore, that the flank attack of the 52d alone overthrew the Imperial Guard, he is speaking without any personal knowledge of what took place in the front of that column, and we are thrown back on the evidence of the officers of Maitland's brigade.

Leeke has a curious theory on this matter. He says that the advance of the Guard was preceded and covered by "a mass of skirmishers,"[11] and that it was these skirmishers and these only that were driven off by Maitland's brigade.

In order to maintain this contention, Leeke is compelled to assume the presence in front of the main body of the Imperial Guard of "massed skirmishers" thrown out by the Guard, and also that the battalions of the Guard never got nearer to Maitland's brigade than 300 yards.[12]

But this is mere guess work. Sharpin, an officer in Napier's battery, which was stationed close to Maitland's brigade, says:—[13]

"We saw the French bonnets just above the high corn and within 40 or 50 yards of our guns. I believe they were in close columns of grand divisions."

Says Captain Powell of the 1st Foot Guards:—[14]

"A close column of grenadiers (about seventies in front) * * * were seen ascending the rise * * * They continued to advance till within 50 or 60 paces of our front."

---

[10]Lord Seaton, then Sir John Colborne, who commanded the 52d, admits that he did not himself see, and could not have seen, any movement of the guards. He simply claims that the Imperial Guard halted when his skirmishers opened fire on their flank. Leeke, vol. 1, p. 101.

[11]Ib., pp. 43, 44, 84.

[12]Leeke, vol. 1, p. 84. See also his letter to the Editor of the Army and Navy Gazette, August 17, 1867.

[13]Waterloo Letters, p. 229. *Cf.* a statement of an officer in the same battery,— Jones, p. 177,— probably Sharpin.

[14]Waterloo Letters, pp. 254, 255.

Says Captain Dirom of the same regiment:—[15]

"The Imperial Guard advanced in close column with ported arms, the officers of the leading division in front waving their swords. The French columns showed no appearance of having suffered on their advance, but seemed as regularly formed as if at a field-day. When they got within a short distance we were ordered to make ready, present and fire."

Leeke's theory of "massed skirmishers" needs no further refutation. There can be no question that the officers of Maitland's guards saw right before them the leading battalions of the Imperial Guard formed in the ordinary manner, in close columns of grand divisions. The skirmishers had all been withdrawn by the time the leading battalions reached the top of the acclivity.

It should, however, be added that the left and rear battalions which Colborne attacked in flank were entirely unaffected by the charge of Maitland's brigade. The British guards did undoubtedly charge the troops in their front, and drove them down the hill a short distance, but on finding other troops, i. e., the four (or, more probably, three) rear and left battalions of the Imperial Guard, on their right flank, they retired to the crest of the hill, and certainly did not assist the 52d and the other regiments of Adam's brigade in their brilliant flank attack. The credit of having overthrown the rear half of the column of the Imperial Guard is due entirely to that brigade; and it assuredly was a most skilfully designed and daringly executed movement. Colborne saw at a glance that the several battalions of the Guard could not be deployed in such a way as to return anything like as destructive a fire as that which the unbroken line of the 52d could deliver. The Guard undoubtedly did its best; the firing was very hot for a time; Gawler says [16] his regiment lost 150 officers and men in four or five minutes. But his

---

[15] Waterloo Letters, p. 257.

[16] Ib., p. 293; *Cf.* Colborne's Letter, p. 285.

men were perfectly steady; their fire was at very close range and well kept up; they had the advantage of position; the loss of the French columns was fearful;[17] and when Colborne, perceiving that the moment had come, ordered a charge, the Guard broke into a confused mass, and were pursued to and across the Charleroi road. The flank attack of Adam's brigade was certainly a most brilliant, and yet a well-justified, manœuvre,—impossible to any but veteran troops, and which none but an experienced, vigilant and daring officer would ever have ordered. Colborne took, it must be admitted, great risks. He says himself[18] that, as his skirmishers opened fire on the Guards, his attention was completely drawn to his position and dangerous advance,—a large mass of cavalry having been seen on the right. Certainly it must have required some nerve to decide to run such a risk as this, and on his own responsibility too, for he advanced his regiment before receiving any order from General Adam. But success justified his decision.

4. Whether Napoleon was warranted in ordering the Guard forward, or rather that portion of it which could be mustered, is a question which has been much discussed, and, we are inclined to think, to no great profit. The answer must depend on the extent of the information possessed by Napoleon as to the actual condition of things at the time when he ordered the movement; and this, of course, must be mainly a matter of conjecture. The order was given somewhere about half-past six o'clock,—an hour before Zieten arrived at Papelotte; and Napoleon certainly did not expect him. Bülow had been forced to retire. The news from the front received by the Emperor when he was conducting the fight against the Prussian flank attack near Planchenoit had been decidedly favorable. The army of Wellington was

---

[17] Leeke, vol. 1, p. 104; Letter of Colonel Brotherton.
[18] Ib., p. 101.

reported as manifestly getting weaker and weaker. The guns placed near La Haye Sainte had done serious damage to the English squares and batteries. The activity and energy of Quiot's and Donzelot's infantry showed no abatement. It seems to us that the Emperor had good reason to think that the English lines would give way before a determined attack made by fresh troops, and those the veterans of the Imperial Guard. He told Ney to mass on the right of Hougomont all the troops of Reille's Corps that he could collect, to concentrate the divisions of Quiot and Donzelot near La Haye Sainte, and to prepare to support the attack with cavalry.[19]

He must, however, have been grievously disappointed as to the execution of this order by Marshal Ney. When the Emperor brought up the Guard, Bachelu's infantry had not been drawn out of the wood of Hougomont.[20] Piré's cavalry, which were in perfectly good condition, had not been brought over from the Nivelles road.[21] No attempt apparently had been made to organize any cavalry force from the wrecks of the splendid divisions which Ney had so obstinately and blindly launched again and again upon the English squares. And the Emperor, who must have expected that an officer of the ability and experience of Marshal Ney would have made some at least of the necessary arrangements for the proper support of the charging column, must have experienced a disappointment as sudden as it must have been bitter, when he saw the battalions of the Guard ascend the plateau without a regiment of cavalry to protect their flanks, or any part of the 2d Corps supporting their attack.

The charge, such as it was, of the Imperial Guard at

---

[19] Charras, vol. 1, p. 321.

[20] Wellington brought up about this time to the right centre of his line Chassé's Dutch-Belgian Division, besides other troops.

[21] Wellington about this time brought over the brigades of Vivian and Vandeleur to the threatened centre of his line, as well as the remnants of Somerset's and Ponsonby's brigades.

Waterloo was most firmly and gallantly met and repulsed. But it should never be forgotten that it was not the sort of charge which Napoleon was in the habit of making with his Guard; that it was, at best, a charge of 8 battalions out of 24, — of 12 guns out of 96, — and that no cavalry at all, light or heavy, supported the charging column. Made, as it was, without supports, except so far as Donzelot's gallant infantry protected its right flank, it was a terrible mistake to make it. And it is all but certain that if proper care and skill had been expended on the preparations and accompaniments of the movement, — if, in a word, Ney had kept his head cool and his hand steady, as did the Duke, — Piré's lancers and Bachelu's division would have given abundant employment to the whole of Adam's brigade, and a few squadrons of horse could have protected the advance on the right. This is not, we submit, going too far in the region of conjecture. Bachelu and Piré, at any rate, were close at hand, and under Ney's command, and were, so far as we know, doing nothing at the time when the charge was ordered.

Ney, in fact, contributed apparently little, except his example of desperate courage, to the success of the day. But courage, though indispensable, does not take the place of judgment and presence of mind.[22] Ney failed most unmistakably to make the most of his resources; he lost sight, practically, of one of the two corps under his orders; he used up all his cavalry; and he neglected to make even the preparations and arrangements which were yet feasible to second the attack of the Guard. It is impossible not to contrast his conduct with that of Wellington whose admirable forethought and coolness gave him the

---

[22] On Marshal Ney's state of mind at this time, see Gourgaud, pp. 48, n 111, 112; Corresp., vol. 31, pp. 249, 250; Muquardt, p. 149, n.; Life of Sir W Napier, vol. 1, p. 505,—where Soult gives his opinion on Ney's conduct Berton, p. 41, where Ney's extraordinary letter to Fouché (Jones, pp. 38 *et seq.*) is examined.

control of the situation, and enabled him to utilize fully all the resources which at the close of this trying day still remained to him.

5. We have not thought it necessary to do more than to call attention to the fact that the Duke of Wellington retained some 18,000 men of Colville's division at Hal and Tubize throughout this perilous and bloody day. The best English authorities [23] unhesitatingly condemn the Duke's action in this regard. Says Sir James Shaw-Kennedy:—[24]

"Wellington certainly ought to have had Colville, with the force under his command, on the field of battle at Waterloo. There was no cause whatever for his being kept in the direction of Hal. It would have been a gross error on the part of Napoleon to have detached any important force on that road, and Colville should, early on the morning of the 18th, have been ordered to march to Waterloo, if he had no information of the advance of the enemy on Hal."

6. It may be thought by some that the effect upon the corps of Bülow and Pirch I. of the appearance of Marshal Grouchy's command, marching from Moustier and Ottignies upon Lasne and St. Lambert, has been stated too strongly in the text. But we cannot think so. Imagine 30,000 or 40,000 men marching in a long column along miry roads to attack an enemy, and still some miles from the field of battle, perceiving a body of troops of apparently equal or nearly equal strength moving right upon their line of march, which is also their line of communications. How many officers in Bülow's position would not have halted to resist such an attack?

It is to be observed, that the dilemma in which Bülow and Pirch I. were placed by knowing that Grouchy was attacking Wavre was quite a different one. In the first place, they, as we now know, estimated Grouchy's force

---

[23] Chesney, p. 217; Hamley, p. 198.
[24] Kennedy, p. 174.

at only half its strength,—they never, it must be remembered, actually saw it; and in the second place, Grouchy might well be detained by Thielemann at and about Wavre until the battle of Waterloo had been won.

If, however, Grouchy had been observed marching from the Dyle directly on their columns *en route* for Planchenoit, the Prussian commanders almost certainly would have been compelled to halt and to give him battle. And this they must have done even although they might have been satisfied that their forces were superior in numbers. A smaller force, if it is directed on the line of march of a larger one, almost inevitably must detain it.

7. The complete ruin which overtook the French army at Waterloo is to be attributed mainly to the unexpected appearance and vigorous attack of Zieten's Corps at the close of the day, when the French had become thoroughly exhausted, and when, owing to the darkness, it was impossible for the Emperor to accomplish anything in the way of rallying them or making new dispositions. The English had certainly won a great success in routing the Imperial Guard; but they were not strong enough to drive the French army from the field, even with the assistance which Bülow and Pirch I. afforded on the side of Planchenoit. They had cleared their front of the enemy from Hougomont to the turnpike; but they were in no condition to attack the strong position of the French, defended by the troops of the 2d Corps, and crowned with many and powerful batteries. The French centre, Müffling tells us,[25] remained immovable after their right wing was in full retreat, and it was not until some of Zieten's batteries, which had been brought over to the west of La Haye Sainte, opened fire, that it began to retire. Then Wellington ordered his whole line to advance. But it was a very thin line indeed, consisting, as Müffling says, only of small bodies, of a few hundred

---

[25] Müffling; Passages, p. 249.

men each, and at great intervals from each other. Müffling goes on to say:—[26]

"The advance of such weak battalions, with the great gaps between, appeared hazardous, and General Lord Uxbridge, who commanded the cavalry, drew the Duke's attention to the danger; the Duke, however, would not order them to stop. * * *
The Duke with his practised eye perceived that the French army was no longer dangerous; he was equally aware, indeed, that, with his infantry so diminished, he could achieve nothing more of importance: but if he *stood still*, and resigned the pursuit to the Prussian army *alone*, it might appear in the eyes of Europe as if the English army had defended themselves bravely indeed, but that the Prussians alone decided and won the battle."

The rout of the divisions of Durutte and Marcognet was entirely due to Zieten's attack; this is universally admitted. Had it not been for Zieten, then, the only contest that would have gone on that evening would have been at and near Planchenoit; and it is hard to suppose that Napoleon could not have maintained his position there, if he had had his whole army to draw from when the Young Guard and Lobau needed reinforcements. To the unexpected irruption of Zieten's Corps,— or rather of his leading division of infantry, all his cavalry, and most of his artillery,— arriving at the close of the day, on the flank of the army, and in perfectly open ground, is the rout of the French army, therefore, principally to be attributed.

8. It only remains to discuss the question of the responsibility for the intervention of the Prussians, as between the Emperor and Marshal Grouchy. It may fairly be said that if either of them had taken all the steps which the situation, as it presented itself to his mind, demanded, this intervention might have been prevented. If the Emperor, when he thought it possible that the Prussians might be intending to unite with the English,

---

[26] Müffling; Passages, p. 250.

had taken Grouchy with him, and had stationed his two corps, or one of them, on the day of the battle, at or near Lasne and St. Lambert, or if he had employed one or both of Grouchy's corps in attacking the English, Blücher, it is safe to say, would not have interfered in the duel between Napoleon and Wellington.

If, after sending Grouchy off, Napoleon had informed him of the impending battle, and had charged him to return to the main army by way of Moustier if he found that the Prussians had gone to Wavre, it is altogether probable that the march of the Prussians would have been arrested.

On the other hand, if Grouchy had acted of his own motion on sound military principles at daybreak of the 18th, or even had been willing to follow the counsel of Gérard at noon, the same result would probably have been attained.

Napoleon took a wholly unnecessary risk when he detached Grouchy with such a large force, after he had reason to apprehend that the Prussians were intending to unite with the English, and he negligently omitted to take the usual means to reduce this risk by supplying his lieutenant with the necessary information, and with precise orders in case he should find that Blücher intended to coöperate with Wellington. He trusted to Grouchy to take the right course, and Grouchy failed to do so. Both Napoleon and Grouchy are therefore responsible for the intervention of the Prussians and the loss of the battle.

CHAPTER XVII.

CONCLUDING OBSERVATIONS.

THE justification for this book on the well-worn subject of the campaign of Waterloo is to be found, if at all, in its treatment of certain topics to which we now propose very briefly to advert.

1. First among them is Napoleon's plan of campaign.[1] In regard to this we have followed his own account, and have pointed out the difference between it and the plan which it has been claimed he either really did entertain or ought to have entertained.

2. In regard to the much-vexed question of the alleged verbal order to Marshal Ney to seize Quatre Bras on the afternoon of the 15th of June, new light, it is submitted, has been thrown.[2] The contemporaneous evidence of the bulletin, and the statement made by Marshal Grouchy in 1818, make it very difficult to disbelieve Napoleon's account of this matter.

3. The true cause of the delay on the morning of the 16th of June has been, we submit, pointed out.[3] The fact that d'Erlon's Corps was so far in the rear seems to have been the chief reason for delaying the forward movement both of the left wing and of the main army.

4. It has been shown by Marshal Ney's orders to his command, and from other evidence furnished by his

---

[1] Chapter I, and Notes: Notes to Chapter IV.

[2] *Ante*, pp. 64 *et seq.*

[3] *Ante*, pp. 131. 132; 139.

defenders, that his arrangements for carrying out his instructions on the 16th were extremely defective, and, in fact, that he perversely departed from the letter and spirit of his orders.[4] It has also been shown that a vigorous and unhesitating compliance with the orders which he received would in all probability have changed the issue of the campaign.[5]

5. In regard to the movements of d'Erlon's Corps on the 16th, it has been shown that its leading division was two hours and a half behind the rear divisions of the 2d Corps on the road to Quatre Bras; and that if d'Erlon's Corps had closely followed the rear division of the 2d Corps, it could not have been turned aside by the staff-officer's blunder.[6]

6. Attention has been called to Napoleon's plan of battle at Ligny, and to the criticisms which it has met with.[7]

7. The view of those writers who regard it as great negligence on the part of Napoleon that on the morning of the 17th he did not take adequate measures to ascertain the direction of the Prussian retreat, is fully adopted.[8]

8. It is also maintained that Napoleon should on that morning at daybreak have marched with the 6th Corps and the Guard to attack the English at Quatre Bras in conjunction with Ney's forces,—a point on which most writers strongly insist.[9]

9. The connection between the injunction contained in the Bertrand order and the new idea as to the projects of Marshal Blücher, which Berton's discovery of a Prussian corps at Gembloux had started in Napoleon's

---

[4] Chapter VIII., and Notes.

[5] *Ante*, pp. 184–186.

[6] *Ante*, p. 181.

[7] *Ante*, pp. 164 *et seq.*

[8] *Ante*, p. 205.

[9] *Ante*, pp. 197 *et seq.*

mind, is brought out;[10] and Napoleon is censured for having on the afternoon of the 17th detached so large a force from his army when he had reason to apprehend that a movement by Blücher with the intention of co-operating with Wellington had been in operation since the previous evening.[11]

10. The warning contained in the Bertrand order is given its due prominence; and the fact that Marshal Grouchy was acting under that order, and therefore had entire liberty to take any steps which his own judgment might approve to frustrate the attempt of the Prussians to act in conjunction with the English, is strongly insisted on.[12]

11. It is shown that Grouchy was at Walhain, and not at Sart-à-Walhain when he heard the sound of the cannon of Waterloo and rejected the counsel of Gérard.[13]

12. That Napoleon expected Grouchy to arrive on the left bank of the Dyle by crossing it at the bridge of Moustier is shown by Marbot's testimony; and attention is called to the inference which this fact warrants, that Napoleon was not cognizant of the language used in the 10 A. M. order to Marshal Grouchy, which seemed to imply that Grouchy was expected to reach Wavre first.[14]

13. It is pointed out that from about four o'clock in the afternoon of the 18th of June to about half-past six, Napoleon's attention was absorbed by the attack of Bülow's Corps upon the right and rear of the French army; and that, for the mistakes committed during this period in the assaults on the English army, Ney is mainly responsible.[15] It is furthermore shown that by

---

[10]*Ante*, p. 209.

[11]Chapter XV., note 1.

[12]*Ante*, p. 211; pp. 249 *et seq.*

[13]*Ante*, p. 255; pp. 286 *et seq.*

[14]*Ante*, pp. 268 *et seq.*

[15]*Ante*, pp. 311 *et seq.*; p. 330.

reason of this distraction of the Emperor's attention from the operations in his front, valuable opportunities for success against Wellington's army were lost.[16]

14. Marshal Ney is censured for having done so little in the way of preparation for the successful charge of the Imperial Guard.[17]

15. The questions relating to the formation of the Imperial Guard in its charge against the English, and of its repulse and defeat by the English guards and the light brigade, have received particular attention. It is believed that the view here presented will be found to harmonize nearly all the conflicting statements.[18]

16. It is maintained that Marshal Grouchy, if he had started for the bridge of Moustier at daybreak,[19] or had followed the advice of Gérard at noon,[20] would probably have stopped Bülow and Pirch I. by engaging them, and that Zieten, in all probability, would not have proceeded further than Ohain;[21] in which case Napoleon would have been able to employ his whole army against that of Wellington, and would have defeated it.

Coming now to the Allies:—

17. It is contended that the definite understanding as to the steps to be taken in the event of a French invasion, which has generally been attributed to the Duke of Wellington and Marshal Blücher, did not exist.[22]

18. That the Duke, in the early morning hours of the 16th, ordered a general concentration of his army at Quatre Bras, as he says in his Report he did, is shown by

---

[16]*Ante*, pp. 314, 330.

[17]*Ante*, pp. 337, 338.

[18]*Ante*, pp. 316 *et seq.*; pp. 331 *et seq,*

[19]*Ante*, pp. 281 *et seq.*

[20]*Ante*, pp. 259 *et seq.*

[21]*Ante*, p. 328.

[22]*Ante*, pp. 70 *et seq.*; p. 91.

an examination of his letter to Marshal Blücher, and a comparison of that letter with the statement as to the situation and destination at 7 A. M. of the 16th of the different divisions of his army, known as "The Disposition," drawn up by Sir William De Lancey, the Deputy Quartermaster General, before the Duke left Brussels.[23]

19. That the Duke, in issuing the order for concentrating at Quatre Bras after he had become satisfied that Napoleon was concentrating in front of Blücher, was acting in strict accordance with the demands of the situation, is maintained:[24] but it is shown that it was several hours after Wellington received this information as to Blücher and Napoleon before he issued the order, and that this delay was not only uncalled for, but that it gravely imperilled the success of the allies.[25]

20. It is shown that it is not true that Blücher's decision to fight at Ligny was based on a promise of support from Wellington.[26]

21. Attention is called to the now generally admitted fact that it was not until the early morning hours of the 18th that Blücher was able to give Wellington definite assurance of his support in the battle of Waterloo.[27]

22. The evidence in regard to the story that the Duke rode over to Wavre on the evening of the 17th is given,[28] and, on that evidence, the story is rejected.

A few words in conclusion.

1. It does not seem to us that Napoleon can be charged with any lack of activity or decision of character, except on the morning after the battle of Ligny, when he was, as we imagine, pretty well tired out. But his energy

---

[23] *Ante*, pp. 87 *et seq.*
[24] *Ante*, p. 94.
[25] *Ante*, p. 89.
[26] Chap. X.
[27] *Ante*, p. 234.
[28] *Ante*, pp. 238 *et seq.*

speedily returned, and we find him conducting the pursuit of the English during the afternoon, and making an examination of their position in the mud and rain in the middle of the night.

2. Nor was there any defect in his plan of campaign. Had Ney executed his orders with promptness and without hesitation, the campaign would have been finished on the 16th of June, either by Ney's furnishing the needed force to take the Prussians in rear at Brye and Wagnelée, or by his defeating Wellington badly by the help of the 1st Corps. If either of these things had happened, there could not possibly have been any battle of Waterloo; the Prussian and English armies would have been definitely separated; one, and perhaps both, would have been beaten; and never, in all probability, would they have acted together again. For this failure to achieve success on the second day of the campaign, Ney and not Napoleon was responsible.

3. But for not overwhelming at Quatre Bras on the early morning of the 17th the two-thirds of his army which Wellington had collected there, no one but Napoleon was responsible; and his failure to do this must be attributed to his excessive fatigue.

4. Then, for his neglect to ascertain the direction of the Prussian retreat on the same morning, Napoleon is responsible; and although Soult ought to have attended to this, in his capacity of chief-of-staff, yet, as the Emperor does not appear to have blamed him for not having reconnoitred in the direction of Wavre, we must consider Napoleon as open to this censure. It is true, it was not likely that Blücher had retired in the direction of Wavre; but it was of vital importance to know whether he had or not. Hence it was a great neglect not to find out.

5. Napoleon is also solely responsible for having persisted in his original design of detaching Grouchy in pursuit of the Prussians after he had reason to believe that they

were intending to unite with the English, and to suspect, in fact, that they had been approaching the English during the previous night and morning; and for contenting himself with merely giving Grouchy a warning that this might be their intention. He laid upon Grouchy, in fact, a burden which to that officer, as Napoleon was well aware, was entirely new; hence, the Emperor was not warranted in risking so much on the chance of Grouchy's being able to sustain it. It is this that Napoleon is to blame for in this connection; for having, when he saw that the Prussians might (as the Bertrand order expresses it) be "intending to unite with the English to cover Brussels in trying the fate of another battle," persisted in adhering to his original plan,— devised when he and Grouchy and everybody else supposed that the Prussians had gone to Namur,— of sending Grouchy in pursuit of them with two *corps d'armée*. Many writers will have it that "Napoleon did not in the least foresee the flank march of the Prussians."[29] This,—if to foresee be equivalent to expect,— may be true. But Napoleon certainly did, at 1 P. M. of the 17th, recognize the possibility of the Prussians uniting with the English; and the true criticism on him is, as it seems to us, that, having this in mind, as a possibility, he should have detached Marshal Grouchy with 33,000 men from the main army, and have been content to rely on Grouchy's being able to prevent this project of the Prussians from being carried out. It must be added to this, that his neglect to send Grouchy any information of his own situation, and any orders as to what he expected him to do if he found the Prussians were marching to join Wellington or to attack the main French army, showed an unjustifiable reliance on the favors of fortune.

6. To Marshal Grouchy belongs the blame of having entirely failed to apprehend his mission, as indicated to

---

[29] Chesney, p. 207; Kennedy, pp. 163, 164.

him by the express warning contained in the Bertrand order. Had he acted intelligently in accordance with the information which he acquired in the night of the 17th and 18th, he could have prevented the Emperor from being overwhelmed by both the allied armies. At daybreak, as appears from his letter to Pajol, he knew that the Prussians had retired towards Wavre and Brussels. But the meaning of this fact he utterly failed to grasp. He made no change in his previously ordered dispositions, which this news should have shown him were wholly unsuited to the situation as now ascertained. Nor did the sound of the cannon of Waterloo produce on him a greater effect. He would not accept the suggestion of Gérard. He persisted in a course which completely isolated his command, and prevented it from playing any part in the events of that memorable day. Napoleon, as we have pointed out, made a great mistake in trusting so much to Grouchy's good judgment; he took a wholly unnecessary risk; he might, as well as not, have taken Grouchy, with far the larger part of his command, with the main army; had he done so, the catastrophe of Waterloo could not, so far as we can judge, have happened. But had Grouchy acted up to the demands of the situation in which he found himself, he also would have averted the ruin which the unhindered union of the allies brought upon Napoleon and his army.

APPENDIX A.

ON SOME CHARACTERISTICS OF NAPOLEON'S MEMOIRS.

Probably no military narratives that ever were written have been subjected to more harsh and unjust criticism than the two accounts of the campaign of Waterloo, which, under the names of the Gourgaud Narrative and the Memoirs, were dictated or written by Napoleon at St. Helena. To read the remarks of Charras, Chesney, Hooper, and others, about these books, one would suppose that a military narrative is the easiest, plainest sort of narrative to write, and that if a general wished to compose it properly he would isolate himself from his fellow-officers and subordinates, and get into some secluded corner of the world thousands of miles from the records of the war-department. For if this is not the view of these writers and of others like them, they are either ignorant of the extreme difficulty which attends the composition of a military narrative, or else are bent upon treating the fallen Emperor with gross injustice.

For instance, Napoleon says in his "Memoirs"[1] that "on the 14th *in the evening*,"[2] General Bourmont deserted to the enemy. The whole army broke camp in the early hours of the 15th. When the 4th Corps moved at five o'clock, it was discovered that Bourmont had left. Charras states that the staff-records of the 4th Corps, to which Bourmont belonged, mention that he deserted on the 15th, and that he wrote a letter to Gérard announcing his desertion dated at Philippeville on the 15th. But

---
[1] Corresp., vol. 31, p. 251.
[2] The italics are ours.

Napoleon at St. Helena had neither the staff-records of the 4th Corps to go by, nor the letter of Bourmont to Gérard. Yet Charras[3] calls the Emperor's statement a designed misstatement (*une inexactitude calculée*).

But we have no disposition to dwell on harsh criticisms of this kind. Our purpose at present is to call attention to a peculiarity of Napoleon's which may serve to explain the existence in his Memoirs of very definite statements which are apparently very wide of the truth. This peculiarity is, that while his orders to his lieutenants were often very general in their character, — pointing out clearly enough, it is true, the thing to be aimed at, or the danger to be feared, — but leaving entirely to the officer the course to be adopted if the emergency should arise, — yet these orders never seem to have been retained in Napoleon's memory in the shape in which they were given, but what he did recall about them was his expectation that, on receiving his order, his lieutenant would act in such or such a manner. This expectation, that such or such action would be taken by his lieutenant on receiving such or such an order, was all that was left of the order in his mind; and, when he came to write his narrative, he would often (at any rate) state that he had given definite instructions to such or such an effect, when all he had really done was to give a general order, from the giving of which he expected such or such a course of action to be taken by his subordinate.

Thus, take the orders to Ney, issued on the afternoon of the 16th, at 2 and 3.15 P. M.[4] They were, as we have seen, very general in character; Ney was directed, after he should have beaten, or, at least, checked, the English, to turn round, and manœuvre so as to take the Prussians in flank and rear. But the "Memoirs"[5] say: —

---

[3] Charras, vol. 1, p. 104, n. 1.

[4] Doc. Inéd., XIII., p. 40; XIV., p. 24; App. C, xxv., xxvi; *post*, pp. 383, 384.

[5] Corresp., vol. 31, p. 204.

"He [Napoleon] reiterated the order for him to push on in front of Quatre Bras; and, as soon as he should have taken position there, to detach a column of 8,000 infantry, with the cavalry-division of Lefebvre-Desnouettes, and 28 pieces of cannon, by the turnpike which ran from Quatre Bras to Namur, which he was to leave at the village of Marbais, in order to attack the heights of Brye, in the enemy's rear."

It is to be observed that the Memoirs make no mention of the orders which were actually sent to Ney that afternoon. And Napoleon sent to Ney no such order as this. What he here calls an order was really what he expected Ney to do when he should get the 2 and 3.15 P. M. orders. That this was so, appears from what follows: —

"After having made this detachment, there would still remain to him [Ney] in his position of Quatre Bras 32,000 men and 80 pieces of cannon, which would be sufficient to hold in check all the English troops which could be expected to arrive from their cantonments during the day of the 16th."

That is, — the Emperor had figured it all out in his own head, as if he were in Ney's place. Ney could spare so many men and so many guns; he would have so many men and so many guns left. But, in fact, the orders to Ney left it to him to make these calculations for himself.

Let us apply now this mode of working of Napoleon's mind to his statements in regard to the orders which he says in his "Memoirs" he sent to Grouchy.[6]

"At ten o'clock in the evening the Emperor sent an officer to Marshal Grouchy, whom he supposed to be at Wavre, to inform him that there would be a great battle the next day; that the Anglo-Dutch army was in position in front of the Forest of Soignes, its left resting on the village of La Haye; that he ordered him to detach before daybreak from his camp at Wavre a division of 16,000 men of all arms and 16 pieces of cannon on St. Lambert, in order to connect with the main army and operate with it; that as soon as he should be assured that Blücher had evacuated Wavre, whether to continue his retreat on Brussels or to move in any other

---

[6] Corresp., vol. 31, p. 216; see, also, p. 212.

direction, he (Grouchy) was to march with the larger part of his troops to support the detachment which he had sent to St. Lambert."

Thiers[7] finds in the minuteness of detail in which this supposed order is stated in the Memoirs a proof that it could not have been invented. We do not so regard the matter. To our mind, the terms in which Napoleon has, in the extract given above, framed what he says was the order which he sent to Grouchy, simply express the expectations formed in his own mind of what Grouchy would do, when, after having received the Bertrand order, he found that Blücher had fallen back towards the English. We think the orders sent to Ney on the afternoon of the battle of Ligny should serve as a guide to us here. We do not believe that Napoleon sent to Grouchy any such order as that which he gives in his Memoirs; but then we do believe that he sent him the Bertrand order, which he does not even mention in his Memoirs, and which in fact he no doubt forgot all about. And we believe that, having a distinct recollection of having sent Grouchy an order, and also a very distinct recollection of what he expected Grouchy would do when he got the order, he has fused the two things in his mind, and has given us his order in the terms of his expectations.

There is nothing very uncommon about this. It is certainly to be distinguished from deliberate misrepresentation. It is partly, at any rate, the result of an active imagination working on facts imperfectly recollected, but which have been dwelt upon until the mind has become disturbed and warped.

---

[7] Thiers, vol. xx, p 95, n.

APPENDIX B.

ON MARSHAL GROUCHY AND THE BERTRAND ORDER.

We have stated (*ante*, p. 208) that Marshal Grouchy "denied, over and over again, in his pamphlets written about the battle, ever having received any written order, whether from Napoleon or Soult, until the next day (the 18th)"; and we have pointed out the grave misconceptions of the conduct of Napoleon which have been the result of these denials on the part of Marshal Grouchy, which, for many years, were very generally credited. We now propose to prove the truth of our statement.

In 1818 Marshal Grouchy published in Philadelphia his "*Observations sur la Relation de la Campagne de 1815 publiée par le Général Gourgaud.*" After giving an account of the verbal orders which Napoleon gave him, of his observations in regard to them, and of the Emperor's reply (*ante*, p. 207), he says:—[1]

"Such are the only dispositions which were communicated to me; the only orders which I received."

In the same pamphlet he says:—[2]

"But why, unceasingly repeats this 'Combatant of Waterloo,' — why does not Marshal Grouchy publish the text of the orders which he received?

"The reason is simple. It is that they were only transmitted to

---

[1] Observations, Phila. ed. 1818, p. 13. In the Philadelphia edition of 1819, p. 12, and in the Paris edition, 1819, p. 13, the statement is made somewhat stronger by the insertion of the words "word for word."

[2] Obs., Phila. ed., 1818, pp. 26, 27; ed. 1819, pp. 24, 25; Paris ed., pp. 30, 31.

me verbally. Those who have served under Napoleon know how rarely he gives them in writing. * * * If it is of any consequence to show that they were only verbal, I can find if not a proof, certainly a strong indication of it in the letter of the Major-General, Marshal Soult, in speaking of my march on Sartavalin. He expresses himself in these terms:—

"'This movement is conformed to the dispositions which have been communicated to you.'

"He would not have failed to say to the instructions or the orders which I have transmitted to you, and which you are acting under, if I had received any except verbal orders."

The point of this argument is fully seen only when we remember that the Bertrand order was dictated by the Emperor in the absence of Soult, the chief-of-staff, and therefore no copy of it was likely to be found on the regular official files. But fortune enabled Grouchy to make sure of this, for he had, soon after Waterloo, an opportunity of examining the records of the chief-of-staff.

Accordingly, we find him, soon afterwards,[3] in support of his denial of having received the orders alleged in the Memoirs to have been sent to him, saying, not, as he ought to have done, that he did receive an order through Bertrand, which, however, was entirely different in its tenor from those given in the Memoirs, but that he received on the 17th no written order at all.

'The proof of this is in the order-book and correspondence of the major-general, the organ of communication of the General-in-chief with his lieutenants. This irrefutable document, which, when I received the command of the army after the loss of the battle of Waterloo, came into my possession, shows that no orders or instructions except those contained in the two letters given herewith, and dated at 10 A. M. and 1 P.M. of the 18th, were ever sent to me."

In a work published in Paris in 1829, speaking of the 10 A. M. order to him of the 18th of June, he says:—[4]

---

[3] Doutes sur l'authenticité des Mémoires Historiques attribués à Napoléon. Par le Cte de Grouchy. Philadelphie; Avril, 1820.

[4] Fragments Historiques: Lettre à MM. Méry et Barthélemy, p. 5, note.

"This letter, and that dated from the field of battle of Waterloo, at one o'clock, are the only ones which I received and which were written to me on the 17th and 18th. The book of the orders and correspondence of the major-general, which I possess, proves this. It gives the hours at which orders are given, and the names of the officers who carry them; and its details do not permit a suspicion of an omission any more than of a misstatement."

It is rather remarkable, to say the least, that General Bertrand should not have stated what he recollected about the matter. But he does not appear to have done so; unless the mention in Jomini's "Political and Military History of the Campaign of Waterloo,"[5] that General Bertrand sent Grouchy a positive order to march on Gembloux, may be attributed to information received from Bertrand.

The Bertrand order first saw the light in 1842,— twenty-seven years after the battle of Waterloo. It was printed in a work entitled "*Notice Biographique sur le Maréchal de Grouchy, &c.*,"[6] by E. Pascallet, editor of a Review treating of Biography, Politics and Letters. The biography is eulogistic. The order is accompanied by no explanation of the repeated denials, to which we have called attention above, of any such order ever having been received by the Marshal.[7]

After this publication, however, the Bertrand order was acknowledged in the memoirs of Marshal Grouchy. It is found in the work of the Marquis de Grouchy, published in 1864, entitled "*Le Maréchal de Grouchy du 16 au 19 juin, 1815*,"[8] written to refute the accusations of Thiers, and in the 4th volume[9] of the "*Mémoires du Maréchal de Grouchy*," by his son, the Marquis. In neither of

---

[5]Jomini, p. 149. Jomini's Preface is dated in 1838.

[6]Pascallet, p. 79.

[7]*Cf.* Napoléon à Waterloo, p. 199, n.

[8]Le Mal de Grouchy en 1815, pp. 26-28.

[9]Grouchy Mém., vol. 4, pp. 50, 51.

these books is there any attempt at explaining away the point blank denials of the Marshal's having received any written order on the 17th of June. It would certainly not be easy to conjecture what explanation could be given. The order reads as follows (Pascallet, p. 79):—

"*Rendez-vous à Gembloux avec le corps de cavalerie de général Pajol, la cavalerie légère du quatrième corps, le corps de cavalerie du général Excelmans, la division du général Teste, dont vous aurez un soin particulier, étant détachée de son corps d'armée, et les troisième et quatrième corps d'infanterie. Vous vous ferez éclairer sur la direction de Namur et de Maestricht, et vous poursuivrez l'ennemi. Eclairez sa marche, et instruisez-moi de ses manoeuvres, de manière que je puisse pénétrer ce qu'il veut faire. Je porte mon quartier-général aux Quatre-Chemins, où ce matin étaient encore les Anglais. Notre communication sera donc directe par la route pavée de Namur. Si l'ennemi a évacué Namur, écrivez au général commandant la deuxième division militaire à Charlemont, de faire occuper Namur par quelques bataillons de garde nationale et quelques batteries de canon qu'il formera à Charlemont. Il donnera ce commandement à un maréchal-de-camp.*

Il est important de pénétrer ce que l'ennemi veut faire: ou il se sépare des Anglais, ou ils veulent se réunir encore, pour couvrir Bruxelles et Liége, en tentant le sort d'une nouvelle bataille. Dans tous les cas, tenez constamment vos deux corps d'infanterie réunis dans une lieue de terrain, et occupez tous les soirs une bonne position militaire, ayant plusieurs débouchés de retraite. Placez détachemens de cavalerie intermédiaires pour communiquer avec le quartier-général.

Ligny, le 17 juin, 1815.

(*Dicté par l'empereur, en l'absence du major-général, au grand-maréchal Bertrand.*)

Passing now to Marshal Grouchy's report to the Emperor, dated Gembloux, June 17, 1815, 10 P.M. This was printed for the first time in the Count Gérard's "*Dernières Observations sur les Opérations de l'Aile Droite de l'Armée Française à la Bataille de Waterloo,*" published in Paris in 1830. It reads as follows:—[10]

---

[10] Gérard: Dern. Obs., p. 15.

" *Sire:*

" *J'ai l'honneur de vous rendre compte que j'occupe Gembloux, et que ma cavalerie est à Sauvenières. L'ennemi, fort d'environ trente mille hommes, continue son mouvement de retraite; on lui a saisi ici un parc de 400 bêtes à cornes, des magasins et des bagages.*

" *Il paraît d'après tous les rapports, qu'arrivés à Sauvenières, les Prussiens se sont divisés en deux colonnes: l'une a dû prendre la route de Wavres, en passant par Sart-à-Wallain; l'autre colonne paraît s'être dirigée sur Perwès.*

" *On peut peut-être en inférer qu'une portion va joindre Wellington, et que le centre, qui est l'armée de Blücher, se retire sur Liége: une autre colonne avec de l'artillerie ayant fait son mouvement de retraite par Namur, le général Excelmans a ordre de pousser ce soir six escadrons sur Sart-à-Wallain, et trois escadrons sur Perwès. D'après leur rapport, si la masse des Prussiens se retire sur Wavres, je la suivrai dans cette direction, afin qu'ils ne puissent pas gagner Bruxelles, et de les séparer de Wellington.*

" *Si, au contraire, mes renseignements prouvent que la principale force prussienne a marché sur Perwès, je me dirigerai par cette ville à la poursuite de l'ennemi.*

" *Les généraux Thielman et Borstell faisaient partie de l'armée que Votre Majesté a battue hier; ils étaient encore ce matin à 10 heures ici, et ont annoncé que vingt mille hommes des leurs avaient été mis hors de combat. Ils ont demandé en partant les distances de Wavres, Perwès et Hannut. Blücher a été blessé légèrement au bras, ce qui ne l'a pas empêché de continuer à commander après s'être fait panser. Il n'a point passé par Gembloux.*

       Je suis avec respect
        de Votre Majesté,
   Sire,   *Le fidèle sujet,*
   (*Signé*) *Le Maréchal Comte de Grouchy.*"

This version of Grouchy's report from Gembloux has been adopted textually by all writers on the campaign,—Charras,[11] Siborne,[12] La Tour d'Auvergne,[13] Chesney,[14] Quinet,[15] the author of "Napoléon à Waterloo,"[16] and others.

---

[11]Charras, vol. 1, p. 244.
[12]Siborne, vol. 1, p. 297.
[13]La Tour d'Auvergne, p. 230.
[14]Chesney, p. 153.
[15]Quinet, p. 430.
[16]Napoléon à Waterloo, p. 219.

The salient thing in this report is its response to the Bertrand order. That directed Grouchy to find out what the Prussians were intending to do, whether to separate from the English, or to unite with them to cover Brussels or Liége in trying the fate of another battle. Grouchy says in this despatch, that, if the mass of the Prussians retires on Wavre he will follow them in that direction *in order that they may not be able to gain Brussels and to separate them from Wellington;* but if on the contrary his information proves that their principal force is marching on Perwès he will march on that city in pursuit of the enemy. But in the Grouchy Memoirs this expression of intention is supplanted by another.[17]

The whole clause reads as follows: —
"*Si j'apprends par des rapports qui, j'espère, me parviendront pendant la nuit, que de fortes masses prussiennes se portent sur Wavre, je les suivrai dans cette direction, ET LES ATTA-- QUERAI DES QUE JE LES AURAI JOINTES.*"[18]

This substitution of an expressed intention to attack the Prussians as soon as he should have caught up with them, if he finds them going to Wavre, is a radical departure from the received text. It is not difficult to see the motive for making this mutilation. Grouchy and his defenders were unwilling to allow that he had, in this despatch, expressed his intention of manœuvring with the object of separating the Prussians from Wellington, for that was exactly what he distinctly refused to do on the next day. And the reason which he alleged for refusing to follow Gérard's advice was, that he had been told by the Emperor to follow the Prussians up closely, and attack them as soon as he should catch up with them. Hence, to admit that the received text of his 10 P. M.

---

[17]Grouchy Mém., p. 58; see, also, p. 263, where the writer says that he has the original under his eyes. See, also, the same thing in the "Mal de Grouchy en 1815," p. 37; and also p. 194, where Thiers is sharply taken to task for following the generally received version.

report on the 17th is correct, is to admit that Grouchy, at the time he wrote it, took a different view of his task from that which he put forward the next day, and ever afterwards maintained; it is, in fact, to admit that he had received, understood, and was intending to act under the Bertrand order, which warned him that the Prussians might be intending to unite with the English; that on that evening of the 17th, at any rate, he fully recognized the real danger to be feared, and regarded, as his great task, not the following on the heels of the Prussians, and attacking their rear guard, but manœuvring so as to prevent them from carrying out their purpose of joining the English.[19]

That the changes in the two Grouchy books are wilful mutilations of the correct text, made for the purpose stated above, appears sufficiently from the fact that the statement of what Grouchy was going to do, if he found the Prussians retiring on Perwès is entirely omitted, apart from the fact that not a single writer adopts the Grouchy version.

Charras puts it mildly in our opinion when he says of Grouchy,[20]—"He has not always been very exact, or very sincere."

---

[18] The capitals are ours.
[19] *Cf.* Clausewitz, ch. 48, p. 131; ch. 50, p. 146.
[20] Charras, vol. 2, p. 53.

APPENDIX C.

I.

ADDRESS TO THE ARMY: June 14, 1815.

Corresp. Vol. 28, p. 324.

22052.— À L'ARMÉE.

Avesnes, 14 juin 1815.

Soldats, c'est aujourd'hui l'anniversaire de Marengo et de Friedland, qui décidèrent deux fois du destin de l'Europe. Alors, comme après Austerlitz, comme après Wagram, nous fûmes trop généreux; nous crûmes aux protestations et aux serments des princes que nous laissâmes sur le trône! Aujourd'hui, cependant, coalisés contre nous, ils en veulent à l'indépendance et aux droits les plus sacrés de la France. Ils ont commencé la plus injuste des agressions. Marchons donc à leur rencontre : eux et nous ne sommes-nous plus les mêmes hommes ?

Soldats, à Iena, contre ces mêmes Prussiens aujourd'hui si arrogants, vous étiez un contre trois ; à Montmirail, un contre six.

Que ceux d'entre vous qui ont été prisonniers des Anglais vous fassent le récit de leurs pontons et des maux affreux qu'ils ont soufferts !

Les Saxons, les Belges, les Hanovriens, les soldats de la Confédération du Rhin, gémissent d'être obligés de prêter leurs bras à la cause des princes ennemis de la justice et des droits de tous les peuples. Ils savent que cette coalition est insatiable. Après avoir dévoré douze millions de Polonais, douze millions d'Italiens, un million de Saxons, six millions de Belges, elle devra dévorer les états de deuxième ordre de l'Allemagne.

Les insensés! Un moment de prospérité les aveugle. L'oppression et l'humiliation du peuple français sont hors de leur pouvoir. S'ils entrent en France, ils y trouveront leur tombeau.

Soldats, nous avons des marches forcées à faire, des batailles à livrer, des périls à courir ; mais, avec de la constance, la victoire sera à nous : les droits, l'honneur et le bonheur de la patrie seront reconquis.

Pour tout Français qui a du cœur, le moment est arrivé de vaincre ou de périr !

NAPOLÉON.

D'après la copie. Dépôt de la guerre.

II.

ORDER OF MOVEMENT: June 14, 1815.

Corresp. vol. 28, p. 325.

22053—ORDRE DE MOUVEMENT.

BEAUMONT, 14 juin 1815.

Demain 15, à deux heures et demie du matin, la division de cavalerie légère du général Vandamme montera à cheval et se portera sur la route de Charleroi. Elle enverra des partis dans toutes les directions pour éclairer le pays et enlever les postes ennemis; mais chacun de ces partis sera au moins de 50 hommes. Avant de mettre en marche la division, le général Vandamme s'assurera qu'elle est pourvue de cartouches.

A la même heure, le lieutenant général Pajol réunira le 1er corps de cavalerie et suivra le mouvement de la division du général Domon, qui sera sous les ordres du général Pajol. Les divisions du 1er corps de cavalerie ne fourniront point de détachements; ils seront pris dans la 3e division. Le général Domon laissera sa batterie d'artillerie pour marcher après le 1er bataillon du 3e corps d'infanterie; le lieutenant général Vandamme lui donnera des ordres en conséquence.

Le lieutenant général Vandamme fera battre la diane à deux heures et demie du matin; à trois heures, il mettra en marche son corps d'armée et le dirigera sur Charleroi. La totalité de ses bagages et embarras seront parqués en arrière, et ne se mettront en marche qu'après que le 6e corps et la Garde impériale auront passé. Ils seront sous les ordres du vaguemestre général, qui les réunira à ceux du 6e corps, de la Garde impériale et du grand quartier général, et leur donnera des ordres de mouvement.

Chaque division du 3e corps d'armée aura avec elle sa batterie et ces ambulances; toute autre voiture qui serait dans les rangs sera brûlée.

M. le comte de Lobau fera battre la diane à trois heures et demie, et il mettra en marche le 6e corps d'armée à quatre heures pour suivre le mouvement du général Vandamme et l'appuyer. Il fera observer, pour les troupes, l'artillerie, les ambulances et les bagages, le même ordre de marche qui est prescrit au 3e corps.

Les bagages du 6e corps seront réunis à ceux du 3e, sous les ordres du vaguemestre général, ainsi qu'il est dit.

La jeune Garde battra la diane à quatre heures et demie, et se mettra en marche à cinq heures; elle suivra le mouvement du 6e corps sur la route de Charleroi.

Les chasseurs à pied de la Garde battront la diane à quatre heures, et se mettront en marche à cinq heures et demie pour suivre le mouvement de la jeune Garde.

Les grenadiers à pied de la Garde battront la diane à cinq heures et demie, et partiront à six heures pour suivre le mouvement des chasseurs à pied.

Le même ordre de marche pour l'artillerie, les ambulances et les bagages, prescrit pour le 3e corps d'infanterie, sera observé dans la Garde impériale.

Les bagages de la Garde seront réunis à ceux des 3e et 6e corps d'armée, sous les ordres du vaguemestre général, qui les fera mettre en mouvement.

M. le maréchal Grouchy fera monter à cheval, à cinq heures et demie du matin, celui des trois autres corps de cavalerie qui sera le plus près de la route, et il lui fera suivre le mouvement sur Charleroi; les deux autres corps partiront successivement à une heure d'intervalle l'un de l'autre. Mais M. le maréchal Grouchy aura soin de faire marcher la cavalerie sur les chemins latéraux de la route principale que la colonne d'infanterie suivra, afin d'éviter l'encombrement et aussi pour que sa cavalerie observe un meilleur ordre.

Il prescrira que la totalité des bagages restent en arrière, parqués et réunis, jusqu' au moment où le vaguemestre général leur donnera l'ordre d'avancer.

M. le comte Reille fera battre la diane à deux heures et demie du matin, et il mettra en marche le 2e corps à trois heures; il le dirigera sur Marchienne-au-Pont, où il fera en sorte d'être rendu avant neuf heures du matin. Il fera garder tous les ponts de la Sambre, afin que personne ne passe; les postes qu'il laissera seront successivement relevés par le 1er corps; mais il doit tâcher de prévenir l'ennemi à ces ponts pour qu'ils ne soient pas détruits, surtout celui de Marchienne, par lequel il sera probablement dans le cas de déboucher, et qu'il faudrait faire aussitôt réparer s'il avait été endommagé.

A Thuin et à Marchienne, ainsi que dans tous les villages sur sa route, M. le comte Reille interrogera les habitants, afin d'avoir des nouvelles des positions et forces des armées ennemies. Il fera aussi prendre les lettres dans les bureaux de poste et les dépouillera pour faire aussitôt parvenir à l'Empereur les renseignements qu'il aura obtenus.

M. le comte d'Erlon mettra en marche le 1er corps à trois heures du matin, et le dirigera aussi sur Charleroi, en suivant le mouvement du 2e corps, duquel il gagnera la gauche le plus tôt possible, pour le soutenir et l'appuyer au besoin. Il tiendra une brigade de cavalerie en arrière, pour se couvrir et pour maintenir par de petits détachements ses communications avec Maubeuge. Il enverra des partis en avant de cette place, dans les directions de Mons et de Binche, jusqu' à la frontière, pour avoir des nouvelles des ennemis et en rendre compte aussitôt; ces partis auront soin de ne pas se compromettre et de ne pas dépasser la frontière.

M. le comte d'Erlon fera occuper Thuin par une division; et, si le pont de cette ville était détruit, il le ferait aussitôt réparer, en même temps qu'il fera tracer et exécuter immédiatement une tête de pont sur la rive gauche. La division qui sera à Thuin gardera aussi le pont de l'abbaye d'Aulne, où M. le comte d'Erlon fera également construire une tête de pont sur la rive gauche.

Le même ordre de marche prescrit au 3e corps pour l'artillerie, les ambulances et les bagages, sera observé aux 2e et 1er corps, qui feront réunir et marcher leurs bagages à la gauche du 1er corps sous les ordres du vaguemestre le plus ancien.

Le 4e corps (armée de la Moselle) a reçu ordre de prendre aujourd'hui position en avant de Philippeville. Si son mouvement est opéré et si les divisions qui composent ce corps d'armée sont réunies, M. le lieutenant général Gérard les mettra en marche demain à trois heures du matin, et les dirigera sur Charleroi. Il aura soin de se tenir à hauteur du 3e corps, avec lequel il communiquera, afin d'arriver à peu près en même temps devant Charleroi; mais le général Gérard fera éclairer sa droite et tous les débouchés qui vont sur Namur. Il marchera serré en ordre de bataille, et fera laisser à Philippeville tous ses bagages et embarras, afin que son corps d'armée, se trouvant plus léger, se trouve à même de manœuvrer.

Le général Gérard donnera ordre à la 14e division de cavalerie, qui a dû aussi arriver aujourd'hui à Philippeville, de suivre le mouvement de son corps d' armée sur Charleroi, où cette division joindra le 4e corps de cavalerie.

Les lieutenants généraux Reille, Vandamme, Gérard et Pajol se mettront en communication par de fréquents partis, et ils régleront leur marche de manière à arriver en masse et ensemble devant Charleroi. Ils mettront, autant que possible, à l'avant-garde des officiers qui parlent flamand, pour interroger les habitants et en prendre des renseignements; mais ces officiers s'annonceront comme commandant des partis, sans dire que l'armée est en arrière.

Les lieutenants généraux Reille, Vandamme et Gérard feront marcher tous les sapeurs de leurs corps d'armée (ayant avec eux des moyens pour réparer les ponts) après le premier régiment d'infanterie légère, et ils donneront ordre aux officiers du génie de faire réparer les mauvais passages, ouvrir des communications latérales et placer des ponts sur les courants d'eau où l'infanterie devrait se mouiller pour les franchir.

Les marins, les sapeurs de la Garde et les sapeurs de la réserve marcheront après le premier régiment du 3e corps. Les lieutenants généraux Rogniat et Haxo seront à leur tête; ils n'emmèneront avec eux que deux ou trois voitures; le surplus du parc du génie marchera à la gauche du 3e corps. Si on rencontre l'ennemi, ces troupes ne seront point engagées, mais les généraux Rogniat et Haxo les emploieront aux travaux de passages de rivière, de têtes de pont, de réparation de chemins et d'ouverture de communications etc.

La cavalerie de la Garde suivra le mouvement sur Charleroi et partira à huit heures.

L'Empereur sera à l'avant-garde, sur la route de Charleroi. MM. les lieutenants généraux auront soin d'envoyer à Sa Majesté de fréquents rapports sur leurs mouvements et les renseignements qu'ils auront recueillis. Ils sont prévenus que l'intention de Sa Majesté est d'avoir passé la Sambre avant midi, et de porter l'armée à la rive gauche de cette rivière.

L'équipage de ponts sera divisé en deux sections; la première section se subdivisera en trois parties, chacune de 5 pontons et 5 bateaux d'avant-garde, pour jeter trois ponts sur la Sambre. Il y aura à chacune de ces subdivisions une compagnie de pontonniers.

La première section marchera à la suite du parc du génie après le 3e corps.

La deuxième section restera avec le parc de réserve d'artillerie à la colonne des bagages; elle aura avec elle la 4e compagnie de pontonniers.

Les équipages de l'Empereur et les bagages du grand quartier général seront réunis et se mettront en marche à dix heures. Aussitôt qu'il seront passés, le vaguemestre général fera partir les équipages de la Garde impériale, du 3e corps et du 6e corps; en même temps, il enverra ordre à la colonne d'équipages de la réserve de cavalerie de se mettre en marche et de suivre la direction que la cavalerie aura prise.

Les ambulances de l'armée suivront le quartier général et marcheront en tête des bagages; mais, dans aucun cas, ces bagages, ainsi que les parcs de réserve de l'artillerie et la seconde section de l'équipage de ponts, ne s'approcheront à plus de trois lieues de l'armée, à moins d'ordres du major général, et ils ne passeront la Sambre aussi que par ordre.

Le vaguemestre général formera des divisions de ces bagages, et il y mettra des officiers pour les commander, afin de pouvoir en détacher ce qui sera ensuite appelé au quartier général ou pour le service des officiers.

L'intendant général fera réunir à cette colonne d'équipages la totalité des bagages et transports de l'administration, auxquels il sera assigné un rang dans la colonne.

Les voitures qui seront en retard prendront la gauche, et ne pourront sortir du rang qui leur sera donné que par ordre du vaguemestre général.

L'Empereur ordonne que toutes les voitures d'équipages qui seront trouvées dans les colonnes d'infanterie, de cavalerie ou d'artillerie, soient brûlées, ainsi que les voitures de la colonne des équipages qui quitteront leur rang et intervertiront l'ordre de marche sans la permission expresse du vaguemestre général.

A cet effet, il sera mis un détachement de 50 gendarmes à la disposition du vaguemestre général, qui est responsable, ainsi que tous les officiers de la gendarmerie et les gendarmes, de l'exécution de ces dispositions, desquelles le succès de la campagne peut dépendre.

Par ordre le l'Empereur:

Le maréchal de l'Empire, major général,

Duc de Dalmatie.

D'après l'original. Dépôt de la guerre.

III.

Doc. Inéd., p. 22.

15 Juin.

A M. LE COMTE REILLE.

Commandant le 2e Corps d'Armée.

Monsieur le comte Reille, l'empereur m'ordonne de vous écrire de passer la Sambre, si vous n'avez pas de forces devant vous, et de vous former sur plusieurs lignes, à une ou deux lieues en avant, de manière à être à cheval sur la grande route de Bruxelles, en vous éclairant fortement dans la direction de Fleurus. M. le comte d'Erlon passera à Marchiennes et se formera en bataille sur la route de Mons à Charleroi, où il sera à portée de vous soutenir au besoin.

Si vous êtes encore à Marchiennes lorsque le présent ordre vous parviendra, et que le mouvement par Charleroi ne pût avoir lieu, vous l'opéreriez toujours par Marchiennes, mais toujours pour remplir les dispositions ci-dessus.

L'empereur se rend devant Charleroi. Rendez compte immédiatement à Sa Majesté de vos opérations et de ce qui se passe devant vous.

Le maréchal d'empire, major général,

Duc de Dalmatie.

Au bivouac de Jumignon, le
  15 juin, 1815, à 8 heures et
  demie du matin.

Doc. Inéd., p. 24.

IV.

A M. LE COMTE D'ERLON.

Bivouac de Jumignon, 15 juin,
  10 heures du matin.

Monsieur le Comte, l'empereur m'ordonne de vous écrire que M. le comte Reille reçoit ordre de passer la Sambre à Charleroi, et de se former sur plusieurs lignes à une ou deux lieues en avant, à cheval sur la grande route de Bruxelles.

L'intention de Sa Majesté est aussi que vous passiez la Sambre à Marchiennes, ou à Ham, pour vous porter sur la grande route de Mons à Charleroi, où vous vous formerez sur plusieurs lignes, et prendrez des positions qui vous rapprocheront de M. le comte Reille, liant vos communications et envoyant des partis des toutes les directions : Mons, Nivelles, etc. Ce mouvement aurait également lieu si M. le comte Reille était obligé d'effectuer son passage par Marchiennes. Rendez-moi compte de suite de vos opérations et de ce qui se passe devant vous ; l'empereur sera devant Charleroi.

V.

ORDER TO THE COUNT D'ERLON: 3 P.M., June 15, 1815.

Doc. Inéd., p. 25.

A M. LE COMTE D'ERLON.

(EXTRAIT DU REGISTRE DU MAJOR GÉNÉRAL.)

En avant de Charleroi, à 3 heures du soir,
  15 juin 1815.

Monsieur le comte d'Erlon, l'empereur ordonne à M. le comte Reille de marcher sur Gosselies, et d'y attaquer un corps ennemi qui paraissait s'y arrêter. L'intention de l'empereur est que vous marchiez aussi sur Gosselies, pour appuyer le comte Reille et le seconder dans ses opérations. Cependant, vous devrez toujours faire garder Marchiennes, et vous enverrez une brigade sur les routes de Mons, lui recommandant de se garder très militairement.

VI.

SUBSEQUENT ORDER TO THE COUNT D'ERLON:
June 15, 1815.

Doc. Inéd., p. 25.

A M. LE COMTE D'ERLON,

COMMANDANT LE 1ER CORPS.

Charleroi, le 15 juin 1815.

Monsieur le Comte, l'intention de l'empereur est que vous ralliez votre corps sur la rive gauche de la Sambre, pour joindre le 2e corps à Gosselies, d'après les ordres que vous donnera à ce sujet M. le maréchal prince de la Moskowa.

Ainsi, vous rappellerez les troupes que vous avez laissées à Thuin, Sobre et environs; vous devrez cependant avoir toujours de nombreux partis sur votre gauche pour éclairer la route de Mons.

Le maréchal d'empire, major général,
Duc de Dalmatie.

VII.

ORDER TO GENERAL NOGUÈS: 3 A. M., June 16, 1815.

"Napoléon à Waterloo," p. 144.

Ordre de mouvement adressé par l'adjudant commandant, chef d'état-major de la 3e division du 1er corps, au général Noguès, commandant la 1er brigade de cette division.

Quartier général à Marchienne-au-Pont:
16 juin (trois heures du matin).

D'après l'intention du général en chef, le lieutenant général me charge de vous inviter à faire partir de suite votre brigade pour être rendue à six heures du matin, et plus tôt s'il était possible, à Gosselies.

L'adjudant commandant,
chef d'état-major:
Ch. d'Arsonval.

P. S.

La 2e brigade reste ici jusqu'à l'arrivée de la première division, pour se rendre ensemble à la même destination.

This indicates that at 3 A. M. of the 16th, while the 4th division (Durutte's) was in bivouac beyond Jumet (Doc. Inéd., Durutte's statement, p. 71, where he gives Gosselies, where the Second Corps was, by mistake for Jumet), the 2d Division (Donzelot's) must also have crossed the river, the 3d division (Marcognet's) was at Marchienne, and the 1st (Allix') had not yet reached the Sambre.

VIII.

BULLETIN OF THE ARMY: June 15, 1815: Evening.

Corresp. vol. 28, p. 331.

22056.—BULLETIN DE L'ARMÉE.

CHARLEROI, 15 juin 1815, au soir.

Le 14, l'armée était placée de la manière suivante :
Le quartier impérial à Beaumont.
Le 1er corps, commandé par le général d'Erlon, était à Solre, sur la Sambre.
Le 2e corps, commandé par le général Reille, était à Ham-sur-Heure.
Le 3e corps, commandé par le général Vandamme, était sur la droite de Beaumont.
Le 4e corps, commandé par le général Gérard, arrivait à Philippeville.
Le 15, à trois heures du matin, le général Reille attaqua l'ennemi et se porta sur Marchienne-au-Pont. Il eut différents engagements dans lesquels sa cavalerie chargea un bataillon prussien et fit 300 prisonniers.
A une heure du matin, l'Empereur était à Jamioulx-sur-Heure.
La division de cavalerie légère du général Domon sabra deux bataillons prussiens et fit 400 prisonniers.
Le général Pajol entra à Charleroi à midi. Les sapeurs et les marins de la Garde étaient à l'avant-garde pour réparer les ponts; ils pénétrèrent les premiers en tirailleurs dans la ville. Le général Clary, avec le 1er de hussards, se porta sur Gosselies, sur la route de Bruxelles, et le général Pajol sur Gilly, sur la route de Namur.
A trois heures après midi, le général Vandamme déboucha avec son corps sur Gilly.
Le maréchal Grouchy arriva avec la cavalerie du général Exelmans.
L'ennemi occupait la gauche de la position de Fleurus. A cinq heures après midi, l'Empereur ordonna l'attaque. La position fut tournée et enlevée. Les quatre escadrons de service de la Garde, commandés par le général Letort, aide-de-camp de l'Empereur, enfoncèrent trois carrés; les 26e, 27e et 28e régiments prussiens furent mis en déroute. Nos escadrons sabrèrent 400 ou 500 hommes et firent 1,500 prisonniers.
Pendant ce temps, le général Reille passait la Sambre à Marchienne-au-Pont, pour se porter sur Gosselies avec les divisions du prince Jérôme et du général Bachelu, attaquait l'ennemi, lui faisait 250 prisonniers et le poursuivait sur la route de Bruxelles.
Nous devînmes ainsi maîtres de toute la position de Fleurus.
A huit heures du soir, l'Empereur rentra à son quartier général à Charleroi.
Cette journée coûte à l'ennemi cinq pièces de canon et 2,000 hommes, dont 1,000 prisonniers. Notre perte est de 10 hommes tués et de 80 blessés, la plupart des escadrons de service, qui ont fait les charges, et des trois escadrons de 20e de dragons,[1] qui ont aussi chargé un carré avec la plus grande intrépidité. Notre perte, légère quant au nombre, a été sensible à l'Empereur, par la blessure grave qu'a reçue le général Letort, son aide-de-

camp, en chargeant à la tête des escadrons de service. Cet officier est de la plus grande distinction. Il a été frappé d'une balle au bas-ventre, et le chirurgien fait craindre que sa blessure ne soit mortelle.

Nous avons trouvé à Charleroi quelques magasins. La joie des Belges ne saurait se décrire. Il y a des villages qui, à la vue de leurs libérateurs, ont formé des danses, et partout c'est un élan qui part du cœur.

Dans le rapport de l'état-major général, on insérera les noms des officiers et soldats qui se sont distingués.

L'Empereur a donné le commandement de la gauche au prince de la Moskova, qui a eu le soir son quartier général aux Quatre-Chemins, sur la route de Bruxelles.

Le duc de Trévise, à qui l'Empereur avait donné le commandement de la jeune Garde, est resté à Beaumont, malade d'une sciatique qui l'a forcé de se mettre au lit.

Le 4e corps, commandé par le général Gérard, arrive ce soir à Châtelet. Le général Gérard a rendu compte que le lieutenant général Bourmont, le colonel Clouet et le chef d'escadron Villoutreys ont passé à l'ennemi. Un lieutenant du 11e de chasseurs a également passé à l'ennemi. Le major général a ordonné que ces déserteurs fussent sur-le-champ jugés conformément aux lois.

Rien ne peut peindre le bon esprit el l'ardeur de l'armée. Elle regarde comme un événement heureux la désertion de ce petit nombre de traîtres, qui se démasquent ainsi.

Extrait du Moniteur du 18 juin 1815.

IX.
WELLINGTON'S FIRST MEMORANDUM OF ORDERS: June 15, 1815.

Gurwood, vol. xii, p. 472.

MEMORANDUM

For the Deputy Quarter Master General.
Movements of the Army.

Bruxelles, 15 June, 1815.

General Dornberg's brigade of cavalry, and the Cumberland Hussars, to march this night upon Vilvorde, and to bivouac on the high road near to that town.

The Earl of Uxbridge will be pleased to collect the cavalry this night at Ninhove, leaving the 2d hussars looking out between the Scheldt and the Lys.

The 1st division of infantry to collect this night at Ath and adjacent, and to be in readiness to move at a moment's notice.

The third division to collect this night at Braine le Comte, and to be in readiness to move at the shortest notice.

The 4th division to be collected this night at Grammont, with the exception of the troops beyond the Scheldt, which are to be moved to Audenarde

The 5th division, the 81st regiment, and the Hanoverian brigade of the 6th division, to be in readiness to march from Bruxelles at a moment's notice.

The Duke of Brunswick's corps to collect this night on the high road between Bruxelles and Vilvorde.

The Nassau troops to collect at daylight to-morrow morning on the Louvain road, and to be in readiness to move at a moment's notice.

The Hanoverian brigade of the 5th division to collect this night at Hal, and to be in readiness at daylight to-morrow morning to move towards Bruxelles, and to halt on the high road between Alost and Assche for further orders.

The Prince of Orange is requested to collect at Nivelles the 2d and 3d divisions of the army of the Low Countries; and, should that point have been attacked this day, to move the 3d division of British infantry upon Nivelles as soon as collected.

This movement is not to take place until it is quite certain that the enemy's attack is upon the right of the Prussian army, and the left of the British army.

Lord Hill will be so good as to order Prince Frederick of Orange to occupy Audenarde with 500 men, and to collect the 1st division of the army of the Low Countries and the Indian brigade at Sotteghem, so as to be ready to march in the morning at daylight.

The reserve artillery to be in readiness to move at daylight.

WELLINGTON.

X.

WELLINGTON'S LETTER TO THE DUC DE FELTRE: 10 P.M., June 15, 1815.

Gurwood, vol. xii, p. 473.

TO THE DUC DE FELTRE.

à BRUXELLES, ce 15 juin, 1815.

à 10 heures du soir.

MONSIEUR LE DUC:

Je reçois les nouvelles que l'ennemi attaqua les postes Prussiens ce matin à Thuin sur la Sambre, et il paraissait menacer Charleroi. Je n'ai rien reçu depuis neuf heures du matin de Charleroi. * * * *

WELLINGTON.

XI.

WELLINGTON'S "AFTER ORDERS": 10 P.M., June 15, 1815.

Gurwood, vol. xii, p. 474.

MOVEMENT OF THE ARMY.

AFTER ORDERS, 10 O'CLOCK P.M.

BRUXELLES, 15th June, 1815.

The 3d division of infantry to continue its movement from Braine le Comte upon Nivelles.

The 1st division to move from Enghien upon Braine le Comte.

The 2d and 4th divisions of infantry to move from Ath and Grammont, also from Audenarde, and to continue their movements upon Enghien.

The cavalry to continue its movement from Ninhove upon Enghien.

The above movements to take place with as little delay as possible.

WELLINGTON.

XII.

EXTRACT FROM WELLINGTON'S REPORT OF THE OPERATIONS; June 19, 1815.

Gurwood, vol. xii, p. 478.

TO EARL BATHURST.

WATERLOO, 19th June, 1815.

MY LORD,

Buonaparte, having collected the 1st, 2d, 3d, 4th, and 6th corps of the French army, and the Imperial Guards and nearly all the cavalry, on the Sambre, and between that river and the Meuse, between the 10th and 14th of the month, advanced on the 15th and attacked the Prussian posts at Thuin and Lobbes, on the Sambre, at daylight in the morning.

I did not hear of these events till in the evening of the 15th; and immediately ordered the troops to prepare to march, and afterwards to march to their left, as soon as I had intelligence from other quarters to prove that the enemy's movement upon Charleroi was the real attack.

The enemy drove the Prussian posts from the Sambre on that day; and General Ziethen, who commanded the corps which had been at Charleroi retired upon Fleurus; and Marshal Prince Blücher concentrated the Prussian army upon Sombref, holding the villages in front of his position of St Amand and Ligny.

The enemy continued his march along the road from Charleroi toward Bruxelles; and, on the same evening, the 15th, attacked a brigade of the army of the Netherlands, under the Prince de Weimar, posted at Frasne, and forced it back to the farmhouse, on the same road, called Les Quatre Bras

The Prince of Orange immediately reinforced this brigade with another of the same division, under General Perponcher, and, in the morning early regained part of the ground which had been lost, so as to have the command of the communication leading from Nivelles and Bruxelles with Marshal Blücher's position.

In the meantime, I had directed the whole army to march upon Les Quatre Bras; and the 5th division, under Lieut.-General Sir Thomas Picton arrived at about half-past two in the day, followed by the corps of troop under the Duke of Brunswick, and afterwards by the contingent of Nassau

At this time the enemy commenced an attack upon Prince Blücher with his whole force, excepting the 1st and 2d corps, and a corps of cavalry under General Kellermann, with which he attacked our post at Les Quatre Bras.

* * *

I should not do justice to my own feelings, or to Marshal Blücher and the

Prussian army, if I did not attribute the successful result of this arduous day to the cordial and timely assistance I received from them. The operation of General Bülow upon the enemy's flank was a most decisive one; and, even if I had not found myself in a situation to make the attack which produced the final result, it would have forced the enemy to retire if his attacks should have failed, and would have prevented him from taking advantage of them if they should unfortunately have succeeded.

* * *

I have the honor to be, &c.
WELLINGTON.

EARL BATHURST.

XIII.

WELLINGTON'S CONVERSATION WITH THE DUKE OF RICHMOND: June 16, 1815.

Letters of the First Earl of Malmesbury, London; Bentley. 1870. vol. 2, p. 445.

CAPTAIN BOWLES * TO LORD FITZHARRIS.

ORIGINAL MEMORANDUM BY THE WRITER.

At the Duchess of Richmond's ball at Brussels the Prince of Orange, who commanded the 1st division of the army, came back suddenly, just as the Duke of Wellington had taken his place at the supper table, and whispered some minutes to his Grace, who only said he had no fresh orders to give, and recommended the Prince to go back to his quarters and go to bed.

The Duke of Wellington remained nearly twenty minutes after this, and then said to the Duke of Richmond, "I think it is time for me to go to bed likewise;" and then, whilst wishing him good-night, whispered to ask him if he had a good map in his house. The Duke of Richmond said he had, and took him into his dressing-room, which opened into the supper-room. The Duke of Wellington shut the door and said, "Napoleon has *humbugged* me (by G——), he has gained twenty-four hours' march on me." The Duke of Richmond said, "What do you intend doing?"

The Duke of Wellington replied, "'I have ordered the army to concentrate at Quatre Bras; but we shall not stop him there, and if so I must fight him *here*" (at the same time passing his thumb-nail over the position of Waterloo). He then said adieu and left the house by another way out. He went to his quarters, slept six hours and breakfasted, and rode at speed to Quatre Bras, where he met Hardinge and went with him to Blücher, who took him over the position at Ligny. The Duke of Wellington suggested many alterations, but Blücher would not consent to move a man.

The conversation in the Duke of Richmond's dressing-room was repeated to me, two minutes after it occurred, by the Duke of Richmond, who was to

---

*Captain George Bowles (Guards).

have had the command of the reserve, if formed, and to whom I was to have been aide-de-camp. He marked the Duke of Wellington's thumb-nail with his pencil on the map, and we often looked at it together some months afterwards.

XIV.
WELLINGTON'S ORDERS TO LORD HILL: June 16, 1815.
Gurwood, vol. xii, p. 474.

INSTRUCTIONS
For the Movement of the Army on the 16th.*

Signed by Colonel Sir W. DeLancey, Deputy Quarter Master General.

To General Lord Hill, G. C. B.

16th June, 1815.

The Duke of Wellington requests that you will move the 2d division of infantry upon Braine le Comte immediately. The cavalry has been ordered likewise on Braine le Comte. His Grace is going to Waterloo.

To General Lord Hill, G. C. B.

16th June, 1815.

Your Lordship is requested to order Prince Frederick of Orange to move, immediately upon the receipt of this order, the 1st division of the army of the Low Countries, and the Indian brigade, from Sotteghem to Enghien, leaving 500 men, as before directed, in Audenarde.

* The original instructions issued to Colonel DeLancey were lost with that officer's papers. These memorandums of movements have been collected from the different officers to whom they were addressed.

XV.
EXTRACT FROM WELLINGTON'S "MEMORANDUM ON THE BATTLE OF WATERLOO."
SUPPLEMENTARY DESPATCHES, &c., of the Duke of Wellington: vol. x, pp. 523 *et seq.*

But what follows will show that, notwithstanding the extension of the Allied army under the command of the Duke of Wellington, such was the celerity of communication with all parts of it, that in point of fact [1] *his orders reached all parts of the army in six hours after he had issued them;* and that he was in line in person with a sufficient force to resist and keep in check the enemy's corps which first attacked the Prussian corps under General Zieten at daylight on the 15th of June; having received the intelligence of that attack *only at three o'clock in the afternoon of the 15th, he was at Quatre Bras before the same hour on the morning of the 16th,*[2] *with a sufficient force to engage the left of the French army.*

---

[1] The italics are ours.

[2] The text cited is from the Supplementary Despatches; but it seems to us quite possible that the reading of this passage given in the Appendix to C. D. Yonge's "Life of Wellington,"—London; Chapman & Hall, 1860,—is the correct one. It there reads as follows:—

"He was at Quatre Bras before twenty-four hours on the 16th,"—that is by 3 P. M., on the 16th,—which was the fact. There are other points where these versions differ, but this is the most important one. See *ante*, p. 90.

It was certainly true that he had known for some days of the augmentation of the enemy's force on the frontier, and even of the arrival of Buonaparte at the army; but he did not deem it expedient to make any movement, excepting for the assembly of the troops at their several alarm posts, till he should hear of the decided movement of the enemy.

The first account received by the Duke of Wellington was from the Prince of Orange, who had come in from the out-posts of the army of the Netherlands to dine with the Duke at three o'clock in the afternoon. He reported that the enemy had attacked the Prussians at Thuin; that they had taken possession of, but had afterwards abandoned, Binch; that they had not yet touched the positions of the army of the Netherlands. While the Prince was with the Duke, the staff officer employed by Prince Blücher at the Duke's headquarters, General Müffling, came to the Duke to inform him that he had just received intelligence of the movement of the French army and their attack upon the Prussian troops at Thuin.

It appears by the statement of the historian[3] that the posts of the Prussian corps of General Zieten were attacked at Thuin at four o'clock on the morning of the 15th; and that General Zieten himself, with a part of his corps, retreated and was at Charleroi at about ten o'clock on that day; yet the report thereof was not received at Bruxelles till three o'clock in the afternoon. The Prussian cavalry of the corps of Zieten was at Gosselies and Fleurus on the evening and night of the 15th.

Orders were forthwith sent for the march of the whole army to its left.

The whole moved on that evening and in the night, each division and portion separately, but unmolested; the whole protected on the march by the defensive works constructed at the different points referred to, and by their garrisons.

The reserve, which had been encamped in the neighborhood and cantoned in the town and in the neighborhood of Bruxelles, were ordered to assemble in and in the neighborhood of the park at Bruxelles, which they did on that evening; and they marched in the morning of the 16th upon Quatre Bras, towards which post the march of all the troops consisting of the left and centre of the army, and of the cavalry in particular, was directed.

The Duke went in person at daylight in the morning of the 16th to Quatre Bras, where he found some Netherland troops, cavalry, infantry, and artillery, which had been engaged with the enemy, but lightly; and he went on from thence to the Prussian army,[4] which was in sight, formed on the heights behind Ligny and St. Amand. He there communicated personally with Marshal Prince Blücher and the headquarters of the Prussian army.

In the meantime the reserve of the Allied army under the command of the Duke of Wellington arrived at Quatre Bras. *The historian asserts that the Duke of Wellington had ordered these troops to halt at the point at which they quitted the Forêt de Soignies. He can have no proof of this fact,*[5] *of*

---

[3] Clausewitz.

[4] About 1 o'clock, at the Windmill of Bussy, between Ligny and Brie: so Hardinge told me. — J. G.

[5] *Cf.* Siborne, vol. 1, p. 102, n.; Gomm, p. 352; Waterloo Letters; Gomm; p. 23.

which there is no evidence; ⁶ and in point of fact the two armies *were united about mid-day* of the 16th of June, on the left of the position of the Allied army under the command of the Duke of Wellington. These troops, forming the reserve, and having arrived from Bruxelles, were *now* joined by those of the *1st division of infantry,*⁷ *and the cavalry;* and notwithstanding the criticism of the Prussian historian on the positions occupied by the army under the command of the Duke of Wellington, and on the march of the troops to join with the Prussian army, *it is a fact,* appearing upon the face of the History, *that the Allied British and Netherland army was in line at Quatre Bras, not only twenty-four hours sooner than one whole corps of the Prussian army under General Bülow, the absence of which is attributed by the historian to an accidental mistake, but likewise before the whole of the corps under General Zieten, which had been the first attacked on the 15th, had taken its position in the line of the army assembled on the heights behind Ligny, and having their left at Sombref.*

It was perfectly true that the Duke of Wellington did not at first give credit to the reports of the intention of the enemy to attack by the valleys of the Sambre and the Meuse.

The enemy had destroyed the roads leading through those valleys, and he considered that Buonaparte might have made his attack upon the Allied armies in the Netherlands and in the provinces on the left of the Rhine by other lines with more advantage. But it is obvious that, when the attack was made, he was not unprepared to assist in resisting it: and, in point of fact, did, on the afternoon and in the evening of the 16th June, repulse the attack of Marshal Ney upon his position at Quatre Bras, which had been commenced by the aid of another corps d'armée under General Reille. These were the troops which had attacked on the 15th, at daylight, the Prussian corps under General Zieten, which corps the Allied troops, under the Duke of Wellington, relieved in resistance to the enemy.

XVI.

WELLINGTON'S LETTER TO BLUCHER: 10.30 A. M., June 16, 1815.

Ollech, opposite p. 124.

Sur les hauteurs derrière
Frasne le 16me Juin 1815
à 10 heures et demi.

Mon cher Prince :

Mon armée est situé comme il suit :

Le Corps d'Armée du Prince d'Orange a une division ici et à Quatre Bras ; et le reste à Nivelles.

La Reserve est en marche de Waterloo sur Genappe ; ou elle arrivera à Midi.

---

⁶ The italics are ours.

⁷ The 1st division did not arrive on the field until after 6 P M. (*ante*, pp. 183, 184), and the cavalry, not at all.

La Cavalerie Anglaise sera à la même heure à Nivelles.
Le Corps de Lord Hill est à Braine le Comte.

Je ne vois pas beaucoup de l'ennemi en avant de nous; et j'attends les nouvelles de votre Altesse, et l'arrivée des troupes pour décider mes opérations pour la journée.

Rien n'a paru du côté de Binch, ni sur notre droite.

Votre très obéissant serviteur
Wellington.

XVII.

SOULT'S FIRST ORDER TO NEY: June 16, 1815.

Doc. Inéd., p. 26.

A M. LE MARÉCHAL
PRINCE DE LA MOSKOWA.

Charleroi, le 16 juin 1815.

Monsieur le maréchal, l'empereur vient d'ordonner à M. le comte de Valmy, commandant le 3e corps de cavalerie, de le réunir et de le diriger sur Gosselies, où il sera à votre disposition.

L'intention de Sa Majesté est qui la cavalerie de la garde, qui a été portée sur la route de Bruxelles, reste en arrière et rejoigne le restant de la garde impériale; mais, pour qu'elle ne fasse pas de mouvement rétrograde, vous pourrez, après l'avoir fait remplacer sur la ligne, la laisser un peu en arrière, où il lui sera envoyé des ordres dans le mouvement de la journée. M. le lieutenant général Lefebvre Desnoëttes enverra, à cet effet, un officier pour prendre des ordres.

Veuillez m'instruire si le 1er corps a opéré son mouvement, et quelle est, ce matin, la position exacte des 1er et 2e corps d'armée, et des deux divisions de cavalerie qui y sont attachées, en me faisant connaître ce qu'il y a d'ennemis devant vous, et ce qu'on a appris.

Le major général,
Duc de Dalmatie.

XVIII.

THE EMPEROR'S LETTER TO NEY: June 16, 1815.

Doc. Inéd., p. 32.: Corresp. vol. 28, p. 334.

AU MARÉCHAL NEY.

Mon cousin, je vous envoie mon aide de camp, le général Flahaut, qui vous porte la présente lettre. Le major général a dû vous donner des ordres; mais vous recevrez les miens plus tôt, parce que mes officiers vont plus vite que les siens. Vous recevrez l'ordre de mouvement du jour, mais je veux vous en écrire en détail parce que c'est de la plus haute importance. Je porte le maréchal Grouchy avec les 3e et 4e corps d'infanterie sur Sombref.

Je porte ma garde à Fleurus et j'y serai de ma personne avant midi. J'y attaquerai l'ennemi si je le recontre, et j'éclairerai la route jusqu' à Gembloux. Là, d'après ce qui se passera, je prendrai mon parti, peut-être à trois heures après midi, peut-être ce soir. Mon intention est que, immédiatement après que j'aurai pris mon parti, vous soyez prêt à marcher sur Bruxelles. Je vous appuierai avec la Garde, qui sera à Fleurus ou à Sombref, et je désirerais arriver à Bruxelles demain matin. Vous vous mettriez en marche ce soir même, si je prends mon parti d'assez bonne heure pour que vous puissiez en être informé de jour et faire ce soir 3 ou 4 lieues et être demain à 7 heures du matin à Bruxelles. Vous pouvez donc disposer vos troupes de la manière suivante. Première division à deux lieues en avant des Quatre-Chemins, s'il n'y a pas d'inconvénient. Six divisions d'infanterie autour des Quatre-Chemins et une division à Marbais, afin que je puisse l'attirer à moi à Sombref, si j'en avais besoin. Elle ne retarderait d'ailleurs pas votre marche. Le corps du comte de Valmy, qui a 3,000 cuirassiers d'élite, à l'intersection du chemin des Romains et de celui de Bruxelles, afin que je puisse l'attirer à moi, si j'en avais besoin; aussitôt que mon parti sera pris, vous lui enverrez l'ordre de venir vous rejoindre. Je désirerais avoir avec moi la division de la Garde que commande le général Lefebvre Desnoëttes, et je vous envoie les deux divisions du corps du comte de Valmy pour la remplacer. Mais, dans mon projet actuel, je préfère placer le comte de Valmy de manière à le rappeler si j'en avais besoin, et ne point faire faire de fausses marches au général Lefebvre Desnoëttes, puisqu'il est probable que je me déciderai ce soir à marcher sur Bruxelles avec la Garde. Cependant, couvrez la division Lefebvre par les deux divisions de cavalerie d'Erlon et de Reille, afin de ménager la Garde; s'il y avait quelque échauffourée avec les Anglais, il est préférable que ce soit sur le ligne que sur la garde. J'ai adopté comme principe général pendant cette campagne, de diviser mon armée en deux ailes et une réserve. Votre aile sera composée des quatre divisions du 1er corps, des quatre divisions du 2e corps, de deux divisions de cavalerie légère, et de deux divisions du corps du Comte de Valmy. Cela ne doit pas être loin de 45 à 50 mille hommes.

Le maréchal Grouchy aura à peu près la même force, et commandera d'aile droite. La Garde formera la réserve, et je me porterai sur l'une ou l'autre aile, selon les circonstances. Le major général donne les ordres les plus précis pour qu'il n'y ait aucune difficulté sur l'obéissance à vos ordres lorsque vous serez détaché; les commandants de corps devant prendre mes ordres directement quand je me trouve présent. Selon les circonstances, j'affaiblirai l'une ou l'autre aile en augmentant ma réserve. Vous sentez assez l'importance attachée a la prise de Bruxelles. Cela pourra d'ailleurs donner lieu a des incidents, car un mouvement aussi prompt et aussi brusque isolera l'armée anglaise de Mons, Ostende, etc. Je désire que vos dispositions soient bien faites pour qu'au premier ordre, vos huit divisions puissent marcher rapidement et sans obstacle sur Bruxelles.

Charleroi, le 16 juin 1815.
N.

XIX.

COUNT REILLE'S LETTER TO NEY: June 16, 1815.

Doc. Inéd., p. 37.

A M. LE MARÉCHAL
Prince de la Moskowa.

Gosselies, le 16 juin 1815,
10 heures et quart du matin.

Monsieur le Maréchal,

J'ai l'honneur d'informer Votre Excellence du rapport que me fait faire verbalement le général Girard par un de ses officiers.

L'ennemi continue à occuper Fleurus par de la cavalerie légère qui a des vedettes en avant; l'on aperçoit deux masses ennemis venant par la route de Namur et dont la tête est à la hauteur de Saint-Amand; elles se sont formées peu à peu, et ont gagné quelque terrain à mesure qu'il leur arrivait du monde : on n'a pu guère juger de leur force à cause de l'éloignement; cependant ce général pense que chacune pouvait d'être de six bataillons en colonne par bataillon. On apercevait des mouvements de troupes derrière.

M. le lieutenant général Flahaut m'a fait part des ordres qu'il portait à Votre Excellence; j'en ai prévenu M. le comte d'Erlon, afin qu'il puisse suivre mon mouvement. J'aurais commencé le mien sur Frasnes aussitôt que les divisions auraient été sous les armes; mais d'après le rapport du général Girard, je tiendrai les troupes prêtes à marcher en attendant les ordres de Votre Excellence, et comme ils pourront me parvenir très vite, il n'y aura que très peu de temps de perdu.

J'ai envoyé à l'empereur l'officier qui m'a fait le rapport du général Girard.

Je renouvelle à Votre Excellence les assurances de mon respectueux dévouement.

Le général en chef du 2e corps.

Comte Reille.

XX.

NEY'S ORDERS TO REILLE AND D'ERLON: June 16, 1815.

Doc. Inéd., p. 38.

A M. LE COMTE REILLE,
Commandant le 2e Corps d'Armée.
Ordre de Mouvement.

Frasnes, le 16 juin 1815.

Conformément aux instructions de l'empereur, le 2e corps se mettra en marche de suite pour aller prendre position, la cinquième division[1] en arrière de Gennapes, sur les hauteurs qui dominent cette ville, la gauche appuyée à la grande route. Un bataillon ou deux couvriront tous les débouchés en

---

[1] That of Bachelu.

avant sur la route de Bruxelles. Le parc de réserve et les équipages de cette division resteront avec la seconde ligne.

La neuvième division[2] suivra les mouvements de la cinquième, et viendra prendre position en seconde ligne sur les hauteurs à droite et à gauche du village de Banterlet[3].

Les sixième et septième divisions[4] à l'embranchement de Quatre-Bras, où sera votre quartier général. Les trois premières divisions du comte d'Erlon viendront prendre position à Frasnes; la division de droite s'établira à Marbais avec la deuxième division de cavalerie légère du général Piré; la première couvrira votre marche, et vous éclairera sur Bruxelles et sur vos deux flancs. Mon quartier à Frasnes.

Pour le Maréchal prince de la Moskowa,

Le Colonel, premier aide de camp,

Heymès.

Deux divisions du comte de Valmy, s'établiront à Frasnes et à Liberchies. Les Divisions de la garde des généraux Lefebvre Desnoëttes et Colbert resteront dans leur position actuelle de Frasnes.

XXI.

SOULT'S FORMAL ORDER TO NEY TO CARRY QUATRE BRAS: June 16, 1815.

Doc. Inéd., p. 27.

A M. LE MARÉCHAL

PRINCE DE LA MOSKOWA.

Charleroi, le 16 juin 1815.

Monsieur le Maréchal, l'empereur ordonne que vous mettiez en marche les 2e et 1er corps d'armée, ainsi que le 3e corps de cavalerie, qui a été mis à votre disposition, pour les diriger sur l'intersection des chemins dits les Trois-Bras (route de Bruxelles), où vous leur ferez prendre position, et vous porterez en même temps des reconnaissances, aussi avant que possible, sur la route de Bruxelles et sur Nivelles, d'où probablement l'ennemi s'est retiré.

S. M. désire que, s'il n'y a pas d'inconvénient, vous établissiez une division avec de la cavalerie à Genappe, et elle ordonne que vous portiez une autre division du côté de Marbais, pour couvrir l'espace entre Sombref et les Trois-Bras. Vous placerez, près de ces divisions, la division de cavalerie de la garde impériale, commandée par le général Lefebvre Desnoëttes, ainsi que le 1er régiment de hussards, qui a été détaché hier vers Gosselies.

Le corps qui sera à Marbais aura aussi pour objet d'appuyer les mouve-

---

[2]That of Foy.

[3]A village on the Brussels turnpike half a mile north of Quatre Bras.

[4]Those of Jerome and Girard. This shows that Ney expected that Girard's division would be returned to him.

ments de M. le maréchal Grouchy sur Sombref, et de vous soutenir à la position des Trois-Bras, si cela devenait nécessaire. Vous recommanderez au général, qui sera à Marbais, de bien s'éclairer sur toutes les directions, particulièrement sur celles de Gembloux et de Wavre.

Si cependant la division du général Lefebvre Desnoëttes était trop engagée sur la route de Bruxelles, vous la laisseriez et vous la remplaceriez au corps qui sera à Marbais par le 3e corps de cavalerie aux ordres de M. le comte de Valmy, et par le 1er régiment de hussards.

J'ai l'honneur de vous prévenir que l'empereur va se porter sur Sombref, où, d'après les ordres de Sa Majesté, M. le maréchal Grouchy doit se diriger avec les 3e et 4e corps d'infanterie, et les 1er, 2e et 4e corps de cavalerie. M. le maréchal Grouchy fera occuper Gembloux.

Je vous prie de me mettre de suite à même de rendre compte à l'empereur de vos dispositions pour exécuter l'ordre que je vous envoie, ainsi que de tout ce que vous aurez appris sur l'ennemi.

Sa Majesté me charge de vous recommander de prescrire aux généraux commandant les corps d'armée de faire réunir leur monde et rentrer les hommes isolés, de maintenir l'ordre le plus parfait dans la troupe, et de rallier toutes les voitures d'artillerie et les ambulances qu'ils auraient pu laisser en arrière.

Le maréchal d'empire, major général,
Duc de Dalmatie.

XXII.

SOULT'S SECOND ORDER TO NEY TO CARRY QUATRE BRAS: June 16, 1815.

Doc. Inéd., p. 31.

A M. LE MARÉCHAL
PRINCE DE LA MOSKOWA.

Charleroi, le 16 juin 1815.

MONSIEUR LE MARÉCHAL,

Un officier de lanciers vient de dire à l'empereur que l'ennemi présentait des masses du côté des Quatre-Bras. Réunissez les corps des comtes Reille et d'Erlon, et celui du comte de Valmy, qui se met à l'instant en route pour vous rejoindre; avec ces forces, vous devrez battre et détruire tous les corps ennemis qui peuvent se présenter. Blücher était hier à Namur, et il n'est pas vraisemblable qu'il ait porté des troupes vers les Quatre-Bras; ainsi, vous n'avez affaire qu'à ce qui vient de Bruxelles.

Le maréchal Grouchy va faire le mouvement sur Sombref, que je vous ai annoncé, et l'empereur va se rendre à Fleurus; c'est là où vous adresserez vos nouveaux rapports à Sa Majesté.

Le maréchal d'empire, major général,
Duc de Dalmatie.

XXIII.

FLAHAUT'S LETTER TO THE DUKE OF ELCHINGEN.
Doc. Inéd., p. 63.

A M. LE DUC D'ELCHINGEN.

Paris, 24 novembre 1829.

Je voudrais, mon cher Duc, pouvoir répondre d'une manière plus précise à vos questions; mais, n'ayant pas pris de notes, il m'est impossible, après un intervalle de quinze années, de me rappeler les détails que vous tenez à savoir.

C'est moi qui ai porté, le 16, à monsieur votre père, l'ordre de marcher aux Quatre-Bras et de s'emparer de cette position. L'empereur me l'a dicté le matin de bonne heure, autant qu'il m'en souvienne, entre huit et neuf heures.

Quant à celle à laquelle je l'ai remis à M. le maréchal Ney, il me serait impossible de le dire, n'y ayant pas attaché d'importance dans le moment.

Après le lui avoir remis, j'ai pris les devants et ai été rejoindre le général Lefebvre Desnoëttes, qui commandait l'avant-garde. L'infanterie s'est fait longtemps attendre, mais dès que monsieur votre père nous a rejoints, et avant qu'elle fût arrivée, il a fait attaquer les troupes anglaises. Voilà tout ce dont je puis me souvenir; je regrette que ce ne soit pas plus circonstancié, puisque vous tenez à avoir des détails plus précis.

Croyez, mon cher Duc, à la sincérité de l'amitié que je vous ai vouée.

Comte Ch. FLAHAUT.

XXIV.

NAPOLEON'S LETTER TO GROUCHY: June 16, 1815.
Corresp. vol., 28, p. 336.

22059.— AU MARÉCHAL COMTE GROUCHY
COMMANDANT L'AILE DROITE DE L'ARMÉE DU NORD.

Charleroi, 16 juin 1815.

Mon Cousin, je vous envoie Labédoyère, mon aide de camp, pour vous porter la présente lettre. Le major général a dû vous faire connaître mes intentions; mais, comme il a des officiers mal montés, mon aide de camp arrivera peut-être avant.

Mon intention est que, comme commandant l'aile droite, vous preniez le commandement du 3e corps que commande le général Vandamme, du 4e corps que commande le général Gérard, des corps de cavalerie que commandent les généraux Pajol, Milhaud et Exelmans; ce qui ne doit pas faire loin de 50,000 hommes. Rendez-vous avec cette aile droite à Sombreffe. Faites partir en conséquence, de suite, les corps des généraux Pajol, Milhaud, Exelmans et Vandamme, et, sans vous arrêter, continuez votre mouvement sur Sombreffe. Le 4e corps, qui est à Châtelet, reçoit directement, l'ordre de se rendre à Sombreffe sans passer par Fleurus. Cette observation est importante, parce que je porte mon quartier général à Fleurus et qu'il faut éviter les encombrements. Envoyez de suite un officier au général Gérard pour lui faire connaître votre mouvement, et qu'il exécute le sien de suite.

Mon intention est que tous les généraux prennent directement vos ordres; ils ne prendront les miens que lorsque je serai présent. Je serai entre dix et onze heures à Fleurus; je me rendrai à Sombreffe, laissant ma Garde, infanterie et cavalerie, à Fleurus; je ne la conduirais à Sombreffe qu'en cas qu'elle fût nécessaire. Si l'ennemi est à Sombreffe, je veux l'attaquer; je veux même l'attaquer à Gembloux et m'emparer aussi de cette position, mon intention étant, après avoir connu ces deux positions, de partir cette nuit, et d'opérer avec mon aile gauche, que commande le maréchal Ney, sur les Anglais. Ne perdez donc point un moment, parce que plus vite je prendrai mon parti, mieux cela vaudra pour la suite de mes opérations. Je suppose que vous êtes à Fleurus. Communiquez constamment avec le général Gérard, afin qu'il puisse vous aider pour attaquer Sombreffe, s'il était nécessaire.

La division Girard est à portée de Fleurus; n'en disposez point à moins de nécessité absolue, parce qu'elle doit marcher toute la nuit. Laissez aussi ma jeune Garde et toute son artillerie à Fleurus.

Le comte de Valmy, avec ses deux divisions de cuirassiers marche sur la route de Bruxelles; il se lie avec le maréchal Ney, pour contribuer à l'opération de ce soir, à l'aile gauche.

Comme je vous l'ai dit, je serai de dix a onze heures à Fleurus. Envoyez-moi des rapports sur tout ce que vous apprendrez. Veillez à ce que la route de Fleurus soit libre. Toutes les données que j'ai sont que les Prussiennes ne peuvent point nous opposer plus de 40,000 hommes.

NAPOLÉON.

D'après la copie. Dépôt de la guerre.

XXV.

THE 2 P. M. — June 16th — ORDER TO NEY.

Doc. Inéd., p. 40.

A M. LE MARÉCHAL
PRINCE DE LA MOSKOWA.

En avant de Fleurus,
le 16 juin à 2 heures.

Monsieur le Maréchal, l'empereur me charge de vous prévenir que l'ennemi a réuni un corps de troupes entre Sombref et Bry, et qu'à deux heures et demie M. le maréchal Grouchy, avec les troisième et quatrième corps, l'attaquera; l'intention de Sa Majesté est que vous attaquiez aussi ce qui est devant vous, et qu'après l'avoir vigoureusement poussé, vous rabattiez sur nous pour concourir à envelopper le corps dont je viens de vous parler.

Si ce corps était enfoncé auparavant, alors Sa Majesté ferait manœuvrer dans votre direction pour hâter également vos opérations.

Instruisez de suite l'empereur de vos dispositions et de ce qui se passe sur votre front.

Le maréchal d'empire, major général,
Duc de Dalmatie.

Au dos de cet ordre est écrit:
    A M. le Maréchal Prince de la Moskowa,
    A Gosselies, sur la route de Bruxelles.
Et au crayon: Wagnée
    Bois de Lombuc.
Un duplicata de cet ordre porte
    A M. le Maréchal Prince de la Moskowa,
    A Gosselies, sur la route de Bruxelles.

Wagnée.
Ransart.

XXVI.

THE 3.15 P. M. — June 16th — ORDER TO NEY.

Doc. Inéd., p. 42.

Monsieur le Maréchal, je vous ai écrit, il y a une heure, que l'empereur ferait attaquer l'ennemi à deux heures et demie dans la position qu'il a prise entre le village de Saint-Amand et de Bry: en ce moment l'engagement est très prononcé; Sa Majesté me charge de vous dire que vous devez manœuvrer sur-le-champ de manière à envelopper la droite de l'ennemi et tomber à bras raccourcis sur ses derrières; cette armée est perdue si vous agissez vigoureusement; le sort de la France est entre vos mains. Ainsi n'hésitez pas un instant pour faire le mouvement que l'empereur vous ordonne, et dirigez vous sur les hauteurs de Bry et de Saint-Amand, pour concourir à une victoire peut-être décisive. L'ennemi est pris en flagrant délit au moment où il cherche à se réunir aux Anglais.

Le major général,
Duc de Dalmatie.

En avant de Fleurus, le 16 juin 1815, à 3 heures un quart.

XXVII.

SOULT'S LETTER TO NEY: June 17, 1815.

Doc. Inéd., p. 45.

A M. LE MARÉCHAL
Prince de la Moskowa.

Fleurus, le 15 [17] juin 1815.

Monsieur le Maréchal, le général Flahaut, qui arrive à l'instant, fait connaître que vous êtes dans l'incertitude sur les résultats de la journée d'hier. Je crois cependant vous avoir prévenu de la victoire que l'empereur a remportée. L'armée prussienne a été mise en déroute, le général Pajol est à sa poursuite sur les routes de Namur et de Liége. Nous avons déjà plusieurs milliers de prisonniers et 30 piéces de canon. Nos troupes se sont bien conduites: une charge de six bataillons de la garde, des escadrons de service et la division de cavalerie du général Delort a percé la ligne ennemie, porté le plus grand désordre dans ses rangs et enlevé la position.

L'empereur se rend au moulin de Bry où passe la grande route qui conduit de Namur aux Quatre-Bras; il n'est donc pas possible que l'armée anglaise puisse agir devant vous; si cela était, l'empereur marcherait directement sur elle par la route des Quatre-Bras, tandis que vous l'attaqueriez de front avec vos divisions qui, à présent, doivent être réunies, et cette armée serait dans un instant détruit. Ainsi, instruisez Sa Majesté de la position exacte des divisions, et de tout ce qui se passe devant vous.

L'empereur a vu avec peine que vous n'ayez pas réuni hier les divisions; elles ont agi isolément; ainsi, vous avez éprouvé des pertes.

Si les corps des comtes d'Erlon et Reille avaient été ensemble, il ne réchappait pas un Anglais du corps qui venait vous attaquer. Si le comte d'Erlon avait exécuté le mouvement sur St. Amand que l'empereur a ordonné, l'armée prussienne était totalement détruite, et nous aurions fait peut-être 30,000 prisonniers.

Les corps des généraux Gérard, Vandamme et la garde impériale ont toujours été réunis; l'on s'expose à des revers lorsque des détachements sont compromis.

L'empereur espère et désire que vos sept divisions d'infanterie et la cavalerie soient bien réunies et formées, et qu'ensemble elles n'occupent pas une lieue de terrain, pour les avoir bien dans votre main et les employer au besoin.

L'intention de Sa Majesté est que vous preniez position aux Quatre-Bras ainsi que l'ordre vous en a été donné; mais si, par impossible, cela ne peut avoir lieu, rendez-en compte sur-le-champ avec détail, et l'empereur s'y portera ainsi que je vous l'ai dit; si, au contraire, il n'y a qu'une arrière-garde, attaquez-la, et prenez position.

La journée d'aujourd'hui est nécessaire pour terminer cette opération, et pour compléter les munitions, rallier les militaires isolés et faire rentrer les détachements. Donnez des ordres en consequence, et assurez-vous que tous les blessés sont pansés et transportés sur les derrières: l'on s'est plaint que les ambulances n'avaient pas fait leur devoir.

La fameux partisan Lutzow, qui a été pris, disait que l'armée prussienne était perdue, et que Blücher avait exposé une seconde fois la monarchie prussienne.

Le maréchal d'empire, major général,
Duc de DALMATIE.

XXVIII.

SOULT'S ORDER TO NEY: 12 M., June 17, 1815.

Doc. Inéd., p. 44.

A M. LE MARÉCHAL
Prince de la Moskowa.

[1]4e corps d'armée [*sic*], à Gosselies.

En avant de Ligny, le 17 à midi.

Monsieur le Maréchal, l'empereur vient de faire prendre position, en avant

---

[1] This mention of the 4th Corps, Gérard's, must be an error.

de Marbais, à un corps d'infanterie et à la garde impériale; S. M. me charge de vous dire que son intention est que vous attaquiez les ennemis aux Quatre-Bras, pour les chasser de leur position, et que le corps qui est à Marbais secondera vos opérations; S. M. va se rendre à Marbais, et elle attend vos rapports avec impatience.

Le maréchal d'empire, major général,
Duc de Dalmatie.

XXIX.

CAPTAIN BOWLES' STORY OF WELLINGTON AT QUATRE BRAS: June 17, 1815.

Captain Bowles in Lord Malmesbury's Letters, vol. 2, p. 447.

"On the morning of the 17th, my company being nearly in front of the farmhouse at Quatre-Bras, soon after daybreak the Duke of Wellington came to me, and, being personally known to him, he remained in conversation for an hour or more, during which time he repeatedly said he was surprised to have heard nothing of Blücher. At length, a staff-officer arrived, his horse covered with foam, and whispered to the Duke, who without the least change of countenance gave him some orders and dismissed him. He then turned round to me and said, 'Old Blücher has had a d——d good licking and gone back to Wavre, eighteen miles. As he has gone back, we must go too. I suppose in England they will say we have been licked. I can't help it; as they are gone back, we must go too.'

He made all the arrangements for retiring without moving from the spot on which he was standing, and it certainly did not occupy him five miuutes."

XXX.

GROUCHY'S REPORT TO NAPOLEON FROM SART-À-WALHAIN: 11 A. M., June 18, 1815.

Grouchy Mém. vol. 4, p. 71.

Sart-à-Walhain le 18 juin, onze heures du matin.

Sire:

Je ne perds pas un moment à vous transmettre les renseignements que je recueille ici; je les regarde comme positifs, et afin que Votre Majesté les reçoive le plus promptement possible, je les lui expédie par le major La Fresnaye, son ancien page; il est bien monté et bon écuyer.

Les 1er, 2e et 3e corps de Blücher marchent dans la direction de Bruxelles. Deux de ces corps ont passé à Sart-à-Walhain, ou à peu de distance, sur la droite; ils ont défilé en trois colonnes, marchant à peu près de même hauteur. Leur passage a duré six heures sans interruption. Ce qui a défilé en vue de Sart-à-Walhain peut-être évalué à trente mille hommes au moins, et avait un matériel de cinquante à soixante bouches à feu.

Un corps venant de Liége a effectué sa jonction avec ceux qui ont combattu à Fleurus. (Ci-joint une réquisition qui le prouve.) Quelques-uns des Prussiens que j'ai devant moi se dirigent vers la plaine de la Chyse, située près de la route de Louvain, et à deux lieues et demie de cette ville.

Il semblerait que ce serait à dessein de s'y masser ou de combattre les troupes qui les y poursuivraient, ou enfin de se réunir à Wellington, projet annoncé par leurs officiers, qui, avec leur jactance ordinaire, prétendent n'avoir quitté le champ de bataille, le 16, qu'afin d'opérer leur réunion avec l'armée anglaise sur Bruxelles.

Ce soir, je vais être massé à Wavres, et me trouver ainsi entre Wellington, que je présume en retraite devant Votre Majesté, et l'armée prussienne.

J'ai besoin d'instructions ultérieures sur ce que Votre Majesté ordonne que je fasse. Le pays entre Wavres et la plaine de la Chyse est difficile, coupé, et marécageux.

Par la route de Wivorde, j'arriverai facilement à Bruxelles avant tout ce qui sera arreté à la Chyse, si tant il y a que les Prussiens y fassent une halte.

Daignez, Sire, me transmettre vos ordres; je puis les recevoir avant de commencer mon mouvement de demain.

La plupart des renseignements que renferme cette lettre me sont fournis par la propriétaire de la maison où je me suis arreté pour écrire à Votre Majesté; cet officier a servi dans l'armée française, est decoré, et parait entièrement dévoué à nos intérêts. Je les joins à ces lignes.

XXXI.

GENERAL ORDER OF PREPARATION FOR THE BATTLE OF WATERLOO: June 18, 1815.

Doc. Inéd. p. 52.

A M. LE MARÉCHAL PRINCE DE LA MOSKOWA.

L'empereur ordonne que l'armée soit disposée à attaquer l'ennemi à 9 heures du matin; MM. les commandants des corps d'armée rallieront leurs troupes, feront mettre les armes en état, et permettront que les soldats fassent la soupe; ils feront aussi manger les soldats; afin qu'à 9 heures précises chacun soit prêt et puisse être en bataille avec son artillerie et ambulances, à la position de bataille que l'empereur a indiquée par son ordre d'hier soir.

MM. les lieutenants-generaux, commandant les corps d'armée d'infanterie et de cavalerie, enverront sur-le-champ des officiers au major-général pour faire connaitre leur position et porter des ordres.

Au quartier-général imperial,

le 18 juin 1815.

Le maréchal d'empire, major-général,

Duc de Dalmatie.

APPENDIX C.

XXXII.

ORDER FOR THE ATTACK TO BEGIN AT 1 P. M., June 18, 1815.

Doc. Inéd. p. 53.

Une fois que toute l'armée sera rangée en bataille, à peu près à 1 heure après midi, au moment où l'empereur en donnera l'ordre au Maréchal Ney, l'attaque commencera pour s'emparer du village de Mont St. Jean où est l'intersection des routes. A cet effet, les batteries de 12 du 2me corps et celle du 6me se réuniront à celle du 1er corps. Ces 24 bouches à feu tireront sur les troupes du Mont St. Jean, et le comte d'Erlon commencera l'attaque, en portant en avant sa division de gauche et la soutenant, suivant les circonstances, par les divisions du 1er corps.

Le 2e corps s'avancera à mesure pour garder la hauteur du comte d'Erlon.

Les compagnies de sapeurs du 1er corps seront prêtes pour se barricader sur-le-champ à Mont St. Jean.

Au crayon et de l'écriture du Maréchal Ney.

Ajouté par M. le Maréchal Ney.

Le comte d'Erlon comprendra que c'est par la gauche que l'attaque commencera, au lieu de la droite.

Communiquer cette nouvelle disposition au général en chef Reille.

AU DOS.

Ordres dictés par l'empereur, sur le champ de bataille du Mont St. Jean, le 18, vers onze heures du matin, et écrits par le maréchal Duc de Dalmatie, major général. Paris, le 21 juin 1815. Le Maréchal Prince de la Moskowa Pair de France, Ney.

XXXIII.

THE 10 A. M. — JUNE 18th — ORDER TO GROUCHY.

Grouchy Mémoires, vol. 4, p. 79.

En avant de la ferme de Caillou, le 18 juin, 1815, à dix heures du matin.

Monsieur le maréchal, l'Empereur a reçu votre dernier rapport, daté de Gembloux.

Vous ne parlez à Sa Majesté que de deux colonnes prussiennes qui ont passé à Sauvenière et à Sart-à-Walhain. Cependant des rapports disent qu'une troisième colonne, qui était assez forte, a passé par Géry et Gentines, se dirigeant sur Wavres.

L'Empereur me charge de vous prévenir qu'en ce moment Sa Majesté va faire attaquer l'armée anglaise, qui a pris position à Waterloo, près de la forêt de Soignes. Ainsi, Sa Majesté désire que vous dirigiez vos mouvements sur Wavres, afin de vous rapprocher de nous, vous mettre en rapport d'opérations et lier les communications, poussant devant vous les corps de l'armée prussienne qui ont pris cette direction et qui auraient pu s'arrêter à Wavres, où vous devez arriver le plus tôt possible.

Vous ferez suivre les colonnes ennemies, qui ont pris sur votre droite, par quelques corps légers, afin d'observer leurs mouvements et ramasser leurs traînards. Instruisez-moi immédiatement de vos dispositions et de votre marche, ainsi que des nouvelles que vous avez sur les ennemis, et ne négligez pas de lier vos communications avec nous. L'Empereur désire avoir très-souvent de vos nouvelles.

Le maréchal duc de DALMATIE.

For translation, see *ante* p. 265.

XXXIV.
THE 1 P. M. — JUNE 18th — ORDER TO GROUCHY.

La Tour d'Auvergne, p. 270.

Du champ de bataille de Waterloo, le 18 juin,
à une heure après midi.

Monsieur le Maréchal,

Vous avez écrit, ce matin à deux heures, à l'Empereur, que vous marcheriez sur Sart-lez-Walhain; donc votre projet était de vous porter à Corbais ou à Wavre. Ce mouvement est conforme aux dispositions de Sa Majesté, qui vous ont été communiquées. Cependant, l'Empereur m'ordonne de vous dire que vous devez toujours manœuvrer dans notre direction. C'est à vous de voir le point où nous sommes pour vous régler en conséquence et pour lier nos communications, ainsi que pour être toujours en mesure de tomber sur les troupes ennemies qui chercheraient à inquiéter notre droite et de les écraser.

Dans ce moment, la bataille est engagée sur la ligne de Waterloo; le centre ennemi est à Mont-Saint-Jean; ainsi manœuvrez pour joindre notre droite.

P. S. Une lettre qui vient d'être interceptée porte que le général Bülow doit attaquer notre flanc. Nous croyons apercevoir ce corps sur les hauteurs de Saint-Lambert; ainsi, ne perdez pas un instant pour vous rapprocher de nous et nous joindre, et pour écraser Bülow, que vous prendrez en flagrant délit.

Le maréchal duc de DALMATIE.

For translation, see *ante*, p. 270.

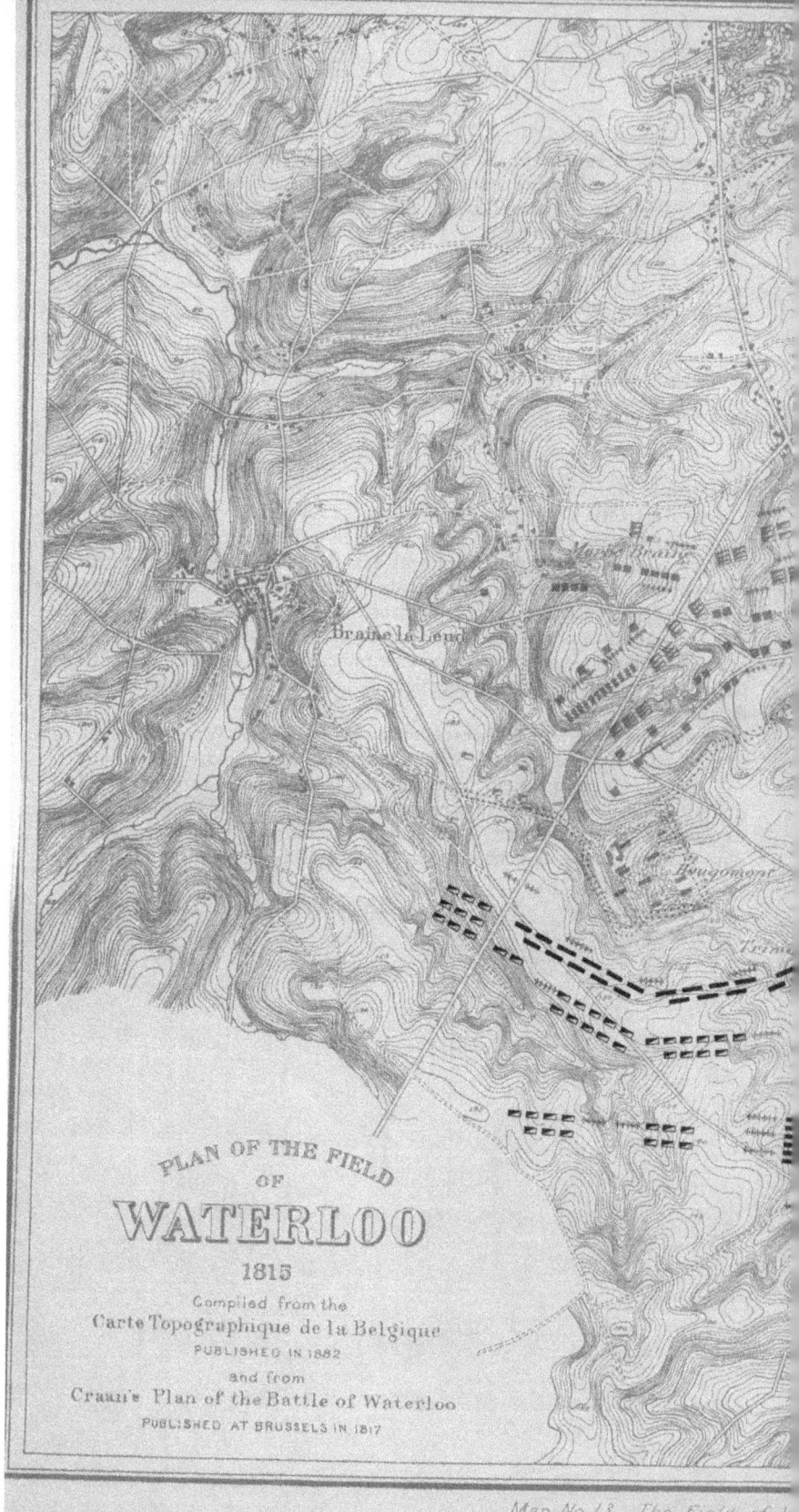

Scale, 1 English mile

Scale of metres
0   500   1000

Contour Interval 1 metre

Ohain

La Haye

Smohain

Frischermont

Wood of Paris

Papelotte

Maison du Roi

Couture

Planchenoit

Maransart

Chantelet

The positions of the troops are
taken from Map No 1 in Siborne's
Waterloo Letters.

at 11.15 A.M. June 18, 1815

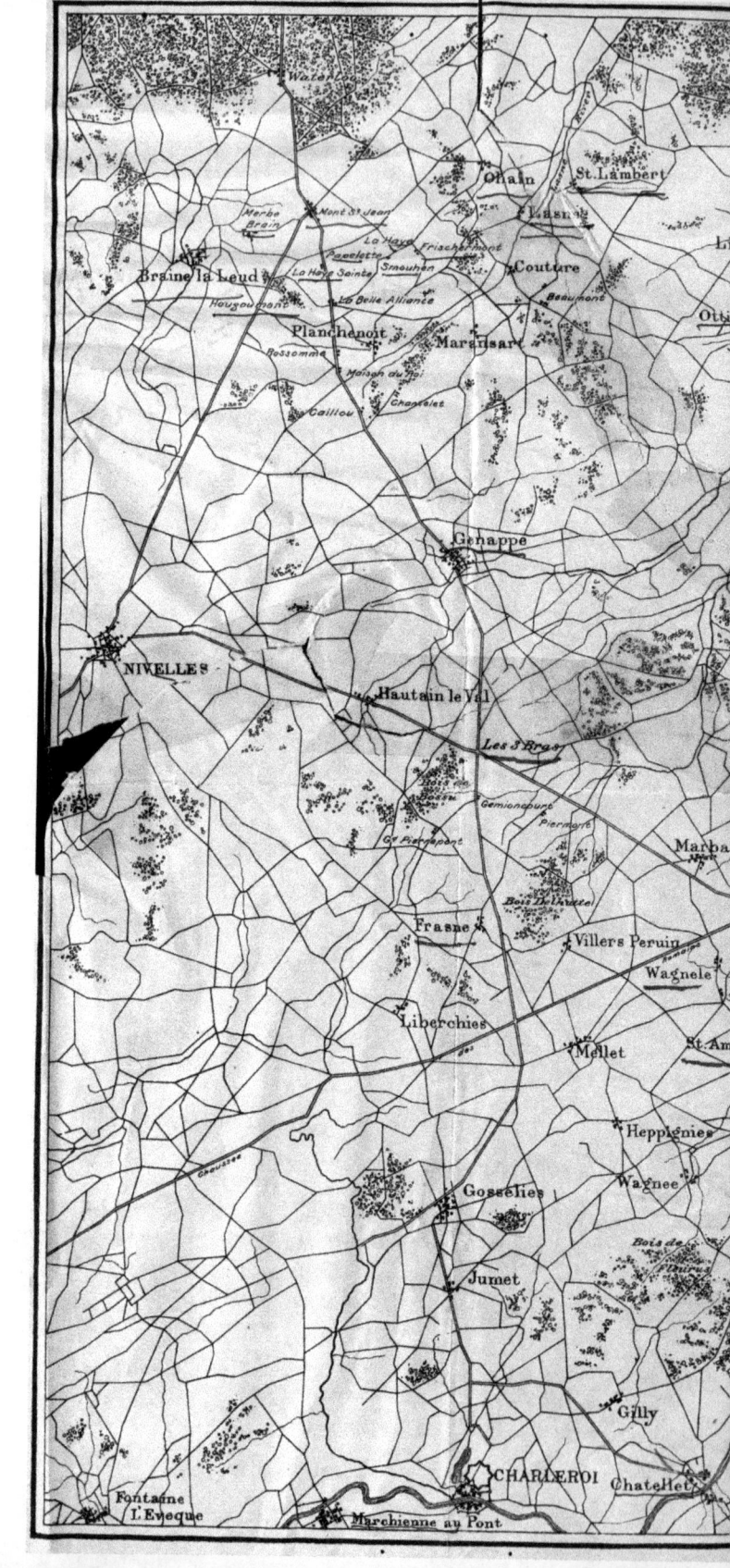

INDEX.

A.

Adam, General Sir Frederick, commander British brigade, 35; his troops of the best quality, 315; his light brigade at Waterloo, 323-324, 332, 333, 335, 336.

Albemarle, Earl of, his *Fifty Years of My Life*, reports story of Napoleon's secluding himself on forenoon of battle of Waterloo, 30.

Alison, Sir Archibald, his *History of Europe* criticised by Wellington and the Earl of Ellesmere, 10; not a military authority, 10; his view that Napoleon intended to throw himself between the allied armies, 10.

Allies. (See ARMIES.)

Allix, General, commander division 1st French corps, 25; his division at Waterloo, commanded by Quiot, 302, 305.

Alten, Lieutenant-General Count, commander 3d British division, 38; arrival of two of his brigades gives Wellington an equality of force at Quatre Bras, 179, 183; position at Waterloo, 300; wounded, his division rallied by Wellington, 314.

Anglesea, Marquis of. (See UXBRIDGE.)

Anthing, commander brigade Dutch-Belgians, 36; his brigade ordered to Enghien, 83, 89; reported near Audenarde, at 7 A.M., June 16th, 108.

Appendices: —
 A. On some Characteristics of Napoleon's Memoirs, 351-354.
 B. On Marshal Grouchy and the Bertrand Order, 355-361.
 C. Orders and Despatches, 362-389.

Arentsschildt, Colonel Sir F., commander cavalry brigade King's German Legion, 35, 36.

ARMIES: —

ALLIED, in concert of action against Napoleon; troops of England, Belgium, Holland, Hanover, Brunswick, Nassau, and Prussia, 2-4; their cantonments on and behind the Belgian frontier, 3, 96; strength, organization, and internal economy of, 32-43.

ANGLO-DUTCH, positions in Belgium before the campaign, 2-4; their extended cantonments, 2, 96; commanded by the Duke of Wellington, 34; heterogeneous character of, 34, 294; organization, 34-35; troops employed on garrison duty, 35; strength and composition in detail, 35-37, 39; location of the various divisions, 38-39; merits and defects of, 39-40, 43; principal officers, 40; Wellington as a commander, 40-41; internal economy of, 41-42; positions of troops as given in the "Disposition," at 7 A.M., June 16, 85, n. 54; actual positions, 111-113; badly served with information from the front, 114; at Quatre Bras, 178-179, 183; strength at Quatre Bras 184; losses, 184; at Quatre Bras morning of 17th, 214; position, composition, and strength at Waterloo, 297-299; in the battle of Waterloo, 294 *et seq.*; 18,000 men detached at Hal and Tubize, 339.

British, strength and composition in detail, 35; mainly relied upon by Wellington, 39, 298; at Quatre Bras, 178-179, 184; steadiness of infantry, 179; in the skirmish at Genappe, 216; strength at Waterloo, 298; positions at Waterloo, 299-300; charge of the Union brigade, 306-307; suffered severely in d'Erlon's assault, 310; the brigades of Vivian and Vandeleur brought to the centre at a critical moment, 314; repulse of the Imperial Guard by the Guards, 319-321; skilful use of troops by Sir Colin Halkett and Colonel Elphinstone in support of the Guards, 322; services of the light brigade, 323-324, 332-336.

Brunswick contingent (see also BRUNSWICK, DUKE OF); strength and composition in detail, 37-38; in the action

INDEX. 391

at Quatre Bras, 178–179, 183; broke in disorder, the Duke being killed, 179; strength at Waterloo, 299; position at Waterloo, 299–300; brought into action, 314; driven back by the French divisions of Donzelot and Quiot, 318.

Dutch-Belgians, strength and composition of, in detail, 36; positions of, 38; raw troops, 39; occupation of Quatre Bras, 101; occupation criticised by Maurice, 103; fully justified, 104; the first troops to receive the attack at Quatre Bras, 101, 178; suffered severely, 183; strength and composition at Waterloo, 299, 314; Bylandt's brigade badly placed, 299; breaks in confusion, 306; Chassé's division supports the British guards, 314; opportune employment of Van der Smissen's battery, 320.

Hanoverians, strength and composition in detail, 36; raw troops, 39; at Quatre Bras, 179; fought stubbornly, 179; strength at Waterloo, 298; in the battle, 312.

King's German Legion, strength and composition in detail, 35–36; positions, 38–39; relied upon by Wellington, 39, 298; strength at Waterloo, 298; position, 300.

Nassau contingent, strength and composition in detail, 37; in the reserve, 38; strength at Waterloo, 299; position, 300; suffered severely, 310; driven back by divisions of Donzelot and Quiot, 318.

PRUSSIANS (allied), positions in Belgium before the campaign, 2–4; extended cantonments, 2, 96; strength and composition in detail, 32–33; locations of different corps, 33; composed mainly of veterans, 33; temper and spirit of, 34; Marshal Blücher, 34; internal economy of, 42; ordered to concentrate at Sombreffe on the 14th, 70, 143; strength and positions at Ligny, 143–144, 151–152, 172; in the battle of Ligny, 154–159; losses, 159; Blücher disabled, 158, 226, 229; retreat towards Wavre, 159, 226 *et seq.*; Blücher decides to join Wellington, 230; admirable conduct of commanders after the battle of Ligny, 231; pledged to support Wellington, 234, 237; delay in the march to support Wellington, 262, 264; the combat at Wavre, 264–265; in the battle of Waterloo, 307–309, 311, 313–314, 324–328, 336, 339–342. (See also Battles of LIGNY, WAVRE, and WATERLOO.)

FRENCH, condition of, upon Napoleon's return from Elba, 1, 16, 17; Soult made chief of staff, 17; confidence in Napoleon, 17; the corps commanders, 18; estimates of general officers, 19; what Napoleon expected of his lieutenants, 20; Ney sent for at last moment, 20; Grouchy suddenly appointed to command of right wing, 21; Napoleon's mistake in leaving Davout at Paris, 22; estimate of the army, 24–25; strength and composition in detail, 25–28; internal economy of, 41; assembled near Charleroi, 44–45; addressed by Napoleon at Avesnes on the 14th, 45; general order of movement, 45–46; desertion of Bourmont, 47; operations on the 15th, 47–69; arrival of Ney, 49; delays in movement, 46, 50–53, 55, 118–119, 121–122, 125–127, 130–132, 138, 139–140, 157, 161, 163 *et seq.*, 176–178, 180–187, 197 *et seq.*, 211–212, 252–254, 256–257; the 2d corps attacks the Dutch-Belgians at Quatre Bras on the 15th, 101; operations on the morning of the 16th, 116–142; in the battle of Ligny, 152–175; strength at Ligny, 154, 171; losses, 159; in the battle of Quatre Bras, 176–196; strength at Quatre Bras, 184; losses, 184; operations on the 17th, 197–225; force detached with Grouchy, 212, 220; pursuit of the English on the 17th led by the Emperor in person, 214; skirmish at Genappe, 216; Grouchy's march on Wavre, 211–213, 245–262, 264–267, 272, 279, 288; the combat at Wavre, 264–265; position at Waterloo, 301; strength and composition, 301; in the battle of Waterloo, 289–342; unwieldy formation of d'Erlon's troops, 304–307; the great cavalry charges upon the English centre, 308–311; the charge of the Imperial Guard, 315–326, 331–338; tactics employed at Waterloo, 329–331; the rout of the French army due to vigorous attack of Zieten's corps at close of the day, 340. (See also Battles of LIGNY, QUATRE BRAS, WAVRE, and WATERLOO.)

Audenarde, on the Scheldt, one limit of Lord Uxbridge's cantonment, 79.

Austria, concentrates a formidable force on the eastern frontier for ultimate co-operation against Napoleon, 2.

Auvergne. (See LA TOUR D'AUVERGNE.)

Avesnes, Napoleon issued stirring order here "to conquer or die," on the evening of June 14th, 45; Marshal Mortier detained here by illness, June 14th, 46.

B.

Bachelu, General, commander division 2d French corps, 25; advance to Frasnes, 49; at Quatre Bras, 178; position at Waterloo, 302; in the attack upon Hougomont, 304; Ney neglects to use this division to support his cavalry charge, 309; or in support of the charge of the Guard, 337.

Baring, Major, his battalion of the King's German Legion occupies farmhouse of La Haye Sainte, 300.

Battle of Ligny, 143–175; Prussian strength and position, 143–144, 151; Napoleon's plan of battle, 152, 153; position of the French, 153, 154; battle begins at 2.30, 154; orders to Ney, 154, 155; fought with determination on both sides, 156; nearly all the Prussian divisions under fire, 156; Napoleon decides to put in the Guard, 156, 157; delay caused by d'Erlon's corps, 157; the Guard breaks Prussian centre, 158; Prussians fall back to Brye and Sombreffe, 159; Prussian desertions, 159; losses, 159; non-employment of the 6th French corps, 159, 160; extent of the French victory, 161, 162; discussion of the battle, 163–175.

Battle of Quatre Bras, 176–196; attack begun by Ney at 2 P.M., 178; at that hour only Perponcher's Dutch-Belgian division opposed him, 178; at 2.30 Wellington arrived and took command, 178; arrival an hour later of Picton's division followed by the Duke of Brunswick's corps, 178; the Dutch-Belgians retire after two hours' fighting, 179; the Brunswickers break, the Duke being killed, 179; at 5 P.M. two brigades of Alten's division arrive, 179, 183; Ney even then has in action only half the force assigned him, 179; and is therefore unable to execute Napoleon's orders, 183; Kellermann's gallant charge, 183, 184; arrival of Cooke's division of the English guards, 184; the French retire, 184; forces engaged, 184; losses, 184; defeat of the French due to diversion of d'Erlon's corps, 184; and to Ney's disregard of orders, 187; Wellington's skilful handling of his troops, 187, 188; discussion of the battle, 189–196.

Battle of Waterloo, 289–342; the field surveyed before the campaign by English engineers, 296; strength and composition of the Anglo-Dutch army, 298, 299; positions, 297, 299–301; strength of the French army engaged, 301; position, 301, 302; relative strength and efficiency of the two armies, 302; Napoleon's plan of battle, 302; the French attack upon Hougomont, 303–304; d'Erlon's assault upon the allied centre, 304–307; unwieldy formation of his troops, 305, 306; gains the crest of the British position, 306; deadly fire and bayonet charge of Picton's division, 306, 307; the charge of Ponsonby's British cavalry, 306, 307; repulse of d'Erlon's charge, 307; the French capture La Haye Sainte at great sacrifice, 307; Bülow's corps (Prussian) advances and threatens Planchenoit, requiring Napoleon's withdrawal from the field, 309; Ney left in command, 309; splendid onsets of French cavalry, 309–311; repulse of Bülow, 311; return of Napoleon to the front, 314; Alten's British division rallied by Wellington, 314; the Brunswick troops brought forward, 314; Chassé's Dutch-Belgian division placed in rear of British guards, 314; the light cavalry brigades of Vivian and Vandeleur brought to the centre, 314; the English troops exhausted, the allies discouraged, much artillery dismounted, 314; the reserves, with Maitland's guards and Adam's brigade combined at centre, 315; Ney ordered to collect infantry and cavalry to support an attack by the Imperial Guard, 315; the attack upon the Anglo-allied line by Donzelot and Quiot, 318; the broken lines rallied by Wellington, 318; steady advance of the Imperial Guard, 318, 319; destructive repulse of the Guard, 319 *et seq.*; persistency of the rear battalions of the Guard, 323–324; timely charge of the 52d regiment, supported by the rest of Adam's brigade, 324; the rout of the Guard complete, 324; Zieten's attack, 324, 325; the French right wing shattered, 325; charge of the British cavalry brigades of Vivian and Vandeleur, 325; Wellington orders his whole line to advance, 325; the French routed, 326; Napoleon borne away in one of the squares of the Guard, 326; the victory of the allies complete, 326; discussion of the battle, 329–342.

Battle of Wavre, Thielemann's corps left to defend the town, 264; Grouchy's

INDEX. 393

attack without skill, 264; the troops of Vandamme entangle themselves in the attempt to carry the lower bridges, 264-265; the 4th French corps in vain attack the Mill of Bierges, above the town, 265; Gérard wounded, 265; Pajol carried the bridge of Limale, 265; battle conducted gallantly by the French, but without method, 265; resistance of the Prussians worthy of all praise, 265.

Batty, Captain, *Historical Sketch of Campaign of 1815*, cited, 333.

Baudus, Lieutenant-Colonel de, his *Études sur Napoléon*, cited, 193, 194, 195, 196, 279, 292.

Beaumont, headquarters of Napoleon on the evening of June 14th, 45.

Belgium, acts in concert with other nations of Europe against France and Napoleon, 2-4 (see also ARMIES ALLIED); territory occupied by the cantonments of the allied armies, 3, 74; Brussels the headquarters of Wellington, 3; daylight in, from before sunrise at 4 A.M. until 9 P.M., 52, 251.

Bernhard, Prince. (See SAXE-WEIMAR.)

Berthier, Marshal, Napoleon's old chief of staff, retired into Belgium with Louis XVIII., 17.

Berton, General, commander French brigade, reports to Napoleon the discovery of a Prussian corps at Gembloux, 209; his *Précis, historique, militaire et critique, des batailles de Fleurus et de Waterloo*, cited, 258, 286, 338.

Bertrand, Grand Marshal (French), to whom Napoleon dictated order to Grouchy, 209, 210. (See GROUCHY.)

Bierges, Mill of, Gérard wounded in attack upon, 265.

Blücher, Field-Marshal Prince, commander of the Prussian army, 32; his character as an officer, 34; hatred of Napoleon, 34; chose the line of the brook of Ligny as a possible battle-field, 70; orders concentration of his army at Sombreffe, 70, 143; his understanding with Wellington, 70 *et seq.;* 91, 100, 143-145; advises Müffling of the concentration of the Prussian army at Sombreffe, 78; his cantonments too greatly extended, 96 *et seq.;* hears from Wellington, 144; determines to fight Napoleon at Ligny on independent grounds, 143-147; his reasons for accepting battle, 148-150; his position, 151; battle formation and force, 151, 152; his position criticised by Wellington, 155, n. 15; leads cavalry charge against the French and narrowly escapes capture, 158; key to his position taken by the French Guard, 158; falls back to Brye and Sombreffe, 159; result of accepting battle with but three-fourths of his force unsupported by Wellington, 162; held Brye and Sombreffe until after midnight, 204; his retreat toward Wavre, 159, 226, 231-233; not in communication with Thielemann and Bülow after defeat of the corps of Zieten and Pirch I., 226, n. 3; his age at time of the battle, 229, n. 14; carried from the field, 229; decides to join Wellington, 230, 234; assures Wellington of support at Waterloo, 234, 237 *et seq.;* he as well as Wellington desired to close the campaign with a great battle, 235; advises Müffling that though ill he will lead his army in person at Waterloo, 263.

Bonaparte, Jerome, commander French division, 2d corps, 25; had nominal command only, 25, n. 13; at Quatre Bras, 178, 179; his division in the attack on Hougomont, 303, 304.

Bonaparte, Joseph, advised by Napoleon on morning of June 14th of his intended movement on Charleroi, 45.

Bourmont, General, deserted with his staff to the enemy, succeeded by Hulot, 26, n. 14, 47.

Braine-le-Comte, sixteen miles west of Quatre Bras, 82; headquarters of the Prince of Orange, 102.

Braine-la-Leud ordered to be intrenched by Colonel Smyth, 296, 297.

Brunswick, Duke of, commander Brunswick corps, 38; arrives opportunely at Quatre Bras, 178; killed at Quatre Bras, 179.

Brussels, Wellington's headquarters, 3, 74; chief objective of Napoleon next to the dispersion of the allied armies, 142.

Brye, place of conference between Wellington and Blücher, 108, 144, 146.

Bullock, R. H., *Journal of*, cited, 113.

Bülow, General, commander 4th Prussian corps, 33; had in 1813 won the battle of Dennewitz against Ney, 34; ordered to Ligny, 70; not fully informed of situation, delayed execution of order, 73; his arrival expected by Blücher, 151, 172; his non-arrival, 231; on the march to Waterloo, 262, 263; attacks the right flank of the French army, 308, 309; attacks Planchenoit and is repulsed, 311; capture of Planchenoit, 325; assures the allied victory, 340.

394 INDEX.

Bylandt, Major-General Count de, commander Dutch-Belgian brigade, 36; at Quatre Bras, 102, 114; dangerous position of his brigade at Waterloo, 299, 300.

Byng, Major-General Sir John, commander brigade British guards, 35; position at Waterloo, 300.

C.

Caillou house, on the Brussels road near tavern of La Belle Alliance, Napoleon's headquarters evening of June 17th, 30, 245, 289.

Charleroi, the general objective point June 15th, 46; occupied by the main French column at noon, June 15th, 47, 114; headquarters of Napoleon, 48.

Charras, Lieutenant-Colonel, his *Histoire de la Campagne de 1815*, cited, 13, 17, 19, 25, 28, 29, 30, 32, 34, 46, 47, 48, 49, 50, 51, 52, 56, 57, 58, 59, 63, 67, 69, 70, 71, 73, 77, 80, 94, 96, 97, 98, 106, 122, 123, 124, 125, 136, 139, 144, 151, 152, 153, 154, 156, 157, 158, 159, 160, 163, 170, 171, 177, 178, 179, 183, 184, 189, 190, 193, 195, 201, 209, 212, 213, 214, 217, 222, 251, 252, 253, 258, 259, 262, 265, 270, 280, 282, 283, 284, 285, 289, 291, 292, 293, 298, 301, 304, 305, 306, 307, 312, 313, 316, 317, 319, 321, 324, 325, 326, 337, 352; admits no merit in Napoleon, iv.

Chassé, General, commander Dutch-Belgian division, 38; position at Waterloo, 300; opportunely brings into play Van der Smissen's battery, 308; ordered to the rear of the British guards, 314.

Chesney, Colonel Charles C., his *Waterloo Lectures*, cited, 25, 29, 51, 69, 70, 71, 73, 74, 76, 77, 90, 95, 101, 104, 128, 141, 188, 219, 221, 268, 278, 280, 339, 349.

Clausewitz, General Carl von, his *Der Feldzug von 1815*, etc., cited, 3, 10, 11, 13, 14, 58, 59, 70, 71, 73, 96, 97, 98, 139, 154, 163, 164, 165, 166, 167, 169, 170, 171, 172, 173, 205, 208, 217, 218, 219, 243, 253, 262, 280.

Clinton, Lieutenant-General Sir Henry, commander 2d British division, 38; position at Waterloo, 300.

Clinton, H. R., his *The War in the Peninsula*, etc., concurs with Hooper in opinion as to Napoleon's intention to wedge himself between the opposing armies, 11, n. 7, 141.

Colborne, Lieutenant-Colonel Sir John (afterward Lord Seaton), commander British 52d regiment, 324; resists advance of the Imperial Guard, 324, 331–336.

Cole, Sir Lowry, commander British 6th division, 38; position at Waterloo, 299; not in the action, 299, n. 25.

Colville, General Sir Charles, commander British 4th division, 38; his division withheld from the field of Waterloo by Wellington, 339.

Communication between allied armies, lines of, not to be confounded with lines of supplies, 14.

Cooke, Major-General, commander 1st division, 38; at Quatre Bras, 184; position at Waterloo, 300.

Correspondance de Napoléon, cited, 5, 14, 19, 45, 47, 52, 53, 54, 57, 64, 65, 66, 68, 96, 98, 99, 100, 134, 135, 141, 142, 165, 180, 191, 215, 243, 289, 317, 332, 338, 351, 352, 353.

D.

Dalton, Charles, his *Waterloo Roll Call* cited, 86.

Damitz, Major, his *Histoire de la Campagne de 1815*, cited, 144, 148, 149, 227, 285, 316, 317.

D'Auvergne. (See LA TOUR D'AUVERGNE.)

Davout, Marshal, desired field service, but was left at Paris, 22; would probably have prevented defeat at Waterloo, if in place of Ney or Grouchy, 22; Napoleon writes him, anticipating battle or retreat of Prussians, 45; his *Histoire de la Vie Militaire*, etc., cited, 22, 164, 166, 173.

Daylight in Belgium, through June from before sunrise at 4 A.M. until 9 P.M., 52, 251.

De Lancey, Colonel Sir William, Wellington's chief of staff, 81; instructions to, lost, 81–82; his "Disposition" of the British army at 7 A.M., June 16th, 85–86, n. 54; hurriedly drawn up, 114, n. 9; is furnished copy of Wellington's survey-sketches, 296.

Delbrück, Hans, his *Das Leben des Feldmarschalls Grafen Reithardt von Gneisenau*, cited, 34, 73, 78, 81, 109, 144, 145, 146, 149, 159, 204, 226, 228, 234.

D'Erlon, Count, commander 1st French corps, 18; position in the advance, 46; backwardness of his corps, 50–56, 94, 118, 119, 124, 127, 131, 132, 137–140,

156, 198; his wandering march, 157–161, 170–172, 174–175, 180–182, 193–196; ordered to halt at Frasnes, 177–178, 183; presence of his corps at Quatre Bras would have assured Ney's victory, 184–186; ordered to pursue the English rear guard, 215; in the first line at Waterloo, 289, 301; his grand assault upon the allied line, 304–307; unwieldy formation of his troops, 305, 329; rallied to support the Guard, 318, 330; his corps hopelessly disorganized, 325.
Dirom, Captain, of 1st British foot-guards, describes advance of Imperial Guard, 335.
Documents Inédits sur la Campagne de 1815, cited, 48, 49, 50, 51, 55, 67, 116, 117, 119, 120, 121, 122, 123, 124, 129, 131, 134, 141, 154, 155, 156, 169, 178, 180, 182, 189, 190, 191, 195, 196, 201, 203, 292, 302, 307, 308, 314, 326, 352.
Domon, General, commander cavalry division 3d French corps, 26; with Napoleon on march to Waterloo, 212; reported retreat of the Prussians, 246; at Waterloo, 301.
Donzelot, General, commander division 1st French corps, 25; in d'Erlon's assault at Waterloo, 305; supports cavalry charge, 310; brilliant attacks upon the allied line in support of the Guard, 318, 322, 330, 337, 338.
Dörnberg, Major-General Sir William, commander British cavalry brigade, 35, 36; reports Napoleon as having turned towards Charleroi, 80, 83; as to Wellington's pledge of support to Blücher on the 16th, 145.
Drouot, General, Adjutant-General of the Imperial Guard, an officer of great merit, 20; advised Napoleon to delay battle at Waterloo, 292.
Du Casse, A., *Le Général Vandamme et sa Correspondance*, cited, 139.
Durutte, General, commander division 1st French corps, 25; in the advance, 50, 129, 176, 179 *et seq.;* position at Waterloo, 302; in d'Erlon's assault, 305; his division routed, 325, 341.

E.

Elchingen, Duke of. (See NEY.)
Ellesmere, Earl of, *Essays on History*, etc., cited, 10, 43, 74, 139, 239.
Elphinstone, Colonel, skilfully supports the British guards at Waterloo, 322.
Erckmann-Chatrian, *Waterloo*, cited, 306.

Exelmans, General, commander 2d French cavalry corps, 27; at Ligny, 154; in the march to Wavre, 212, 251 *et seq.*

F.

Flahaut, General, on Napoleon's staff, the bearer to Ney of the Emperor's plans for the operations of the 16th, 121, 131, 134, 135; returns, bringing news of the result at Quatre Bras, 200.
Fleurus, point of retreat of the Prussians on the 15th, 48, 70; occupied by the French army on the 16th, 153–154; headquarters of Napoleon after battle of Ligny, 159, 200.
Foy, General, his *History of the War in the Peninsula*, portrait of Napoleon, 23; commander division 2d French corps, 25; in the advance to Quatre Bras, 49, 122, 129, 130; at Quatre Bras, 178; at Waterloo, 301–302; joins in attack upon Hougomont, 304.
Fraser, *Letters of Colonel Sir A. S.*, cited, 30.
Fraser, Sir William, *Words on Wellington*, cited, 105.
Friant, General, commander division Old Guard, 26; at Waterloo, 316.

G.

Gardner, Mr. Dorsey, his *Quatre Bras, Ligny, and Waterloo*, cited, 29, 105, 249, 268.
Gawler, an officer of the British 52d regiment, his *Crisis and Close of the Action at Waterloo*, cited, 333.
Genappe, a smart skirmish at, 216; after the battle of Quatre Bras Wellington spent the night at, 233; the French retreat blocked at, 326.
Gérard, General Count, commander 4th French corps, 18; in the advance, 44, 46; at Ligny, 153, 154, 157–159; 165; in the march to Wavre, 211; urged Grouchy to march to the sound of the cannon, 256, 257, 262; wounded in the attack on Wavre, 265; his *Quelques Documents* and *Dernières Observations*, etc., cited, 212, 247, 251, 252, 258, 259, 267, 271.
Girard, General, commander division 2d French corps, 25; in pursuit of the Prussians, 49; at Ligny, 153, 154; mortally wounded, 203; his division left at Ligny to care for the wounded, 203.

396 INDEX

Gleig, Rev. G. R., his *Life of the Duke of Wellington*, cited, 92, 93.

Gneisenau, General, chief of staff to Blücher, an able administrator, 34; remiss in not fully informing Bülow of the situation, 73; believed that Wellington had given assurance of support at Ligny, 145, 149; assumed command after Blücher's injury, 226; gave order for the retreat on Wavre, 226, 227; his want of confidence in Wellington, 229, 264.

Gomm, Sir William Maynard, *Letters and Journals of*, cited, 83, 112, 178, 299.

Gore, Captain Arthur, *An Historical Account of the Battle of Waterloo*, cited, 316, 319, 332.

Gourgaud, General, *Campagne de 1815*, cited, 4, 19, 52, 56, 63, 64, 66, 195, 215, 216, 338.

Grouchy, Marshal, commander French cavalry reserve, 18, 21; a veteran, 18; unfit for independent command, 208, 273; given command of the right wing, 21, 22, 135; in the first day's advance, 47, 48; in the battle of Ligny, 154; given verbal orders by Napoleon to pursue the Prussians, 206, 209; his objections to order, 207, 208; the order dictated to General Bertrand, 209–211, 218–221, 223, 249 *et seq.*, 345, 350, 358; force given him for pursuit, 209, 212, 220; his letter to Napoleon from Gembloux, 212–213, 245, 250; his movement on Wavre, 211–213, 245–262, 264–267, 272, 279, 288; issues orders for the morning of the 18th, 250; his letter to Pajol morning of 18th, 251; makes no change in his orders, 252; should have marched for the bridge of Moustier at daybreak, 253; neglects proper reconnoissance, 254; his despatch from Walhain, 255, 256; heard the sound of the cannon of Waterloo at Walhain, not Sart-à Walhain, 256, 259, 287, 288, 345; refused to accept Gérard's advice, 256, 257; was expected to arrive on left bank of the Dyle by the bridge of Moustier, 268 *et seq.*, 345; probable result had he marched for Moustier at daybreak, 281, 283, 284, 326–328, 339, 342; or had followed the counsel of Gérard at noon, 261, 339, 342; in the battle of Wavre, 264–265; receives further orders from Napoleon, 265, 270; is supposed to be bearing toward the main army, 271, 272; carried the bridge of Limale, 271; expected to keep off Blücher, not to fight Wellington, 278; not solely responsible for defeat at Waterloo, 328, 342.

Guard. (See IMPERIAL GUARD.)

Gudin, General, Napoleon's page at Waterloo, credited with story as to Napoleon's health on morning of battle of Waterloo, 30.

Guilleminot, General, according to Charras, the real commander of Jerome Bonaparte's division, 25, n. 13, 304.

Gurwood, Lieutenant-Colonel, *The Despatches of Field-Marshal the Duke of Wellington*, cited, 39, 71, 77, 78, 79, 80, 81, 82, 295, 328.

Guyot, General, commander cavalry division Imperial Guard, 27; at Ligny, 157; in Ney's charge upon the allied centre, 310, 311.

H.

Halkett, General Sir Colin, commander British brigade, 35; assists in opposing charge of Imperial Guard at Waterloo, 320, 322, 331.

Hamilton, Lieutenant-General Sir F. W., his *Grenadier Guards*, cited, 111.

Hamley, General Edward Bruce, *The Operations of War*, etc., cited, 221, 222, 280, 281, 339.

Hardinge, General Sir Henry, English military *attaché* at Blücher's headquarters, gives Wellington's criticism of Blücher's position, 155; lost his left hand at Ligny, 229; story of discussion between Blücher and Gneisenau as to remaining in communication with the English, 230.

Harlet, General, commander 4th regiment grenadiers of the Guard at Waterloo, 316.

Henrion, General, commander 4th regiment chasseurs of the Guard at Waterloo, 316.

Heymès, Colonel, Ney's aide-de-camp, 67; regarding interview between Ney and Napoleon, 49, n. 18, 67, 68; reports account of Ney's interview with Napoleon at midnight of the 15th, 116; reports conference between Ney and Reille, 116; as to the inactivity of Ney on morning of 16th, 119; as to arrival of the 3.15 P.M. order to Ney from Napoleon, 195, n. 19; overestimates Napoleon's loss in taking La Haye Sainte, 307, n. 41; denies that Ney ordered Guyot to charge upon the allied centre, 311.

Hill, Lieutenant-General Lord, commander 2d British corps, 38; a valuable man, 40; orders to, morning of the 16th, 82, 88, 89.

Histoire de l'Ex-Garde, cited, 326.

Hooper, George, his *Waterloo*, cited, 11, 77, 104, 155, 182, 183, 184, 190, 222, 282, 307.

Hougomont, Chateau of, description of, 297; occupied by the English, 300; French attack upon, 303, 304, 329, 330.

Hulot, General, succeeded General Bourmont to command of division 4th French corps, 26; at Ligny, 153, n. 7, 154.

I.

Imperial Guard, strength of, 26; leaves Paris, 44; ordered to advance 45-46; leaves its commander, Marshal Mortier, behind, ill, 46; a division of cavalry of, supports Ney at Frasnes, 49, 157; in reserve near Fleurus at beginning of battle at Ligny, 154; led by Napoleon in person at Ligny, 157, 158; loss, 161, 197; pursues the retreating English, 214-216; position at Waterloo, 301; in defence of Planchenoit, 309, 311; attack on the English line by the cavalry of, 309, 311; the *élite* of the army, 312; position, condition, and strength of, 315-318; charge of, and repulse by British guards and Adam's brigade, 318-324; the attack pressed, but again repulsed, 323, 324; resisted heroically to the last, 326; the Emperor finally forced to take refuge in one of its squares, 326; the charge of, reviewed, 331, 332, 335-338.

Inniskilling Dragoons, a part of the British Union brigade at Waterloo, 300.

J.

Jomini, General Baron de, *The Political and Military History of the Campaign of Waterloo*, cited, 12, 56, 59, 63, 66, 71, 139, 142, 153, 158, 170, 176, 177, 186, 192, 193, 200, 205, 253, 280, 281, 357.

Jones, George, *The Battle of Waterloo*, cited, 125, 144, 146, 200, 235, 317, 332, 334, 338.

K.

Kellermann, Count of Valmy, commander 3d French cavalry corps, 27; at Quatre Bras, 183, 184, 197; in reserve at Waterloo, 301; in the charge upon the allied centre, 309-310.

Kempt, Major-General Sir James, commander British brigade, 35; at Waterloo, 306, 312.

Kennedy, General Sir James Shaw,—his *Notes on the Battle of Waterloo*, cited, 96, 97, 99, 100, 250, 268, 274, 278, 280, 284, 294, 299, 301, 308, 310, 312, 339, 349.

Kielmansegge, Count, commander Hanoverian brigade, 36; his brigade unable to hold its position at the close of the battle of Waterloo, 312.

Kruse, General von, commander Nassau contingent, 37; did not arrive at Quatre Bras in time to take part in the action, 113.

L.

La Haye Sainte, farm-house on Brussels road, 301; attack upon, by the French, 305, 307; captured shortly before 4 P.M., 307, n. 42, 308, 312.

La Tour d'Auvergne, Lieutenant-Colonel Prince Édouard de, his *Waterloo: Étude de la Campagne de 1815*, cited, 13, 46, 51, 56, 59, 63, 69, 71, 118, 130, 136, 146, 154, 157, 158, 177, 202, 248, 250, 251, 257, 270, 304, 306.

Leeke, Rev. William, an officer of the British 52d regiment, 333; his *History of Lord Seaton's Regiment at the Battle of Waterloo*, cited, 111, 333, 334, 336.

Lefebvre-Desnouettes, General, commander division of cavalry Imperial Guard, 27; in support of troops at Frasnes, 49, 157; in the charge upon the allied centre at Waterloo, 309.

L'Heritier, General, commander of division 3d French cavalry corps, 27; his division at Quatre Bras, 183.

Life Guards, Historical Record of the, cited, 113.

Ligny. (See BATTLE OF.)

Lines of supply, 4.

Lobau, Count of (Mouton), commander French 6th corps, 18, 26; in the advance on the 15th, 46; delayed in reaching Ligny, 160; as to non-employment of his corps at Ligny, 160; at Waterloo, 301; made gallant defence of Planchenoit, 311, 325, 331.

Lockhart, J. G., his *History of Napoleon Buonaparte*, cited, 238, 239.

M.

Mackworth, Sir Digby, on Lord Hill's staff at Waterloo, describes advance of Imperial Guard, 332.

398   INDEX.

Maitland, •Major-General, commander brigade British guards, 35; repulses attack of Imperial Guard at Waterloo, 319-323, 331-335.
Malmesbury, *Letters of the First Earl of*, cited, 81, 233.
Marbot, Colonel, his *Mémoires*, cited, 247, 254, 258, 268, 269, 270.
Marcognet, General, commander division 1st French corps, 25; position at Waterloo, 302; in d'Erlon's assault 305; forced to abandon his position, 325, 341.
Marette, Chateau, at Walhain, 255, 288.
Marmont, Marshal, *Mémoires*, cited, 246, 247.
Maurice, Colonel J. F., his *Articles on Waterloo*, cited, 46, 47, 55, 71, 73, 74, 75, 76, 80, 83, 84, 85, 86, 94, 103, 106, 167, 204, 220, 221, 224, 227, 230, 237, 238, 241, 250, 262, 263.
Memorandum on the Battle of Waterloo, cited, 72, 74, 90, 95.
Mercer, General Cavalié, *Journal of the Waterloo Campaign*, cited, 216, 310.
Michel, General, commander brigade chasseurs of Imperial Guard at Waterloo, 316.
Milhaud, General Count, commander French 4th cavalry corps, 27; at Ligny, 154, 157-159; at Waterloo, 301; in the charge upon the allied centre, 309.
Morris, William O'Connor, his *Great Commanders of Modern Times, and the Campaign of 1815*, cited, 69, 307.
Morvan, General Poret de, commander 3d regiment grenadiers of the Imperial Guard at Waterloo, 316, 317.
Mortier, Marshal, commander Imperial Guard, taken ill just before the opening of the campaign, 20, 46.
Mouton. (See Lobau.)
Mudford, William, his *Historical Account of the Campaign in the Netherlands in 1815*, cited, 105.
Müffling, General Baron von, his *Passages from my Life*, cited, 39, 42, 71, 77, 78, 80, 81, 105, 109, 144, 145, 146, 159, 229, 233, 340, 341.
Muquardt, his *Précis de la Campagne de 1815*, cited, 118, 159, 177, 338.

N.

Napier, General Sir William, *Life of*, cited, 24, 191, 338.
Napier's battery at Waterloo, 317, 318.
Napoleon, his return to Paris from Elba, 1; general military situation, 2; his reasons for taking the offensive, 2, 3; his plan of campaign, 4-15, 45, 59 *et seq.*, 343, 348; his army, 16-28; gives Ney command of the left wing, 21, 49; his bodily strength and vigor, 23, 24, 29-31, 140, 200, 202, 290, 347, 348; leaves Paris for the field, 44; assembles his army near Charleroi, 44, 45; issues general order of movement, 45, 46; the advance to Fleurus, 46-53, 55 *et seq.*; fixes his headquarters at Charleroi, 48; as to verbal orders to Ney to seize Quatre Bras, 52, 62-69, 343; midnight conference, with Ney on the 15th, 54, 116, 129, 130, 132, 140; orders to Ney on the 16th, 120-125, 130, 131, 134, 141-142, 154-156; his reasons for delay on morning of 16th, 132-142, 163; his arrival at Fleurus about 11 A.M., 152; examines the position at Ligny, 152; his plan for the battle, 152-153, 164 *et seq.*; battle of Ligny, 152-175; delays decisive blow upon the unexpected appearance of d'Erlon's corps, 157-158, 160, 161, 170, 171, 174, 198; spends the night after the battle of Ligny at Fleurus, 159, 200; his skill conspicuous at Ligny, 171; not responsible for d'Erlon's wandering, 182, 193 *et seq.*; his delay on the morning of the 17th, 197 *et seq.*; loses the opportunity of overwhelming Wellington at Quatre Bras, 199-202, 344, 348; orders to Ney on the 17th, 201, 203 (see Ney); his march to join Ney, 203, 213-214; misconceives movement of Blücher, 203-206; his neglect of proper reconnoissance on the morning of the 17th, 205, 217, 218, 223-225, 344, 348; gives verbal order to Grouchy to pursue the Prussians, 206, 209 (see Grouchy); the Bertrand order to Grouchy, 209-211, 218-223, 248, 249, 274, 345; leads pursuit of the English from Quatre Bras, 214, 215; not to blame for not pursuing the Prussians on the early morning of the 17th, 217; expects Grouchy to arrive by the bridge of Moustier, 247, 268 *et seq.*, 290, 293, 294, 345; orders to Grouchy on the 18th, 265-272, 291; his headquarters at the Caillou house, 289; reconnoitres the field of battle of Waterloo at 1 A.M., 289; his conduct on the morning of the 18th, 289-294; his plan of battle, 292, 302 (see Battle of Waterloo); decides to defer the main attack until about 1 P.M., 292, 302; the attack upon Hougomont, 303, 304, 329; called from

INDEX. 399

the front to resist Prussian attack upon his right flank, 308–309, 311 *et seq.*, 330, 345, 346; returns to the front, 314; organizes general advance upon the British position, 315–317, 336; the attack of the Guard repulsed, 318–324, 331–338; his efforts to rally the Guard, 325; his army routed, 326; borne from the field in a square of the Guard, 326.

Napoléon à Waterloo, cited, 48, 50, 51, 69, 157, 181, 214, 215, 222, 247, 269, 270, 314, 319, 357.

Ney, Marshal, placed in the field at the last moment, 20, 21, 49, 55; given command of the left wing, 21, 49; overtakes the army near Charleroi, 49; movement on Quatre Bras on the 15th, 49–54, 55, 56, 62, 69, 139; verbal orders from Napoleon on the 15th to seize Quatre Bras, 52, 62–69, 343; midnight interview with Napoleon on the 15th, 54, 116, 129, 130, 132, 140; lacks a competent staff, 55, 119, 129, 140; his defective preparations and disobedience of orders on the 16th, 116–128, 140, 176–183, 186–187, 191, 344, 348; orders from Napoleon on the 16th, 120–125, 130, 131, 134, 141–142, 154–156; in the battle of Quatre Bras, 178–196; prevented Wellington's aiding Blücher, 187; makes no report of the result of the battle to Napoleon, 200, 202; orders from Napoleon on the 17th, 201, 203; his neglect to pursue Wellington on the morning of the 17th, 214; with Napoleon in pursuit of Wellington to Waterloo, 214 *et seq.*; his great attack with d'Erlon's infantry upon the allied line, 304–307; the capture of La Haye Sainte, 307; cavalry attacks upon the allied centre, 309–311; non-employment of infantry, 309, 311, 318, 324, 337; responsible for mistakes in assaults upon the allied line, 311 *et seq.*, 329, 330, 345; his lack of preparations for an attack by the Imperial Guard, 315, 317, 337, 338, 346; leads the charge of the Imperial Guard, 318–324, 331–338; contrasted with Wellington, 338.

O.

O'Connor Morris, William (see MORRIS).
Oldfield, Major John, his *Letters on the Battle of Waterloo*, cited, 89, 105, 296, 301.
Ollech, General von, *Geschichte des Feldzuges von 1815*, cited, 72, 73, 76, 77, 83, 84, 85, 106, 109, 134, 136, 143, 144, 145, 149, 154, 205, 208, 209, 226, 227, 228, 229, 231, 232, 233, 238, 258, 262, 263, 285.
Ompteda, Colonel von, commander brigade King's German Legion, 35; his brigade nearly annihilated near La Haye Sainte, 312.
Orange, Prince of, commander British 1st corps, 38; character as an officer, 40; hears of the French advance, 76; notifies Wellington at Brussels, 77; at Quatre Bras, 102, 178.

P.

Pack, Major-General Sir Denis, commander British brigade, 35; at Waterloo, 306.
Pajol, General, commander 1st French cavalry corps, 27; in the advance on the 15th, 46, 47; at Ligny, 154; in pursuit of the Prussians after Ligny, 205; with Grouchy in the march on Wavre, 212; in the battle of Wavre, 265.
Papelotte, small village in front of Wellington's position at Waterloo, 297; occupied by Zieten's corps, 324.
Pascallet, M. E., *Notice Biographique sur M. le Maréchal Marquis de Grouchy*, cited, 209, 357.
Perponcher, General, commander division Dutch-Belgians, 38; at Quatre Bras, 102, 103, 112, 178; his position at Waterloo, 299.
Picton, Sir Thomas, commander 5th British division, 38; a man of energy and capacity, 40; at Quatre Bras, 178; in battle of Waterloo, 299; repulses d'Erlon's charge, 306, 307.
Pirch I., General von, commander 2d Prussian corps, 32; headquarters at Namur, 33; at Ligny, 143, 151, 159; falls back towards Wavre, 159, 226, 232, 246, 339, 340, 346; delayed in leaving Wavre, 262, 263, supports Bülow's assaults upon Planchenoit, 325, 340.
Piré, Lieutenant-General, commander cavalry division 2d French corps, 25; in the advance, 49; at Quatre Bras, 178; at Waterloo, 301, 337.
Planchenoit, 313, n. 52; attacked successfully by Bülow, retaken by Napoleon, 311; gallantly defended by the Young Guard and Count de Lobau, 311.
Ponsonby, Major-General Sir William, commander Union brigade English cavalry, 35; his charge at Waterloo, 306, 307, 313.

Porter's *History Royal Engineers*, cited, 296, 312.
Powell, Captain, 1st British footguards, 334; describes advance of Imperial Guard at Waterloo, 319, 324.

Q.

Quatre Bras, value of the position, 3 *et seq.*, 12, 13, 61 *et seq.*, 94 *et seq.* (See BATTLE OF.)
Quinet, Edgar, *Histoire de la Campagne de 1815*, cited, 11, 58, 282.
Quiot, General, commanded Allix's division at Waterloo, 302; assigned to the task of capturing La Haye Sainte, 305; brilliant attacks upon the allied line in support of the Guard, 318, 330, 337.

R.

Raguse, Duc de, *Mémoires*, see MARMONT.
Rebecque, General Constant, chief of staff to the Prince of Orange, orders Perponcher to the support of Prince Bernhard's brigade at Quatre Bras, 101–103.
Reille, General Count, commander 2d French corps, 18; in the advance, 44, 46, 48, 50, 101; conference with Ney on the 16th, 116; his *Notice Historique*, cited, 121; disobedience of orders, 121–122, 168, 176, 192–193; his corps at Quatre Bras, 178; position at Waterloo, 301; attacks Hougomont, 303–304, 314, n. 54, 329, 330, 337; failed to realize his opportunity for retreat, 326.
Relation Belge sur la Bataille de Waterloo, cited, 320.
Rogniat, his *Considérations de l'Art de la Guerre*, and *Réponse aux Notes Critiques de Napoléon*, cited, 12, 56, 57, 58, 164.
Roguet, General, commander brigade Imperial Guard at Waterloo, 316.
Royal Dragoons, a part of the British Union Brigade at Waterloo, 300.
Russia, sets her army in motion for the general attack upon France, 1; expected to reinforce the Austrian army, 2.

S.

Saint Hilaire, Émile Marco de, *Histoire de la Garde*, cited, 319.

Saltoun, Lord, at Waterloo, 320.
Sart-à-Walhain, Grouchy orders troops there, 250; erroneously supposed to be the place where he heard the cannon of Waterloo, 255, 286–288.
Saxe-Weimar, Prince Bernhard of, commander brigade Dutch-Belgians, 36, 36, n. 5; driven from Frasnes, 49, 101; at Quatre Bras, 90, 101–103; his position at Waterloo, 299.
Scots Greys, a part of the British Union brigade at Waterloo, 300.
Scott, Sir Walter, *Life of Napoleon*, cited, 93.
Siborne, Captain W., *History of the War in France and Belgium in 1815*, cited, 13, 34, 35, 71, 73, 75, 77, 80, 82, 83, 84, 91, 111, 112, 114, 139, 154, 158, 159, 179, 183, 184, 191, 192, 199, 205, 212, 229, 232, 234, 237, 238, 254, 258, 261, 262, 270, 279, 283, 284, 285, 298, 301, 306, 310, 312, 319, 322, 333.
Sidney, Rev. Edwin, *The Life of Lord Hill*, cited, 332.
Sombreffe, its military value, 12–14; 57 *et seq.*; point of concentration for the Prussian army, 70; the centre of the Prussian army at the battle of Ligny, 151.
Somerset, Major-General Lord Edward, commander cavalry brigade British guards, 35; position at Waterloo, 300; charge of his brigade, 307, 313.
Soult, Marshal, succeeds Berthier as Napoleon's chief of staff, 17; unfit for the position, 18; told Sir W. Napier that Napoleon fought Waterloo without examination of the enemy's position, 24, n. 10; not at fault on the morning of the 16th, 128; orders Ney to envelop the enemy's right, 155; told Sir W. Napier that Ney neglected his orders at Quatre Bras, 191; of no assistance to Napoleon on morning of 17th, 202; opposed to detaching Grouchy with so large a force, 279, n. 7; negligent as a staff officer, 246, 348.
Stanhope, Philip Henry, 5th Earl, *Notes of Conversations with the Duke of Wellington*, cited, 42, 46, 155, 230.
Steinmetz, General von, commander division Prussian 1st corps, 32; at Waterloo, 324–325.
Supplementary Despatches of the Duke of Wellington, edited by his son, cited, 72, 74, 85, 90, 374 *et seq.*
Supplies, lines of, not to be confounded with lines of communication between the allied armies, 14.

INDEX.

T.

Thielemann, General von, commander 3d Prussian corps, 33; at Ligny, 144, 151, 159; his corps placed where it could not aid Zieten and Pirch I., 204; in the retreat to Wavre, 231, 232, 234, 261; his corps left alone, defended Wavre against Grouchy, 264-265. (See BATTLE OF WAVRE.)

Thiers, M. A., his *History of the Consulate and the Empire of France under Napoleon*, cited, 10, 24, 29, 30, 66, 154, 193, 292, 354.

U.

Union Brigade, British, commanded by Major-General Ponsonby, composed of the Royal Dragoons, Scots Greys, and the Inniskilling Dragoons, at Waterloo, 300, 306, 307, 313.

Uxbridge, Lord (afterwards Marquis of Anglesea), commander of combined cavalry of British and King's German Legion, 38; leads charge of Somerset's cavalry at Waterloo, 307; calls Wellington's attention to danger of pursuit of the French with weakened battalions, 341.

V.

Vandamme, Count, commander 3d French corps, known as a hard fighter, 18; delayed in the advance on the 15th, 47; at Ligny, 153, 154, 157-159; delayed in the march with Grouchy to Gembloux, 211, 252; his troops entangled in attempt to carry bridges at Wavre, 264, 265.

Vandeleur, Major-General Sir John, commander British light cavalry brigade, 35; his position at Waterloo, 299; brought to the centre with Vivian's brigade at a critical time, 314; in the final charge, 325.

Van Löben Sels, E., *Précis de la Campagne de 1815 dans les Pays-Bas*, cited, 49, 76, 77, 92, 101, 102, 112, 279, 280, 284, 291, 310, 312, 317.

Vaudoncourt, General Guillaume de, *Histoire des Campagnes de 1814 et 1815 en France*, cited, 59, 289, 291.

Vivian, Major-General Sir Hussey, commander British light cavalry brigade, 35; his position at Waterloo, 299; brought into action at a critical moment, 314; in the final charge, 325.

W.

Walhain, where Grouchy heard the cannon of Waterloo, 255, 256, 259, 286-288.

Waterloo, the field of, 296; surveyed by English engineers before the opening of the campaign, 296. (See BATTLE OF.)

Waterloo Letters,' cited, 83, 112, 233, 299, 300, 310, 312, 319, 321, 322, 323, 324, 332, 333, 334, 335.

Wavre, regarded by Napoleon as the proper point of concentration for the Prussian army, 98; the Prussian rendezvous after battle of Ligny, 233. (See BATTLE OF.)

Weather, 198, 211, 216, 289, 291, 292, 348.

Wellington, Duke of, headquarters at Brussels, 3, 74; his qualifications as a commander, 40, 41; his army, 34-40, 43, 294, 302; anticipates French advance by way of Mons, 74-77; his understanding with Blücher, 70 *et seq.*, 91, 346; delays advance upon Quatre Bras, 77-115, 346-347; at Quatre Bras on the 16th, 106, 109; his conference with Blücher at Brye, 108, 144-146, 150; disapproves of Blücher's position at Ligny, 155, n. 15; in the battle of Quatre Bras, 178, 179, 183-185, 187, 188; retreats from Quatre Bras, 214, 233, 297; learns of Prussian defeat at Ligny, 233; did not receive assurance of support from Blücher until the morning of the 18th, 234, 238, 347; his ride to Wavre to consult with Blücher, 238 *et seq.*, 347; his preparations for the battle of Waterloo, 294-297; occupies Hougomont, 297; his command at Waterloo, 297-300; fortifies La Haye Sainte, 301; his justification in accepting battle based upon assurance of support from Blücher, 294, 295, 302, 327; his efforts to restore his shattered line, 310, 312, 314, 318; his imminent peril, 314; repulses charge of the Imperial Guard, 318-325, 332-336; final advance of his whole line, 325, 340, 341; his retention of 18,000 men at Hal and Tubize, 339; contrasted with Ney, 338, 339.

Y.

Yonge, C. D., *Life of Wellington*, cited, 296.

Young, Rev. Julian Charles, *A Memoir of Charles Mayne Young, Tragedian* cited, 239-241.

Z.

Zieten, General von, commander 1st Prussian corps, 32; headquarters at Charleroi, 33; resists French advance on the 15th, 47, 70, 77; at Ligny, 143, 151; falls back toward Wavre, 159, 226, 232; delay in movement on the 18th, 262; arrival of his corps at Waterloo, 324; his probable course indicated if Grouchy had detained Bülow and Pirch I., 328; his intervention not anticipated, 336; his appearance and decisive attack upon the right flank of French army assured the allied victory, 340, 341.

www.ingramcontent.com/pod-product-compliance
Lightning Source LLC
Chambersburg PA
CBHW070833160426
43192CB00012B/2181